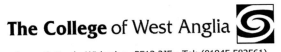

THE DADA MOVEMENT

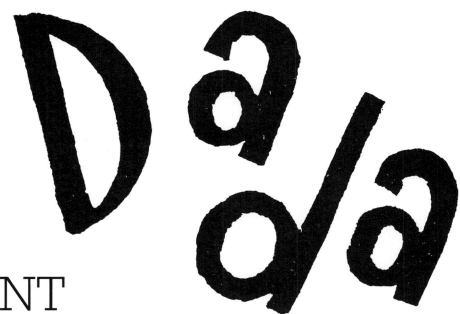

THE DADA MOVEMENT

1915 - 1923

by Marc Dachy

SKIRA

RIZZOLI
NEW YORK

017897

The Chronology and Bibliography in this book were compiled by the author.

Grateful acknowledgment is made to the publishers for permission to quote from the following books: *Dialogues with Marcel Duchamp*, Thames and Hudson, London, and The Viking Press, New York, 1971, by permission of Viking Penguin, a division of Penguin Books USA Inc.; *The Museum of Modern Art Bulletin*, Vol. XIII, Nos. 4-5, New York, 1946; William Carlos Williams, *Autobiography*, New Directions Publishing Corporation, New York, 1948; *The Dada Painters and Poets: An Anthology*, edited by Robert Motherwell, Wittenborn, Schultz, Inc., New York, 1951; Hugo Ball, *Flight Out of Time*, The Viking Press, New York, 1974, by permission of Viking Penguin, a division of Penguin Books USA Inc.; Man Ray, *Self Portrait*, Little, Brown and Company, Boston, 1963; László Moholy-Nagy, *Vision in Motion*, Paul Theobald and Co., Chicago, 1947; Gertrude Stein, *The Autobiography of Alice B. Toklas*, Harcourt, Brace, New York, 1933, by permission of Random House, Inc., New York; William S. Burroughs, *Nova Express*, Grove Press, New York, 1964. For further acknowledgments, see pages 201-203.

Published in the United States of America in 1990 by

Rizzoli International Publications, Inc.
300 Park Avenue South, New York 10010

Translated from the French by Michael Taylor

Printed in Switzerland

Library of Congress Cataloging-in-Publication Data

Dachy, Marc.
   [Journal du Mouvement Dada. English]
   The Dada Movement. 1915-1923 / Marc Dachy.
      p.   cm.
   Translation of: Journal du Mouvement Dada.
   Includes chronology, bibliography and index.
   ISBN 0-8478-1110-7
   1. Dadaism.   2. Arts, Modern—20th century.   I. Title.
NX456.5.D3D32513   1990
700'.9'04—dc20   89-42797
                                      CIP

Contents

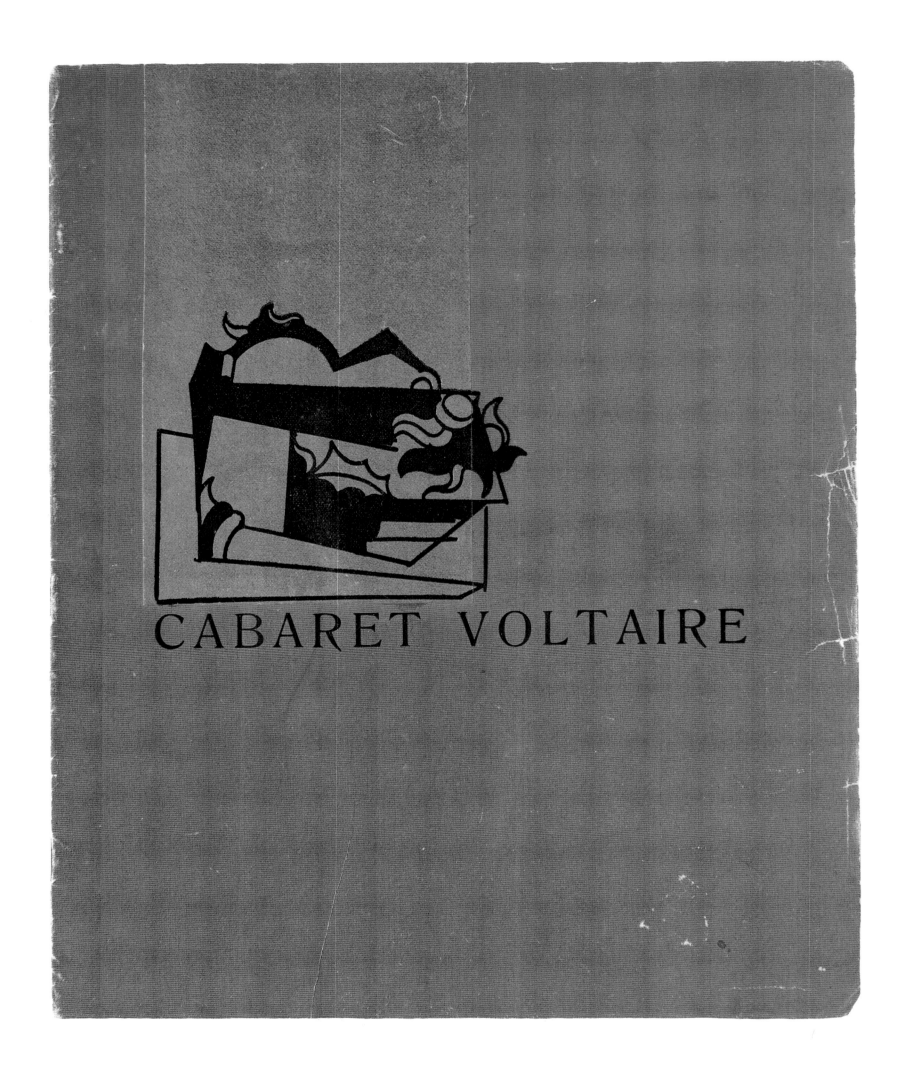

Introduction

"An art more art"

Out of an exceptional conjunction of circumstances, the First World War, the neutrality of Switzerland, the chance meeting in Zurich of some rare artists and some free young men who set their face against "the furious folly of these times," sprang DADA. Under that emblematic, ironic and rather baffling name, there came together an international constellation of artists, groups, periodicals, books and works, radically affirming the freedom of man and the irrepressible claims of the life impulse in all its manifestations.

All too often it is treated by historians as an interlude between Cubism and Surrealism or, at best, between Futurism and Constructivism. By a defense mechanism inherent in the values it challenged, the history of the Dada Movement has been presented again and again as a negation of culture, a school of nihilist derision arising unwanted, unneeded, out of the postwar confusion, fomenting scandals and provocations under cover of the collapse of civilizing values.

Such a view of the artistic and international reality of this movement has consigned the Dadaists to the limbo of provocation. For decades, history has seen no more of Dada than the spectacular or humorous flair with which it made its sweeping protest against the role and significance of culture. An interpretation which ignored the real scope of the movement, which took no account of its very telling relevance, in both artistic and theoretical terms, to the historical moment in which it arose and to the art of the twentieth century as a whole.

Critical report was not far from paraphrasing the famous stage direction of Alfred Jarry: the scene is set in the Cabaret Voltaire, in other words nowhere; enter Dada, in other words, no matter what. And of course it is true that at the end of the nineteenth century provocation and humor had made their mark in French literature with Jarry's comedy *Ubu Roi* (1896), his "pataphysics," his mind-boggling songs, his cast of burlesque figures. The misunderstanding in fact, at least initially, had been deliberately instigated by Dada, its members seeking above all to show their disapproval.

The first evenings at the Cabaret Voltaire in Zurich heralded the birth of the Movement. Already Dadaistic, they were at once artistic and critical, polemical and contradictory. In his *Zurich Chronicle* Tzara describes the events of that summer of 1916: "The Cabaret lasted six months, every night we thrust the triton of the grotesque of the god of the beautiful into each and every spectator, and the wind was not gentle—the consciousness of so many was shaken—tumult and solar avalanche—vitality and the silent corner close to wisdom or folly—who can define its frontiers?—slowly the young girls departed and bitterness laid its nest in the belly of the family man... In the presence of a compact crowd Tzara demonstrates, we demand we demand the right to piss in different colors, Huelsenbeck demonstrates, Ball demonstrates, Arp Erklärung, Janco meine Bilder, Heusser eigene Kompositionen, the dogs bay and the dissection of Panama on the piano on the piano and dock—shouted Poem—shouting and fighting in the hall, first row approves second row declares itself incompetent the rest shout, who is the strongest, the big drum is brought in, Huelsenbeck against 200, Ho osenlatz accentuated by the very big drum and little bells on his left foot—the people protest shout smash windowpanes kill each other demolish fight here come the police interruption."

Such was the atmosphere. Behind it lies this fact, that it was through art that Dada made good its insurrection. Dada is a "protest," explains Tzara, a revolt, adds Arp, against the "puerile mania for authoritarianism [which] would use art itself for the stultification of mankind." Far from keeping to a superficial attack on the culture of a bankrupt society, the men and women of the Dada Movement, in a period rich in social and cultural problematics, proved themselves intensely and abundantly creative, bringing about a violent renewal of meanings.

From Zurich, where it had emerged, the Dada Movement reached out to the capitals of the Western world. The German members of the Zurich group exported Dada to Berlin, while the war was still on, then after the Armistice to Hanover and Cologne in a ruined and divided Germany, tense with revolutionary aspirations. In Barcelona and New York, havens untouched by the war, artists and periodicals were also won over to Dada. Finally, those members of the Zurich group who were devoted to French culture, Tzara in particular, extended the Movement to postwar Paris. There Dada created a great stir before slowly dying out, as it broke down into various tendencies (one of them was to merge with Surrealism). In addition to its Parisian success, Dada enjoyed a second run on the international level, winning over active groups of Constructivist artists, some at the Weimar Bauhaus, others on the staff of the periodicals *De Stijl* in Holland and *MA* in Budapest-Vienna; and thanks to the untiring activity of its founder, it exerted a major influence on the whole avant-garde.

Artists and writers rallied to Dada and turned away now from alienating procedures directly visible in the actual making of cultural objects, in particular in the structure of historically determined art forms. They laid sign systems bare and did away with the mediations that condition expression. For the old forms invested with a social authority void now of any content, they substituted new, shifting, transient, unfinished forms, any potential form in progress, in the making, being considered noteworthy and preferable to an idealized perfection.

There was negation of culture because the latter subjects art to a language which is not its own, but there was a revolutionary affirmation of this new freedom: the Dadas released art from the constraint of a pre-established meaning. They liberated materials (reliefs, pasted papers, object-sculptures), words (free prose, automatic poems), language and letters (poster poems, concrete poems, sound poems), light (photograms, abstract films), signs (typography). All these elements they released from the illustrational and anecdotal purposes they had served. And thus freed the Dadas used them to produce new pictorial and verbal forms whose meaning is revealed by the way they are handled, while these stylistic procedures went to determine a new status and new analytical criteria.

It was an unprecedented reversal in the production of meaning: the material was not reduced to a pre-established narrative line within the cultural order. Painting told no more stories, it displayed a fulfillment peculiar to itself. Language was not reduced to convention, to the narrative sequence, its constituent elements were thrown into relief for the beauty and bloom that they admitted of. The exercise of these new liberties was accompanied moreover by great skill in the handling of forms.

Not content with mere aesthetic contemplation, the Dadas thus refused a set place within the scheme of an evolution along historicist lines. They cared too much about art to wish for their own to be modern, while to the increasing triteness of all the talk about the death of art, Tzara could reply in his *Manifesto on Feeble Love and Bitter Love*: "The (ever impending) annihilation of art is being envisaged. What is wanted here is an art more art."

To the annoyance and bewilderment of a cultural establishment wedded to prewar values, the Dadaists peppered their output with polemical manifestoes designed to counter any purely aesthetic interpretation of their works. Generally published in the magazines of the period or in the form of booklets or broadsheets, these statements have for the most part never been reprinted; hence the extracts from them quoted here. The writers of these manifestoes combine critical precision and theoretical pertinence with distinction, independent thinking, and banter, which seemed to them the most telling forms of communication in their hostile surroundings.

Dada said No to logic, hierarchies, prophets, the future; and Yes to spontaneity, the freedom of each individual in the "folly of the moment," the "elegant leap," the freedom and contradictions of life. In art it called for "works that are strong straight precise and forever beyond understanding."

The creation of new and spontaneous works, made directly out of wood, iron, stone or tin, led on to assemblages, sculptures, and collages which are a self-contained reality and a direct critique of the previous art forms. These latter were compromised along with the culture of a world which Tzara describes in the *Dada Manifesto 1918* as being "abandoned to the hands of bandits, who rend one another and destroy the centuries."

Just as they eagerly derided an art shaped by outworn models of thought, so the Dadaists eagerly founded their own periodicals, galleries, and cabarets, for the sole purpose of removing the new creation from the old official circuits. They were bent not only on overriding the arbitrary character of any backing or endorsement, and denouncing its uselessness, but also on showing up the incoherence of officialdom, its obsolete and dictatorial biases, especially when it is camouflaged behind a liberal or allegedly modern façade, as demonstrated so glaringly by Marcel Duchamp with his *Fountain* at the 1917 Independents exhibition in New York.

The history of Dada falls into several periods. The first, with the birth of the Movement in 1916-1917, is a syncretic, utopian, social phase. Hugo Ball, Tristan Tzara, and Hans Arp set out to gather together the constructive forces indicative of the "New Spirit" then on the rise in Europe. A few Cubists and Futurists contributed to the periodicals *Cabaret Voltaire* and *Dada* in Zurich, and to *SIC* and *Nord-Sud* in Paris. The first issues of *Dada* still proposed a constructive vision. In them something was even said about "building the cathedral of the future." The Italian Futurist Boccioni saw Cubism as "the cathedral of the future." The Dadaist Picabia dismissed Cubism as "a cathedral of shit."

The second phase, 1918-1921, following on Tzara's *Dada Manifesto 1918*, marks a clean break. After assimilating Parisian Cubism and Italian Futurism, the Dadas refused to go on tamely in their wake. Dada was not an "ism." Rejecting any functionalism, any idea of Future or Progress as well as any overall political scheme, the Dadas relied on chance, on the throw of the dice, on irony and playfulness, on childhood, in the name of life and against the desiccating idea of modern art whose formalistic character they denounced.

The third phase sprang from the first. The concept of elementary art had arisen with Arp in Zurich in 1916-1917. The pure vocal and visual gestures, which at first were a way of breaking out of their confinement in a given historical situation, a way of deconstructing the Western linguistic grip, now found an extension in the theoretical statements shared by Dadas and Constructivists, whether in the *Call for an Elementary Art* of 1921 or in syllabic poetry.

Art, redefined as a law unto itself, autonomous, answering its own purposes, entered a new conceptual era. Pure plasticism, the existential level of form, sealed the clearing away of literary narrative metaphor and any metapictorial baggage.

When they openly display the procedures at work in the making of a montage, a collage or a poem, the discontinuities, disruptions or tallyings, the form, color, nature and density of the materials fitted together, implying the viewer or reader within the making up of the pictured or written statement, the Dadaists are not only laying emphasis on formal procedures but exalting the boldness of their attitude to both art and life. Thus stripped of imaginary or symbolic connotations, the work not only sets out forms for their own sake, but enhances them by the transforming energy which it releases.

In this sense construction and deconstruction meet, announcing the follow-up of Dada in the work of the Constructivists, notably in Holland, Germany, and Russia in the years 1922-1923. For the artists of this tendency were the only ones who shared with the Dadaists their rejection of psychologism, of ideological inspiration, of metaphysical and literary archaism, of the naturalistic and realistic aesthetic; but they were also the first to tackle the new stylistic problems stemming from innovative practices. Stemming, for example, from the extension by the Bauhaus artists, chiefly Moholy-Nagy, of the Dada invention of photograms, which Schad, Man Ray, and Hausmann had already exploited.

In the literary field, both Raymond Roussel and Mallarmé had opened up new perspectives for narration. A fresh approach to typography, page design, lettering, an untrammeled play of the imagination, these prefigured the non-logic of the Dada discourse and, in Russia, the transrational manipulations of language, the inner declensions of words, the new linguistic ways invented by Khlebnikov. If the language procedures of Roussel find a particular extension in the entire work of Marcel Duchamp (and later that of Michel Leiris), Tzara for his part questions logical trains of association and by the same token the whole organization of society. He deliberately sets out "to disorder meaning." For him "every page must explode, either by profound heavy seriousness, the whirlwind, poetic frenzy, the new, the eternal, the crushing joke, enthusiasm for principles, or by the way in which it is printed."

In Zurich, joining together in a "limited company for the exploitation of the Dada vocabulary," Arp, Serner, and Tzara discovered automatic writing and wrote prose and poems in a mixture of French and German, weaving polysemic effects into the very tissue of language. James Joyce, author of *Ulysses* (1922), was not far away.

The Dada deconstruction of models, ideologies, identities and behaviors was carried out in a libertarian spirit, bringing to the surface the transforming energies at work within the individual, energies buried and repressed beneath the conventions imposed by the social polity. That its ludic and aleatory attitude, even in art, was well founded is confirmed by its accord and interaction with the Constructivist artists, for the latter, intent on a strict development of art forms and language, had arrived at very similar conclusions by ways of their own.

Voicing its negation of the systems and forms of power opposed to life, Dada in the space of a few years displayed a wild and creative energy, fundamentally positive in its thrust, and asserted the absolute supremacy of art and life as experienced by free men.

Paris, August 9, 1989

Marcel Duchamp:
*Nude Descending a
Staircase, No. 2, 1912*

Chapter 1

The Armory Show of 1913:
From the recognition of modern art to the transcending of any artistic formulation

Marcel Duchamp had surely no idea that he was inaugurating a new era in twentieth century art when, in February 1913, he exhibited his *Nude Descending a Staircase* at the Armory of the Sixty-Ninth Infantry, which had been converted to a gallery for the occasion, on Lexington Avenue in New York City. He was even unaware that he had become an instant celebrity in the United States. A year earlier, in Paris, his canvas had been rejected by the selection committee of the Salon des Indépendants, which included Archipenko, Le Fauconnier, Gleizes, Metzinger and Léger, who are said to have considered the work's title a criticism of Cubism. The committee left it to Duchamp's brothers Gaston (the painter Jacques Villon) and Raymond (the sculptor Duchamp-Villon) to inform him of its negative decision. This refusal, voiced by exponents of Cubist ''orthodoxy,'' was only the first in the long series of rejections that marks the history of the Dada Movement.

So, after being shown at the Dalmau Gallery in Barcelona, where it received scant attention, Duchamp's picture was sent on to New York. There it created a sensation. The Armory Show, which Mabel Dodge described as ''the most important event in the nation since the signing of the Declaration of Independence,'' revealed a new artistic reality to the American public.

Less well-off than Picabia, who traveled to New York for the show, Duchamp stayed behind in Paris where he was eventually informed that the three canvases he had sent to America had all been sold. Only in 1915, when summoned to New York and greeted on his arrival there by one of the organizers of the Armory Show, Walter Pach, was Duchamp able to measure the full extent of his success on the other side of the Atlantic. Pach introduced him to Walter Arensberg. Visiting the Armory Show on its closing day, Arensberg had found himself suddenly propelled on to the modern art scene. He had been so overwhelmed by this experience that he had neglected to return to his home in Boston for three days and had decided then and there to move to New York City. Arensberg the Imagist poet had become Arensberg the collector of Marcel Duchamp. He was to donate his patiently amassed Duchamp collection to the Philadelphia Museum of Art in 1950.

In a matter of days, Duchamp gained the position of authority that he was to hold with serenity for the rest of his life. ''When I met Marcel Duchamp in New York in 1916,'' wrote Henri-Pierre Roché, ''he seemed, at the age of twenty-nine, to have a kind of aura, and for me he has always kept this aura. What did it consist of? A limpidness, an easiness, a swiftness, an unselfishness, an openness to everything that seems new, a spontaneousness and a boldness. His presence was a grace and a gift, and he didn't realize it even though he was surrounded by a growing crowd of disciples. There he was, youthful, alert, inspired. The memory of his personality is even more present than the recollection of his works, a definitive sampling of which he gave us from 1911 to 1923 without ever once repeating himself—his only direct offering.''

Duchamp's presence in New York helped to speed the growth of modern art in America, which would in fact be a step ahead of European art throughout the twentieth century. Witness the publications and exhibitions assembled by Alfred H. Barr Jr. at the Museum of Modern Art (notably *Cubism and Abstract Art* in 1936). In 1920 Duchamp, who by then was advising the collector and patron Katherine S. Dreier, founded the Société Anonyme, Inc. (Its pleonastic title was a find of Man Ray's, ''Inc.'' being the

A view of the Armory Show, New York, 1913

The Rude Descending a Staircase, caricature in the New York Evening Sun of Duchamp's Nude Descending a Staircase, 1913

equivalent of the French "Société Anonyme.") This remains one of the best modern art collections in the world and a model for any museum of modern art; in fact, through its Brooklyn Museum exhibition in 1926, it indirectly inspired the birth of New York's Museum of Modern Art in 1929. Two other models, rivaling the Société Anonyme, were the collection of Sergei Shchukin in Moscow (Picasso, Matisse, Gauguin, Monet, Derain, Renoir),

Living room in Walter Arensberg's New York apartment, c. 1918

brought together before the First World War; and, in Paris, the collection of Gertrude Stein (a friend of Marcel Duchamp's from as early as 1913).

To come back to the *Nude Descending a Staircase*. The idea for it goes back to a drawing Duchamp made in 1911 to illustrate a poem by Jules Laforgue (*Encore à cet astre*) which continues a theme developed in an earlier poem, *Un mot au soleil pour commencer*. Laforgue's impact on the younger generation in the early 1900s is no longer remembered, though Ezra Pound declared that the French poet's "intelligence ran through the whole gamut of his time." The figure climbing the stairs is almost certainly "the first idea in reverse" of the 1912 canvas, just as the *Bride Stripped Bare by Her Bachelors, Even* was later conceived as a "delay in glass" ("*retard en verre*") of the *Nude*.

The canvas presents itself at once as an irreverent variation on the reclining academic nude and as a static image of a body in motion. It is contemporary with the rediscovery of Etienne Marey's "chronophoto-graphs" and Muybridge's sequences of galloping horses and duelling fencers. The different positions and trajectories of the body are rendered with white dotted lines and arcs. Duchamp's breakdown of forms has more in common with the spatial experiments of Cubism than with the dynamic purport of Italian Futurism.

Duchamp was acquainted with Severini, who had exhibited in Paris with the Futurists in 1912, but *Nude Descending a Staircase, No. 1*, an oil sketch more colorful than the famous *Nude No. 2*, was painted earlier, in 1911. The latter, with its parcimonious colors deriving from the Cubist aesthetic (so little do they have in common with Delaunay's simultaneous colors, Léger's palette, Kupka's pure color surfaces or the American Synchromists), is thus a provocation to both traditional and avant-garde values. The Italian Futurists had banned the nude from painting, dismissing it as a survival of obsolete academicism. Duchamp checkmates both the academic tradition and the Futurists' dogmatic rejection of it. Unwilling to relinquish a perennial pictorial theme, he gave it a new plastic formulation, austere and forceful. He set the female anatomy in motion—thus accentuating the nude's immodesty —and stripped down the articulations between the various representational elements, thereby raising his art to a new level. From there he would go

Kasimir Malevich: *The Knife Grinder, 1912*

What contributed to the interest provoked by that canvas was its title.
One just doesn't do a nude woman coming down the stairs, that's
ridiculous. It doesn't seem ridiculous now, because it's been talked
about so much, but when it was new, it seemed scandalous. A nude
should be respected.
It was also offensive on the religious, Puritan level, and all of this
contributed to the repercussions of the picture. And then there were
painters over there who were squarely opposed to it. That triggered a
battle. I profited. That's all.
— What do you,,more than a half century away, think of that "Nude"?
I like it very much. It held up better than "The King and the Queen."
Even in the old sense, the painterly sense. It's very involved, very
compact, and very well painted, with some substantial colors a German
gave me. They've behaved very well, and that's very important.

Marcel Duchamp, 1967

beyond the conventions of figurative art and would soon wholly abandon
"retinal painting."

Nude No. 2 has more in common with Russian Cubo-Futurism (in
particular with Malevich's *Knife Grinder* of 1912) than with Italian Futurism,
which Duchamp regarded as an "Impressionism of the mechanical world."
Like the Moscow artists, who were then feeling their way toward
Suprematism, but unlike the Italian Futurists, Duchamp wanted to do away
with the "physicalness" of painting.

Duchamp himself has remarked on the colors of his stunning *Nude No. 2.*
In talks with Pierre Cabanne (*Dialogues with Marcel Duchamp*, 1971) he
observed that the picture is "very well painted, with some substantial
colors." He adds that these colors have "behaved very well." Now Duchamp
had studied color in Munich in 1912, in what was in effect a second break with
the Puteaux Cubists. Moreover, unlike *Nude No. 2*, *Nude No. 1* is highly
colored. It seems from one of Duchamp's notes (used later in the famous
Green Box of 1934) that the colors of the earlier painting were worked out

during an automobile excursion the artist made with Picabia and Apollinaire in the Jura mountains. "*Wood* is the pictorial material of the Jura-Paris road; to me wood translates the feeling of chipped flint. Try to ascertain whether it's necessary to choose a particular kind of wood (pine or varnished mahogany)."

Duchamp wrote a great deal. Among his early friends in the Puteaux group was the writer Georges Ribemont-Dessaignes who later belonged to the first generation of Paris Dadaists, along with Picabia and Duchamp himself. Almost from the start, Duchamp's written oeuvre—his ephemeral notes and outlines for projects, his titles and puns, the 1934 *Green Box*, the *White Box* (*A l'infinitif*)—reflected the artist's involvement with novel ideas about language pioneered by, on the one hand, the "Douanier Rousseau of philology," that "prince of thinkers," Jean-Pierre Brisset and, on the other, Raymond Roussel, whose *Impressions d'Afrique* in its stage version had been seen by Duchamp, Picabia and Apollinaire together in 1911. (Like Duchamp, Roussel was an avid chess player.)

"It was fundamentally Roussel who was responsible for my glass, *La Mariée mise à nu par ses célibataires, même.* From his *Impressions d'Afrique* I got the general approach . . . I saw at once I could use Roussel as an influence. I felt that as a painter it was much better to be influenced by a writer than by another painter. And Roussel showed me the way. My ideal library would have contained all Roussel's writings—Brisset, perhaps Lautréamont and Mallarmé. Mallarmé was a great figure. This is the direction in which art should turn: to an intellectual expression, rather than to an animal

The three Duchamp brothers at Puteaux, near Paris, 1912. Left to right: Jacques Villon, Marcel Duchamp, and Raymond Duchamp-Villon

Man Ray: *Marcel Duchamp's Bottlerack, 1914*

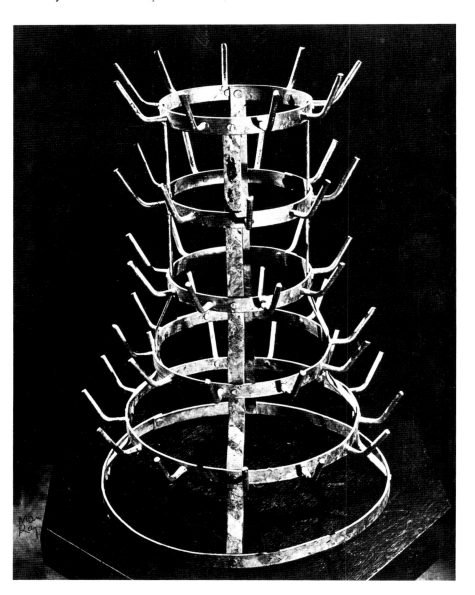

Marcel Duchamp: *"Rose Sélavy considers that an incesticide should lie with his mother before killing her; the bedbugs are indispensable."*

expression. I am sick of the expression *'bête comme un peintre'*—stupid as a painter."

From the first, then, the issue of language coincided with the issue of pure painting (as formulated by the De Stijl artists or the Russian Constructivists). It also reflected Duchamp's autobiography. For that born bachelor, what counted most was family (his two brothers, his sister Suzanne and her husband, Jean Crotti) and convivial relationships (chess tournaments and associations, the Bride and her bachelors).

Duchamp's oeuvre draws its energy from the driving force of language. Its tangled skein of alliterations, signs, phonemes, puns and word-plays (like the inclusion of the artist's first name in the title *La* MAR*iée mise à nu par ses* CEL*ibataires, même*) has provided ample material for commentators. Duchamp even declined to take part in the Dada Salon of 1921 merely for the pleasure of firing off a one-word cable to his brother-in-law Crotti: *Podebal.* And the *Nude Descending a Staircase* was refused by the selection committee of the Salon des Indépendants because of its title. Not unlike the unconscious as defined by Jacques Lacan, Duchamp's whole oeuvre is "structured like a language" or like a "system of invisible signs and subtle zigzag lines of defense" (Michel Foucault on Raymond Roussel). "*What is the most poetic word?*[Cabanne asked Duchamp]. — I have no idea. I don't have

one handy. In any case, they would be words distorted in their sense. — *Word games?* — Yes, word games. Assonances, things like that, like the 'delay' in the 'Glass'; I like that very much. 'Backward,' that means something. — *Even the word 'Duchamp' is very poetic.* — Yes. Nevertheless, Jacques Villon didn't waste any time changing names, not only 'Duchamp' into 'Villon,' but also 'Gaston' into 'Jacques'! There are periods when words lose their salt. — *You're the only brother to keep his name.* — I was sort of obligated to. One of us had to!'' (*Dialogues with Marcel Duchamp*, 1971).

So even while moving irreversibly toward the series of extra-pictorial works by which he would soon overthrow the ''retinal'' art he rejected, Duchamp nevertheless stayed within the limits of meaning, erotic symbolism and literary narrativity (the *Large Glass*). Meanwhile, in Russia, Malevich was transgressing those very limits by radically asserting the total self-sufficiency of pure painting.

Both artists were breaking free from the rigid perspectivist system of late Cubism, yet each did so in his own way; each approached in his own manner the point sometimes referred to as the ''death of art.'' Duchamp challenged art's ontological status with his Readymades (the *Bicycle Wheel* of 1913, the *Fountain* of 1917). Malevich broke with Analytical Cubism by means of alogical compositions which paved the way for Suprematism in 1913-1915 (the so-called ''Black Square''). Simultaneously both became interested in the fourth dimension. Duchamp read Gaston de Pawlowski's *Voyage au pays de la quatrième dimension* (1912) and Malevich pored over Ouspenski's more philosophical *Tertium Organum* (1911).

Cover of Gaston de Pawlowski's ''Journey to the Land of the Fourth Dimension,'' Paris, 1912

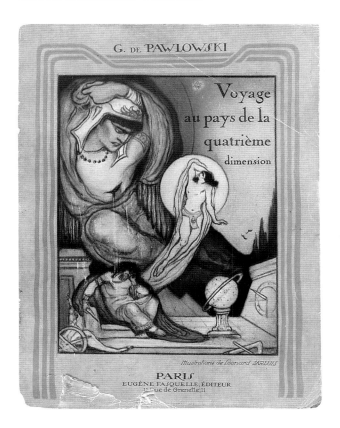

Having already reached the land of the fourth dimension for some time now, I feel, as I write my anticipated recollections, that it is strangely difficult to translate them into the vernacular. For its vocabulary is based on the data of three-dimensional space. It has no words capable of exactly defining the bizarre impressions that a man feels when he rises forever above the world of the usual sensations. The vision of the fourth dimension opens up horizons absolutely new. It completes our understanding of the world; it enables us to carry out the definitive synthesis of everything we know; it justifies that knowledge, even when it seems contradictory, and we then realize that synthesis is a total idea which partial expressions cannot contain. By the very fact of stating an idea in the words of common use, one thereby limits it to the preconception of three-dimensional space.

Gaston de Pawlowski, 1912

Through the abundance of critical commentary it has inspired, Duchamp's *Nude*, which is both Cubist and Futurist without quite being either, a rejection of Futurism as it was in turn rejected by the Cubists, has engendered its own history. However, notwithstanding its immense success, it does not explain the birth of what Gabrielle Buffet-Picabia termed the New York "pre-Dada group." Still, the strategy suggested to Duchamp by the aura of scandal and respect surrounding this painting foreshadowed the tactics adopted by the Dadaists a few years later.

For his part Picabia, who came to New York City in January 1913 for the Armory Show, immediately struck up a friendship with Alfred Stieglitz. Their meeting was no accident. Picabia had been initiated into photography at an early age by his grandfather, and Stieglitz was a master photographer.

Stieglitz ran the Little Gallery of the Photo-Secession at 291 Fifth Avenue, later called 291 Gallery; and Stieglitz's photography magazine, *Camera Work*, was later renamed *291*. In 1917 Picabia, by then in Barcelona, founded the most representative of the Dada periodicals, and he called it *391*, to stress his connection with Stieglitz.

The fact that Stieglitz was a photographer is significant inasmuch as photography played a leading role in the "crisis of painting" between 1910

Francis Picabia, Gabrielle Buffet and Guillaume Apollinaire at the Luna Park amusement grounds, Paris, 1913

Constantin Brancusi: *Endless Columns, 1920-1930*

Cover of Camera Work, *Nos. 34-35, New York, 1911*

à Francis Picabia

Tristan TZARA

Tristan Tzara: *A Francis Picabia – 1920*

and 1920. It was in fact in the Photo-Secession Gallery that modern art made its appearance in America. It was there that Stieglitz's friend Edward Steichen (the photographer who made the famous stills of Rodin's *Balzac* in the sunset at Meudon) introduced American viewers not only to Rodin's work but to Matisse, Picasso and Brancusi as well. Stieglitz published the first Gertrude Stein text to appear in print anywhere. A few days before the opening of the Armory Show he proclaimed his admiration for "a group of painters who refuse to do what the camera can do far better. . . who have banded together to declare their independence. . . to the angry shouts of those who continue to copy old masters on both continents and their adjacent islands."

A great deal of thought went into the organization of the Armory Show. Arthur B. Davies had studied the catalogue of the important international Sonderbund exhibition in Cologne in 1912. He and his friends had then decided to mount an even better exhibition. Their efforts were such that Gabrielle Buffet-Picabia later wrote: "A greater number of painters were represented, and more works exhibited, than ever before in the world (and for once this expression is no exaggeration). From Europe came a torrent of dazzling art works that were incomprehensible to most of the crowd that packed into the Armory. But their quantity at least suggested a strong *raison d'être*, it helped to give the benefit of the doubt to a totally different concept of art, and it held in check even the most adverse reactions."

It was an aesthetic *coup d'état*. On the eve of the First World War, in an armory of all places, art works briefly replaced guns. Only twenty years later the books of "degenerate" writers were being burned in Nazi Germany. But for the moment the critics were magnanimous. (Or foiled: Raoul Hausmann would soon make clear, in a stunning collage, just how brutal they could be.) Invited by the artists to an unscheduled luncheon at the end of the show, they observed the rules of fair play. "A good show," one of them declared, "but don't do it again."

It took a massive exhibition like this for the new trend in art to triumph over Cubist dogma. There was as yet no term for this art; later the word Dada would be coined, its success amply confirming the need for it. But for the time being there was no term to adequately describe the powerful transformation manifest in the new art, and so the press used the word "cubist" to designate every new aesthetic form.

Significantly, in the March 1915 issue of *291* Stieglitz disregarded (as Picabia was to do two years later in *391*) the labels and instant descriptions that were affixed to the new art. For to him and to other innovators, they were charged with discredited literary and artistic overtones. In short, artists, writers and photographers everywhere were covertly, and sometimes even unwittingly, building a movement that might never become a movement at all; or if it did eventually become recognized as one, it would appear as an anti-movement. Thus Marcel Duchamp and Man Ray went through the motions of requesting permission from Tristan Tzara to call the magazine they published in April 1921 *New York Dada*.

And the Dada Movement: what would it be? At first it was only a name, a label that distinguished those bold enough to adopt it (and to publicize it by performing certain characteristic Dada activities) from those who recoiled from it. "Tristan Tzara had been one of the first to grasp the suggestive power of the word Dada," wrote Richard Huelsenbeck in 1920. "From here on he worked indefatigably as the prophet of a word, which only later was to be filled with a concept."

Just as Picabia decided to call his Barcelona magazine *391*, the first Dada exhibition opened in Zurich. The word Dada, a nonsense vocable that had no cultural connotation, had been hit on a few weeks earlier in a random search through a dictionary. (The sight of an open book's pages turning haphazardly in the wind inspired the *Unhappy Readymade* that Marcel Duchamp sent to his sister when she married Jean Crotti: a geometry text-book that was meant to be hung from a string outdoors.)

But in 1915 the word Dada did not exist. Rejecting all labels and "isms," Stieglitz called the new artists "revivifiers" since each of them was giving life to his own pictorial practice. For lack of any better term, Picabia used the term "Cubist" to describe his own feelings about New York City (unless this is a misprint of the newspaper which interviewed him).

Francis Picabia: *New York, 1913*

The spirit of your New York is so elusive, so wonderfully and immensely atmospheric, while the city itself is so concrete, that it is difficult to describe with words alone the effect that it has on me. My pictures will say it better than I can myself...
On my return to Paris, I'll set down on canvas my impressions of the post-Cubist qualities of your New York. These studies I have made are only the foundations of a larger picture.
If I were still an Impressionist, I would turn your New York into a picture of what I see materially, like an Impressionist. But as you know, I've gone beyond that stage, and already I no longer even regard myself as a Cubist.

Francis Picabia, 1913

New York was modernizing at full speed. A week before the Armory Show opened, Grand Central Station was inaugurated. With its forty-two tracks and its underground passages to adjacent hotels and streets, it was the largest train station in the world.

Picabia expressed his fascination with New York in a series of watercolors painted on the spot. Stieglitz exhibited them in his gallery two days after the Armory Show ended. The critics dubbed Picabia's work "rebel art." *The New York Times* wrote that the artist was "recubing the Cubists" and "refuturizing the Futurists." This brings to mind the intensity that Tristan Tzara advocates in his *Manifesto on Feeble Love and Bitter Love:* "The (ever impending) annihilation of art is being envisaged. What is wanted here is an art more art." A more Cubist Cubism, a more Futurist Futurism, an art more art, a Picabia who was more Picabia than ever in New York. Tzara's intensity was of course not just a matter of transforming representation ever more radically. It also reflected a more abstract preoccupation, a need to go beyond art that verged on the end of art in its ultimate "realization," as embodied by Duchamp's *Fountain* of 1917.

Picabia's two outstanding canvases of 1913, *Udnie* and *Edtaonisl*, were not shown at the Armory; they were painted after he returned to Paris, in the afterglow of his American experience. Crucial works in the history of abstract painting, both were acquired by American museums, at the insistence of André Breton and Marcel Duchamp, when art historians and curators, after World War Two, were re-examining the beginnings of abstraction. But in Paris, at the Salon d'Automne of 1913, they went unnoticed, save for some insulting remarks by critics.

Replete with surprises, reflecting a variety of Picabia's phases and manners (his Impressionist style, his mechanical drawing and Dada "machinist" style, his transparency, his brutality), *Udnie* is a major accomplishment. Like Duchamp's *Nude*, it can be read as an ultimate expression of the Cubist sensibility, though Picabia always denied having been influenced by it, just as he claimed to have bypassed Cézanne. The fact is that in 1909-1910, on emerging from his Impressionist phase, Picabia moved freely toward a grammar of intensely personal abstract forms, in an interspace between Cubism and Futurism.

Within this trend, *Udnie* displays a chromatic boldness and formal mastery rarely equalled by Picabia. The planes delimited by straight lines and angles combine in space with flexible curved forms, which prompted Apollinaire to describe this canvas as a "crazy ardent work" filled with "astonishing conflicts" between the paintwork and the artist's imagination.

Udnie remains something of a mystery. Is it a pictorial translation of the Hindu dancer from Montmartre, Napierkowska, who performed on the liner that took Picabia to America? A rendering of the bewilderment sometimes experienced by passengers when they look out over a watery world bereft of fixed points? Or does it simply express the excitement of New York recollected in the tranquillity of the artist's Paris studio?

Here is what Picabia himself had to say in 1913: "*Udnie* is no more the portrait of a girl than *Edtaonisl* is the picture of a prelate, as commonly conceived. They are recollections of America, evocations of the country. As such, subtly set out like musical chords, they become representative of an idea, a nostalgia, a fleeting impression."

Francis Picabia: *Udnie, 1913*

Pablo Picasso:
Head, 1913-1914

Chapter 2

Tired of This Old World

European abstraction had triumphed in New York, but in Paris the situation was very different. In one of his most famous poems, *Zone*, published in the December 1912 issue of *Les Soirées de Paris*, Guillaume Apollinaire lamented the fact that Europe was still buried under archaic conventions:

> You're tired of this old world at last
> The flock of bridges is bleating this morning o shepherdess Eiffel Tower
> You've had enough of living in the Greek and Roman past
> Even the cars look ancient here

Are these lines an allusion to F.T. Marinetti's provocative statement, in the *Futurist Manifesto* (1909), that a "roaring automobile...is more beautiful than the *Victory of Samothrace*"? At all events, the poem expresses the weariness with things of the past felt by a poet and critic who hungered for new excitements, one of the first voices in this century, both in poetry and in criticism (his *Aesthetic Meditations*), to celebrate the seduction of modernity.

Apollinaire's lassitude was not only caused by the inevitable resistance that every innovator encounters, but also by his clashes with his own circle at *Les Soirées de Paris* where he was frequently blamed for his artistic choices. It was only after the periodical's original owner, André Billy, sold the title to Serge Jastrebzoff (the painter Serge Férat) that the poet finally felt he could express himself freely.

Zone (initially entitled *Cri*), the first poem in Apollinaire's book *Alcools*, broke with the conventions of literary Symbolism and announced a new poetry. In the fall of 1912 he gave up the use of punctuation. (So did the Italian Futurists that same year.) The facsimile edition of the corrected galley proofs of *Alcools* (published in 1953 at the prompting of Tristan Tzara who had obtained them from Sonia Delaunay) makes it clear that Apollinaire actually took the historic decision to remove the punctuation from his poems only after they had been set in type.

Then, in the summer of 1913, Apollinaire agreed to put his name to *L'Antitradition futuriste*, a gesture that came under sharp criticism from French literary men. He is generally considered to be the author of this manifesto, in spite of the fact that it was printed in Milan and is apparently a celebration of the Italian Futurists.

The latter were very active. Marinetti published his *Technical Manifesto of Futurist Literature* in May 1912. A year later he published *Immaginazione senza fili. Parole in libertà*. He later viewed all subsequent avant-garde writing, including Molly Bloom's interior monologue in James Joyce's *Ulysses*, as stemming from his influence. In February 1912 the Italian Futurist painters exhibited at the Bernheim-Jeune Gallery in Paris. A few months later the Futurist composer Luigi Russolo published his manifesto, *The Art of Noises*, opening up the field of music to include "non-musical" sounds and noises. Around the same time, Boccioni's mixed material sculptures were shown at La Boétie Gallery in Paris. And, finally, Boccioni and Severini's former painting teacher, Giacomo Balla, was meanwhile extending the range of the subtle Pointillist and Divisionist technique and using it in his "velocity landscapes."

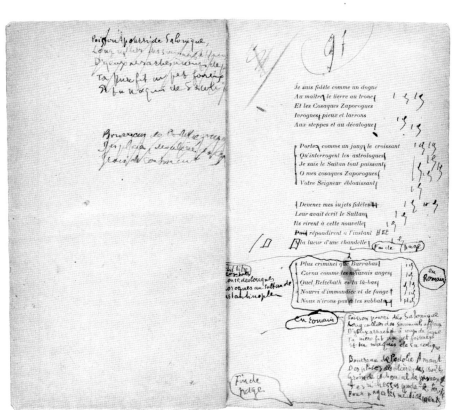

Proofs of Guillaume Apollinaire's Alcools, *from which he has removed all the punctuation, 1913*

Around the time of the fertile encounters between Sonia Delaunay and Blaise Cendrars, Apollinaire and Robert Delaunay, a group of Russians, dubbed *Budetlyane* by Velimir Khlebnikov to distinguish them from the Marinettian Futurists, began producing works that sprang from a cross-fertilization between painting and poetry.

The poet Alexei Kruchenykh issued the first chapbooks of Russian Futurist poetry jointly with the painter Mikhail Larionov. In *Pomada* (Pomade, January 1913) the latter's collages and lithographs combine his primitivist manner with his Rayonist style.

The Russian Futurist "book" is generally a slender mimeographed pamphlet illustrated by a radical artist (usually Larionov, Kasimir Malevich or Natalia Goncharova). Art work and typography are interwoven, and are equally intense, as if they sprang from the same hand. Some of the finest examples of this art-combined-poetry are: *Igra v Adu* (A Game in Hell), with poems by Khlebnikov and Kruchenykh and art by Goncharova; *Starinnaya Lyubov* (Old-Time Love), *Mirskontsa* (Worldbackwards) and especially *Vselenskaya voina* (Universal War), a selection of poems by Kruchenykh illustrated with transparent cut-outs by Olga Rozanova, the first book of abstract collages ever made.

Together with other artists in the Union of Youth, Malevich and David Burliuk staged fertile, eventful creative soirées preparing, with much hot debate, a public declaration of their theoretical position. Olga Rozanova was given the task of writing the group's manifesto as well as an important background article entitled "On the New Creation and the Reasons Why it is Not Understood." It was now, too, that the Union of Youth absorbed an earlier group called Hylaea.

Russian Futurism was launched in the summer of 1913 when Malevich and Kruchenykh met at the summer home of their mutual friend, the composer

Natalia Goncharova: Illustrations for Igra v Adu *(A Game in Hell) by Kruchenykh and Khlebnikov, 1916*

and painter Mikhail Matiushin, at Ussikirko near the Finnish border. They gave their budding friendship and newly formed association a coloring that was both strangely formal and playfully ironic by publishing a manifesto solemnly entitled "First Pan-Russian Congress of the Bards of the Future." This was the founding document of the Russian Futurist movement.

The two friends next collaborated on a Futurist opera, *Pobeda nad solntsem* (Victory over the Sun). Kruchenykh wrote the libretto, Matiushin composed the music and Malevich designed the sets. The trio followed the guidelines laid down in Moscow a few weeks earlier (December 1912) in a

Olga Rozanova: *Illustration for Kruchenykh's* Universal War, *1916*

Kasimir Malevich: *The Gravedigger, 1913*

manifesto entitled "A Slap in the Face of Public Taste," signed by Burliuk, Kruchenykh, Khlebnikov and Mayakovsky:

> We *order* that the poet's rights be revered:
> (1) to enlarge the *scope* of the poet's vocabulary with arbitrary and derivative words (word-novelty);
> (2) to feel an insurmountable hatred for the language existing before their time;
> (3) to push with horror off their proud brow the wreath of cheap fame that you have made from bathhouse switches;
> (4) to stand on the rock of the word "we" amidst the sea of boos and outrage.
>   And if *for the time being* the filthy stigmas of your "common sense" and "good taste" are still present in our lines, these same lines *for the first time* already glimmer with the Summer Lightnings of the New Coming Beauty of the Self-Sufficient (self-centered) Word.

The prologue to the opera was penned by Velimir Khlebnikov, one of the signers of the manifesto, who was the inventor of the "transrational" language, Zaum. In the same spirit, Khlebnikov was also investigating the mathematical basis of history (which led him, in 1912, to predict the downfall of a "certain empire" five years later). Influenced by Khlebnikov's inventions, Kruchenykh became a leading exponent of verbal creation, in particular with a text entitled *Novye puti slova* (The New Ways of the Word in the anthology *Troe*, The Three, 1913) which begins with the statement:

> No one will gainsay me if I declare that we have no
> literary critics (judges of verbo-creation)
> for the vampires who feed on the blood of dead celebrities can hardly be called critics, nor can those who throttle all that is young and alive
> vampires gravediggers cossacks parasites these are the only names
> our critics deserve

Khlebnikov and Kruchenykh were jointly responsible for yet another manifesto, *Deklaratsiya slova kak takovogo* (The Word as Such, 1913). Using various methods of composition, Khlebnikov had begun to elaborate his own language several years earlier. His poems are the measure of this language's possibilities. In "The Laughter Plot," for example, a single phoneme, the root *smiekh* (to laugh), serves as the basis for an "inner declension" which activates "meanings lying dormant in the word" (Benedikt Livchits):

> *The Laughter Plot*
>
> O forthlaugh, you laughers!
>   O laugholate, laughers!
> You who laugh with laughter, who mockster laughingly.
>   O laugholate smilingly!
> O smiling supermocking—laughter of smilaughing laughlers!
> O smilent terlaughs—mockling laughloud laughters!
>   Laughesse, laughesse,
> Terla, terli, laughette, laughette,
>   Laugholators, laugholators!
>   O forthlaugh, you laughers!
>   O laugholate, laughers!

Henceforth, write Kruchenykh and Khlebnikov, "a work can be composed from a single word, and a complete expressive artistic image can be obtained merely by skillfully manipulating that word." One is tempted to say that the language of the Russian Futurists is "illuminated from within," like the characters in *Victory over the Sun*. Refusing to be caught up in the deception of figuration (symbolized by the sun), they declare: "Our light is internal." The opera's poetic demythification of the sun, which is portrayed as an old-fashioned idealistic curiosity, goes hand in hand with a Copernican revolution in language which frees words from their referential function and allows them to become purely emotional units ("self-sufficient words").

We know from Matiushin's account of the performance that it was a shock to the public, "such was the inner force of the words, the power and awesomeness of the sets and the Futurist (actors), the tenderness and sinuousness of the music which twined itself around the words, the tableaux, the Futurist Hercules triumphing over the sun of cheap appearances and lighting their inner light."

On the occasion of the opera's performance at the Luna Park theater at St Petersburg in December 1913, Malevich exhibited for the first time his famous black square, the "royal child," that "icon of our time." The gravedigger wore this square on his torso: it could be viewed as a coffin seen endwise. The square also appeared in some of the artist's sketches for the sets and on the curtain, where it was bisected by a diagonal line, perhaps to symbolize a partial eclipse of appearances.

The characters in the opera were burlesque caricatures who trampled on theatrical conventions. The cast includes: Nero-Caligula, a Fat Man, A Man With Evil Intentions, an Intrepid Voyager Through the Centuries (played by Kruchenykh himself), several Cowards, as well as a number of New Men and Futurist Hercules. The sets on the other hand had an extreme plastic sobriety, with sharp contrasts between the severe geometric surfaces of the white walls and black floor (and between the austere setting and the colorful characters).

Light was the active element in the setting, where it was conceived as a "creative source of forms legitimizing the existence of things in space" (Livchits). As for the sun, the fact that it is captured by the Futurist Hercules suggests a number of interpretations above and beyond the literal explanation of the opera, the most obvious one being that the sun is clearly an image of paternal authority. (Robert Delaunay was then experimenting in Paris with various methods of decomposing sunlight, chiefly by filtering it through a persienne, in an endeavor to capture the colors of the spectrum on canvas.)

How much was known about the Russian Futurists in Paris and Zurich? Very little. Though *Les Soirées de Paris* was financed by Apollinaire's Russian friend Jastrebzoff, there was little contact between French writers

Vladimir Tatlin: *Corner Counter-Relief, 1915*

and artists and their Russian counterparts. There was one exception, though. In the summer of 1913 Vladimir Tatlin visited Paris and met Picasso and Archipenko in their respective studios. Picasso's Cubist assemblages clearly inspired the non-objective reliefs that the Russian artist began to construct after his return to Moscow. Tatlin borrowed the concept of the independent assembled object to create his "synthetico-static compositions," though in fact Picasso conceived his constructions with the purpose of later transferring them on to canvas. Tatlin did sketches of a stunning formal precision (compositions of rhythmical lines) for the forest scene in the opera *Ivan Sussanin* (which was never staged). It is worth noting that in 1920, during the Berlin Dada Fair, George Grosz and John Heartfield brandished a panel bearing the slogan: "*Die Kunst ist tot. Es lebe die neue Maschinenkunst TATLINS*" (Art is dead. Long live Tatlin's new machine art). Malevich, for his part, never visited Paris. He left the Union of Youth in 1914, and both he and Tatlin moved away from Russian Futurism.

In Russia the transrational poet Ilya Zdanevich (jointly with Michel Ledentu) launched a new movement: *Vsechestvo* (Everythingism). Its aesthetic program, which Larionov and Goncharova shared, consisted in "utilizing and combining all the known art forms of the past." Somewhat later, Larionov and Zdanevich (the latter was also the biographer of the former) proclaimed the birth of Futurist body painting, in a manifesto published in the magazine *Argus (Pochemu my raskrashivaemsya*, "Why We Paint Our Faces").

Larionov began a correspondence with Ukrainian-born Sonia Delaunay who had left Russia at the age of twenty to settle in Paris (1905). Thanks to

Alexandra Exter (who lived in Paris off and on between 1909 and 1914) and the expatriate Russians connected with *Les Soirées de Paris*, Larionov showed his Rayonist compositions at the Galerie Paul Guillaume in 1914. Apollinaire prefaced the catalogue. Later, settling in Paris, Larionov and Goncharova designed costumes and sets for Diaghilev's Ballets Russes.

In "The Year 1915" exhibition in Moscow a number of Futurist works were shown by Larionov, Mayakovksy and Wassily Kamensky. They anticipated Dada: one of them was an electric fan in motion. Then, in June, the poet Mayakovsky declared that Russian Futurism was dead.

The link between the Russian avant-garde and the Dada Movement was Ilya Zdanevich, better known as Iliazd. In Paris in 1921 he struck up a friendship with Tristan Tzara, then with Robert and Sonia Delaunay. Tzara and Iliazd collaborated on the former's *Cœur à gaz* performances. Iliazd contributed his own brand of Zaum writing to the friendship and his own publishing venture, the University of Degree 41. As a poet and creative typographer he was later to play a discreet but important role on the Paris art scene (see Chapter 6).

Iliazd and Serge Charchoune took part in various Dada activities, hence the term Russian Dadaism or "Russian Surdadaism" (André Germain), taken up by contemporary critics and still used today to describe Russian Futurism, including the pre-Dada period. Tzara himself included Iliazd and Charchoune in the Dada Movement. In *Some Memoirs of Dadaism* (1922) he writes: "In Russia the Dadaists call themselves '41°': Zdanevich, Kruchenykh and Terentiev. They are abstract and very productive. The first mentioned is professor of Dadaism at the University of Tiflis."

*Before the bell rings take your places on the clouds, the
trees, and the whaling beds.
The blare of the trumpetries will be wafted up to you.
The useman will welcome you.
The singalist's dreamy whining will fill the contemplier.
The bellringlets comply with the impromptu stroller.
The seeds of Futuroslavl will fly off into life.
The contemplier is a mouth!
Hark, be all hearkened to, contemplookerson!
And steal a glance.*

Velimir Khlebnikov, 1913

△ **Georgi Yakulov:** *The Picturesque Café in Moscow, 1917*

▷ **Iliazd:** *Poster for his lecture* New Schools in Russian
Poetry, *Paris, 1921*

Iliazd photographed in Paris in 1922

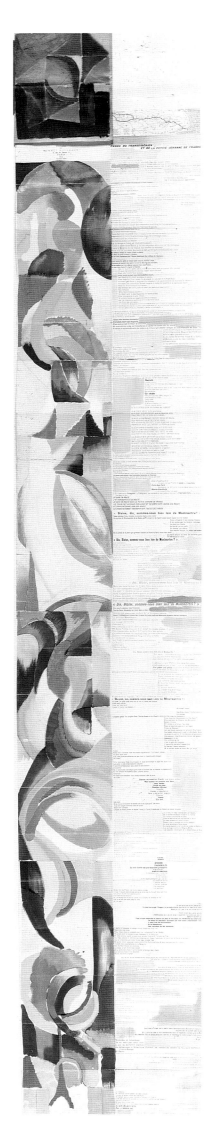

Sonia Delaunay and Blaise Cendrars:
La Prose du Transsibérien et
de la Petite Jehanne de France, *1913*

Photograph of Sonia Delaunay, undated

Simultaneism: from autonomous colors to autonomous words

In Paris simultaneity was the order of the day. In an essay on "The Aesthetics of Dramatic Poetry" (1912-1914), published in his own periodical *Poème et Drame*, Henri Barzun set forth the theory of *simultanéisme*. Barzun was also responsible for a short article, signed by some alleged "antagonists," violently accusing Apollinaire, whose mother was Polish, of "half-caste plagiarism" for appropriating ideas that Barzun considered— retrospectively—as his own! One of the founders of the Abbaye de Créteil group (1906-1908), Barzun advocated a program of adapting the musical technique of polyphony to literary creation. He composed odes that later took the form of "dramas" consisting of poems (dramatism) and songs alternating three groups of four voices each.

Simultaneism can be defined as the attempt to express reality under all its aspects, not in succession but simultaneously. Viewed thus, it can be seen as an extension of the Cubist rendering of objects and figures from several angles at once. Delaunay was fond of speaking of reality as "rhythmical simultaneousness," and he emphasized its role in color and light: "Simultaneity in light is harmony, the rhythm of colors that creates the vision of men."

The attempt to render simultaneously the perceptions impinging on the modern consciousness is one of the fundamental points of the new aesthetic.

Most of the creations dating from these years reflect this preoccupation: Apollinaire's conversation-poems ("*Lundi rue Christine*"), the first Dada events at the Cabaret Voltaire in Zurich. These latter opened with African chants (abstract poetry) and a simultaneous German and French recitation of the poem "The Admiral's in Search of a House to Rent."

In a note appended to the printed text of this poem, Tzara outlined a brief theoretical history of simultaneism and acknowledged the graphic, typographic and linguistic experiments of precursors like Apollinaire, Barzun, Marinetti and Mallarmé. He also evoked the beginnings of Cubism: "The experiments with transmuting objects and colors conducted by the first Cubist painters (1907), Picasso, Braque, Picabia, Duchamp-Villon, Delaunay, prompt one to apply the same principle of simultaneity to poetry."

This principle was being put to the test in painting by Robert and Sonia Delaunay and in poetry by Blaise Cendrars. In the latter's poem *Crépitements* (Cracklings), we read:

> The rainbow dissonances of the Tower's
>   wireless telegraphy
> Midday
> Midnight
> People saying *merde* to each other from every corner of the universe
>
> Sparks
> Chrome yellow
> We're in touch
> Ocean liners approaching from every quarter
> Sailing into the distance
> All the watches are set
> And the bells are ringing
> *Paris-Midi* headlines a German professor was
>   devoured by cannibals in the Congo
> Serves him right
> The evening *Intransigeant* prints postcard verses
> This is crazy when the astrologers are all housebreaking
> the stars

Simultaneism "sets all the watches" and imparts ubiquity to Cendrars' lines which seem to reach out to all the great cities of the world, challenging the old metaphoric poetry with chance encounters between simultaneous images and places.

How does Robert Delaunay define simultaneity? "The simultaneous," he wrote, "was fully brought out for the first time in 1912, being completely expressed in my painting *The Windows* for which Apollinaire wrote his famous poem... Intimations of it had already appeared in 1910 in the picture of my destructive period, *The Eiffel Tower... The Windows* was far more significant in its sensibility, its pictorial and poetic novelty. For if one compares it with the past, the time when it was painted or even the present, it is a real creation. I mean that there is nothing like it in traditional art, there is nothing like it at present, and I think it has been misunderstood. When I compare it to other works, I find no trace of it in the intention or physical appearance of any painting by another artist, not even in mosaics, which resemble it superficially. The first time I noticed a trace of this thought was in the notes Leonardo da Vinci wrote concerning the difference between the art of painting and literature, but his observation applies only to the eye function. He tries to demonstrate the intellectual superiority resulting from the simultaneous perceptions of the eyes, those *windows of the soul*, over the successive auditory function of the ear. But, as you can see in *The Windows*, what I was driving at was simply color for color's sake."

The Windows (one motif of which was reproduced in *Dada 2*, Zurich, December 1917) inspired one of Guillaume Apollinaire's most famous poems, of the same name. In a letter to Madeleine Pagès, the poet confides: "My *Windows* stems from a wholly new aesthetic, whose workings I have not been able to enter into again."

The term "simultaneous" was not new in art. Robert Delaunay borrowed it from Chevreul's treatise, *De la loi du contraste simultané des couleurs et de l'assortiment des objets colorés considéré d'après cette loi* (1839). Nor was Chevreul, then director of the Gobelins tapestry works in Paris, the only influence on the Delaunays. Sonia made no secret of her debt to Seurat and Signac; she had met the latter and read his book *D'Eugène Delacroix au néo-impressionnisme* (1899).

Adopted first by the Delaunays and then by Blaise Cendrars, who proclaimed himself a "simultaneous poet," the term *simultané* soon became a Delaunay trademark. The couple used it for their first "simultaneous disks" (1912), for solar prisms, and for the dresses, costumes and accessories they designed for the Paris Exhibition of Decorative Arts in 1925.

The finest result of the collaboration between the Delaunays and Blaise Cendrars, and the symbol of their friendship, is *La Prose du Transsibérien et de la petite Jehanne de France* (October 1913), a sequence of images (simultaneous colors) and poetry on a continuous strip of paper some six feet high that unfolds in the manner of the first automobile maps, which began to appear around the same time. To the color rhythm is added a typographical rhythm combining some ten different typefaces and offering the viewer a supplementary series of simultaneous contrasts.

Robert Delaunay: *Windows over the City (1st part, 2nd motif), 1912*

Just as Duchamp and Picabia's paintings were viewed as (for lack of a better word) "Cubist" works when first shown in New York, the pure color movement, despite the fact that it had nothing in common with the muted tones of the Cubist palette, was regarded as a "poetic" branch of that movement by Apollinaire who dubbed it "Orphic Cubism."

In his *Méditations esthétiques* (1913), Apollinaire distinguishes four kinds of Cubism, which he groups into two pairs: Scientific Cubism and Physical Cubism, Orphic Cubism and Instinctive Cubism. To be sure, there were good reasons to simplify, given the general lack of understanding for avant-garde art at the time and the need (or so the poet thought) to make a united front of all the new artistic trends.

These years were rich in literary-artistic friendships. "Zeppelins and Big Berthas were being hailed by poets as new images," wrote Paul Morand; "trust and cheerfulness greeted the first American soldiers; one worked in an atmosphere of cameraderie, endless talk and mutual admiration which I have never encountered again. One even saw writers liking each other!" It was at the Delaunays' that Apollinaire took refuge after being wrongly accused (and imprisoned for one week) of stealing the Mona Lisa and some statuettes from the Louvre. (It is true that the poet's secretary did actually commit one of these thefts!)

Not long after, the Delaunays met Blaise Cendrars at one of Apollinaire's regular Wednesday gatherings in his apartment on the Boulevard Saint-Germain or at the Café de Flore. Cendrars had just returned from New York where he had spent several months, mostly reading in the New York Public Library. He had written his first long poem, *Les Pâques à New York* (Easter in New York), in a single night in April 1912. And he had then hurried back to Paris, as if his sole purpose in crossing the Atlantic had been to write this poem. He had then had a hundred copies of it run off on an anarchist press in the 19th arrondissement.

Gino Severini: *North-South, 1912*

It was from one of these copies that Cendrars read the poem to Apollinaire and the Delaunays. So deeply impressed was the author of *Alcools*, who was seven years Cendrars' senior, that some critics believe Cendrars' poetry had a decisive influence on Apollinaire's style. In any event, he assured Cendrars that *Les Pâques à New York* was "better than all the poems published in *Le Mercure* [*de France*] in the last ten years."

In 1913 Sonia Delaunay, before setting to work with Blaise Cendrars on the first simultaneous book, *La Prose du Transsibérien*, devised a simultaneous binding for *Les Pâques à New York*. She had already done bindings for an edition of Rimbaud (1909) and for a book by the Italian writer Ricciotto Canudo, who marked the period by helping to make the cinema the seventh art.

Marie Laurencin:
Apollinaire and his Friends, 1909; left to right, Gertrude Stein, Fernande Olivier, a muse, Guillaume Apollinaire, the dog Fricka, Pablo Picasso, Marguerite Gillot, Maurice Cremnitz, Marie Laurencin

Pablo Picasso: *Caricature of Apollinaire, undated*

LES PÂQUES À NEW YORK

... Seigneur, l'aube a glissé froide comme un suaire
Et a mis tout à nu les gratte-ciel dans les airs.

Déjà un bruit immense retentit sur la ville.
Déjà les trains bondissent, grondent et défilent.

Les métropolitains roulent et tonnent sous terre.
Les ponts sont secoués par les chemins de fer.

La cité tremble. Des cris, du feu et des fumées,
Des sirènes à vapeur rauquent comme des huées.

Une foule enfiévrée par les sueurs de l'or
Se bouscule et s'engouffre dans de longs corridors.

Trouble, dans le fouillis empanaché des toits,
Le soleil, c'est votre Face souillée par les crachats...

Blaise Cendrars, 1912

EASTER IN NEW YORK

.... Lord, the dawn has glided in cold as a shroud/And has laid bare the skyscrapers in the air./Already an immense noise resounds over the city./Already the trains are bounding forward, rumbling and filing past./The subways roll and thunder underground./The bridges are shaken by the railroads./The city trembles. Outcries, fire and smoke,/Steamer sirens blow hoarsely like hootings./A crowd fevered by the toiling for gold/Hustles and surges into long corridors./Dim, in the gaudy jumble of roofs,/The sun, it's your Face sullied by spittle ...

Cast of Guillaume Apollinaire's play Les Mamelles de Tirésias, *produced in Paris on ▷ June 24, 1917. Lower right, the author*

Cendrars and Canudo, close as their poetic position was to Apollinaire's, also shared some of his other preoccupations, in particular his patriotism and his commitment to defending France militarily. Canudo's periodical *Montjoie!* (1913) bore the ambiguous subtitle: "The Organ of French Imperialism." When the First World War broke out the two writers jointly wrote an "Appeal to France's Foreign Friends," urging the latter to enlist in the French forces. Published in most of the Parisian newspapers, this open letter is said to have prompted some eighty thousand volunteer enlistments. Cendrars was not among those who could admit that Braque, Léger or Derain should be at the front and not Picabia or Picasso.

The war divided Apollinaire's generation and opposed it to the pacifism of the next. Despite the young Dadaists' admiration for Apollinaire, they were uncomfortable with the poems in which, perhaps influenced by the bellicose aesthetics of the Italian Futurists ("War is the world's only hygiene," wrote Marinetti in 1911), he celebrated armed conflict. They all looked up to him, but their pacifism bothered him (see Chapter 3) and prevented him from having close ties with the Zurich Dadaists. He expressed his disagreement with their ideas about the war by mail, but in rather guarded terms owing to the postal censorship.

Apollinaire's reservations about Dada, like his commitment to fighting for France, must be viewed in the context of the First World War and in the light of the poet's personal problems. He was moved to enlist by a number of things: his high moral standards (which often made life difficult for him), his deep attachment to France, a desire for integration certainly, together with the desire to atone for the dishonor of his imprisonment (though he was soon cleared and released). Finally, his precarious relationship with Lou, the young woman of *Calligrammes* and the melancholy *Poèmes à Lou*, precipitated his decision to enlist. He applied for French citizenship, then requested to be sent to the front. He died in November 1918 of the Spanish flu, weakened by a severe head wound sustained in action.

JEAN THILLOIS   HOWARD   EDMOND VALLÉE   J. NORVILLE

Une Manifestation "Sic": *Les Mamelles de Tirésias*

EDMOND VALLÉE   JULIETTE NORVILLE   LOUISE MARION   HOWARD   GUILLAUME APOLLINAIRE

The provocativeness and sense of fun of the Dada artists owed more to its few precursors than to the aesthetic doctrines that emerged with the beginnings of abstraction. Foremost among them was the poet Arthur Cravan, whose name is linked enduringly with bravado, high spirits and tenderness. An appealing, impulsive figure, Cravan was not only a poet but also, if we are to believe him—and Cravan's statements have proved to be trustworthy — "a swindler, a seaman on the Pacific Ocean, a mule driver, an orange picker in California, a snake charmer, a hotel thief, Oscar Wilde's nephew, a logger in the giant forest, a former French boxing champion, the grandson of the Queen's chancellor, a chauffeur in Berlin, a housebreaker, etc., etc."

In April 1912 Cravan published the first issue of the periodical *Maintenant* (Now), a title that was a manifesto in its own right. Proclaiming himself an ardent champion of the present, Cravan distanced himself not only from "this old world" but also from Italian Futurism, of which the American collector Walter Arensberg had quipped that it "would always be a thing of the future." The English poetess Mina Loy, soon to become Cravan's companion, was equally scathing about the Italian Futurists. They were, she said, simply "fighting evil with evil." Mina Loy first attracted notice with some "Aphorisms on Futurism" published in *Camera Work* in 1914. Her most

important book, *Lunar Baedecker*, was published in 1923 by Robert McAlmon's Contact Press in Paris.

Anticipating some of the later Dada magazines, *Maintenant* was small in format, sober in appearance and designed with care, with a running title and thin black line at the top of each page. It would probably not have drawn much attention had it not been for the fact that it was hawked from a baby carriage parked by the exit of the Gaumont race course by the publisher himself accompanied by either the boxing champion Silver Sivre, the Hungarian painter Jacobi, or Cravan's best friend Jourdan, the son of a restaurant proprietor from the Auvergne whose tongue-in-cheek advertising slogans added spice to the little magazine: "Where can one see Van Dongen putting food into his mouth, masticating it, digesting it and smoking? At Jourdan's restaurant."

All the articles in *Maintenant* appear to have been written by Cravan himself. Like the Portuguese poet Fernando Pessoa, Cravan chose different pseudonyms for different topics: W. Cooper for articles on Oscar Wilde, Edouard Archinard (almost a phonetic anagram of *anarchie*) for a poem in classical alexandrines, Marie Lowitska for aphorisms, Robert Miradique for literary criticism. The boxer-poet signed his own name to his apocryphal encounters with André Gide and to his detailed, mordant comments about the artists exhibiting at the Salon des Indépendants.

The opening lines of W. Cooper's article on Oscar Wilde, soberly entitled "Unpublished Documents Concerning Oscar Wilde," set the tone—a scathingly ironic and polemical one—for the little magazine, and warned the unwary reader that here was a periodical unlike any other. Oscar Wilde, as everyone knows, was convicted for having committed "immoral acts" and was thrown into prison in 1895 by a hypocritical society that, after applauding his genius, had then found his conduct criminal. This clearly called for a head-on attack: "Oscar Wilde, who was favored, some say, with a well developed though receding forehead, while his nobly ovoid skull swelled out at the back, held that the seat of man's true faculties was not the front of the skull but its hindmost part, and averred that men of great ability got their ideas. . . from the back of their mind."

Cravan's claim to be the nephew of Oscar Wilde was long thought to be merely a provocation, and the best biographies of Wilde have ignored Cravan's many writings about his uncle. Yet the fact is that Oscar Wilde was

Every great artist has the sense of provocation.
Dullards only see the beautiful in beautiful things.

Marie Lowitska (Arthur Cravan)

*I prefer all the eccentricities of even a commonplace mind
to the tame works of a bourgeois fool.*

Arthur Cravan

Genius is an extravagant manifestation of the body.

Arthur Cravan

married to the sister of Otho Lloyd, who was none other than the father of Fabian Lloyd (Cravan's real name). The boxer-poet always fondly remembered his cousins, Oscar Wilde's two sons, whose childhood games he had shared.

Like most of what he wrote, Cravan's account of his alleged encounters with Oscar Wilde is a masterpiece of humorous and tender irreverence. Its slapstick bluster ('' 'Shut up, you old sot,' I bellowed, pouring us another drink And then, going utterly beyond the pale, I began to question him thus: 'You old rotter, tell me immediately where you've been! How did you find out what floor I live on!' '') is a counterpoise to the author's nostalgia for a great writer he undoubtedly would have liked to know and whom he wished to rescue from the dishonor heaped upon him.

Cravan's mystifications, his knack of placing art and literature on the same plane as ordinary life, his sarcastic dismissal of certain artists and writers ("All Books, Periodicals and Manuscripts addressed to Robert Miradique will be subjected to merciless criticism. Nothing will be returned") and, finally, his way of making scandalous behavior an element of art—all this makes him a major forerunner of the polemical side of Dada. From an artistic standpoint, he deserves credit for the invention of the "prosopoem," the autobiographical narrative combining poetry and prose.

Cravan's mysterious disappearance off the coast of Mexico in 1918 helped to give him a place in what Aragon calls the "fluorescent realm of myths," where he was joined, only a few weeks later (January 1919), as if wafted there on the smoke from his opium pipe, by the poet Jacques Vaché (whose personality made a lasting impression on André Breton).

Shortly before he vanished, Cravan had married Mina Loy, the English poetess who had befriended Djuna Barnes, Marcel Duchamp, James Joyce, Man Ray, Sylvia Beach, Louis Aragon and William Carlos Williams. In his *Autobiography* the latter writes: "Never shall I forget our fascination with Mina's 'Pig Cupid, his rosy snout rooting erotic garbage.'. . . Mina was very English, very skittish, an evasive long-limbed woman. . . Marianne Moore was in awed admiration of Mina's long-legged charms. . . Later Mina married Cravan and went to Central America with him where he bought and rebuilt a seagoing craft of some sort. One evening, having triumphantly finished his job, he got into it to try it out in the bay before supper. He never returned.

Pregnant on the shore, she watched the small ship move steadily away into the distance. For years she thought to see him again."

At least, this is how the literary version goes. To it André Breton adds the following: "There are reports of him teaching physical education at the Athletic Academy in Mexico City in 1919 [*sic*]; he is said to have been working on a lecture on Egyptian art. We lose trace of him shortly thereafter in the Gulf of Mexico where he had ventured out one night in the frailest of crafts" (*Anthologie de l'humour noir*, 1940). According to Tzara, "a sixth issue of *Maintenant* is said to have appeared in Mexico City," and Blaise Cendrars states that "Cravan was assassinated in a boxing academy he had set up in Mexico City. A dagger that went straight to his heart. Nobody knows why, or who did it."

Cravan's disappearance corresponds almost too perfectly to one of the author's literary fantasies; moreover it recalls the death of Shelley almost a century earlier, who disappeared in the Gulf of Spezia while his wife and Lord Byron waited vainly for him to return. Toward the end of 1912, Cravan had in fact written to his mother, telling her that he was intending to disappear in such a way that people would think he was dead. "There will presumably be a committee for the publication of my posthumous works." In another variation of this idea, Cravan had reported in a special issue of *Maintenant* that his uncle Oscar Wilde was actually still alive. (Wilde had died in 1900 when Cravan was thirteen).

Both a poet and an adventurer, Cravan, that "mystical colossus," as Mina Loy called him, embodied an ideal sketched by Tristan Tzara in his "Open Letter to Jacques Rivière," editor of the *Nouvelle Revue Française*: "I do not write professionally, and I have no literary ambitions. I might have become a dashing adventurer with refined gestures, had I had the physical strength and stamina to accomplish this sole prowess: not being bored."

Cravan did not display the whole range of his talents in *Maintenant*, far from it. Though he did not actually join the Dada movement, he took part all the same in some of its events (see Chapter 4 for the role he played in Barcelona and New York). He did so with such *éclat* that Blaise Cendrars was later able to write: "It was in New York that he made his real début and that his way of behaving, of making himself liked and of being scandalous brought him success. His stay there was short but he made a lasting impact."

Otto van Rees: *Poster for the exhibition Arp/Adya van Rees-Dutilh/Otto van Rees at the Tanner Gallery, Zurich, 1915*

Chapter 3

Zurich: A Justifiable Enthusiasm
Beyond war and nationalities

Hugo Ball and Emmy Hennings, Zurich, 1918

In 1915 several young men, revolted by the butchery of the First World War and the social and cultural systems that had spawned it, banded together in Zurich, Switzerland. From their friendships, their pooling of common, though sometimes conflicting, energies channeled into artistic activities, there emerged the Cabaret Voltaire. A small theater which saw the birth of the first events staged by the members of the Dada Movement, the Cabaret Voltaire was located in a back room of the Meierei tavern on Spiegelgasse. Almost immediately, a group, a periodical and an art gallery followed in its wake.

In fact, the review *Cabaret Voltaire* had barely made its appearance under Hugo Ball's guidance when Tristan Tzara galvanized the Dada Movement into life. In his editorial in the first and only issue of this little magazine (15 May 1916), Ball announced the birth of another periodical: *Dada*. "When I founded the Cabaret Voltaire," he wrote, "I was sure that there were a number of young men in Switzerland who, like myself, were determined not only to enjoy their independence, but also to demonstrate it." And he concluded: "With the help of our French, Italian and Russian friends, we are publishing this little magazine. Its purpose is to detail the activities of the Cabaret. The Cabaret's role is to remind us that, beyond the war and nationalities, there are independent men who live by other ideals. The artists who are gathered here intend to publish an international review. It will appear in Zurich and will be called DADA, Dada Dada Dada Dada."

The presence of so many artists, writers and independent thinkers in Switzerland, that peaceful oasis in strife-torn Europe, can be explained by their common rejection of the war. In the distance they heard the booming of guns. In two weeks alone, in February 1916, six million shells were fired at Verdun, and eighty thousand men were killed. In Berlin, where the population was on the brink of starvation, there were riots. In Dublin, a nationalist uprising spearheaded by the clandestine Irish army, the Irish Volunteers, was crushed by British troops.

Meanwhile, only a stone's throw from the Cabaret Voltaire, Lenin was planning the Russian Revolution. (It broke out a year later, in two stages—February and October 1917.) Hans Richter claimed jokingly that the authorities in Zurich "were far more suspicious of the Dadaists, who were liable to pull off some unexpected stunt at any moment, than of those quiet, scholarly Russians" [Lenin, Radek, Zinoviev]. Zurich also harbored the Irish writer James Joyce, then working on that *magnum opus* of modern fiction, *Ulysses*, which like the Dada Movement was to gain recognition in Paris a few years later. For the moment, the artistic capital of the world—a devastated world, to be sure—was the tranquil, respectable lakeside city of Zurich.

Geneva, for its part, was the base of a pacifist group led by Romain Rolland, which included Henri Guilbeaux, Frans Masereel and Pierre-Jean Jouve. But even in neutral Switzerland this group had trouble publishing its declarations. Jouve was writing (*Poème contre le grand crime*, *Hôtel-Dieu*, *Récits d'hôpital en 1915*). The young Jorge Luis Borges was learning French and German, discovering the Expressionist writers, reading Max Stirner (*Der Einzige und sein Eigentum*, 1845). Stravinsky, in exile near Geneva, was composing. One of his keyboard compositions is dedicated to a young pianist who performed Saint-Saëns at the Cabaret Voltaire: Arthur Rubinstein.

A great negative work of destruction to be accomplished

Had it not been for their intense creative activity, the handful of Zurich Dadaists would have been just another short-lived pacifist group. Ironically, their primary goal was not to launch a new art movement, but to engage in radical protest for the sake of life itself—a protest that went beyond the issues of art.

"In Zurich," wrote Hans Arp, "unconcerned with the slaughterhouses of the world war, we gave ourselves up to the Fine Arts. While the thunder of guns sounded in the distance, we pasted, we recited, we versified, we sang with all our soul. We searched for an elementary art that would, we thought, save mankind from the furious folly of these times. We aspired to a new order that might restore the balance between heaven and hell. This art rapidly became an object of general reprobation. It is not surprising that the 'bandits' were unable to understand us. Their puerile mania for authoritarianism leads them to use art itself as a means to stultify mankind" ("Dadaland" [1948] in *On My Way*).

Though their group included some of the major future artists of this century, it was mainly the Dadaists' distrust of art and the complacencies that go with it that characterized them in the eyes of the public. Dada was not intended to be the tip of the avant-garde in modern art. "And so Dada was born of a need for independence, of a distrust towards society. Those who are with us preserve their freedom. We recognize no theory. We have enough Cubist and Futurist academies: laboratories of formal ideas." So wrote Tristan Tzara in his *Dada Manifesto 1918* (July 23, 1918). "Let each man proclaim: there is a great negative work of destruction to be accomplished. We must sweep and clean. Affirm the cleanliness of the individual after the state of madness, aggressive complete madness of a world abandoned to the hands of bandits, who rend one another and destroy the centuries. Without aim or design, without organization, indomitable madness, decomposition."

Commenting on the efforts of Parisian critics to pigeon-hole Dada and give it a place among the modern movements, Tzara explained to Roger Vitrac in 1923: "If what you are talking about is that intellectual tendency that

Tristan Tzara: *Astronomy-Calligram, 1916*

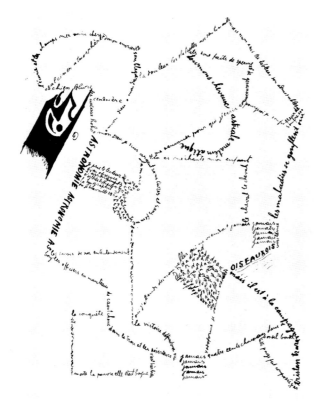

has always existed and that Apollinaire called *l'Esprit nouveau*, I'm not at all interested in modernism. And I think that it was wrong to say that Dadaism, Cubism and Futurism have a common foundation. The last two were mainly based on a principle of intellectual or technical progress, whereas Dadaism was not based on any theory and was simply a protest.''

The first Dada group: Arp, Ball, Huelsenbeck, Janco, Tzara, Serner, Van Rees

The Dada protest was born in the free, unprogrammatic, collective space of the Cabaret Voltaire, which was the creation of the writer and theater director Hugo Ball. Ball had come to Switzerland in 1915, at the beginning of the war. ''He belonged to the race of thinkers and poets who had several lines of occupation in those days,'' writes Hans Richter. ''Ball was interested in everything: he was at once a philosopher, a novelist, a cabaret artist, a poet, a journalist and a mystic.'' An outstanding personality, Ball very soon moved away from Dada, and, as early as 1919, wrote *Zur Kritik der deutschen Intelligenz* (Critique of the German Intelligence) which already contains a foreboding of Hitler's rise. In his diary *Die Flucht aus der Zeit* (Flight Out of Time), published by his companion Emmy Hennings soon after his death in 1927, he gives a detailed account of the formation of the first Dada group.

Ball's announcement of the opening of the Cabaret Voltaire, published as a press communiqué, was promptly answered by Arp and his future companion Sophie Taeuber; the Rumanian painter Marcel Janco and his friend the poet Tristan Tzara, who had recently arrived from the ''Paris of the Balkans,'' Bucharest. They were followed by a young German poet and medical student, Richard Huelsenbeck. A few months later, Huelsenbeck was to start another Dada group in Berlin (early 1918). Worth mentioning too is the fascinating and mysterious Walter Serner who, in the wake of Tzara's celebrated *Dada Manifesto 1918*, composed a witty, fiery manifesto of his own, entitled *Letzte Lockerung* (Last Loosening).

Jean (Hans) Arp and his brother François were drawn to Zurich and the haven of Swiss neutrality partly for autobiographical reasons: their father was German, their mother Alsatian. To evade conscription in Germany, Arp succeeded in convincing the German consulate in Zurich that he was insane.

Arp, before joining the Cabaret Voltaire, spent some time at the Monte Verità colony in Ascona, in Italian Switzerland. Lying on the frontier between the Germanic and Mediterranean cultures, at the northern tip of Lago Maggiore, near Locarno, the libertarian community of Monte Verità was a retreat for artists and thinkers. Mikhail Bakunin had sojourned there as early as 1869; so had Erich Mühsam. By turns a lay monastery for theosophists, a vegetarian commune and a school for the ''art of living'' (an idea of Rudolf von Laban's whose female dancers took an active part in the Dada soirées), Monte Verità was a seed-bed of anarchist thinking. Its rejection of the standard social values being ushered in by industrialization, urbanization and technological progress was reflected in a variety of creeds and ideals: the back to nature movement, Oriental philosophy, vegetarian cooking, libertarian socialism and diverse forms of personal liberation, including sexual liberation. The school of natural expressive dancing which Mary Wigman developed there is the source of modern choreography.

The guests at Monte Verità included the dissident psychoanalyst Otto Gross (see Chapter 5), Carl Gustav Jung, Marianne von Werefkin, Jawlensky, the leader of the Dutch labor movement Ferdinand Domela Nieuwenhuis, and his son, the future Constructivist César Domela. Most of the Zurich Dadaists, in particular Ball, Hennings and Richter, spent some time at Monte Verità as well. During the First World War Joyce, Rilke and Hermann Hesse stayed briefly at the colony as did, in the twenties, El Lissitzky and the Bauhaus artists Albers, Bayer, Breuer, Gropius, Moholy-Nagy, Klee, Schawinsky.

Arp joined his friend, the Rumanian painter Arthur Segal, at Monte Verità, where he also met the Dutch painter Otto van Rees and his wife Adya van Rees-Dutilh. Even before the Cabaret Voltaire and Dada came into

existence, Arp, Otto and Adya mounted an assault on traditional tastes with a group show at the Galerie Tanner in Zurich (November 1915). Otto van Rees's poster for the show combines an abstract composition of cut-out pasted papers with letters and numerals printed from wooden characters in thick black (Werkman would later use them in Holland for his periodical *The Next Call*). It is a major work of the Zurich period and a forerunner of countless compositions that mix painting and typography. Arp, Segal and the van Reeses all took part in the first Cabaret Voltaire events.

At the first soirée the future Dada group took shape. ''The place was jammed,'' wrote Hugo Ball. ''Many people could not find a seat. At about six in the evening, while we were still busy hammering and putting up futuristic posters, an Oriental-looking deputation of four little men arrived, with portfolios and pictures under their arms; repeatedly they bowed politely. They introduced themselves: Marcel Janco the painter, Tristan Tzara, Georges Janco, and a fourth gentleman whose name I did not quite catch. Arp happened to be there also, and we were able to communicate without too many words. Soon Janco's sumptuous *Archangels* was hanging with the other beautiful objects, and on that same evening Tzara read some traditional-style poems, which he fished out of his various coat pockets in a rather charming way.''

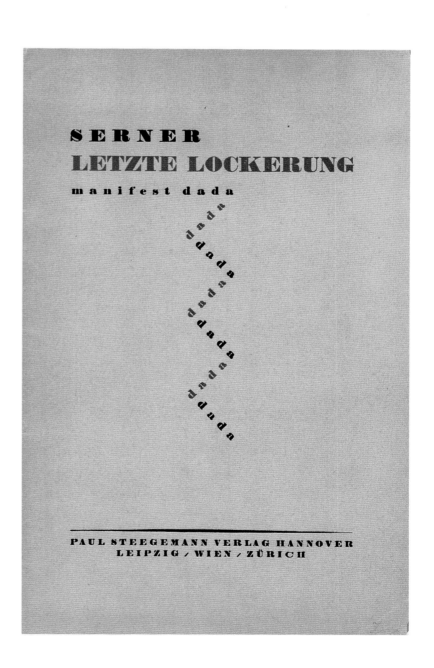

A few days after the Cabaret Voltaire opened on February 5, 1916, the word Dada suddenly appeared. Its birth has become a legend. Several artists and poets claim to have discovered it. Huelsenbeck was so insistent that it was he who came up with the word that, in 1921, Arp felt obliged to come to the aid of Tristan Tzara when André Breton tried to discredit him: "I hereby declare that Tristan Tzara discovered the word Dada on February 8, 1916, at six o'clock in the afternoon; I was present with my twelve children when Tzara for the first time uttered this word which filled us so justifiably with enthusiasm. This took place at the Café de la Terrasse in Zurich, and I was wearing a brioche in my left nostril. I am convinced that this word is of no importance and that only half-wits and Spanish professors [a hit at Picabia] can be interested in the dates."

Though Arp playfully undercuts the strictly historical nature of this declaration, it is nonetheless a valuable testimonial insofar as one of the later Zurich Dadaists, Christian Schad, addressed a bitter letter to Picabia, following a visit to Paris in 1921, in which he attributes the discovery of the movement and its ideas to Walter Serner. However, Serner himself never made such a claim and always remained on good terms with Tzara. But this does not mean that Arp's declaration is the final word on the matter.

Huelsenbeck says: "The word Dada was hit on by chance in a German-French dictionary by Ball and myself while we were looking for a stage name for Madame Le Roy, a singer at our cabaret. Dada is also

Tristan Tzara in Zurich, 1917

contained in the French word *cheval à dada*" (hobby horse). A letter from Ball to Huelsenbeck, dated November 28, 1916, seems to support this version: "... and finally I also described Dada therein: the Cabaret and the Gallery. You would then have the last word on the matter, as you had the first." Nevertheless, Ball writes in his diary, on April 18, 1916: "Tzara keeps on worrying about the periodical. My proposal to call it *Dada* is accepted. We could take turns at editing, and a general editorial staff could assign one member the job of selection and layout for each issue."

Tzara never bothered to claim that it was he who had discovered the word Dada; his authority and the decisive role he played in the birth of the movement were recognized everywhere (see Chapter 4 regarding the New York group's request to him to call their magazine *New York Dada*).

When he wrote his "Zurich Chronicle" for the *Dada Almanac* (see Chapter 5) published by Huelsenbeck in Berlin in 1920, Tzara's intention may have been to forestall any future controversy about the invention or discovery of the word. He notes in passing: "A word was born, no one knows how DADA DADA we took an oath of friendship on the new transmutation that signifies nothing, and was the most formidable protest, the most intense armed affirmation of salvation liberty blasphemy mass combat speed prayer tranquillity private guerilla negation and chocolate of the desperate."

Perhaps the true explanation lies in the phrase "a word born, no one knows how." There was at this time a cosmetic called "Dada" cream, manufactured by Bergmann & Co. in Zurich. If this hypothesis is correct, the divers claims about who actually discovered the word Dada would all seem to be wrong. And if that is the case, they amount to a sort of collective conspiracy to confuse historians and critics and to amuse the public, always delighted by the spectacle of Dadaists wrangling over historical details which they are supposed to despise—some of them getting so nettled as to fall out with each other (Tzara and Huelsenbeck).

Tzara: from *Mr. Antipyrine* to the *Dada Manifesto 1918*

In his teens, in Rumania, Tzara published poems in the Symbolist vein, heavily influenced by the verse of Emile Verhaeren. Not much else is known about this young poet who suddenly appeared in the firmament of avant-garde art in Zurich in 1916, taking the lead in this most spontaneous and unpredictable of movements. All the energy of Dada seems to have been concentrated in his small frame. From the outset he took on most of the movement's tasks: organizing events, publishing *Dada*, borrowing art works, mounting exhibitions. By contacting those writers and painters who were capable of sharing the boldness and freedom of the Dadaists, he immediately gave the movement an international dimension.

Relatively tame at first, Tzara's ferocity grew after those early contacts, though as yet they were merely indicative of the gropings of a young poet (Tzara was only nineteen in 1916) searching at once for his own voice and for allies and friends. . .

Création mystérieuse!
revolver magique!
MOUVEMENT DADA

The first two numbers of his little periodical were slender pamphlets entitled *Dada, recueil littéraire et artistique* (July and December 1917). As his means were limited, the reproductions were all in black and white. They included works by the Zurich Dadaists (Arp, Janco, Lüthy, Van Rees) and others for which Tzara succeeded in obtaining halftone blocks abroad: one panel from Delaunay's *Windows*, a Kandinsky watercolor contributed by *Der Sturm* in Berlin, a Chirico by courtesy of the dealer Paul Guillaume in Paris (who also put Tzara in touch with Apollinaire).

Logic is a complication. Logic is always wrong. It draws the threads of notions, words, in their formal exterior, toward illusory ends and centers. Its chains kill, it is an enormous centipede stifling independence.

Tristan Tzara, Dada Manifesto 1918

▽ **Marcel Janco:** *Woodcut illustration for Tzara's "The First Celestial Adventure of Mr. Antipyrine," 1916*

▷ *Letter from Tzara to Pierre Albert-Birot, Zurich, 1917*

▷▽ **Marcel Janco:** *Cover of Tzara's "The First Celestial Adventure of Mr. Antipyrine," Zurich, 1916*

MOUVEMENT·DADA

Zurich,le 12 août 1917.

Cher monsieur,

J'ai lu avec grand plaisir votre carte et je serais heureux de publier quelque chose de vous dans le prochain numéro de " D A D A ".
Je vous envoie quelques pages de moi pour " S I C " que j'apprécie et que j'aime.Je n'ai pas encore reçu votre livre ni la revue,mais je les attends avec impatience.
Recevez,cher monsieur,une bonne poignée de main d'un allié roumain
TRISTAN TZARA
Zurich|Suisse|Bellerivestr.28/VIIIe/.

LA·PREMIÈRE·
AVENTURE·CÉ·
LÉSTE·DE·Mr·AN·
TIPYRINE·PAR·
Tr·TZARA·AVEC·
DES·BOIS·GRA·
VÉS·ET·COLORI·
ÉS·PAR·M·IANCO
COLLECTION·DADA·

Art: the one constructed thing

The most interesting material in the review *Dada* is Tzara's own notes, poems and declarations (*Note 18 sur l'art*, *Saut blanc cristal*, *Marcel Janco*, *Poèmes nègres*, *Chanson du serpent*). The poet pays homage to the German physicist and pacifist Nicolai's "courageous, conscious, revolutionary, absolute, luminous" work, but criticizes an article in verse by Henri Guilbeaux in favor of the Russian revolution: "the cosy pathos of that gentleman sprawls with beatific complacency in a state of sentimental dilettantism and perfumed mediocrity."

The first number of *Dada* opened on a reproduction of an Arp design executed in embroidery by Sophie Taeuber (*Pathetic Symmetry*), followed by the ringing words of Tzara's "Note 18 on Art": "Art is at present the one constructed thing, complete unto itself, concerning which there is nothing more to say, such richness vitality significance wisdom: understanding seeing."

Tzara's poetry placed him in the first rank. He was soon idolized by his young friends. *La Première aventure céleste de M. Antipyrine* (The First Celestial Adventure of Mr. Fire-Extinguisher), with colored woodcuts by Marcel Janco, was the first book to appear under the Dada imprint, which was also to include selections of Tzara and Huelsenbeck's poetry. In December 1916, Apollinaire wrote to Tzara: "I have long admired your talent and I am especially pleased that you have done me the honor of directing it along a road where I precede but do not outstrip you."

Tzara wrote brilliant poems, verbal cataracts that gave French poetry a new impetus, a sudden acceleration. He took unpunctuated free verse, inherited in part from Apollinaire and Blaise Cendrars (both poets were present in the single number of *Cabaret Voltaire*), and transformed it into an extraordinarily powerful instrument. By exciting the latent energies in language he created an extreme poetry filled with vertiginously polysemic meanings and the novel rhythms of substantives flashing by like telephone poles seen from a speeding car. He even went as far as not to choose the words he aligned at random. Duchamp's Readymades leave the artist the responsibility of choice; Tzara, for his part, openly declared that he was renouncing that privilege.

Hans Arp, Tristan Tzara, and Hans Richter in Zurich, 1918

    To make a Dada poem.
    Take a newspaper.
    Take a pair of scissors.
    Choose an article as
long as you are planning to make your poem.
    Cut out the article.
    Then cut out each of the words that make up
this article and put them in a bag.
    Shake it gently.
    Then take out the scraps one after the other
in the order in which they left the bag.
    Copy conscientiously.
    The poem will be like you.
    And here you are a writer, infinitely original and endowed with a sensibility that is charming though beyond the understanding of the vulgar.*

---

* Example: when the dogs cross the air in a diamond like the ideas and the appendix of the meninges shows the hour of awakening program (the title is my own) price they are yesterday agreeing afterwards paintings / appreciate the dream epoch of the eyes / pompously than recite the gospel mode darkens / group the apotheosis imagine he said fatality power of colors / cut arches flabbergasted the reality a magic spell / spectator all to efforts from the it is no longer 10 to 12 / during digression volt right diminishes pressure / render of madmen topsy-turvy flesh on a monstrous crushing scene / celebrate but their 160 adepts in not to the put in my mother-of-pearl / sumptuous of land bananas upheld illumine / joy ask reunited almost / of has the one so much that the invoked visions / of the sing this one laughs / destiny situation disappears describes this one 25 dances salvation / dissimulated the whole of it is not was / magnificent the ascent to the gang better light of which sumptuousness scene me music-hall / reappears following instant shakes to live / business that there is not loaned / manner words come these people

This clearly provocative stance, which is almost always parodied or reduced to its purely anecdotal aspect, has the merit of bringing to the forefront, thanks to the poetic gesture that it assumes, the pre-eminence of language as such; for it designates the whole literary superstructure, especially the essentially manipulative language of journalism, as an arbitrary convention.

Photograph of Marcel Janco, 1916-1917

Cover of the review Dada 3 *with a color woodcut by Marcel Janco and a quotation from Descartes, Zurich, 1918*

Tzara, Richter, and Arp in front of the Elite Hotel, Zurich, 1917

Program of a Zurich Dada evening, July 14, 1916

PROGRAMM

I.

Hans Heusser: „Prelude". „Wakauabluthe", exotische Tanzrytmen.
„Eine Wüstenskizze". (eigene Kompositionen)
Emmy Hennings: „Zwei Frauen" (Prosa)
Verse („Makrele", „Aether", „Gefängnis", „Jütland".)
Hans Arp: Erläuterungen zu eigenen Bildern (Papierbilder I — V)
Hugo Ball: „Gadji Beri Bimba" (Verse ohne Worte, in eigenem Kostüm).
Tristan Tzara: „La fièvre puerpérale" (Poème simultan, interpreté par Ball, Huelsenbeck,
Janco, Tzara.)
Chant nègre I (nach eigenen Motiven aufgeführt von Ball, Huelsenbeck, Janco, Tzara.)
Chant nègre II (nach Motiven aus dem Sudan, gesungen von Huelsenbeck und Janko.)

Marcel Janco: Erläuterungen zu eigenen Bildern.
Hans Heusser: „Bacchanale aus der Oper Chrysis". „Japanisches Theehaus".
„Burlesque". (eigene Kompositionen)
Rich. Huelsenbeck und Tristan Tzara: Poème mouvementiste (Masques par M. Janco) Concert
voyelle. Poème de voyelle. Poème bruitiste.
Drei Dada-Tänze (getanzt von Emmy Hennings. Masques par Marcel Janco. Musik von Hugo
Ball.)
Richard Huelsenbeck: „Mpala Tano" (Verse)
Cubistischer Tanz (Kostüme und Arrangement von Hugo Ball, Musik aus „Leben des Menschen"
von Andrejew. Aufgeführt von Ball, Hennings, Huelsenbeck, Tzara.)

Photograph of Emmy Hennings, c. 1917

L'amiral cherche une maison à louer

Poème simultan par R. Huelsenbeck, M. Janko, Tr. Tzara

HUELSENBECK	Ahoi ahoi	Des Admirals gwirktes	Beinkleid schnell		zerfällt		Teerpappe macht Rawagen	in der Nacht	
JANKO, chant		Where the honny suckle	wine twines ilself		arround	the door a swetheart	mine is waiting patiently	for me l	
TZARA	Boum boum boum Il	déshabilla sa chair	quand les grenouilles		humides	commancèrent à bruler	j'ai mis le cheval	dans l'âme du	

HUELSENBECK	und der	Conciergenbäuche	Klapperschlangengrün sind milde ach		verzerrt	in der Natur		chrza prrrza chrrrza	
JANKO, chant	can hear	the weopour	will arround arround the hill					my great room is	
TZARA	serpent à	Bucarest on	dépendra mes amis dorénavant et		c'est très	intéressant les griffes des morsures équatoriales			

HUELSENBECK	prrrza chrrrza prrrza	Wer suchet dem wird		aufgetan	Der Ceylonlöve ist kein Schwan	Wer	Wasser braucht find	
JANKO, chant	mine admirably confortably	Grandmother said				I	love the ladies	
TZARA		Dimanche : deux éléphants		Journal de Genève au restaurant		Le	télégraphiste assassine	

Intermède rythmique

HUELSENBECK	hihi Yabomm hihi Yabomm hihi hihi hihiiiii				
	ff p cresc ff cresc ff f				
TZARA	rouge bleu rouge bleu rouge bleu rouge bleu rouge bleu				
	f cresc cresc ff				
SIFFLET (Janko)		p cresc f ff fff			
CLIQUETTE (TZ)	rrrrrrrrrr rrrrrrrr rrrrrrrr rrrrrrrr rrrrrrrr rrrrrrrrrr				
	f decrsc f cresc fff uniform				
GROSSE CAISE (Huels.)	O O O O O O O O O O O O O O O O O O O O				
	ff p f fff p p				

						Find was er nötig	
						And when it's five	
HUELSENBECK	im Kloset zumeistens was er nötig hätt ahoi iuché ahoi iuché			Dans l'église après la messe le pêcheur dit à la comtesse : Adieu Mathilde			
JANKO (chant)	I love the ladies I love to be among the girls						
TZARA	la concierge qui m'a trompé elle a vendu l'appartement que j'avais loué						

HUELSENBECK	hätt' O süss gequollnes Stelldichein des Admirals im Abendschein und			uro uru uru uro uru uru uru uro pataclan patablan pataplan uri uri uro			
JANKO (chant)	o'clock and tea is set I like to have my tea with some brunet shai shai			shai shai shai shai shai shai Every body is doing it doing it doing it Every body is			
TZARA	Le train traîne la fumée comme la fuite de l'animal blessé aux			intestins ecrasés			

HUELSENBECK	Der Affe brüllt die Seekuh belit im Lindenbaum der Schräg zerschellt tara-			tata taratata tatatata In Joschiwara dröhnt der Brand und knallt mit schnellen			
JANKO (chant)	doing it doing it see that ragtime couple over there see			that throw there shoulders in the air She said the raising her heart oh dwelling			
TZARA	Autour du phare tourne l'auréole des oiseaux bleuillis en moitiés de lumière vis-			sant la distance des batteaux Tandis que les archanges chient et les oiseaux tombent oh Oh! mon			

HUELSENBECK	Peitschen um die Lenden Im Schlafsack gröhlt der			alte Oberpriester und zeigt der Schenkel volle Tastatur		L'Amiral n'a rien trouvé
JANKO (chant)	oh yes yes yes yes yes yes yes yes yes yes			yes oh yes oh yes oh yes oh yes yes yes oh yes sir		L'Amiral n'a rien trouvé
TZARA	cher c'est si difficile La rue s'enfuit avec mon bagage à travers la ville Un métro mêle			son cinéma la prore de je vous adore était au casino du sycomore		L'Amiral n'a rien trouvé

NOTE POUR LES BOURGEOIS

Les essays sur la transmutation des objets et des couleurs des premiers peintres cubistes (1907) Picasso, Braque, Picabia, Duchamp-Villon, Delaunay, suscitaient l'envie d'appliquer en poésie les mêmes principes simultans.

Villiers de l'Isle Adam eût des intentions pareilles dans le théâtre, où l'on remarque les tendances vers un simultanéisme schématique; Mallarmé essaya une réforme typographique dans son poème: Un coup de dés n'abolira jamais le hazard; Marinetti qui popularisa cette subordination par ses „Paroles en liberté"; les intentions de Blaise Cendrars et de Jules Romains, dernièrement, amenèrent Mr Apollinaire aux idées qu'il développa en 1912 au „Sturm" dans une conférence.

Mais l'idée première, fut en son essence, fut exteriorisée par Mr H. Barzun dans un livre théoretique „Voix, Rythmes et chants Simultanés" où il cherchait une rélation plus étroite entre la symphonie polirythmique et le poème. Il opposait aux principes successifs de la poésie lyrique une idée vaste et parallèle. Mais les intentions de compliquer en profondeur cette t e c h n i q u e (avec le Drame Universel en exagérant sa valeur au point de lui donner une idéologie nouvelle et de la cloitrer dans l'exclusivisme d'une école, — echouèrent.

En même temps Mr Apollinaire essayait un nouveau genre de poème visuel, qui est plus intéressant encore par son manque de système et par sa fantaisie tourmentée. Il accentue les images centrales, typographiquement, et donne la possibilité de commancer à lire un poème de tous les côtés à la fois. Les poèmes de Mrs Barzun et Divoire sont purement formels. Ils cherchent un effort musical, qu'on peut imaginer en faisant les mêmes abstractions que sur une partiture d'orchestre.

Je voulais réaliser un poème basé sur d'autres principes. Qui consistent dans la possibilité que je donne à chaque écoutant de lier les associations convenables. Il retient les éléments caractéristiques pour sa personalité, les entremêle, les fragmente etc, restant tout-de-même dans la direction que l'auteur a canalisé.

Le poème que j'ai arrangé avec Huelsenbeck et Janko) ne donne pas une description musicale mais tente à individualiser l'impression du poème simultan auquel nous donnons par là une nouvelle portée.

La lecture parallèle que nous avons fait le 31 mars 1916, Huelsenbeck, Janko et moi, était la première réalisation scénique de cette esthétique moderne.

TRISTAN TZARA

"The Admiral's in Search of a House to Rent," simultaneous poem by Huelsenbeck, Janco and Tzara, published in Cabaret Voltaire, May 15, 1916

Marcel Janco, Dr. Sterling, and Hans Arp at the Wolfsberg Gallery, Zurich, 1918

We want to make men better, make them understand that the only brotherhood lies in a moment of intensity in which the beautiful is life concentrated on the tip of a wire rising up to bursting point, a blue trembling bound to earth by our loving gaze which covers the peak with snow. The miracle. I open my heart for men to be better.
Many artists no longer look for solutions in the object, in relations with the outside. They are cosmic or primary resolved simple sober-minded serious.
The diversity of today's artists is squeezing the jet of water in a great crystal liberty. And their efforts are creating new bright organisms.

Tristan Tzara, Note 18 on Art, May 1917

Cover of the deluxe edition of the Dada Anthology (Nos. 4-5), 1919

Marcel Janco: *Dadaga, 1920*

Giorgio de Chirico: *The Evil Genius of a King, 1914-1915*

Against the sentimental, romantic swagger of the Futurists

The Italian avant-garde made a fleeting appearance in *Dada*, with woodcuts by Prampolini and poems by Moscardelli, Meriano, Cantarelli, Maria d'Arezzo and Chirico's brother Alberto Savinio. Tzara's short-lived relations with the Futurists must be put down to the young exile's loneliness and to his eagerness to gain allies. Thus, in 1916, he planned to have the Italian poet Meriano see to the publication of the volume of black (i.e. African and Oceanian) oral literature which he had begun working on. However the Italian poets do not seem to have lived up to Tzara's expectations and the Italian connection was soon broken off.

In a letter of autumn 1922 to the French collector Jacques Doucet, Tzara recalled: "I was corresponding with A. Savinio who was living at the time in Ferrara with his brother G. de Chirico. Through him, my address spread through Italy like a contagious disease. I was bombarded with letters from every corner of Italy. Almost all of them began with *caro amico*, but most of my correspondents called me *carissimo e illustrissimo poeta*. That quickly made me decide to sever relations with that overly enthusiastic nation."

Then, too, there is Tzara's ironic clairvoyance in the *Manifesto on Feeble Love and Bitter Love* of 1920: "Is poetry necessary? I know that those who write most violently against it unconsciously desire to endow it with a comfortable perfection, and are working on this project right now; they call this hygienic future." The Futurists' political leanings (the "hygienic future" clearly derives from the bellicosity and political ideas of Marinetti) rested on a conceptual flaw which Tzara complained about in a letter to Meriano, mailed from Zurich in March 1919. In it he deplores the fact that the poems he has received from Italy "do not really go beyond the Futurists' scientific monochromy, the sentimental moment, the busy romantic swagger of conjectures."

Cabaret Voltaire. Under this name a group of young artists and writers has been formed whose aim is to create a center for artistic entertainment. The idea of the cabaret will be that guest artists will come and give musical performances and readings at the daily meetings. The young artists of Zurich, whatever their orientation, are invited to come along with suggestions and contributions of all kinds.

Press notice, Zurich, February 2, 1916

Secretly, in his quiet little room, Janco devoted himself to a "naturalism in zigzag." I forgive him this secret vice because in one of his paintings he evoked and commemorated the Cabaret Voltaire. On a platform in an overcrowded room, splotched with color, are seated several fantastic characters who are supposed to represent Tzara, Janco, Ball, Huelsenbeck, Madame Hennings, and your humble servant. We are putting on one of our big Sabbaths. The people around us are shouting, laughing, gesticulating.

Hans Arp, Dadaland, 1948

Marcel Janco: Cabaret Voltaire, 1916. On the platform, left to right: Hugo Ball at the piano, Tristan Tzara wringing his hands, Hans Arp, behind him Richard Huelsenbeck, behind him Marcel Janco, Emmy Hennings dancing with Friedrich Glauser

Tristan Tzara: "Dada Disgust," last paragraph of his Dada Manifesto 1918 in Dada 3, Zurich, December 1918

Dégoût dadaïste.

Tout produit du dégoût susceptible de devenir une négation de la famille, est *dada* ; proteste aux poings de tout son être en action déstructive : **dada** ; connaissance de tous les moyens rejétés jusqu'à présent par le sexe pudique du compromis commode et de la politesse : **dada** ; abolition de la logique, danse des impuissants de la création : <u>**dada**</u> ; de toute hiérarchie et équation sociale installée pour les valeurs par nos vallets : DADA ; chaque objet, tous les objets, les sentiments et les obscurités, les apparitions et le choc précis des lignes parallèles, sont des moyens pour le combat : DADA; abolition de la mémoire : DADA; abolition de l'archéologie : *DADA* ; aboliton des prophètes : **DADA**, abolition du futur : **DADA** ; croyance absolue indiscutable dans chaque dieu produit immédiat de la spontanéité : **DЯDЯ** ; saut élégant et sans préjudice, d'une harmonie à l'autre sphère ; trajectoire d'une parole jettée comme un disque sonore cri ; respecter toutes les individualités dans leur folie du moment : sérieuse, craintive, timide, ardente, vigoureuse, décidée, enthousiaste ; peler son église de tout accéssoire inutil et lourd ; cracher comme une cascade lumineuse la pensée désobligente ou amoureuse, ou la choyer — avec la vive satisfaction que c'est tout-à-fait égal — avec la même intensité dans le buisson, pur d'insectes pour le sang bien né, et doré de corps d'archanges, de son âme. Liberté : **DADA DADA DADA**, hurlement des couleurs crispées, entrelacement des contraires et de toutes les contradictions, des grotesques, des inconséquences : **LA VIE.**

TRISTAN TZARA.

crier! CRIER!

Hugo Ball: from vowels to elephants. Primitivism

A like rejection underlies the genesis of Hugo Ball's abstract poems, his "poetry of unknown words" (as Iliazd called it in 1949): "In these phonetic poems we totally renounce the language that journalism has abused and corrupted. We must return to the innermost alchemy of the word, we must even give up the word too, to keep for poetry its last and holiest refuge."

This program was to have innumerable repercussions. It was even to change the face of language, which is, as the Russian theorist Mikhail Bakhtin reminds us, "the ideological phenomenon *par excellence*."

Within a few months the Cabaret Voltaire and the Dada Gallery became laboratories where the new plastic and literary language was being forged. In his poem *La Victoire*, which appeared in the first number (March 1917) of Pierre Reverdy's review *Nord-Sud*, where it acquired the force of a manifesto, Apollinaire hailed the advent of this new language.

> O Mouths man is searching for a new idiom
> Which no grammarian of any language can make out
> And the old tongues are so near to extinction
> That it's really just out of habit and lack of daring
> That they're still being used for poetry

Apollinaire ends the poem by calling for new sounds, vowel-less consonants, tongue clicking, phonemes deep as the tolling of bells. "Language," says the poet, "requires shaking up."

In his memoir *Flight Out of Time*, Hugo Ball relates a legendary moment when, wearing a "Cubist" costume, he gave a reading of his "sound poems" at the Cabaret Voltaire.

> I had made myself a special costume for it. My legs were in a cylinder of shiny blue cardboard, which came up to my hips so that I looked like an obelisk. Over it I wore a huge coat collar cut out of cardboard, scarlet inside and gold outside. It was fastened at the neck in such a way that I could give the impression of winglike movement by raising and lowering my elbows. I also wore a high, blue-and-white-striped witch doctor's hat...
>
> I could not walk inside the cylinder so I was carried onto the stage in the dark and began slowly and solemnly:
>
> gadji beri bimba
> glandridi lauli lonni cadori
> gadjama bim beri glassala
> glandridi glassala tuffm i zimbrabim
> blassa galassasa tuffm i zimbrabim...

The stresses became heavier, the emphasis was increased as the sound of the consonants became sharper. Soon I realized that, if I wanted to remain serious (and I wanted to at all costs), my method of expression would not be equal to the pomp of my staging... I had now completed "Labadas Gesang an die Wolken" [Labada's Song to the Clouds] at the music stand on the right and the "Elefantenkarawane" [Elephant Caravan] on the left and turned back to the middle one, flapping my wings energetically. The heavy vowel sequences and the plodding rhythm of the elephants had given me one last crescendo. But how was I to get to the end? Then I noticed that my voice had no choice but to take on the ancient cadence of priestly lamentation, that style of liturgical singing that wails in all the Catholic churches of East and West.

In the midst of this hurricane Ball stood as motionless as a tower (for in fact he could not move in his cardboard costume) over the crowd of pretty girls and earnest philistines bursting with laughter and applauding—motionless as Savonarola, fanatical and unmoved.

Hans Richter, 1964

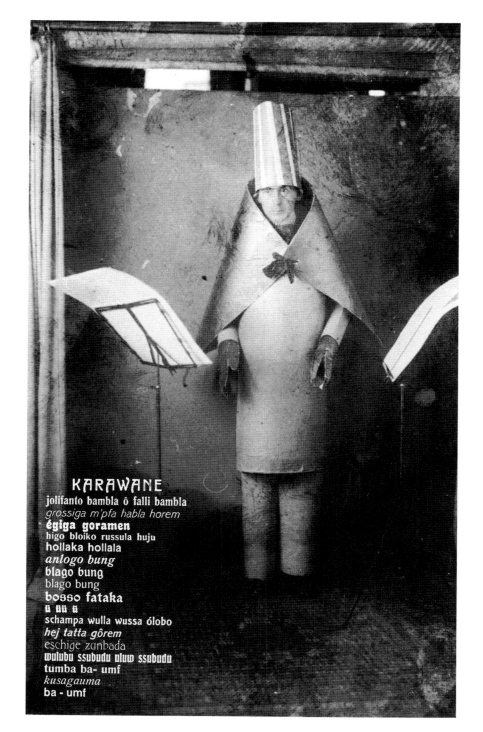

Hugo Ball in "cubist" costume reciting his poem "Caravan" (overprinted, lower left) at the Cabaret Voltaire, Zurich, 1916

Janco's masks and posters: lesbian sardines and ecstatic mice

Ball was not the only Dadaist to recite abstract poems wearing a costume. In Berlin Hausmann danced his "letterist" poems, and in Zurich sound abstraction was combined with dancing and costumes. Sophie Taeuber performed dances wearing costumes and masks designed by Marcel Janco, and she herself designed (or co-designed) tunics suggested by Hopi kachinas for recitals of Ball's poems.

The group's interest in so-called primitive art was evident with Janco's masks, Tzara's negro poems and the abstract verse of Ball and Huelsenbeck. Tzara made a study of oral literature from Africa, Madagascar and the South Seas. The program of the Dada soirées often included recitations of negro poems from the Aranda, Kinga, Loritja and Ba-Konga tribes. Some of these poems were declaimed simultaneously by two or more Dadaists to the accompaniment of drums played by Hugo Ball. The soirée of April 14, 1917, featuring a group of art works lent by the Sturm Gallery in Berlin, comprised negro music and dances performed by two young women (Jeanne Rigaud and Maya Chrusecz) wearing Janco masks.

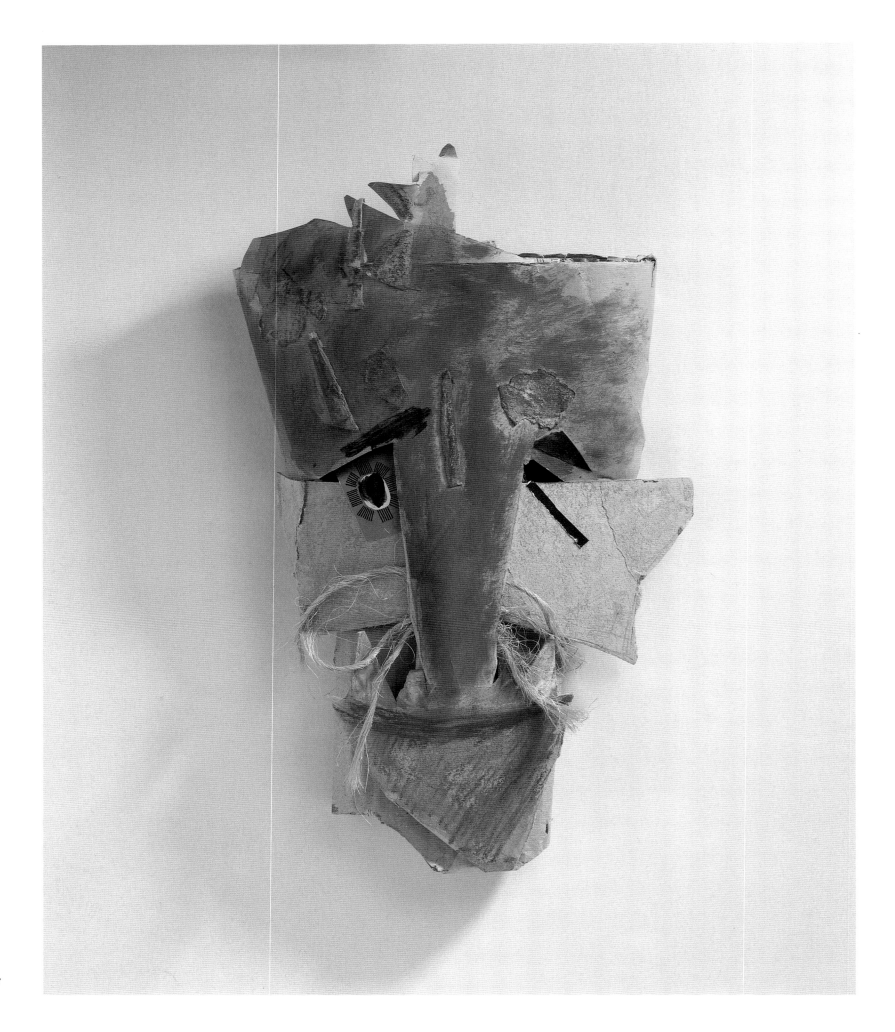

Marcel Janco:
Mask, 1919

These masks were not based on any known models in African or Oceanian art, but were purely the product of Janco's imagination. They were made from ephemeral materials. "Are you still singing that diabolical song about the mill at Hirza-Pirza, shaking your gypsy curls with wild laughter, my dear Janco?" wrote Arp in 1948. "I haven't forgotten the masks you used to make for our Dada demonstrations. They were terrifying, most of them daubed with bloody red. Out of cardboard, paper, horsehair, wire and cloth, you made your languorous foetuses, your Lesbian sardines, your ecstatic mice."

Hans Richter writes that "Janco's negro masks transported the audience from the virgin language of the new poetry to the virgin forest of the artistic vision." Under Janco's masks, under this borrowed Negritude or Indianness, a different personality emerged, Ball noted. The masks required the persons wearing them to dance; they dictated "precise, pathetic gestures verging on madness"; they instantly communicated their formidable power to the group.

Accounts of the times, fragmentary as many of them are, also make it clear that the Dadaists attached considerable importance to choreography. This interest evidently went well beyond their almost daily contact with the students of Rudolf von Laban's dancing studio a few doors away from the Dadaists' regular meeting place. "Sophie dreamt Sophie painted Sophie danced," wrote Arp after his wife's death. Many of the Dadaists, notably Tzara who fell in love with the dancer Maya Chrusecz, were attracted to Laban's female students. It is significant that in the last Dada periodical to appear in Zurich, *Der Zeltweg*, a photograph of Sophie Taeuber's friend the famous dancer Mary Wigman is printed.

The Dadaists' discovery of primitive art and their interest in children's drawings (some were exhibited at the Dada gallery on May 29, 1917) were part and parcel of the counterculture which they evolved in the face of the massive slaughter that the so-called civilized nations of the world were engaged in. The African poems offered them a range of possibilities (new cadences, syllabic repetitions, ellipses and novel syntax) which had an obvious kinship with Huelsenbeck's "vowel concerts" and some of the poems in his *Phantastische Gebete*. Moreover their championing of primitive art contained an unspoken critique of colonialism, which most of the Dadaists disapproved of, though their sentiments on this issue were voiced rather sporadically (for example, Clément Pansaers' title *Le Pan-Pan au cu du Nu Negre*, 1919, which can be translated approximately as: "Pan-Pan on the Ass of the Nude Negro".)

Masks were not Janco's only contribution to Dada. Janco was both a painter and an architect, and his oeuvre reflects these two interests. His small constructions (*Construction 3* in *Dada 1*, 1917) and his painted plaster reliefs, some of which were conceived to be embedded in a wall (*Etude pour Architecture empire brillant*, 1918), are one side of his output. The other side is his painting, which anticipates Abstract Expressionism (*Dadaga*, 1920). To Janco we owe a unique document of the times: the 1916 canvas entitled *Cabaret Voltaire*, which, better than any photograph, captures the atmosphere of the Dada soirées. (The present whereabouts of this painting is unknown.)

Janco's protean artistic activities helped to forge the image of the Zurich Dada group. He designed the movement's first letterhead and engraved the blue and black woodcuts and the dancing characters on the cover of the first volume in the series of Dada books (Tzara's *La Première aventure céleste de M. Antipyrine*, July 1916).

Unlike the charcoal sketch Janco made for the recital of negro songs at the Cabaret Voltaire on March 31, 1916 (and taken over for the invitation card of the Dada Gallery), which was obviously inspired by African sculpture, his engravings for the poster announcing the soirée of July 23, 1918 are a deeply personal work. The richness of the polysemic details is remarkable. The woodcuts are printed in black and were colored in later, probably by means of stencils. Janco seems to have used the same process with his cover for *Dada 3*: there are small differences in coloring and printing with each copy of the poster and each numbered copy of the periodical.

Fancy-dress dances on a poem by Hugo Ball, 1918

Mary Wigman dancing, 1919

Marcel Janco:
*Poster for the
Dada evening at the
Zur Meise hall, Zurich,
July 23, 1918,
where Tzara read his*
Dada Manifesto 1918

In his *Dada Manifesto 1918*, which he read in public on July 23, Tzara stresses the broad scope of the poetic act: "I destroy the drawers of the brain and of social organization: spread demoralization wherever I go and cast my hand from heaven to hell, my eyes from hell to heaven, restore the fecund wheel of a universal circus to objective forces and the imagination of every individual."

Though this act has a place of its own on the artistic register, Tzara specifies: "What we need is works that are strong straight precise and forever beyond understanding." For him, abstraction is a struggle, a requisite that is not limited to painting, to abstract creation or even to the "formal laboratory" of aesthetics, as Tzara brands it. Tzara's proclamation restores all the power of evocation and critical strength of the word "abstraction." In his use of the word we hear both its original sense (to draw away, to separate, to isolate) and the meaning it has come to have in art (the highest requirement of thought: material, color and line for their own sake). "Dada is the signboard of abstraction." This supposes taking ordinary reality and transforming it artistically ("advertising and business are also elements of poetry").

Elsewhere in the manifesto, Tzara raises the issue of the art work's space proper. He defines abstraction simultaneously as a space for independent creation, liberated from bygone concepts of art, and as an artistic protest against traditional modes of representation (the old rules of art) through the use of elementary materials: "The new painter creates a world, the elements of which are also its implements, a sober, definite work without argument. The new artist protests: he no longer paints (symbolic and illusionist reproduction) but creates—directly in stone, wood, iron, tin, boulders—locomotive organisms capable of being turned in all directions by the limpid wind of the momentary sensation."

When he wrote these lines, Tzara almost certainly had in mind Marcel Janco's reliefs and small constructions, Hans Arp's random pasted papers, reliefs and painted wooden shapes. And no doubt, too, Arp and Schwitters, the one in Zurich, the other in Hanover, were in agreement with Tzara's ideas about elementary materials (see Chapter 7).

Kurt Schwitters states in *i* (*a manifesto*), written in 1922:

> i finds the work of art in nature. Artistic creation in this case means recognizing the rhythms and expressivity in one part of nature. There is therefore no need to fear any loss through transference, that is to say that there is nothing to disturb the creation. I demand i, not because it is an artistic form but because it is a specific form... More knowledge is required to carve out a work of art from nature, which is not formed from an artistic viewpoint, than to construct a work of art from its proper artistic rules... The material is unimportant in art; it is enough to give it shape for it to become a work of art. For i, however, the material is far from being unimportant, inasmuch as a fragment of nature does not necessarily become a work of art.

Hans Arp: *Before my Birth, 1914*

Marcel Janco:
Construction 3, 1917

A picture is the art of making two lines geometrically ascertained as parallel meet on a canvas, before our eyes, in the reality of a world transposed according to new conditions and possibilities.

Tristan Tzara, Dada Manifesto 1918

Hans Arp and Sophie Taeuber-Arp: the laws of chance

Before his Zurich period, Arp had already exhibited his work, notably in 1912, with the Blaue Reiter group in Munich; he was acquainted with Kandinsky, Marc, Macke, Klee, as well as Herwarth Walden, editor of the Berlin periodical *Der Sturm*, in which some of his drawings had been reproduced; he had met Max Ernst in Cologne. But it was in Zurich that his genius flowered, in part, no doubt, as a result of his meeting Tristan Tzara and Sophie Taeuber. Sophie taught at the Zurich School of Applied Arts and was an artist in her own right. When Arp first met her in 1915, she was moving towards pure plasticity. They became intimate in 1917 and were married in 1922.

Arp's œuvre, and the brilliance of his elementary approach to art, made him the first Dada artist, the very prototype of the Dada creator-cum-inventor-cum-propagator. His extreme sensitivity for natural forms and details oscillated between two poles: biomorphic abstraction (*Enoch's Tears, The*

Entombment of the Birds and Butterflies or Portrait of Tzara) and pasted papers composed according to the laws of chance, which have an obvious affinity to the pure plastic works of Sophie Taeuber, Otto and Adya van Rees. Or, more exactly, Arp's sensibility seemed to soar in great sweeping circles, retaining creative principles and approaches that other artists have traditionally rejected: chance, spontaneity, play, nonconformity, the absence of any system.

Arp began to contrive reliefs out of pieces of wood screwed together and painted; he made pasted papers, embroideries, woodcuts for Tzara's *Vingt-cinq poèmes* (Twenty-five Poems). Sophie Taeuber did embroideries with glass beads; made marionettes (which remind one of Hannah Höch's dolls for the first international Dada fair in Berlin in 1920), gouaches on paper, oils on canvas, reliefs, painted wooden objects (*Dada Head*, c. 1918); and wove wool rugs.

Hans Arp: *i Picture, c. 1920*

Arp became "more and more removed from aesthetics," seeking "another order, another value for man in nature"; "all things and man were to be like nature, without measure," he explained.

His collages openly display the formal procedures that went into their making (*i Picture*, 1920): the discontinuities, breaks and seams; the form, color, nature and texture of the materials, often found materials, that he used. These plunge the spectator into the heart of the plastic statement's production (to borrow a phrase from Marcel Duchamp), involving the eye in an entirely novel way in the process by which a work of art is perceived.

Arp playfully used the "laws of chance" (*According to the Laws of Chance*, 1916) in a series of inspired gestures that had the superb exigency of total spontaneity: he dropped torn bits of paper onto a colored page, allowing them to settle at random (*Untitled*, 1917), in much the same way that Tzara composed aleatory poems by randomly drawing newspaper clip-

Hans Arp: *Automatic Drawing, 1916*

Hans Arp: *White Forms on a Black Ground, c. 1917*

Sophie Taeuber and Hans Arp in their Zurich studio, with her puppets on the wall, 1918

Sophie Taeuber: *Dada Head, c. 1918*

Sophie Taeuber behind her Dada Lamp, 1920

Sophie Taeuber: *Pathetic Symmetry (after a drawing by Hans Arp), 1916-1917*

pings from a top hat and recording them in the order in which they came. Both acts question the arbitrary and ideological nature of language in relation to social structures that had been discredited by the First World War.

Arp was not only a visual artist but a poet as well—one could almost call him a visual poet. He spent five years, from 1915 to 1920, shaping the poems of his *Wolkenpumpe* (Cloud Pump) phrase by phrase, word by word, syllable by syllable. "If it ever happens that I am forced to choose between my plastic work and my written work," he once confided to Marcel Jean, "if I had to give up either sculpture or poetry, I would choose to write poems."

Dada was Arp's natural environment, so much so that when the magazine *L'Art contemporain* asked him in 1927 if his work was rooted in Neo-Plasticism or Surrealism, he replied that it sprang from the affirmation of Dada and declared unequivocally that he did not share the position of the later Surrealists. Surrealist art, he stated, was ignorant of the means that were proper to art, a reproach he did not level, with good reason, at the Neo-Plasticists. He added that if he had happened to exhibit his works with the Surrealists it was because their rebellion stemmed from Dada.

In his literary œuvre, *On My Way* (1912-1947), Arp pays tribute to his Dadaist comrades: Sophie Taeuber, Kurt Schwitters, Francis Picabia, Marcel Janco, Hans Richter. His talent as a critic and polemicist is equalled only by Tzara. His style is "sensitive as a butterfly's antennae" (Picabia to Christine Boumeester in a letter dated July 26, 1950).

Other writings by Arp, notably those devoted to the poet and tireless champion of pure plasticism Michel Seuphor (the leader of the Cercle et Carré group, 1930) and the Hungarian Constructivist Lajos Kassák (editor of the review *MA*), bring to light the importance of the constructivist and elementary current that existed from the outset in the Zurich group. The Dadaists alone were able to combine the discipline of plasticism with ironic detachment and freedom. To this explosive mixture we owe some of the most rigorous works in the movement (Arp, Kurt Schwitters, Raoul Hausmann), the ones that correspond to what Tzara had called for: "works that are strong straight precise and forever beyond understanding."

Although they were very close in artistic matters, like Robert and Sonia Delaunay, Hans Arp and Sophie Taeuber-Arp rarely worked together, with the exception of a few joint drawings and paintings executed in 1939 and their collaboration with their friend Theo van Doesburg on the Aubette in Strasbourg in 1927. Their fee for the Strasbourg commission incidentally allowed them to buy a plot of land in Meudon, near Paris (and a few hundred yards from the building designed by the leader of the De Stijl group) and to build a house there. Designed by Sophie Taeuber, it is now the Jean Arp Foundation in Clamart-Meudon.

Marcel Janco: *Study for* Brilliant Empire Architecture, *1918*

Hans Arp: *Entombment of the Birds and Butterflies (Portrait of Tristan Tzara), 1916-1917*

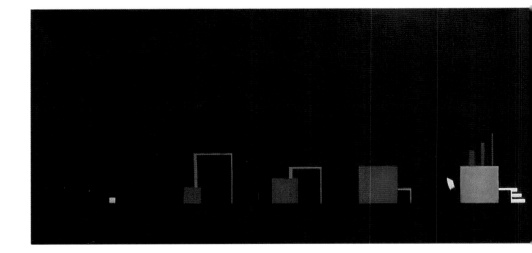

Hans Richter: *Rhythm 23, 1923*

As a corollary to the intense plastic activity within the Dada group, experiments in other fields took place as well: they include Christian Schad's "Schadographs" and the abstract films of Viking Eggeling and Hans Richter (see Chapter 7).

The Swedish artist Viking Eggeling lived in Paris (where Arp met him) before the First World War; he later moved to Ascona and joined the Zurich Dada group in 1918. In Switzerland he renewed his acquaintance with Arp and, through Tristan Tzara, met the painter Hans Richter. Keenly sensitive to line, as shown by his early work (mainly pencil drawings), and little concerned with planes and surfaces, Eggeling was primarily interested in the genesis of forms, in interconnecting lines (some pages in his notebooks are reminiscent of Klee's *Pedagogical Sketchbook*). "Here is Eggeling connecting the wall with the ocean," notes Tzara in his *Zurich Chronicle*, "and telling us the line proper to a painting of the future."

The emergence of a shape and its gradual transformation into another shape: this is the basic "plot" of an Eggeling film sequence. Though he had not envisaged this new art form at the outset, it eventually dawned on Eggeling that film was the only solution to certain pictorial problems he encountered as early as 1915 (according to Arp) while working on a series of linear plates. Towards the end of 1918, Hans Richter joined him in his quest for a universal pictorial vocabulary or, as Eggeling put it, a *Generalbass der Malerei* (basso continuo of painting) or *Eidodynamik* (visual dynamic).

Like other Dadaists, Hans Richter evolved from a fiery, colorful abstract expressionism (*Autumn*, 1917) towards an art imbued with a Constructivist sensibility. First came a series of *Dada Heads* with contrasting white and black values that foreshadow his later film experiments. Then, espousing Eggeling's theories, he moved to Berlin with the latter in 1919. There

Eggeling, Richter, Schad: from painting to abstract photography and film

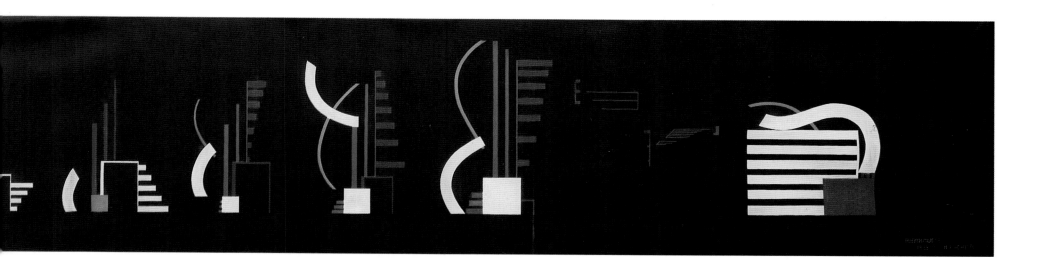

Viking Eggeling: Four drawings for the Diagonal Symphony, *1920-1924*

Photograph of Viking Eggeling, c. 1920

Eggeling became acquainted with Raoul Hausmann; the two artists met in June, just after the publication of the first number of *Der Dada*, either in Hannah Höch's studio or at the home of Arthur Segal, who had settled in Berlin after participating in the Zurich Dada group.

In 1921 Eggeling published, in Lajos Kassák's Viennese periodical *MA*, an article entitled: "Theoretical Introduction to the Art of Movement." It was illustrated with drawings, cross-sections of a dynamic process. What Eggeling wanted to show was the transition from one form to another within the duration of a real movement; a space large enough to accommodate an "orchestration of forms"; a "dynamic mode of expression that differed from easel painting."

At this juncture Eggeling and Richter hit upon an initial solution suggested by Chinese scrolls and ideograms (which articulate time). In 1919 they made their first scrolls (Eggeling's *Horizontal-Vertical Orchestra*, Richter's *Prelude*). These were arrangements of forms that acquired supplementary lines, an elongated curve, the intimation of a surface. The two artists had jointly solved the problem of space, but now felt impelled to tackle movement, and so, in the course of the year 1920, they began working with film, a medium that presented considerable difficulties at first. Eggeling made a second scroll, *Diagonal Symphony*. Richter produced *Fugue* followed, between 1923 and 1925, by *Rhythm 21*, *Fugue 23* and *Orchestration of Color*. Eggeling completed *Diagonal Symphony* only in the fall of 1924; and when his work was given its first public screening in May 1925, he was too ill to attend. He died a few days later.

Eggeling and Hausmann both attended the gatherings held at the home of the painter Arthur Segal in Berlin. Segal too was a former member of the Zurich group. His Zurich period works announce his later experiments with

Arthur Segal: *Port in the Sun, 1918*

light. In *Port in the Sun* (1918), the spectrum is broken up into sheaves of color which not only evoke Delaunay's experiments (see Chapter 2) but produce a distinctive formal stylization: a system of repeating vertical and horizontal bands of color which appear first on the frame and next on the canvas, where they are repeated in contrasting symmetrical movements, in a novel system of repetitions consisting of sixteen (four times four) juxtaposed sequences. The result is an impression of temporal successivity comparable to a comic strip, yet having the colors and contrasts of Léger's first Cubist works or the compositions of the Russian Cubo-Futurists.

In a statement published in the last Dada periodical to appear in Zurich, *Der Zeltweg* (November 1919), Segal outlined a theory of equivalences in which he rejects the concept of an optical hierarchy and advocates a simultaneous reading of art works wherein each part is the equivalent of every other part and no detail is subordinate. (This idea bears some similarity to Gertrude Stein's analysis of Cézanne in her early, pre-1910 writings, as well as to Strzemiński's 1928 theory of Unism).

The fact that Segal's researches led him to use light as a medium, notably in his joint works with Nikolaus Braun (with whom he wrote a book in 1925 on the role of light in art) retrospectively enriches our reading of the prismatic disintegrations of his Dada period canvases, and it also explains why he was friends with Eggeling and Hausmann. Finally, it is interesting to note that Segal, who had got to know the Dutch artist César Domela at the Monte Verità colony in Ascona, later contributed to the Constructivist periodical *i10* (Amsterdam, 1927).

The friendship and artistic collaboration that resulted from Eggeling's encounter with Raoul Hausmann might have proved still more fruitful than they were had Eggeling not died in 1925. Both artists jointly signed a manifesto (written by Hausmann) that was published in Kassák's Viennese review *MA* in 1923. Entitled "Second Declaration of PREsentism," it is a significant document, for it opposes the excessively rigid constructivism put forward by Alfréd Kemény and László Moholy-Nagy at one of the Constructivist Congresses in Berlin.

We fell in with each other again just before the Great War in Zurich where I was studying architecture at the Polytechnic and Tzara was reading philosophy at the University. The hardships of war had cut off all my resources and I had begun earning a livelihood in the nightclubs of Zurich, singing folk songs of France, England and Rumania. My brother accompanied me on the piano. One evening, looking for work in a narrow lane in the old town, I came across the fantastic figure of Hugo Ball. A very long personage, very asymmetrical, equally skilled as a poet and a thinker. He was running a cabaret. When he learned that I was a painter, that I had some connections with the Cubists and Futurists, that I knew some poets and other artists in Zurich, he at once invited me to take part in his project of creating a literary cabaret. The next day I spoke about it to Arp and Tzara, hoping to convince them to join in. Tzara saw immediately that much could be made of this, and Arp was an untiring collaborator. We called the cabaret "Voltaire." Every night new friends were added to our group. The poets chanted, the writers recited their prose and their troubles, the walls glowed with paintings and manifestoes, we listened to the sonatas Ball played on the piano and we danced to Negro or Javanese music in my painted masks, or we read simultaneous poems for four voices in four different languages.

Marcel Janco

Tzara left Zurich at the end of 1919 and moved to Paris. Janco too stayed briefly in the French capital, then returned to Rumania (and settled in Tel Aviv in 1940). He made his living there designing private villas, evolving a clean style not unlike the Bauhaus style. He played a leading role in the Rumanian avant-garde: in June 1922 he founded the periodical *Contimporanul*, edited by his friend Ion Vinea.

Shortly thereafter another little magazine appeared in Bucharest, *75HP*, founded by the Dadaist-Constructivist poet Ilarie Voronca. Its first and only issue was published in October 1924; a month later it was replaced by yet a third avant-garde periodical, *Punct*. The painter Victor Brauner, who had started his career working in the Constructivist vein before moving on to Surrealism, made his first public appearance in *75HP* where, together with Voronca, he invented "pictopoetry." Pictopoetry involved including words and word fragments in painting, using them for their visual and organic properties and giving them as much weight in the composition as the other, purely abstract elements (see the cover of *75HP*).

Brauner and Janco both contributed actively to *Punct*, notably with abstract linoleum cuts. This periodical, edited by the writer Scarlat Callimachi, was subtitled "A Review of Constructivist Art," though in some ways it reflected the Dada spirit. Inspired by Eggeling's films, Janco composed a formal alphabet for *Punct* that resembled the Swedish artist's abstract signs on film. "Eggeling, the Edison of the new art," proclaimed the artist, "will take his cinema (that new music of planes) to every part of the world."

Punct was succeeded by yet another magazine: *Integral*, which appeared in Bucharest from 1925 to 1928. Constructivist in its outlook, it covered a broad spectrum of international art (typography, film, the theater) and campaigned against the burgeoning Rumanian Surrealist group.

▷ *Cover of the review* 75HP *by Victor Brauner, Bucharest, 1924*

▽ *Cover of the review* Punct, *No. 1, Bucharest, 1924*

Schadographs and first automatic poems

Though they had the imprimatur of Tristan Tzara, who coined the name "Schadograph," Christian Schad's pioneering photograms devised in Zurich in 1918, have, like their inventor himself, gone almost unnoticed in the history of the Dada Movement. Unlike Man Ray (see Chapter 6), Schad has left no account of the circumstances which led him to make his discovery—one that appears all the more unexpected in that, as far as we know, the artist had no photographic activities before he began to produce his abstract photograms.

He did not explore all the possibilities offered by this new medium; nevertheless, he used it to great effect, evoking an intangible world of his own, filled with shadows, silhouettes and floating disembodied forms. One of his Schadographs, reproduced in *Dadaphone 7* (Paris, March 1920), bears the caption: "Arp and Val Serner at the London Crocrodrarium," a title that reminds one of the cycle of automatic poems ("transcribed on the spot, unreflectingly and without revising") that Arp, Serner and Tzara jotted down at the Café Odéon and Café Terrasse in Zurich (*Hyperbole of the Crocodile Barber and the Walking Stick*). Schad attained a level of abstraction with his photograms that seems quite foreign to both his earlier and his later plastic output.

Richard Huelsenbeck: Verwandlungen ("Transformations")
Roland Verlag, Munich, 2.50 Marks, bound 3.50 Marks

Cacadou-colored bulging windowpane ears run around Klumbumbus yellow star belly straight through dog lining bursting. Good. Cacadou becomes butter Jamaica cognac steel becomes dance Butter Lane is corkscrew for infantile oteros in bags Chinamen spit for years after petroleum. One from Confidence feeds a semicolon red. Apoplexy. Dragon salad, telegraphically, yet how. Toreador of the green tie before the eyes stuffed cakes at the end of neuralgic threads pette pette says the poet the tribune of the heart and of Geneva par excellence easter. It is not easy to provide speeds with a good conscience. Altogether violent pages. Is for sale.

Hans Arp, Walter Serner, Tristan Tzara, 1918-1919

Christian Schad:
Transmission, 1919

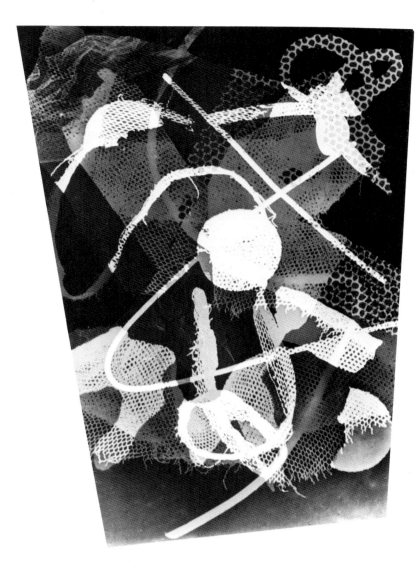

Christian Schad: Schadograph No. 23, c. 1918

In the manner of his wood reliefs, which have a good deal in common with Arp's though at first glance their crisp mechanical appearance gives them a distinctive look of their own, Schad often cut out his finished photograms into rectangles that differ from the standard formats of photographic paper.

Like his friend Walter Serner, author of the manifesto *Letzte Lockerung*, Christian Schad was a discreet and retiring person. Like Arp and Richter, Schad had escaped from wartime Germany and settled in Zurich, having pleaded a weak heart and thus evaded military service: "In the summer of 1915 I left Munich by train, bound for Zurich, passing from a black-white-red cataclysm to an island of peace."

Schad is known mainly for his striking neo-realist portraits painted in the twenties under the banner of Neue Sachlichkeit, a term that gained currency at the 1925 Mannheim Exhibition: in Schad's interpretation it became "the irony of the new objectivity" and a natural sequel to Dada. Schad began his Zurich period with Expressionistic woodcuts, then engraved portraits of most of his fellow Dadaists, while at the same time painting tormented Expressionistic canvases; for example the 1919 picture entitled *Transmission* where we see figures—some of them upside down—caught up in the hullabaloo of a Dada soirée, unless it is a raging battle, scrambling to escape furious spirals and zigzagging lightning bolts.

Christian Schad: Schadograph No. 65, c. 1918

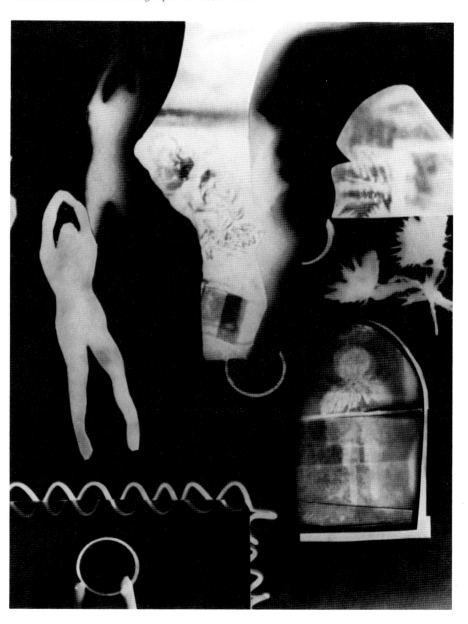

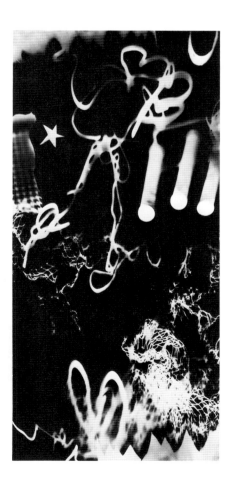

Christian Schad:
Schadograph No. 60, c. 1918

It was Serner who introduced Schad to the Dada group. Before he joined the Dadaists, Schad (who had little taste for riotous soirées and was in any case the kind of person who prefers to remain in the background) had contributed drawings and woodcuts, as had Arp and Otto van Rees, to Serner's Post-Expressionist little magazine *Sirius* (Zurich, 1915-1916). This periodical's other contributors include Else Lasker-Schüler, Max Hermann Neisse, Peter Altenberg, Ivan Goll, Alfred Wolfenstein, Georg Christoph Lichtenberg, Theodor Däubler, and, in German translation, Claudel, Baudelaire and Rabelais, before Serner gave up this editorial activity which Dada rendered pointless.

Arp describes Serner as a legendary figure: "Doctor Serner, the adventurer, author of crime novels, social dancer, skin specialist and gentleman-burglar." Serner read his Dada manifesto *Letzte Lockerung* at

I met Tzara and Serner at the Odeon and at the Café de la Terrasse in Zurich where we wrote a cycle of poems: Hyperbole of the Crocodile Barber and the Walking Stick. This type of poem was later baptized "automatic poetry" by the Surrealists.

Hans Arp, Dadaland, *1948*

1919 — 9 Avril

Non PLUS ultra

Salle Kaufleuten

NON PLUS ULTRA

9. D^ad**A**-SOIRÉE

Metteur en scène: W. SERNER

Dompteur des acrobates: *TZARA*

Handbill for the 9th Dada evening, Zurich, April 9, 1919, with Serner as producer and Tzara as acrobat tamer

Walter Serner in Zurich, 1918

Hans Richter: *Macabre Portrait, 1917*

Walter Serner: *Untitled, 1920*

Kaufleutenauditorium in Zurich on April 9, 1919. Judging from Tzara's report of the event in his *Zurich Chronicle* the audience reacted vehemently:

> tumult hurricane frenzy siren whistles bombardments song the battle starts out sharply, half the audience applaud the protestors hold the hall in the lungs of those present nerves are liquified muscles jump Serner makes mocking gestures, sticks the scandal in his buttonhole / ferocity that wrings the neck / Interruption.
> Chairs torn loose projectiles crackings expected appalling and instinctive outcome.
> NOIR CACADOU, Dance (5 persons) with Miss Wulff, the pipes dance the renovation of the headless pithecanthropes, stifles the rage of the audience. The balance of intensity tips towards the stage. Serner in place of his poems lays a bunch of flowers at the feet of a dressmaker's dummy. Tzara prevented from reading the DADA PROCLAMATION the audience goes wild his voice in tatters trails over the chandeliers, progressive savage madness twines laughter and audacity. Repeat of the previous performance. New dance in 6 enormous dazzling masks. End. Dada has succeeded in connecting the circuit of absolute unconsciousness in the audience which forgot the frontiers of good breeding of prejudices, experienced the commotion of the NEW.
> Final victory of Dada.

Having gained this victory, Tzara left Zurich at the end of 1919 and moved to Paris, where Picabia and Breton were waiting for him. Serner, for his part, settled in Geneva and carried on the group's activities there, organizing the Gustave Buchet/Christian Schad and the Ribemont-Dessaignes/Picabia exhibitions at the Salon Néri (February and April 1920) and the Dada Ball at the Plainpalais municipal hall. On this last occasion he informed the press of several authentic Dada false reports and published a genuine telegram of support from the Paris Dada group.

Serner later became the novelist now being rediscovered in Germany. A similar destiny was in store for two other members of the Zurich Dada group, Otto Flake and Friedrich Glauser.

Poster and invitation for the Great Dada Ball, Geneva, 1920

Chapter 4

Two Havens : New York and Barcelona

If the history of the Dada Movement is restricted to those artists, groups and periodicals that were connected with an active Dada nucleus and bore the official or, rather, "authorized" Dada label, then strictly speaking it is only after April 1921 that the New York group can be termed Dada.

It was then that the single issue of *New York Dada* appeared. The remarkable thing about this periodical, which was edited by Marcel Duchamp and Man Ray, is that, in addition to marking the birth of the American branch of Dada, it gave a retroactive Dada coloring to the two artists' activities in New York between 1915 and 1920, before Paris became the center up to 1923.

As for Barcelona, it can be linked with New York, if not because the artists exiled in these two cities during World War One shared the same state of mind, then because Picabia and Cravan shuttled back and forth between them and because *391*, the "traveling magazine," connected them tangibly. Founded by Picabia in the capital of the jealously independent province of Catalonia, that spawning ground of libertarianism, it was later transferred to New York, the world's most exciting and modern metropolis.

Revolted by the intolerance shown in France to conscientious objectors and men unfit for wartime service, Marcel Duchamp moved in August 1915 to New York, where the success of his *Nude* at the Armory Show had made his name (see Chapter 1). His meeting there with Man Ray led to several years of joint activities and marked the beginning of the New York pre-Dada group. This group came to include Arthur Cravan, the American artists John Covert, Joseph Stella and Morton Schamberg (whose work shows the influence of Duchamp and Picabia), as well as Alfred Stieglitz, Walter Arensberg and Katherine Dreier, who all contributed, with their interest and support, to the growth of the movement.

Richard Boix: *The New York Dada Group, c. 1921*

Duchamp and Picabia in New York and the review *291*

Picabia joined Duchamp in New York in the summer of 1915. He had been called up in the general mobilization of 1914 and had not attempted to evade conscription, though he might easily have done so, by reason of his father's Cuban birth. He had managed to get himself appointed the chauffeur of General de Boissons, a family friend of Gabrielle Buffet's, who was good enough to remember Picabia's passion for automobiles. Then, in 1915, Picabia had been sent to Cuba on a mission to buy molasses for the French army.

He never got there. On the way he stopped off in New York with its rich memories of the Armory Show and the friendships he had formed during his first visit there, and he simply stayed on. He renewed his acquaintance with Arensberg and Stieglitz, met the caricaturist and draftsman Marius de Zayas, Paul Haviland (the representative of Limoges china in the United States) and Mrs. Ernest Meyer, whose husband was the publisher of *The Washington Post*. The artistic activities now ruled out in Paris resumed in New York: witness the publication in March 1915, only four months before Picabia's arrival, of *291* and the slender single number of *The Ridgefield Gazook*.

MAGIC CITY

Un vent dangereux et tentateur de sublime nihilisme
nous poursuivait avec une allégresse prodigieuse.

Idéal inattendu.
Rupture d'equilibre.
Enervement croissant.
Emancipations.

Partout hommes et femmes avec une musique qui me plaît
publiquement ou en secret
déchainent leurs passions stériles.

Opium.
Whisky.
Tango.

Spectateurs et acteurs
de plus en plus subtils
surmontent les satisfactions grossières.

Femmes moins fortes
plus belles et plus inconscientes.

Les hommes avec une silencieuse arrière-pensée
regardent leur plaisir.

Années de génie et de soleil oriental.
1914 - 1915

F. P.

Francis Picabia's poem "Magic City," published in 391, March 1917

◁ **Joseph Stella:** *Chinatown, c. 1912*

Alfred Stieglitz: *The City of Ambition, 1910*

Photograph of Morton Schamberg,
c. 1913-1918

Morton Schamberg: Machine, 1916

John Covert: Vocalization, 1919

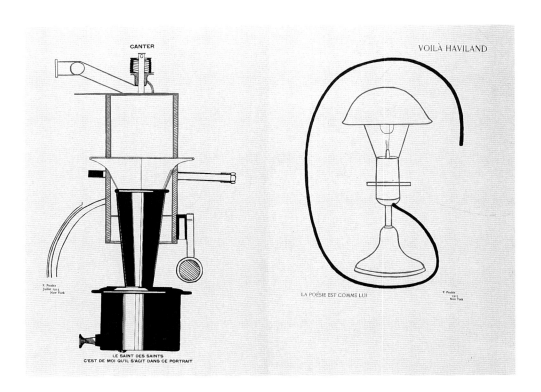

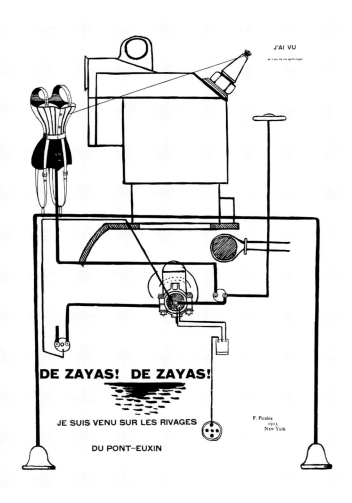

Edited by Paul Haviland, Marius de Zayas and Agnes Meyer, *291* appeared under the auspices of Alfred Stieglitz. It set out to stimulate interest in the modern artists being exhibited at Stieglitz's gallery at a time when the latter, by then in his fifties, was momentarily tired of fighting. Though this monthly stopped publishing after one year, it was related, if only in format and spirit, to *391*, which Picabia was to edit in Barcelona in 1917, and was consequently the ancestor of all the Dada periodicals. And of course it had its own ancestors too: *Les Soirées de Paris*, whose main contributor, Guillaume Apollinaire, was a personal friend of Marius de Zayas's, and *Camera Work*, the quarterly that Stieglitz edited from 1903 to 1917, bringing out a total of fifty numbers.

291 published Marius de Zayas's "psychotypes" (concrete typographical poems), Picasso's Cubist reliefs, and published poems by Apollinaire and Georges Ribemont-Dessaignes. It also included Picabia's "object portrait" of Max Jacob (a flashlight) and his famous *Portrait of a Young American Girl in a State of Nudity* (a spark plug). The side of the spark plug is inscribed with the words "For Ever," beginning a vein of mechanical-erotic imagery that was to culminate in Duchamp's *Large Glass*.

291 also published prose by Apollinaire and Alberto Savinio, and works by Braque, John Marin, Katharine Rhoades and Edward Steichen. The cover of the last number features an African sculpture, a bronze from the Congo, which seems to announce the African and Pre-Columbian art prominently displayed by Marius de Zayas at Stieglitz's Modern Gallery for its opening a few weeks later.

In many ways *291* was related to the Dada magazines that appeared in Zurich the following year. What makes it unique is its generous format and the lasting power of some of the art works reproduced between its broad covers.

Francis Picabia: *Very Rare Picture on Earth, 1915*

Picabia's passion for machines

In New York Picabia began to paint again. The first of his so-called machine pictures, dating from 1915, were "object portraits" with clever titles open to various interpretations. Some of these pictures are quite hard and dry in style: they take a real object and reduce it to a few schematic blue and black contours; for example the 1915 *Here's Haviland/Poetry Is Like Him*, which was reproduced in *291*.

Very Rare Picture on Earth, also 1915, an oil on canvas that is much larger in size, has affinities with the hard-edge painting that developed in America half a century later. The picture seemingly reproduces with extreme fidelity various mechanical elements; some appear to be real (the cylindrical water tanks with their worn copper sheathing), others are obviously stylized (the bottom half of the painting).

The austere somber tones of *Very Rare Picture* point in a new direction for Picabia, in contrast to the big bright exuberant Orphic works *Edtaonisl* and *Udnie*, which have, thanks to their distinctive dimensions, an American rather than a European sense of space (though they were in fact painted in Paris after the artist's first trip to New York).

Usually described as anti-painting, Picabia's new style cloaks a conceptual uncertainty about the avenue opened by *Udnie* and *Edtaonisl*. This was a recurring—and revealing—attitude with Picabia; it is impossible to understand the artist's protean oeuvre, from its Post-Impressionist beginnings to its final flowering in the early fifties, if one overlooks his characteristic propensity for self-questioning. It partly explains Picabia and Duchamp's rejection of oil painting (or, more exactly, the kind of figuration sustained by oil painting). Finally, Picabia's new style announces a sharp break with Cubism and Post-Impressionism, and at the same time it proclaims a new liberty that throws off the constraints of "aesthetics" and classical pictorial procedures. The machines that Picabia began to draw and paint in 1915 were thus the midwives of a new, fresh, and spontaneous creativity.

Man Ray

The first and only issue of *The Ridgefield Gazook* is small in format. Printed on a single sheet folded in four, this flippant, ironical little review was edited by the young Philadelphia-born artist Man Ray, who also did all its drawings and puns.

Man Ray lived and studied in New York, in particular at the Ferrer Center which was founded by sympathizers of the Spanish anarchist Francisco Ferrer executed in 1909. In an open-minded liberal environment comparable in some ways to Monte Verità in Ascona, the Ferrer Center offered courses free of charge in literature, philosophy, painting and drawing; and in addition had an elementary school conceived along libertarian lines, whose classes were an alternative to the pedagogical conventions of the times. The Center's philosophy of encouraging children's self-expression has a parallel in the Zurich Dadaists' interest in children's art.

The existence of the Ferrer Center, like that of the Ridgefield community which Man Ray helped to found, shows us that the American Dada group does not just owe its birth to the influence of Picabia and Duchamp but should be viewed as an episode in the history of the intellectual avant-garde in America. The American tradition of self-reliant thinking goes back to Henry David Thoreau (*Walden*, 1854) and Walt Whitman (*Leaves of Grass*, 1855). Whitman happens to have been Man Ray's favorite poet at the time, just as

Cover of The Ridgefield Gazook, *edited by Man Ray, 1915*

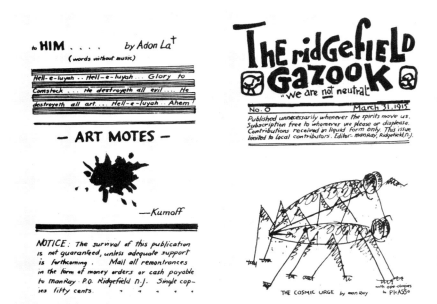

Man Ray: *Figures, 1915* ▷

Man Ray: *The River, 1914*

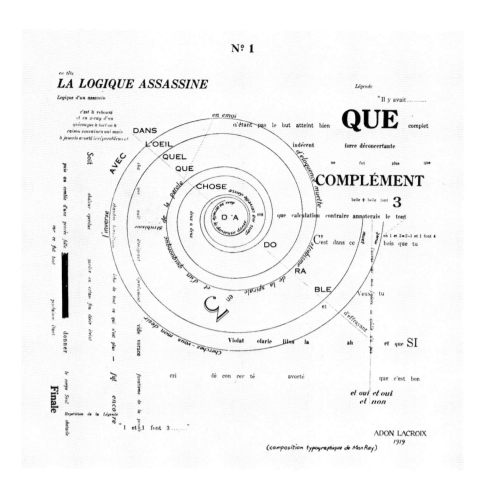

Thoreau, along with Erik Satie and the Dadaists themselves, would later become a crucial influence for John Cage.

Ridgefield was a libertarian artists colony in New Jersey (1913-1915). It was here that Man Ray met William Carlos Williams, Max Eastman (publisher of *The Masses*) and the poet, musician and chess player Alfred Kreymborg, who would later edit the review *Others*. Here too he met his future companion, the Belgian poetess Donna Lacour (Adon Lacroix). She introduced him to the poetry of Mallarmé and Rimbaud, and collaborated with him on typographical experiments like the layout of his *Book of Diverse Writings* (1915) and the plate for *La Logique assassine* (Murderous Logic, a phrase borrowed from Tzara's *Dada Manifesto 1918*). A particularly interesting composition, the latter is echoed in the typography of Man Ray's 1920 poem *L'Inquiétude* and in the "silent" poems of 1924.

After a series of Post-Impressionist canvases (1909-1912) which are merely the first steps of a young artist, there followed a period that was still hesitant but deeply influenced by the Armory Show—Man Ray was twenty-three in 1913—that is to say, by the triumph of Cubism and the avant-garde techniques of decomposing movement. The *Portrait of Stieglitz* (1913) is probably the first picture Man Ray painted after the Armory Show; it is a fitting tribute to the man who ran "291" and introduced Man Ray to photography, which was soon to play a major role in his artistic career.

Man Ray: *Boardwalk, 1917*

However, the first works to reveal Man Ray's own artistic personality, after he outgrew his youthful influences, are the ten collages of his *Revolving Doors* series (1916-1917), of which *Long Distance*, the work reproduced here, is the second.

In November 1915, on the occasion of his first one-man show at the Daniel Gallery, whose art director Hartpence was a friend from Ridgefield, Man Ray found himself obliged to provide friends, collectors and the press with photographs of his works. "The few reproductions done by professionals were unsatisfactory," he wrote. "Translating colors into black and white requires not only technical skill but also a real understanding of the work that is to be copied. No one, I said to myself, is more qualified to do this than the painter himself." Man Ray always declared that he was a painter first, and yet the camera became one of the main instruments of his art. He has left us not only a priceless gallery of photographic portraits of the artists and writers of the twenties, but also a remarkable series of films: *Le Retour à la raison* (1923), *Emak Bakia* (1927), *L'Etoile de mer* (1928), *Les Mystères du château du dé* (1929).

Under the influence of photography Man Ray began to move away from painting. His almost accidental discovery of the aerograph (air brush) was a further step (he had already exchanged the brush for the knife) towards the kind of intangible abstract effects that he was later to seek with his

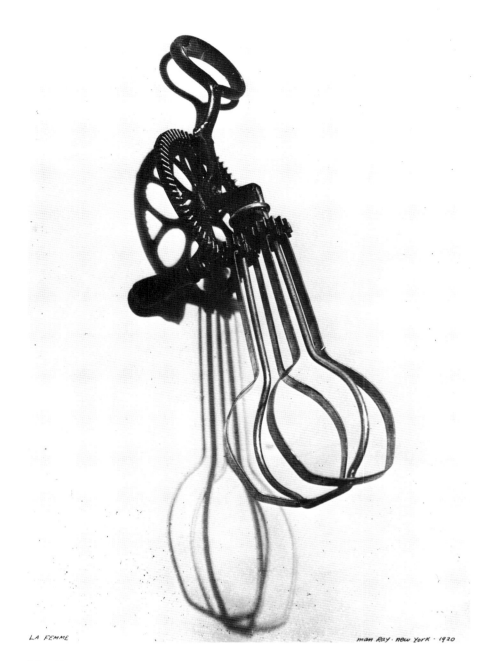

LA FEMME   man Ray · New York · 1920

Man Ray: *Man, 1917 (or Woman, 1920)*

Man Ray: *Lampshade, 1919*

Rayographs (see Chapter 6) and solarizations (*Suzy Solidor*, 1929). The rejection of traditional pictorial techniques is in fact one of the distinctive characteristics of the New York group. The aerograph allowed the artist to paint without actually touching the picture surface. By spraying at different distances he was able to create a variety of effects: "It was like painting in three dimensions," he declared. And because it was impossible to touch up the canvas after it was spray painted, using the aerograph amounted to automatic painting: a first-draft painting that precluded second thoughts.

Works like *Composition With Key and Triangle* (1919) and *Admiration of the Orchestrelle for the Cinematograph* (1919) build up variations in luminosity that are almost indistinguishable from the later Rayographic effects. Not for nothing did the artist—whose real name was Emmanuel Rudnitzki—choose the luminous pseudonym Man Ray.

The discovery of the Rayograph proves, if proof were needed, that of the many discoveries, accidental or otherwise, that an artist makes in the course of his experiments, only those that correspond to his own artistic preoccupations are retained. Of course his judgment depends on the degree of liberty he grants to himself, and on his receptivity, and these are both conditioned by circumstances. Thus it is not surprising that the Dada "phenomenon," which proclaimed freedom in the teeth of conventions, should have fostered the birth of possibilities that would otherwise have been repressed.

There was some rubbish in the vestibule with a broken lampshade on top. I carefully removed the paper, took it back to the room and hung it up by one end. It formed a pleasing spiral. This would be one of my exhibits in the new museum [La Société Anonyme]—my contribution as a sculptor. Looking at a dress form in a corner, I mentally removed the cloth-covered torso—the stand itself would serve as a support. I would also send in my latest painting—an airbrush composition of gear wheels, which had been inspired by the gyrations of a Spanish dancer I had seen in a musical play. The title was lettered into the composition: it could be read either DANCER or DANGER.

Man Ray, 1963

Man Ray: *Long Distance, 1916-1917*

This sensitivity of Man Ray's for the transparent and the ironic reduction of forms relates him to Marcel Duchamp, to whom he was introduced at Ridgefield in 1915 by Walter Arensberg. Together with Duchamp, he threw himself into a feverish creative activity involving photography. Tenuous appearances, cast shadows, ephemeral materials, ''dust farms,'' creations dictated by accidents or circumstances: these are what held the two artists' attention.

Dust Breeding (1920) was first published in the magazine *Littérature*, in Paris, above the caption: ''View from an airplane by Man Ray: This is Rrose Sélavy's territory/How arid it is. How fertile/How joyful. How sad.'' This work is actually a Man Ray photograph of Marcel Duchamp's *Large Glass* lying on the floor of the artist's studio and illuminated by a swinging naked light bulb. The dusty panel is littered with cotton wads and pieces of paper that were used to clean the glass's finished components. It was only later that Duchamp gave the photograph the title *Dust Breeding*.

Man Ray preserved many of Duchamp's ''actions'' for posterity (thus enabling them to influence later art movements like body art): for example, the star-shaped tonsure of 1921, the various disguises of Rrose Sélavy (''*Rose cela vit*,'' as Man Ray wrote at the bottom of a canvas portraying Duchamp), and so forth. Man Ray also took the few photographs we have of Duchamp's atelier, guarded symbolically by nine figures in livery, the Malic Molds of the *Large Glass*, daubed with rust paint and affixed to a glass pane.

The studio contains two other famous Duchamp works: the *Chocolate Grinder* (which was reproduced on the cover of Duchamp's little magazine *The Blind Man* in 1917) and the *Bicycle Wheel* mounted on a stool. This wheel,

Cover of The Blind Man, *No. 2, New York, May 1917*

Marcel Duchamp and **Man Ray:**
Dust Breeding, 1920

Marcel Duchamp's New York studio, 33 West 67th Street, 1917-1918, photograph by Man Ray

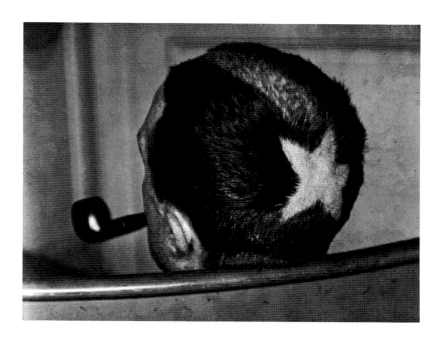

Marcel Duchamp with haircut by George de Zayas, 1921, photograph by Man Ray

Marcel Duchamp as Rrose Sélavy, his alter ego, c. 1920, photograph by Man Ray

In 1913 I had the happy idea to fasten a bicycle wheel to a kitchen stool and watch it turn.

A few months later I bought a cheap reproduction of a winter evening landscape, which I called ''Pharmacy'' after adding two small dots, one red and one yellow, in the horizon.

In New York in 1915 I bought at a hardware store a snow shovel on which I wrote: ''In advance of the broken arm.''

It was around that time that the word ''readymade'' came to mind to designate this form of manifestation.

A point which I want very much to establish is that the choice of these ''readymades'' was never dictated by any aesthetic delectation.

This choice was based on a reaction of visual indifference with at the same time a total absence of good or bad taste . . . in fact a complete anaesthesia.

One important characteristic was the short sentence which I occasionally inscribed on the ''readymade.''

That sentence instead of describing the object like a title was meant to carry the mind of the spectator towards other regions more verbal.

Sometimes I would add a graphic detail of presentation which in order to satisfy my craving for alliterations, would be called ''readymade aided.''

At another time wanting to expose the basic antinomy between art and readymades I imagined a ''reciprocal readymade'': use a Rembrandt as an ironing board!

I realized very soon the danger of repeating indiscriminately this form of expression and decided to limit the production of ''readymades'' to a small number yearly. I was aware at the time, that for the spectator even more than for the artist, art is a habit forming drug and I wanted to protect my ''readymades'' against such contamination.

Marcel Duchamp, 1961

Marcel Duchamp: *The Large Glass (The Bride Stripped Bare by her Bachelors,* ▷
*Even), 1915-1923, photographed in Katherine S. Dreier's home in West Redding,
Connecticut*

Marcel Duchamp behind the Rotary Glass Plates, *1920*

*Dada was an extreme protest against the physical side of painting. It was a
metaphysical attitude. It was intimately and consciously involved with
"literature." It was a sort of nihilism to which I am still very sympathetic. It
was a way to get out of a state of mind—to avoid being influenced by one's
immediate environment, or by the past: to get away from clichés—to get
free. The "blank" force of Dada was very salutary. It told you "don't forget
you are not quite so 'blank' as you think you are." Usually a painter
confesses he has his landmarks. He goes from landmark to landmark.
Actually he is a slave to landmarks—even to contemporary ones.*

Marcel Duchamp, 1946

to which the artist would give a light spin whenever he passed near it,
reminded Duchamp, with its shimmering spokes, of the tranquil wavering of
flames in a fireplace. The studio windows are covered with sheets of
newspaper for the nocturnal shadow theater the artist produced with a
corkscrew, the *Hat Rack* and the *Bicycle Wheel*.

Marcel Duchamp on the other side of painting: from the Readymade to *The Bride*

In New York Marcel Duchamp combined the extemporaneous casualness
of the Readymades with the lengthy process of elaborating his major work,
The Bride Stripped Bare by Her Bachelors, Even, known familiarly as the
Large Glass, which he "incompleted" in 1923.

The Readymade, the ordinary object "found" by Duchamp and then
exhibited as an art object (*Bicycle Wheel*, 1913; *Bottlerack*, 1914), is a protest
against the undue attention paid to certain art works, opposing to them an
equally arbitrary valuation of a routine object (but with the Readymade there
is no routine object).

Duchamp sacralizes and transforms the object. The object's sacral nature
is revealed in Man Ray's photograph of it, making it the object of an aesthetic
contemplation and giving it a metaphorical title (the eggbeater entitled *Man*,
1917, or, in another version, *Woman*, 1920) or including it in a more elaborate
composition (the revolver clinging to a magnet suspended from a string in
Compass, 1920).

Duchamp produced only a few Readymades. As he once said, it is enough
to have chosen a few objects to cast suspicion on all objects. Nevertheless the
fact that he chooses the object—and this choice is the one condition without
which there can be no Readymade—precludes the possibility of a general
principle of equivalence among all objects. The Readymade is singled out by
the artist, just as a picture exists in a sense because it is viewed. It is, so to
speak, a celebration of the artist's strictly personal, free and sovereign
choice.

The Bride should be read as a synthesis of Duchamp's thinking on art
between 1915 and 1923 when he "incompleted" it and then decided, when
the glass was cracked in transit after the Brooklyn exhibition of 1926, not to
restore it. Comprising two large glass panels joined in a metal frame to form
a transparent field about nine feet high and six feet wide, the work is now in
the Philadelphia Museum of Art.

The subject matter of *The Bride* is, in André Breton's words, "a
mechanistic and cynical interpretation of the phenomenon of love." The
forms are applied to the glass in paint and wire. In many ways a deliberately
hermetic work, it has inspired a flurry of notes by Duchamp himself (*The
Green Box*, 1934) as well as numerous attempts to interpret it, notably by
André Breton ("Phare de la mariée," in *Minotaure*, 1935). Michel Carrouges
(*Les Machines célibataires*, 1954), Octavio Paz (*The Castle of Purity*, 1967, and
Appearance Stripped Bare, 1976), Arturo Schwarz and Jean Suquet. The
writings of Katherine Dreier and Robert Lebel are interesting in this regard
too.

Jean Crotti and Suzanne Duchamp: the eye of Tabu

Marcel Duchamp: *To Be Looked at with One Eye, Close to, for Almost an Hour, 1918*

Other artists akin to the group were present in New York: Charles Sheeler first of all, a painter and film-maker whose film *Mana Hatta*, taken to Paris by Duchamp, was shown at the *Cœur à barbe* gala in July 1923 (see Chapter 6); next Jean Crotti, Duchamp's brother-in-law, whose work has a singularity of its own.

Clown (1916), a kind of automaton carefully devised, yet rickety, was made of lead wire and brightly colored red and blue circles. It stood in a white-bottomed glass box. In it one recognized Crotti's characteristic hallmark: a set purpose carried out with deliberately common and makeshift means. It had three artificial eyes, one surmounted by an eyelid with lashes: this he used as a trademark at the Tabu exhibition of his own and Suzanne Duchamp's work, held in Paris at the Galerie Montaigne in April 1921, only a few weeks before the Dada Salon at the same gallery (see Chapter 6). In Picabia's *L'Œil cacodylate*, Crotti was to write: "My glass mourning eye is watching you."

As to his choice of the word Tabu, the artist gives no explanation. What he does say, in an autobiographical text, is that it came to him in a flash, like a "luminous apparition," while he was walking down a street in Vienna. One

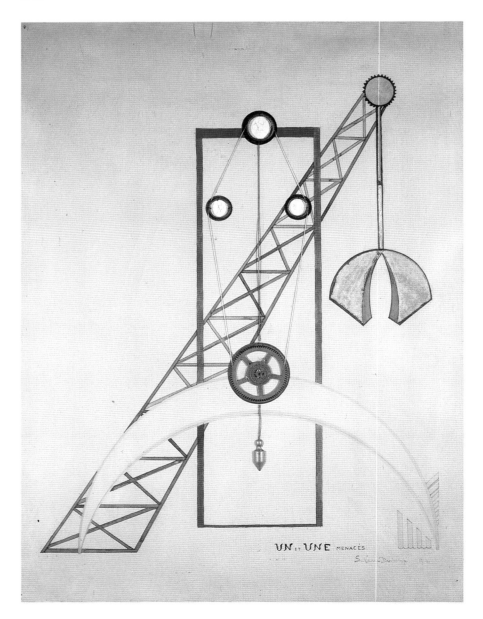

Suzanne Duchamp: *Un et Une menacés (One Man and One Woman Threatened), 1916*

Jean Crotti, Germaine Everling, Francis Picabia and Suzanne Duchamp at Cannes on the Riviera, 1921

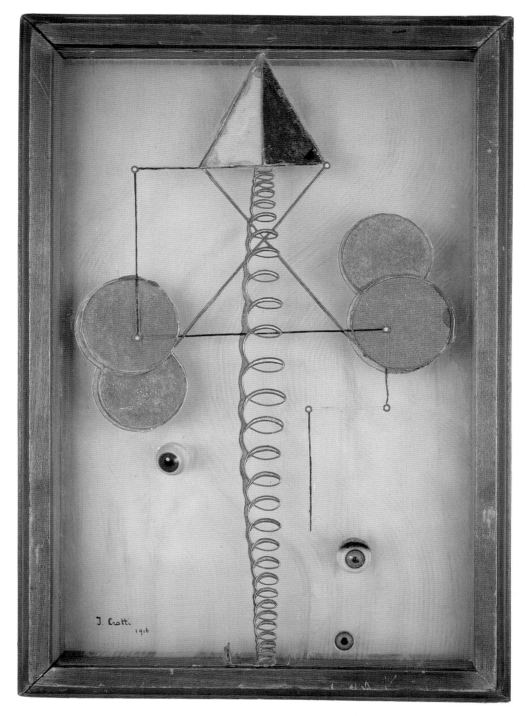

Jean Crotti: *Clown, 1916*

is accordingly tempted to see in it an allusion to Freud's book of 1913, *Totem und Tabu*. Others see in the special *Pilhaou-Thibaou* issue of *391* a borrowing from Tabu or an allusion to it.

The Tabu movement took more definite form in November 1921, when Jean Crotti exhibited his canvas *Mystère acatène* at the Salon d'Automne, held at the Grand Palais in Paris (see Chapter 6). To publicize the Tabu movement as a breakaway from Dada, Crotti and Suzanne Duchamp handed out to visitors a leaflet in which the picture was presented as the first illustration and embodiment of Tabu art. Little came of it, but in the artist's own mind this leaflet laid down a new line of thought and expression, indeed a new religion: the rejection of sensuality and materialism in art, the embracing of mystery, and the opening up of a boundless field of action for whoever wished "to express the Infinite itself."

In many ways the monochromatic purity conjured up by Crotti in this major canvas reminds one of certain compositions by Picabia (with geometric forms floating in space, like *Fixe* of 1921-1922 or *Astrolabe* of 1921) or of the severe simplicity of some of the Russian Constructivists (Puni's *White*

Ball, for example). But while this spareness was an end in itself for the Russian artists, the outcome of all their theorizing and experiments, it was merely a passing phase in the ever renewed pictorial adventure of Dada.

While it breaks away conspicuously from the cycle of machine-inspired works and heralds a new conception of space, Crotti's *Mystère acatène* also embodies the religious convictions and spiritual yearnings peculiar to this discreet and sensitive artist.

Between these two works, *Clown* and *Mystère acatène*, came several delicate paintings. Their very titles, *Virginity on the Move* and *The Mechanical Forces of Love in Movement*, point to preoccupations very similar to those of Duchamp and Picabia in New York. In the fall of 1915 Crotti, Duchamp, Picabia and Gleizes were the subject of a feature article in the *New York Tribune*. Their friendship and family ties (soon after Crotti's divorce from Yvonne Chastel, Duchamp lived with the latter and Crotti married Duchamp's sister) go far to explain the common inspiration behind this group, shared by Suzanne Duchamp in her paintings and also by Ribemont-Dessaignes in his.

The Picabia exhibition at the Dalmau Gallery, Barcelona, 1922

Serge Charchoune: *Catalogue cover for the Grunhoff-Charchoune exhibition, Dalmau Gallery, Barcelona, 1916*

Francis Picabia: *Spanish Night, 1922*

The Barcelona group

Exhausted by his eventful thirteen months' stay in New York, Picabia left America in June 1916 and moved to the sunny climate of Barcelona. Here he met a new group of exiled artists: the Cubist painter Albert Gleizes and his wife Juliette Roche; Marie Laurencin who had recently married Otto von Wätjen; Arthur Cravan, his brother Otho Lloyd and his companion Olga Sacharov who became a friend of Marie Laurencin; the poet Maximilien Gauthier (who signed his contributions to *391* Max Goth); Nicole Groult, the sister of the couturier Paul Poiret. Sonia and Robert Delaunay stayed briefly in Barcelona before moving on to Lisbon.

There were other artists in Barcelona at this time as well, though they were not acquainted with each other, among them Serge Charchoune and his friend Hélène Grunhoff; he was to join the Paris Dada group in 1921. For the moment, Charchoune was sketching out abstract painted films with Ricciotto Canudo and exhibiting with Hélène Grunhoff at the Dalmau Gallery, as did Picabia (who saw in Josep Dalmau a second Alfred Stieglitz, or very nearly). Dalmau was an antique dealer; at his shop on Portaferrissa he sold furniture and stylish objects as well as modern art. After five years in Paris, he had begun exhibiting Cubist painters in 1912. Dalmau was the first to organize a public viewing of Duchamp's *Nude Descending a Staircase* after it had been rejected by the selection jury of the Salon des Indépendants in Paris and before it was sent to the Armory Show in New York.

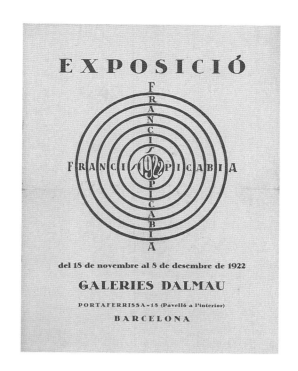

Poster of Picabia's one-man show at the Dalmau Gallery, 1922

Arthur Cravan, poet, boxer, lecturer

Cravan too turned up in Barcelona. He dropped literature and was now a boxing coach. As the director of the Real Club Marítimo, he refereed several boxing matches. Shortly before Picabia's arrival, he challenged the black boxing champion Jack Johnson. The fight caused a considerable stir in the literary world and gave Cravan a legendary aura, but it was hardly a great date in the annals of sport. It took place in the Plaza de Toros Monumental before an audience of four or five thousand and was filmed as part of a feature film on Jack Johnson. Here is the account given by the Barcelona paper *La Veu de Catalunya* on April 24, 1916:

> As soon as Johnson began to attack, Cravan seemed terrified. After wearing him down with a few clinches, the Negro demolished him with three blows to the stomach. The next five attacks exhausted Cravan completely, while the Negro let him get in a few punches for the sake of the movie they were shooting. In the sixth round, after literally playing with his opponent, Johnson demonstrated his overwhelming superiority. He gave him a straight right followed by a sideswipe that knocked him flat. The Negro then put on a display with his trainers and the entertainment ended.

According to some reports, Cravan had challenged Johnson in order to win a fifty thousand franc bet. For that sum, one journalist wrote, "it's worth getting yourself mauled." Other reporters blamed "Johnson's rather shady dealings" or the "unscrupulousness of the impresario, Señor Hernandez."

In a letter of January 1916 to André Level, the director of the Galerie Percier in Paris, Cravan outlined his plans as follows:

> I have fallen ill here and have not yet completely recovered. This means that, having come to Barcelona in order to box, I am obliged to wait some more. Anyway, I don't think I will stay here. I will go first to the Canary Islands, in all probability to Las Palmas, and thence to America, Brazil. . . I will go to see butterflies. This is perhaps absurd, ridiculous, impractical, but I can't help it and if I perhaps have one small virtue as a poet, it is precisely that I have passions, immoderate needs: I would like to see the spring in Peru, befriend a giraffe, and, when I read in the dictionary that the Amazon, which has a course of 6,420 kilometers, is also the river that has the largest discharge in the world, this makes such a powerful impression on me that I couldn't even express it in prose.
>
> You see, it is better not to try and reason with me, especially as I know in advance that I am letting myself in for difficult times and even sufferings because I lack funds. I will always console myself with the thought that I am putting distance between myself and Montparnasse, where art now survives solely through stealing, swindling, and wheeling and dealing, where ardor is calculated, tenderness is replaced by syntax and the heart by reason and not a single noble artist breathes and a hundred people make a living with spurious innovations.

In this state of mind, Cravan had ceased to publish his review and, seemingly, to write. Yet only a few months later, at Arensberg's house in New York, he fell in love with a writer: the poetess Mina Loy. He married her shortly before his mysterious disappearance in the Bay of Mexico in 1918 (see Chapter 2).

Poster for the Johnson-Cravan fight, Barcelona, April 1916

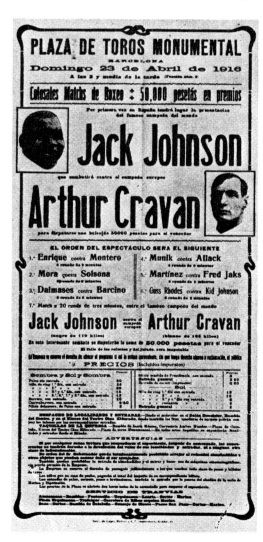

Cover of 391, No. 2, Barcelona, February 10, 1917

291. — *Obviously the 391 of Barcelona is not the 291 of New York. But where are Messrs. Stieglitz, Haviland and de Zayas who ran the already celebrated extinct review whose shapely figure we shall soon see again, shall we not? Not in Barcelona, to be sure. Mr. Stieglitz contents himself, for now, with being the most artistic of photographers; Mr. Haviland, the most meticulous of metalworkers and Mr. Zayas (see* Life*) the shrewdest of caricaturists . . .*
And we resume the work, with our imperfect means.

Francis Picabia, 1917

Letter from Francis Picabia to Alfred Stieglitz, January 22, 1917

Francis Picabia: *Dada Movement, 1919*

Birth of the traveling review *391*

The task of publishing a review in Barcelona thus fell to Picabia—Cravan anyway soon left Spain for America. The painter founded *391*, bringing out four numbers before he returned to New York in April 1917. As the title clearly shows, it was conceived in the tradition of Stieglitz's *291*. "We resume the work," Picabia explained, "with our imperfect means."

The first number appeared in January 1917. There were four pages in all. The cover illustration was a Picabia (*Novia*, 1917); inside was a watercolor by Marie Laurencin and several poems by Picabia and Max Goth. The cover of the second issue, Picabia's *Mirror of Appearances* (1917) is an antipictorial manifesto. On the keyboard of a realistically rendered piano, we read the words "*Miroir de l'apparence*," which denounce the illusionist system and the theory of art as a reflection of external reality. Note the musical motif: Picabia's wife Gabrielle Buffet was a musician, a student of Vincent d'Indy. Musical allusions occur often throughout Picabia's pictorial oeuvre.

The "traveling review," *391* was published by turns in Barcelona (four numbers), New York (three numbers in the summer of 1917), Zurich (one number in February 1919) and Paris (November 1919 to October 1924). It was the most international and adventurous of the Dada periodicals.

Cravan's lecture on art

Not long after Picabia arrived in Barcelona, Arthur Cravan left for New York. A note by "Pharamousse" (the pen name with which Picabia signed his international commentary "*Odeurs de partout*," Smells from Everywhere) in the first issue of *391* confirms the report that Cravan "too has left aboard an ocean liner."

As a matter of fact, Cravan traveled to America aboard the *Montserrat*; and, around the same time that Lenin and Tristan Tzara were both frequenting the Café Terrasse in Zurich, Cravan and his fellow passenger Leon Trotsky were celebrating New Year's eve 1917.

Cravan has left no account of this meeting (one wishes that he had given us something along the lines of his "Encounters with André Gide"), but in his autobiography *My Life* (1929) Trotsky surprisingly mentions the boxer-poet. His evident disapproval of Cravan and other artists of his ilk helps us to understand the stiffness with which Franz Jung and his Berlin Dada friends were received in the Soviet Union after the Revolution. ("*Messieurs les*

Marcel Duchamp (left) with Francis Picabia and Beatrice Wood on Coney Island, 1917

Cravan was late. He was impatiently waited for. Luckily there was a long bar on one side of the hall and everybody was having a drink. Every five minutes the telephone rang and in a well regulated crescendo a voice would announce a traffic jam or a puncture, and would conclude: "Don't worry! He's on the way!" In he came at last like a hunted lion, disheveled, red in the face, his collar wilting, self-assured, and drunk. He sat down at the small table on the platform, tasted a glass of water, made a wry face, and began with a few haughty phrases. Suddenly, in a small altered voice, he declared that the heat was intolerable and, this being so, he would have to give his lecture stark naked.

Henri-Pierre Roché, 1957

révolutionnaires," writes Picabia, "your minds are as narrow as that of a petit bourgeois from Besançon.")

> The ship's population was a mixed lot [says Trotsky] and was on the whole not very prepossessing. There were a number of deserters of diverse nationalities, especially individuals of a higher social rank. For example, there was an artist who was fleeing from the battle front with his paintings, his talent, his fortune and his family under the protection of his aged father. A boxer, also a poet and nephew of Oscar Wilde, who openly pronounced that he preferred to slug Yankees in a noble sport than to get his chest driven in by some ignorant German.

After disembarking in New York, Cravan did another of his legendary performances, this time with a lecture on art. Though to those who attended the lecture at the Independents exhibition Cravan seemed woefully unprepared, the boxer-poet had in fact come to New York partly with the intention of lecturing on art. A note by Pharamousse in the last Barcelona number of *391* specifies that Cravan is expected to give a lecture in America: "Will he be attired as a man of the world or as a cowboy? At the time of his departure he leaned towards the second costume and was planning to make an impressive entry on stage riding a horse and firing three shots at the chandelier with a revolver."

Cravan gave his lecture in June 1917, and he was in fact drunk. He began to undress in front of the ladies who had come to Grand Central Gallery to hear him, was promptly arrested, and was only released after Arensberg agreed to post bail for him. To what extent had he premeditated this scandal? Judging from Gabrielle Buffet-Picabia's account of the event, Cravan seems to have improvised as he went along:

> Cravan arrived very late, pushing his way through the large crowd of very smart listeners. Obviously drunk, he had difficulty in reaching the lecture platform, his expression and gait showing the decided effects of alcohol. He gesticulated wildly and began to take off his waistcoat. A canvas by the American painter, Sterner, was hanging directly behind him, and the incoherence of his movements made us fear that he would damage it. After having taken off his waistcoat, he began to undo his suspenders. The first surprise of the public at his extravagant entrance was soon replaced by murmurs of indignation. Doubtless the authorities had already been notified, for, at that moment, as he leaned over the table and started hurling one of the most insulting epithets in the English language at his audience, several policemen attacked him suddenly from behind, and handcuffed him with professional skill. He was manhandled, dragged out, and would have been thrown into jail, but for the intervention of Walter Arensberg, who bailed him out and took him to his house, while the protesting crowd made a tumultuous exit. . . What a wonderful lecture, said Marcel Duchamp, beaming, when we all met that evening at the home of Arensberg.

What game, if any, was Cravan playing? His manner of sacrificing himself on the altar of scandal, egged on by his friends (the boxer-poet stripped bare by his Dadaists, even), reminds one of the dynamic inter-antics between Johannes Baader and the Berlin Dadaists.

Within a few days of Cravan's New York lecture, Jacques Vaché made a stir at the première of Apollinaire's play *Les Mamelles de Tirésias* (The Breasts of Tiresias) in Paris (June 24, 1917). Annoyed by the "lyrical tone and the Cubist rehash of the sets and costumes" (André Breton), Vaché came to the theater wearing the uniform of an English officer and brandished a gun during the intermission. Had he read Picabia's note in the January issue of *391*?

Fountain by R. Mutt   Photograph by Alfred Stieglitz

THE EXHIBIT REFUSED BY THE INDEPENDENTS

Page from The Blind Man, *New York, 1917*

The *Fountain* of R. Mutt

The uproar caused by Cravan's lecture was not the first scandal to mark the First Annual Exhibition of Independent Artists in New York. It was in a sense the mate to Duchamp's notorious Readymade urinal. Remembering the rejection of his *Nude Descending a Staircase* several years earlier at the Salon des Indépendants in Paris (see Chapter 1), Duchamp set what amounted to a trap, and the Society of Independent Artists fell into it.

With the urinal Duchamp, or rather "R. Mutt," demonstrated publicly that the Society of Independent Artists was not abiding by its own rules ("no jury, no prizes") and had betrayed the ideal of liberty which it claimed to embody. His carefully prepared action resulted in a gradual destabilization of the Society. By questioning the institutionalization of what purported to be a free and open initiative, by challenging the Society's curatorial authority to decide which works were worthy of being included in culture and called art, Duchamp ended by raising an issue whose implications are so sweeping that it has become, under the spectacular terms of anti-art or the death of art, one of the crucial issues underlying all thinking about art in this century.

In 1917 Duchamp's situation in New York was the reverse of what his situation in Paris had been in 1912. Then even his own brothers had sided with the defenders of orthodox Cubism who had rejected the *Nude Descending a Staircase*. Now, ever since the Armory Show, Duchamp had an immense reputation and a unique status. He was thus invited to become one of the twenty-one directors of the Society of Independent Artists. Chuckling to himself, he accepted. He had a surprise in store for his fellow directors, among them Walter Arensberg, Joseph Stella, Katherine Dreier, Man Ray, Morton Schamberg and Walter Pach.

In the spring of 1917 Arensberg, Stella and Duchamp visited, at the latter's suggestion, the J.L. Mott Iron Works in New York and bought a glazed porcelain urinal. A few weeks later a certain "Richard Mutt" from Philadelphia submitted this object to the Independents. It was presented horizontally, entitled *Fountain* and signed "R. Mutt, 1917." As Duchamp had anticipated, the Society's directors rejected it, in violation of their bylaws (free admission). Many of them were shocked by the fact that a vulgar bathroom fixture was being submitted as a work of art (just as the jury of the Indépendants in Paris had been shocked by the *Nude Descending a Staircase*) and were further antagonized by the mocking allusion to the famous comic strip, *Mutt and Jeff*. And of course "mutt" means a stupid person or, more significantly, a mongrel.

At stake here was the extravagant power of naming, of saying what "in the name of the law" of meaning and in the name of art, over this baptismal font (the fountain), would bear the name of art(ist) or *not*. After playing upon exquisite words, Duchamp brought into action the name, both the falsely patronymic proper name (Mutt) and, supreme taboo, the "true" proper name of *art*.

Viewed by most of them as a joke in poor taste, the *Fountain* sparked off an acrimonious debate among the directors. George Bellows (once Man Ray's painting teacher) rumbled: "Do you mean that if an artist put horse manure on a canvas and sent it to the exhibition, we would have to accept it?" "I'm afraid we would," replied Arensberg. Duchamp, protesting the Society's decision, resigned his directorship.

He and his friends then started making hay of the affair. They got Stieglitz to photograph the *Fountain* in front of a Marsden Hartley canvas (*The Warriors*, 1913), and since Stieglitz was the leading promoter of avant-garde European art in the United States, his imprimatur gave the urinal a quasi-official status and made it a symbol. Then *The Boston Evening Transcript* reported, on April 25, 1917, that Richard Mutt intended to take the Society of Independent Artists to court for rejecting his work and had declared that he would not be satisfied merely with a reversal of the Society's decision: he was going to sue for damages.

In May, the second number of *The Blind Man*, the periodical founded by Henri-Pierre Roché, Beatrice Wood and Marcel Duchamp, further increased the pressure on the Society by publishing an editorial on the "Richard Mutt case." (The little magazine's first issue had been entirely devoted to the Independents exhibition.) Accompanying the editorial was a full-page

Portrait of Marcel Duchamp, 1920

reproduction of Stieglitz's photograph of the urinal, with the legend: "Fountain by R. Mutt. Photograph by Alfred Stieglitz. The exhibit refused by the Independents." The phrasing here was somewhat ambiguous. Where does the emphasis lie, on fountain, on photograph, or on exhibit? The editorial, presumably penned by Duchamp himself, reminded the Society's directors that

> Whether Mr. Mutt with his own hands made the fountain or not has no importance. He CHOSE it. He took an ordinary article of life, placed it so that its useful significance disappeared under the new title and point of view—and created a new thought for that object.

The editorial was followed by an article entitled "The Buddha of the Bathroom." Its author Louise Norton (ex-wife of the editor of *Rogue* magazine) put forward an aesthetic approach to the *Fountain*, stressing the urinal's formal properties and pleasing visual qualities. This was the first step in the process by which the *Fountain* has gradually become enshrined in the history of the avant-garde. In Paris Apollinaire spoke up in the *Mercure de France*, also likening the *Fountain* to a seated Buddha and denouncing the Society of Independent Artists.

The emphasis on the aesthetic quality of the Readymade can hardly be underestimated. For in fact the urinal and, in a lesser degree, certain works by Picabia (*Donkey*, 1917) prefigure the industrial aesthetic. Duchamp himself was impressed by industrial design. In Paris in 1912, when he visited the Air Locomotion Show with Fernand Léger and Constantin Brancusi, he was fascinated by the engines and propellers. Turning to Brancusi he said: "Painting is finished. Who can do better than that propeller? Tell me, can you do that?"

As for Louise Norton's article on the *Fountain*, Duchamp himself was probably behind it, as anyone knowing him can guess. The emphasis on the beauty of the object, meant by Duchamp to discourage any aesthetic investment, began when Stieglitz set the spotless urinal up in front of a colorful Marsden Hartley canvas, with carefully adjusted lighting and a keen attention to detail which make this picture of the Readymade a very fine work by the great photographer. From that moment an aesthetic interpretation of the Readymade gained currency, for example in an article by Beatrice Wood: "At Marcel's request, Stieglitz agreed to photograph the *Fountain* for the frontispiece of the magazine. He was greatly amused, but also felt it was important to fight bigotry in America. He took great pains with the lighting,

and did it with such skill that a shadow fell across the urinal suggesting a veil. The piece was renamed: 'Madonna of the Bathroom'."

The urinal was thus transformed into a Madonna, a Virgin, or into a bride or anyhow a female. In this way Duchamp integrated the *Fountain* into the ingeniously devised circuit of his love machinery. Of the effects produced by this Readymade, not the least surprising was that it yielded a variety of metaphors: Buddha, Madonna, and the first one of all, Fountain.

The very shadows, whether they are the metaphor of a Madonna's veil placed there by Stieglitz or were photographed by Duchamp or Man Ray (*Shadows of Readymades*, in Duchamp's studio, 1918), are an integral part of the painter's aesthetic. These shadows reappear enlarged by projection (the *Bicycle Wheel*, the *Coat Stand*, the *Corkscrew*) in *Tu m'*, a canvas painted this same year, 1918, for a strip of wall in Katherine Dreier's library. It is one of the most colorful canvases ever done by Duchamp, a symbolic work, for in it he reverts for the last time to the pleasure of painting and adds several sarcastic elements. From a tear on the right a bottle-washing brush points out at the viewer. In this farewell to painting, clinched with an actual nut and bolt, one also notes a whole chromatic scale (of color samples) receding in perspective in the movement of the wheel.

It was around this time, too, that the rumor spread that *Fountain* had been destroyed by the Society's president, the painter William Glackens. This seems doubtful, but the *Fountain* did in fact disappear. Duchamp later claimed that it had been acquired by Walter Arensberg and subsequently lost. Other sources report that Duchamp was last seen with the *Fountain* at the Grand Central Palace where he and Man Ray brandished it in front of the visitors attending the exhibition.

The Mutt mystery has never been completely elucidated. In a letter to his sister, dated April 11, 1917, Duchamp writes that one of his female friends, using the pseudonym Richard Mutt, "sent in a porcelain urinal by way of a sculpture." But no doubt the artist is indulging his legendary fondness for disguises, female pseudonyms (like Rrose Sélavy) and subverting external reality (the dud check to Dr Tzanck, the beautifully imitated Monte Carlo bond certificate, and so forth). In any event, he seems to have been reluctant to acknowledge in writing, even privately, that he was the real author of the *Fountain*.

In later years Duchamp agreed to sign "R. Mutt" to replicas of the original *Fountain*, secure in the knowledge that no one else would claim authorship of this work, but the fact that he never officially recognized it as his own adds yet another twist to its complex meaning.

The *Fountain* indeed raises multiple issues: What is art? What is an art work? Under what conditions does a work become "art"? What divisions within reality govern those conditions, and what justifies those divisions? What does justify mean? By undermining the strictly conventional boundary between art and non-art, Duchamp poses even more radical questions, perhaps the only ones that are really worth asking, concerning the actual nature of all activity, the reality of the individual, the meaning of power and the power of meaning.

Marcel Duchamp:
Shadows of Readymades, 1918, photograph taken in Duchamp's New York studio

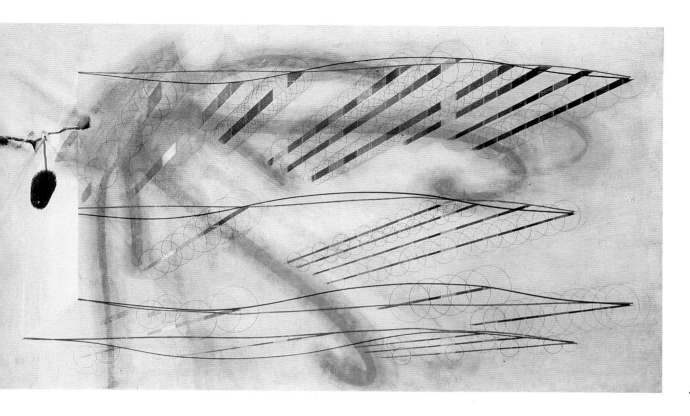

Marcel Duchamp: *Tu m', 1918*

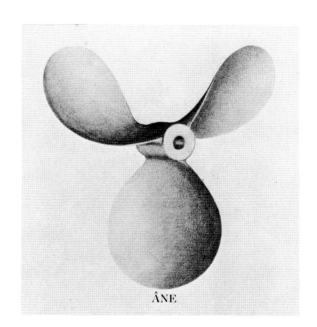

ÂNE

Francis Picabia: *Donkey, cover drawing for 391, No. 5,*
New York, 1917

Morton Schamberg: *God, c. 1917*

Marcel Duchamp: *Cover for* New York Dada, *April 1921*

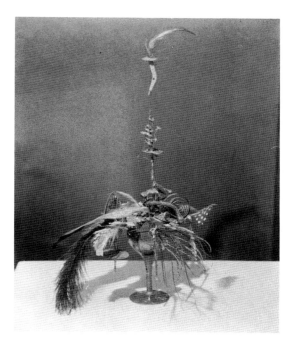

Baroness Else von Freytag-Loringhoven:
*Portrait of Marcel Duchamp, 1922, photographed
by Charles Sheeler*

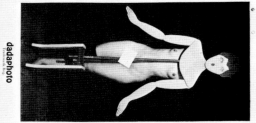

EYE-COVER ART-COVER CORSET-COVER
AUTHORIZATION

NEW YORK-DADA:

You ask for authorization to name your periodical Dada. But Dada belongs to everybody. I know excellent people who have the name Dada. Mr. Jean Dada; Mr. Gaston de Dada; Fr. Picabia's dog is called Zizi de Dada; in G. Ribemont-Dessaigne's play, the pope is likewise named Zizi de Dada. I could cite dozens of examples. Dada belongs to everybody. Like the idea of God or of the tooth-brush. There are people who are very dada, more dada; there are dadas everywhere all over and in every individual. Like God and the toothbrush (an excellent invention, by the way).

Dada is a new type; a mixture of man, naphthaline, sponge, animal made of ebonite and beefsteak, prepared with soap for cleansing the brain. Good teeth are the making of the stomach and beautiful teeth are the making of a charming smile. Halleluiah of ancient oil and injection of rubber.

There is nothing abnormal about my choice of Dada for the name of my review. In Switzerland I was in the company of friends and was hunting the dictionary for a word appropriate to the sonorities of all languages. Night was upon us when a green hand placed its ugliness on the page of Larousse—pointing very precisely to Dada—my choice was made. I lit a cigarette and drank a demitasse.

For Dada was to say nothing and to lead to no explanation of this offshoot of relationship which is not a dogma nor a school, but rather a constellation of individuals and of free facets.

Dada existed before us (the Holy Virgin) but one cannot deny its magical power to add to this already existing spirit and impulses of penetration and diversity that characterizes its present form.

There is nothing more incomprehensible than Dada.

Nothing more indefinable.

With the best in the world I cannot tell you what I think of it.

The journalists who say that Dada is a pretext are right, but it is a pretext for something I do not know.

Dada has penetrated into every hamlet; Dada is the best paying concern of the day.

Therefore, Madam, be on your guard and realize that a really dada product is a different thing from a glossy label.

Dada abolishes "nuances." Nuances do not exist in words but only in some atrophied brains whose cells are too jammed. Dada is an anti "nuance" cream. The simple motions that serve as signs for deaf-mutes are quite adequate to express the four or five mysteries we have discovered within 7 or 8,000 years. Dada offers all kinds of advantages. Dada will soon be able to boast of having shown people that to say "right" instead of "left" is neither less nor too logical, that red and valise are the same thing; that 2765 = 34; that "fool" is a merit; that yes = no. Strong influences are making themselves felt in politics, in commerce, in language. The whole world and what's in it has slid to the left along with us. Dada has inserted its syringe into hot bread, to speak allegorically into language. Little by little (large by large) it destroys it. Everything collapses with logic. And we shall see certain liberties we constantly take in the sphere of sentiment, social life, morals, once more become normal standards. These liberties no longer will be looked upon as crime, but as itches.

I will close with a little international song: Order from the publishing house "La Sirene" 7 rue Pasquier, Paris, DADAGLOBE, the work of dadas from all over the world. Tell your bookseller that this book will soon be out of print. You will have many agreeable surprises.

Read Dadaglobe if you have troubles. Dadaglobe is in press. Here are some of its colloborators:

Paul Citroen (Amsterdam); Baader Daimonides; R. Hausmann; W. Heartfield; H. Hoech; R. Huelsenbeck; G. Grosz; Fried Hardy Worm (Berlin); Clement Pansaers (Bruxelles); Mac Robber (Calcutta); Jacques Edwards (Chili); Baargeld, Armada v. Dulgedalzen, Max Ernst, F. Haubrich (Cologne); K. Schwitters (Hannovre); J. K. Bonset (Leyde); Guillermo de Torre (Madrid); Gino Cantarelli; E. Bacchi, A. Fiozzi (Mantoue); Krusenitch (Moscou); A. Vagts (Munich); W. C. Arensberg, Gabrielle Buffet, Marcel Duchamp; Adon Lacroix; Baroness v. Loringhoven; Man Ray; Joseph Stella; E. Varese; A. Stieglitz; M. Hartley; C. Kahler (New York); Louis Aragon; C. Brancusi; André Breton; M. Buffet; S. Charchoune; J. Crotti; Suzanne Duchamp; Paul Eluard; Benjamin Peret; Francis Picabia; G. Ribemont-Dessaignes; J. Rigaut, Soubeyran; Ph. Soupault, Tristan Tzara (Paris); Melchior Vischer (Prague); J. Evola (Rome); Arp; S. Taeuber (Zurich).

The incalculable number of pages of reproductions and of text is a guaranty of the success of the book. Articles of luxury, of prime necessity, articles indispensable to hygiene and to the heart, toilet articles of an intimate nature.

Such, Madame, do we prepare for Dadaglobe; for you need look no further than to the use of articles prepared without Dada to account for the fact that the skin of your heart is chapped; that the so precious enamel of your intelligence is cracking; also for the presence of those tiny wrinkles still imperceptible but nevertheless disquieting.

All this and much else in Dadaglobe. TRISTAN TZARA.

From *391* to the one issue of *New York Dada*

Upon his return to New York, Picabia resumed publication of *391*, opening it to old friends of *291* like Walter Arensberg, Paul Haviland, Alfred Stieglitz, the composer Edgar Varèse, and Albert Gleizes (who had also left Barcelona for New York, living there in the same building as Picabia). With its large format and striking typography, *391* was one of the handsomest Dada periodicals.

It attained the goal set by Tristan Tzara in the *Dada Manifesto 1918*—a goal the Rumanian-born poet himself never succeeded in reaching with his own periodical: "Every page must explode, either by profound heavy seriousness, the whirlwind, poetic frenzy, the new, the eternal, the crushing joke, enthusiasm for principles, or by the way in which it is printed."

391 was the foremost Dada review published in New York, but it was not the only one. *New York Dada*, edited by Marcel Duchamp and Man Ray, appeared in April 1921, on the fringe of the Dada galaxy. While Duchamp was not a regular member of the Dada movement, as he himself made clear when he sent his famous "Podebal" cable to Jean Crotti declining to take part in the Dada Salon at the Galerie Montaigne in Paris (June 1921), it is nevertheless significant that he and Man Ray chose to bring out their review under the Dada label.

A reproduction of Duchamp's "assisted" Readymade *Belle Haleine, Eau de Voilette* (1921) adorns the magazine's cover against a background of the endlessly repeated words "new york dada april 1921" in typewritten characters printed back to front. The Readymade is a bottle of *eau de toilette* to which a label has been affixed, containing a Man Ray photograph of a transvestite Duchamp as Rrose Sélavy.

The review's contents include photographs by Stieglitz and Man Ray (the *Coat Stand* here entitled *Dadaphoto*); poems by the Baroness Else von Freytag-Loringhoven, a writer close to the Dada group; and Kurt Schwitters' announcement for the Société Anonyme collection founded in April 1920 by Katherine Dreier, at the instigation of Marcel Duchamp and Man Ray, and destined to play a leading role in the dissemination of modern art in the United States (see Chapter 1).

But the most interesting contribution to *New York Dada* is Tzara's "authorization" to use the name Dada, which the editors reproduced in full. For before undertaking to publish their magazine, Duchamp and Man Ray had, not uncalculatingly, put Gabrielle Buffet up to writing Tzara to request permission for Stieglitz to open a Dada branch in New York.

This put the founder of the movement in a difficult position. In theory Dada recognized no hierarchy; its members were all considered presidents of the movement, as was repeatedly proclaimed orally and in print. Asking Tzara for permission to use the word Dada was a way of paying tribute to his moral authority, but in doing so Duchamp and Man Ray automatically placed him in a position of institutional authority. This was contrary to the Dada policy of urging its members to pay no heed to rights and permissions. Tzara wriggled out of the dilemma by replying: "Dada is not a dogma nor a school, but rather a constellation of individuals and of free facets."

Page from New York Dada *with Tristan Tzara's "Authorization" and* Man Ray's Coat Stand, *April 1921*

Chapter 5

Dada in Germany:
Revolution within the Revolution

The Dadaists had challenged the established order of speech, and of the world, on neutral ground in Zurich. Now, in the streets of Berlin, they witnessed the failure to which the old entrenched ideas had led, ideas which in Germany were embodied in the unyielding structure of the Empire, as a virtual caricature of an authoritarian, reactionary and anti-Semitic state. Even before the war, Expressionists such as Ludwig Meidner of the Pathetiker group had painted apocalyptic war scenes (*Revolution*, 1913), burning houses, exploding grenades, wounded men, and so on.

When Richard Huelsenbeck left Zurich for Berlin in February 1917, Germany was conducting an all-out submarine offensive against the allied ships forming the blockade. Mutinies broke out in the German navy. In January 1918, at the same moment as the first Dada evening organized by Huelsenbeck in Neumann's Graphisches Kabinett, 200,000 workers in the Berlin armament factories (soon to be half a million throughout the country) answered the Spartacists' call for a general strike against the war and the government. The military authorities broke the strike by proclaiming martial law and threatening workers who refused to go back to work with war tribunals. In spite of the encouragement of the Spartacists, the workers gave in, while the most active leaders of the revolt were forced to enlist in the armed forces.

For the German offensive against the Allies was continuing. In the spring, while the big Dada evening was taking place in the Berlin Secession Hall (April 1918), the German army, now at the gates of Paris, subjected the city to a heavy bombardment with their massive siege gun Big Bertha. Nevertheless, the allied forces, regrouped and reinforced by American aid, forced Germany to retreat until her defeat and the armistice of November 11, 1918.

Out of this grew the Spartacist revolution which spread to Germany as a whole, both at home and among the occupation forces. German soldier-workers in Brussels publicly ripped the badges of rank from their superior officers. The latter sought refuge in the Italian Embassy to protect themselves from their troops, who made their way home on their own initiative. Two writers played an important role at their head, the German essayist, Carl Einstein, one of the first art critics to write about Cubism and African sculpture, and the Dadaist poet Clément Pansaers (who joined the Paris group shortly afterwards). Contemporary witnesses, among them Max Ernst, an ordinary private, could not get over that "strange fellow" (Carl Einstein) who "speaks French like a Parisian." Einstein, who was an art critic in Paris, dictated his orders to the German Governor of Brussels whose "very junior employee" he had been only the evening before.

Emperor Wilhelm II abdicated: the Berlin chancellery handed over its powers to the SPD (the Social Democratic Party), which formed the provisional Ebert government. The Social Democratic Party proclaimed the German Republic, but the Spartacist leader Karl Liebknecht countered by announcing the birth of the Free Socialist Republic of Germany.

The absence of power was followed by a new phase of rebellion which gave birth to a swarm of committees and people's soviets which the Social Democrats tried to conciliate by setting up a new government. In January 1919, armed Spartacist factions fought in the streets of Berlin, occupied the newspaper district and called for armed struggle against the government.

*Richard Huelsenbeck and Raoul Hausmann
in Prague, March 1920*

The movement met with little support and government troops crushed the insurrection. The Spartacist leaders (Karl Liebknecht and Rosa Luxemburg, as well as the spokesman of the Social Democrats) went underground. Discovered by the militia, Liebknecht and Luxemburg were arrested by the division of the General Staff. After being questioned, during their transfer to the Moabit prison, they were brutally attacked and wounded with a rifle butt by a member of the military escort. Another soldier ''finished Liebknecht off.'' Rosa Luxemburg was murdered in a different vehicle and her body was thrown into the Landwehr canal.

The General Staff issued communiqués; they claimed that Liebknecht was killed while trying to escape and that Rosa Luxemburg was murdered by persons unknown. The government said it would order a ''strict inquiry,'' declaring that ''the victims were entitled to justice'' and that ''this lynching dishonors the German people and everyone condemns it morally.''

Such was the climate in which Huelsenbeck launched Dada in Germany, amid confusion that put the finishing touches to the breaking up of the State. Meanwhile, an extreme right wing was being organized. Hitler and the German ''workers'' party appeared as early as February 1920. A former member of the Reichstag called Kapp and his accomplices tried to seize power; they failed, but went unpunished. France occupied the Ruhr without British approval as a reprisal for German violations of the Treaty of Versailles, and this at a time when the amount of reparations owed by Germany to the Allies was under discussion and the population was still suffering from malnutrition.

The situation in Berlin gave the Dada movement a more popular and more violent impetus; it clashed with the censorship and was banned from publishing on several occasions. It also gave Dada a political overtone that was concrete (public interventions) and publicity-seeking (posters, slogans, false news items, parodies of the press). But the politicization of the Berlin

F.W. Seiwert: *Karl Liebknecht and Rosa Luxemburg, 1919*

Cover of Wieland Herzfelde's ''Tragigrotesques of the Night/Dreams,'' with a drawing by George Grosz, 1920

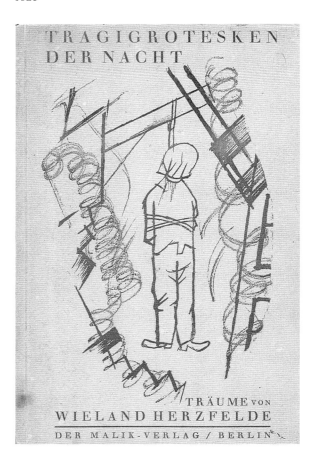

movement could not fit in with established ideological trends, nor could it accept a limited commitment. Two tendencies emerged among the Berlin Dadaists. Huelsenbeck was able to reconcile them in such a way that Dada made use of both of them to increase the effect of a single united protest.

The first, more authentically Dada tendency, anarchistic, individualistic, artistic, crystallized around Raoul Hausmann (the Dadasopher), Hannah Höch and Johannes Baader (the Oberdada). The second, openly political and left-wing, consisted basically of Wieland Herzfelde, the founder of the publishing house Malik Verlag (borrowed from Else Lasker-Schüler's novel *Malik*, the word means prince or bandit leader in Turkish), his brother John Heartfield (Monteurdada, who had anglicized his name) and their close friend, the painter George Grosz (Marshal Dada or Propagandadada Marschall).

In a retrospective article written in 1924 for the Polish review *Blok*, Kurt Schwitters explained: ''Grosz invented a political formula (he never took an active part in Dadaism). There is no doubt that for a time he looked on Dada as an instrument of political warfare, unlike Huelsenbeck who used Communism as an instrument of Dadaist warfare. Today Herzfelde, formerly John Heartfield, is the ultrabourgeois director of the bourgeois Malik publishing house and he has nothing but contempt for Dadaism.''

Divergences between these two tendencies arose on many occasions, especially when Otto Dix, George Grosz, Raoul Hausmann and Hannah Höch, among others, sent an ''Open letter to the November Group'' in which they declared their opposition to that group of radical artists founded during the November 1918 revolution. They felt that the November Group flouted the aspirations of the young members who had ''faith in the proletarian revolution'' on the one hand, and who, on the other hand, did not want to be ''artists in the sense that bourgeois culture uses the word,'' because they did not see in ''the establishment of a so-called revolutionary aesthetic the path towards the liberation of mankind.'' Lastly they accused the leaders of the group of being too preoccupied with ''their own affairs and reputations.''

George Grosz:
*The Monteur
John Heartfield.
After Franz Jung's
attempt to put
him on his feet,
1920*

Year 1 of world peace. Dada notice

Hirsch copper falling. Will Germany starve? Then she will have to sign. Smart young lady, seventeen inch waist for Hermann Loeb. If Germany doesn't sign, then she will probably sign. On the market of standard values the quotations are going down. But if Germany signs, then she will probably sign in order not to sign. Amor halls. Eighto'clockeveningpaperwithblusteringsky. From Viktorhahn. Lloyd George considers it possible that Clemenceau is of the opinion, that Wilson thinks, Germany must sign because she won't be able not to sign. The Dada Club accordingly declares itself in favor of absolute liberty of the press, for the press is the instrument of culture without which it would never be known that Germany will finally sign, merely in order to sign.

(Dada Club, Section for Liberty of the Press, insofar as good manners allow.)

Published on the cover of Der Dada, No. 1, Berlin, June 1919

A few years later in a somewhat less urgent context, the *Proletarian Art Manifesto*, an important document cementing the alliance formed between the Dadaist and Constructivist artists (see Chapter 7), would put an end to all speculation, foreseeing clearly the proletarian or ''socialist-realist'' diversions hostile to their art:

There is no such thing as art relating to a particular class of human beings, and if there were, it would have no relation to life . . .

There is no such thing as art produced by the proletariat, since, when a proletarian produces a work of art, he ceases to be a proletarian and becomes an artist. An artist is neither a proletarian nor a bourgeois, and his work belongs neither to the proletariat nor to the bourgeoisie, but to everyone. Art is a spiritual function of man, the purpose of which is to redeem him from the chaos of life and its tragedy. Art is free in its choice of means but is bound by its own laws and by them alone, and once a work of art is created it far transcends the class distinction between proletarian and bourgeois. If there were a kind of art exclusively for the benefit of the proletariat, then, apart from the fact that the proletariat is infected by bourgeois taste, it would be no less limited than specifically bourgeois art. Such art could not be universal or reflect a sense of world citizenship, but would remain at the level of individual views rooted in social conditions and the restrictions of time and space . . . What we on our part are striving for is the universal work of art that rises above all forms of advertisement, be they for champagne, Dadaism or Communist dictatorship.

Art as we would have it is neither proletarian nor bourgeois: the forces it develops are strong enough to influence the whole of civilization, rather than let themselves be influenced by social conditions. The proletariat, like the bourgeoisie, is a condition that must be superseded.

But if the proletarians imitate the bourgeoisie cult by setting up a rival cult of their own, they are unconsciously helping to preserve the corrupt culture of the bourgeoisie, to the detriment of art and of civilization.

By their conservative attachment to old, outworn forms of expression and by their incomprehensible aversion to modern art they are keeping alive the bourgeois culture which they profess to attack. This is how it happens that bourgeois sentimentalism and romanticism continue to exist and are cultivated anew despite the most strenuous efforts of radical artists to put an end to them. Communism is already just as bourgeois as Majority-Socialism, that is to say capitalism in a new form. The bourgeoisie uses the apparatus of Communism, which was invented by

George Grosz: *Midsummer Night, 1918*

George Grosz: *The Guilty, 1919*

the bourgeois and not by proletarians, simply as a means of rejuvenating its own decayed culture (Russia). Hence the proletarian artist is fighting neither for art nor for the new life of the future, but for the bourgeoisie. Every single proletarian work of art is an advertisement for the bourgeoisie and nothing else.

Signed: Theo van Doesburg, Hans Arp, Christof Spengemann, Kurt Schwitters, Tristan Tzara, The Hague, March 6, 1923.

To come back to 1918. To the Dadaists, the setting up of the Weimar Republic, dependent on a parliamentary system rather than the imperial regime, was in no way a revolution. It brought back the ''values'' which had led to disaster, beginning with the spirit of submission, the bourgeois order, the Church, education and the army. ''Weimar is nothing but a lie, a mask hiding Teutonic barbarism,'' declared Raoul Hausmann, the Dadasopher of the group, author of a manifesto ''Against the Weimar View of Life,'' and George Grosz looked on the new government as a ''revival of the Hohenzollerns.''

In January 1918, a year after his return to Berlin from Zurich, Huelsenbeck organized the first Dada evening in Neumann's Graphisches Kabinett. A second evening was held in the spring to celebrate the foundation of the Dada Club by Huelsenbeck, Raoul Hausmann and George Grosz. This second Dada event took place in the rooms of the Berlin Secession and to mark the occasion Huelsenbeck published the first Berlin *Dada Manifesto*, in the form of a tract:

The highest art will be that which in its conscious content presents the thousandfold problems of the day, the art which has been visibly shattered by the explosions of last week, which is forever trying to collect its limbs from yesterday's crash. The best and most extraordinary artists will be those who every hour snatch the tatters of their bodies out of the frenzied cataract of life, who, with bleeding hands and hearts, hold fast to the intelligence of their time ... You say yes to a life that strives upward by negation. Affirmation—negation: the gigantic hocus-pocus of existence fires the nerves of the true Dadaist—and there he is, reclining, hunting, cycling—half Pantagruel, half St. Francis, laughing and laughing!

Blast the aesthetic-ethical attitude! Blast the bloodless abstraction of expressionism!

Blast the literary hollowheads and their theories for improving the world! For Dadaism in word and image, for all the Dada things that go on in the world! To be against this manifesto is to be a Dadaist!

This manifesto, first issued by the Berlin group, plus Tzara and Janco, had many more signatures when it was revived in the *Dada Almanach* in 1920, namely those of the Zurich Dadaists (Tzara, Janco, Ball, Arp, Van Rees, Lüthy, Glauser) and the Germans (Franz Jung, George Grosz, Huelsenbeck, Preisz, Hausmann, Mehring), as well as others such as Pierre Albert-Birot, poet and guiding spirit of the review *SIC* in Paris, and some Italians, including Cantarelli (a Dadaist poet and painter at Mantua, editor of the reviews *Bleu* and *Procellaria*), and lastly Prampolini who had joined the Dadaists and published the review *Noi*, before becoming the main representative of Italy's "second Futurism."

Huelsenbeck's was one of the first manifestoes of the Dada movement, because it preceded by several days that of Serner in Zurich and Tzara's *Dada Manifesto 1918* of July 1918 by some weeks. It was, however, nearly two years later than the movement's first proclamation, the *Manifesto of Mr. Antipyrine* read by Tzara in Zurich in July 1916 ("Dada is our intensity...")

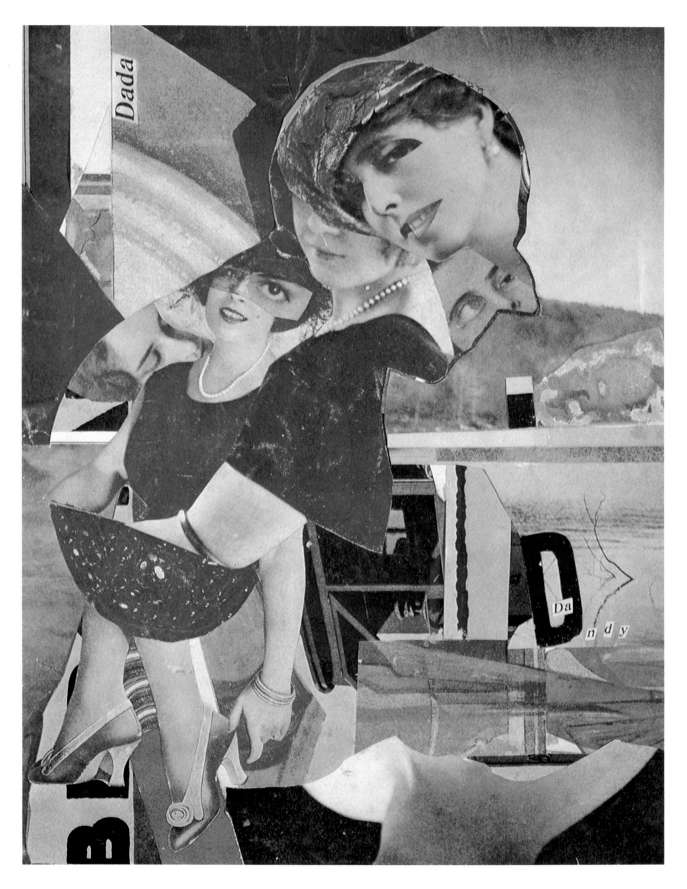

Hannah Höch:
Da-Dandy, 1919

OFFEAHBDC BDQ ,, qjyE!

In 1918 I introduced typography as a picture element and I created my "poster poems," which are "phonetic poems" composed according to the sound sense of the letters, without having had any knowledge of the analogous experiments made by Khlebnikov and Ball.

Raoul Hausmann, 1958

Raoul Hausmann: *OFF..., phonetic poster poem, 1918*

Raoul Hausmann: *Design for "Material of Painting, Sculpture, Architecture," 1918*

Raoul Hausmann: *Woodcut for* Club Dada, *Berlin, 1917*

The event of the second evening in the Berlin Secession Hall, even more than the reading of the manifesto or Huelsenbeck's lecture ("Dadaism in Art and Life") undoubtedly lay in Raoul Hausmann's declaration about the new material in painting. Hausmann emphasized the question of subject matter: it had to be independent of extrapictorial reality in order to bring out its creative potentialities. A decisive step was taken, announcing the elaboration of a radically new conception of the world and matter, consigning to the rubbish heap of the past all anecdotal or literary, social or political considerations which did not contribute to the autonomy of artistic expression, which was revolutionary in itself.

Such ideas, shared by his future friend Kurt Schwitters, were later to bring the Dadaists close to the Constructivist artists. Moreover, they were to inspire the intense creative activity of Raoul Hausmann throughout his life, as painter, draftsman, photographer, creator of photomontages, visual concrete poet, sound poet, theoretician, prose writer, technician, journalist, historian, magazine editor, dancer and performer.

Like Schwitters, Raoul Hausmann was an artist for whom Dada meant more than an artistic movement. It was a "life anchorage and vantage point, a form of internal mobility" which turned him into an explorer of abstraction, moving on eagerly from one discovery to another, from his first collages to his first photomontages (Heartfield recognized his role here as a pioneer) down to the late gouaches of 1965. He also interested himself in the phenomena of sound and light. He wrote a treatise on optophonetics and, together with the Russian engineer Daniel Broido, took out a patent for the invention of the optophone in London in 1935.

Throughout his many-sided activities, Hausmann refused to systematize any particular invention of his, energetically taking the path of multiple researches rather than the unswerving road to the formation of a systematized, set style, an "image" that would favor one aspect of his work and encourage his public recognition as an artist.

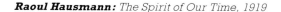

Raoul Hausmann: *The Spirit of Our Time, 1919*

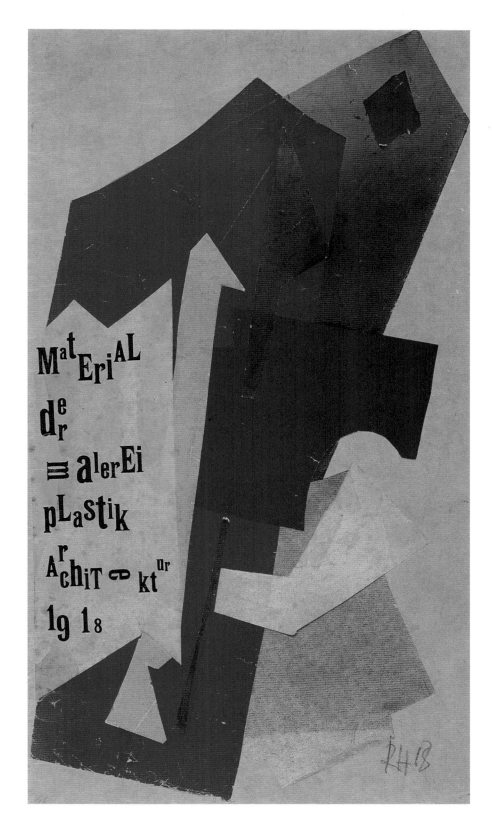

Raoul Hausmann: *Design for "Material of Painting, Sculpture, Architecture," 1918*

And, when Dada was on the wane in Berlin, Hausmann declared that Dada was only a word and that "the individual and intellectual state comprised by the word" continued to exist in him. Everything was always equally present and urgent, with or without Dada, and Hausmann proclaimed himself a "presentist." In February 1921 he drew up the manifesto of PREsentism, published in Van Doesburg's review *De Stijl.* This was a heady text packed with meaning, revealing the wide scope of his investigations. Perhaps its leading sentence was this: "The new man must have the courage to be new."

Each one of the covers of the declaration made at the Dada evening, *Material der Malerei Plastik Architektur,* a few copies of which were published by Hausmann during 1918, was a unique collage of paper cut-outs. One of them, probably preprinted, shows the skillful arrangement of the typography (inversion of letters, mixture of upper and lower case letters) of the title, which became a visual poem of words and letters in itself, while still contributing to the general economy of the composition.

The almost simultaneous invention of the phonetic poem and the poster poem (terms that are far too reductive, but commonly used to designate completely abstract poetry, also known as concrete poetry) led Hausmann to an instrumentalization of the letter (a concrete phenomenon) as a visual and aural element (an abstract phenomenon). The letter should be perceived not only as an alphabetical unit taken from a more complicated organization (Jean Cocteau once compared literature to an alphabet in disorder), but as a material capable of development in itself, the source of possible new departures.

The works of the Expressionist poets Morgenstern, Scheerbart and Stramm have often been seen as forerunners of the Hausmannian poem. But, as also with Hugo Ball, they are better described as an abstract chanting of poetry made up of "unknown words" (to use Iliazd's expression) or invented words. Hausmann's poster poem, on the other hand, consisting of typographical letters of different sizes, put the emphasis on sound and rhythm, abandoning the established order of speech. "In a poem," he said, "it is not the sense and rhetoric of the words, but the vowels and consonants and even the letters of the alphabet that should carry a rhythm." The optophonetic order of the poster poem determines the changes of sound, the alphabetical letter reflecting the expression of a musical attitude. "The two voices, abdominal and guttural-nasal, are the symbols of two psychic natures, the catatonic and the maniacal, but they must be used in a new way."

Hausmann also used to dance his poems. "He had perfected," said Vera Broido-Cohn, the engineer's sister, "an extraordinary technique. He would put out all the lights except one and sit down just below it, throw his head back, his body absolutely motionless, and perform a dance with his face while chanting a bizarre air, without words, but rhythmic . . . According to a contemporary article, 'he opened and closed his eyes, and seemed to be building something. His gestures were neither ugly nor beautiful, they told a kind of strange story and everything about him was set in motion: his face, his eyes, his fingers. In this respect his dance was akin to Balinese dances.' He explained the seriousness of his dance to me and that encouraged me to dance a lot afterwards. 'Everything begins with dancing,' he would repeat. 'Movements come long before verbal expression or even music, for dancing has its own music. When you stand up there, you are not in space, but outside space, you are neither on the earth nor outside the earth, and it is from there that creation begins. Build the walls and limits of your universe yourself.' To him, all forms of artistic expression were interrelated, in this case dancing and architecture or even more than that, a sort of global construction of the world."

Raoul Hausmann: *Phonetic Poem, May 25, 1918*

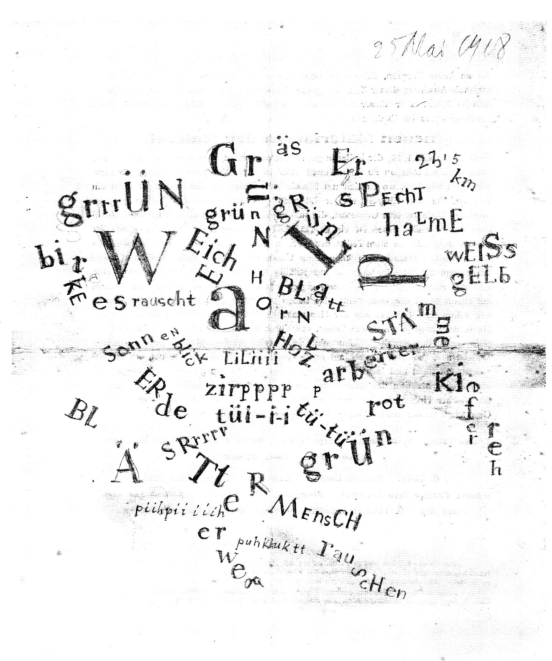

Cover of Raoul Hausmann's book Hurrah! Hurrah! Hurrah!, *12 Satires, Berlin, 1921*

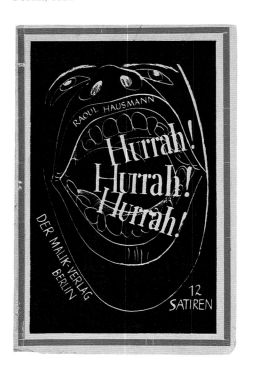

In the summer of 1918 I began making pictures with colored paper cutouts and newspaper and poster clippings. But it was during a stay at the seaside in the Baltic, on the island of Usedom, in the small village of Heidebrink, that I got the idea of photomontage. In almost all the houses, hanging on the wall, was a color lithograph representing a grenadier, with his barracks in the background. To make this military memento more personal, each family had pasted a photograph of its own soldier over the head in the lithograph. It came like a flash, I saw instantly that one could make pictures entirely composed of cutout photographs. Back in Berlin in December, I began working out this new vision by using press and film photos. In my zeal as a renovator, I had to have a name for this technique, and by common consent with George Grosz, John Heartfield, Johannes Baader and Hannah Höch, we decided to call these works photomontages. *This term answered to our aversion for playing the artist and, considering ourselves as engineers (hence our preference for working clothes, for overalls), we professed to build and mount our works. I myself, apart from my different pseudonyms and Dada titles (like Dadasopher), took the name Algernoon Syndetikon. Syndetikon was the trademark of the paste I used.*

Raoul Hausmann, 1958

Raoul Hausmann: *Fiat Modes, 1920*

Photograph of Raoul Hausmann, 1920

Raoul Hausmann's *Fiat Modes* is a montage on several levels, a series of overlayings. On the frontispiece of the set published by Max Ernst (Cologne, 1919), of which he allowed only the title (*Fiat Modes*) to appear, Hausmann pasted a reproduction of one of the watercolors from his set of ''German satires,'' *Hurrah! Hurrah! Hurrah!*. Only a few elements of this watercolor still exist (in the right background a tailor's dummy taken over from Chirico, to the left a door in perspective, in the right foreground the base of a coffee-mill and the hand of the poet grinding his coffee), because Hausmann later cut out a new sheet and pasted it over this image. While serving as a new ground for the collages that gradually accumulated and revolved in the center of the composition, the latter showed a continuous dancing sequence of typographic characters probably obtained by striking a linotype keyboard at random: here was the unprecedented prototype of abstract sound prose, the endless humming language restored to its physical materiality, a telex reeling off its mechanical scriptural signs, letters, figures and punctuation marks.

On this sheet appeared, as a concentric revolving accumulation suggested by the movement of the coffee-mill's handle, not only several women's faces, one of them in the center on the axis of rotation, but also several legs, accentuating the dynamism of the movement and the race, the legs of female athletes on the left, on the right the legs of women wearing shoes and stockings, next to the tailor's dummy (for trying clothes on?). Lastly, at the foot of the montage we still have the ironic remark appearing below the watercolor in Hausmann's original set: *Kutschenbauch dichtet* (Coach belly writes verse). Values are changed and transformed from the bare athletic legs to the legs dressed for town, fashion passes and turns like a coffee-mill, the signs run riot. *Pereat ars*: May art perish. Forget about art, life goes on in a dynamic whirligig.

Johannes Baader, Intertelluric Superdada President

Without that legendary personage, Johannes Baader, the Oberdada (Superdada), a vital piece would have been missing from the German chessboard. Baader had not taken part in the first manifestations, except perhaps as an onlooker; but in February 1918, even before Huelsenbeck founded the Dada Club, he proclaimed himself "President of the League of Intertelluric Superdadaist Nations" (at the same time, the Russian Futurist Khlebnikov announced that he was President of the Terrestrial Globe) and sat "in the saddle of the white horse Dada."

When Huelsenbeck disappeared for a time after the Berlin Secession evening (April 12, 1918), Johannes Baader became Raoul Hausmann's most faithful ally in carrying on the movement. A photomontage shows them head to foot alongside each other, like a single Siamese Dada.

Hausmann, who had met Baader as early as 1905 when he was handing out leaflets in a Berlin tram in the Steglitz district, had immediately recognized him as a man capable of "driving his head through a brick wall in support of an idea," willing to rock the boat "like mad" to bedevil the powers that be. Baader's global, universal, solar and prophetic ambitions, his death followed by instantaneous resurrection on the steps of Leipzig railway station, called for a new spirituality and urged people to go beyond existing reality and the arbitrary frontiers of normality. Baader put poetry into action, by the impact of the outrageous gesture, by protest and revolt, and contributed a supplementary ambiguity pregnant with meaning to the libertarian verve of Berlin Dadaism.

By embodying the myth of a rebirth and a new cosmogony to be recreated on the ruins (ever present in Schwitters' work) of the old, shattered world (he even proposed to establish a new calendar, starting from 1919), Baader fascinated people by the intensity of his desire, combining the Dadaist revolt with mythological and private purposes, although Huelsenbeck, a psychiatrist to be, always treated him ironically, calling Baader an "impostor of Dadaism," a "Swabian pietist," an "amuser of fools," or worse still, "Christus imitator."

In the spring of 1918 the antics of Baader and Hausmann were at their height. They played all kinds of practical jokes, typing news items during the night which they took to the newspaper offices before 6 a.m. so that they would appear the same day: "The Dadaists demand the Nobel Peace Prize," "Minister Scheidemann joins Dada," "Men are angels and live in heaven."

On Sunday, November 17, 1918, in the name of greater respect for Christ's teaching, Baader interrupted Pastor Dryander as he was about to begin his sermon in Berlin's main cathedral: "Just a minute. I'm asking you what Jesus Christ means to you. You don't care a damn about him..." Arrested in the ensuing commotion, Baader could not be charged with blasphemy.

We all want to create a new world of our own!

Dada is the only art form of the present to have striven for a renewal of the means of expression and against the classic ideal of education of the order-loving bourgeois and its latest offshoot, Expressionism.
During the war the Dada Club stood for the internationality of the world. It is an international anti-bourgeois movement!
The Dada Club was the uprising against the "white collar worker," against the "intellectuals"! The Dadaist is against humanism, against historical education!
DADA CALLS ON EACH MAN TO LIVE HIS OWN LIFE!!!

Raoul Hausmann, 1919

Johannes Baader: *Last Manifesto, 1918*

Johannes Baader:
The Author in his Home, 1918-1919

Johannes Baader: *Advertisement for Myself, 1919-1920*

Johannes Baader: *Futur, c. 1920*

George Grosz: *Dada Picture, c. 1919*

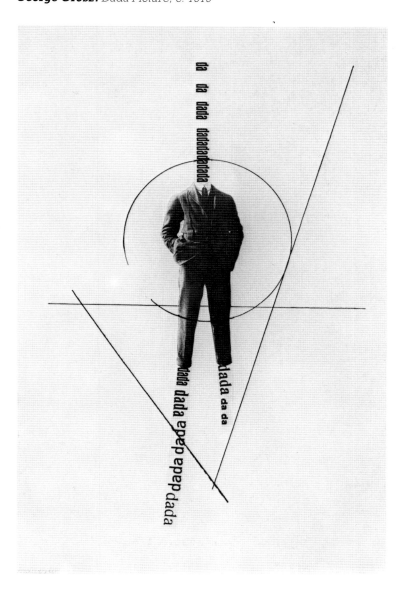

He had on him the text of a speech in which he accused the Church of not respecting the teaching of Christ. The whole of the Berlin press carried the story. A misrepresentation of the facts was answered by Baader in the *Berliner Tageblatt:* "If you read the text of my speech, which is in your possession, it becomes quite clear that the words I spoke yesterday have an entirely different meaning from that imputed to them by the *Berliner Morgenzeitung* today. The other assertion in the papers, according to which a mentally ill person was involved, seems to me to be one of the dirty tricks employed nowadays when anyone becomes troublesome."

In March 1919 Baader and Hausmann even planned the foundation of a Dada Republic at Nikolassee, using posters to proclaim an independent republic, but the project was leaked by one of Baader's friends who had been proposed as Minister of Finance. On the appointed day, the Town Hall was surrounded by troops called in by the anxious authorities.

"Baader," concluded Hausmann (some people thought he used Baader as a punching-ball and manipulated him), "was the man Dada needed, by virtue of his natural unreality which was curiously linked with an extraordinary grasp of practical matters."

Conflict with everything

The driving force of Baader's criticisms, indeed of his whole life, lay in his revolt against the oppression inflicted on the individual, first in childhood and later by social structures on all levels, aesthetic, moral, philosophical and logical. "Logic," wrote Tzara in the *Dada Manifesto 1918*, "is a complication. Logic is always wrong. It draws the threads of notions and words, in their formal exterior, toward illusory ends and centers. Its chains kill, it is an enormous centipede stifling independence." So logic and rationality were shown up and called to account in their various aspects. Beginning with the field of art.

Psychoanalysis also had a part to play in the Berlin group. Hausmann wrote that the Dada group really took off in the pages of the review *Die freie Strasse*, which propagated the ideas of the psychoanalyst Otto Gross, a distinguished pupil of Freud's, "a brilliant man," according to Ernest Jones. The founder of psychoanalysis had seen in Gross a valuable personality and a remarkable mind, but disowned him, as well as other analysts, around 1908. In 1912 Gross announced his intention of editing a journal, "something like a 'Review of the Psychological Problems of Anarchism' in which radically individualistic results would be presented, calling in question all existing institutions, and leading to a determined exploration of the unconscious: that would constitute a sort of internal preliminary to the revolution."

Johannes Baader *and* ***Raoul Hausmann:***
Portrait of Baader and Hausmann, one up,
one down, 1920

Events did not give him time to get started. He was suddenly and illegally detained in a psychiatric home at the instigation of his father, who had assembled a damning file on him. Apparently Otto Gross had acquired the cocaine habit during visits to Latin America when he was ship's doctor on the Hamburg-South America line (Huelsenbeck was also to be a ship's doctor in the early thirties). The campaign launched in the psychoanalyst's favor extended even to France, and Blaise Cendrars addressed a few words of support: "I join with all my heart in your protest stigmatizing the unworthy behavior of a narrow-minded father (all our fathers are narrow-minded) who does not hesitate to destroy the work of one of the minds of contemporary Germany most appreciated in France."

One of Gross's most stalwart defenders was his friend Franz Jung, who published a book about the affair before founding the review *Die freie Strasse* with Gross in 1915. A writer with anarchist tendencies, Franz Jung, who volunteered in August 1914 with the intention of sabotaging the German war machine, must have met with difficulties, because in December when he wanted to get away from the front he prevailed on Walter Serner, then in

Berlin, to issue him with a medical certificate saying that he had a weak heart and sign it "Dr. Serner."

After the murder of Liebknecht and Luxemburg (January 1919), Jung played an important part in the formation and fate of the KAPD (German Communist Workers' Party), of which he was one of the three founders. It stood to the left of the German Communist Party (KPD, formed by the Spartacists), which had excluded Jung and all his left wing in October 1918. In May 1920 the newly formed KAPD denounced the KPD as a "clique of irresponsible leaders placing their personal interests above the interests of the proletarian revolution [and seeking] to impose their personal conception of the 'death' of the German revolution."

It was at this period that the now legendary hijacking of a fishing boat by Franz Jung and a KAPD sailor took place. Anxious to provide the new party with a newspaper and some financial backing, Jung wanted to get it recognized (and no doubt subsidized) as an official member of the Third International. He decided to go to Moscow for the Congress of the Communist International, otherwise known as the Komintern, and, as the land routes were blocked by the Franco-British occupation forces in the frontier regions, he ended up by hijacking a fishing boat. In Moscow, however, the KAPD came up against the manipulation of the delegates to the Congress by the Komintern bureaucracy. No sooner had it been glimpsed than the possibility of a new political avenue was blocked.

Such, following the birth of Dada in Berlin, were the shifting political preferences of some of those friendly to the movement. To this same Franz Jung the Berlin Dadaists were indebted for their first publication in German, as well as for the welcome they were given in his review, in the seventh number of *Die freie Strasse* entitled *Club Dada* in March 1918.

Gross and Hausmann, according to the latter, then made some analytical discoveries that anticipated and outstripped Freud and Carl Gustav Jung. Gross saw in psychoanalysis a means to free men from social and patriarchal structures, to help them in their "conflict with everything" by a revolution in culture and language. Carl Einstein, author of *Bebuquin, oder Die Dilettanten des Wunders* (1912) and an essay on African sculpture (*Negerplastik*, 1915), was very close to the Dadaists; he later edited the review *Der blutige Ernst* with George Grosz. Together with Franz Jung, he attempted to map out a new language. Such ambitions overlapped with those of the Dadaists, especially Hausmann, who, as we have seen, was working towards the total poem, the abstract poem based on letters alone.

At the same time a change in the attitude to insanity was taking place in advanced, but still restricted circles. While insanity, in the best of cases, was beginning to be treated through the medium of analysis instead of being

Leaflet for the satirical weekly Der blutige Ernst,
Berlin, 1919

simply repressed, attention was also being directed to the works produced by so-called lunatics. Two decisive books on the subject appeared successively in Germany: a monograph by Walter Morgenthaler, a doctor at the Waldau Hospital (Bern), about the artistic works by his patient *Adolf Wölfli* (1921); and *Bildnerei der Geisteskranken* (1922), a book commenting on the drawings, paintings and sculptures done in asylums collected by Hans Prinzhorn (Arp and Sophie Taeuber were waiting impatiently for its publication, which, incidentally, caused Max Ernst to give up a similar project).

Nevertheless, these two books had been preceded by the less well-known work by Marcel Réja, *L'Art chez les fous*. Published in Paris in 1907, it can be considered as a pioneer work both among his medical colleagues (Réja was the pseudonym used by Dr. Meunier for his literary work) and among the Dadaists. Réja attributed an important role to the ludic manipulation of words and the priority of sound over sense. He also seems to have been the first person to take an interest in the hallucinatory analyses of words put forward in *La Grammaire Logique* (1883) by Jean-Pierre Brisset, who had announced himself as the "seventh angel of the Apocalypse and the Archangel of the Resurrection."

Advertisement for the Dada atlas Dadaco, *1920*

These books appeared in Germany at a time when the Dadaists were producing both visual works (collages and montages) and auditory works (abstract poetry made up of invented words). The fact that artists were now introducing into the heart of culture a series of creations in which words were consciously and deliberately manipulated threw a new light on the artistry of the mentally ill. The inroads made by the latter on language, the basic medium of social relations (and those inroads were all the more disturbing for that reason), suddenly became audible and legible. They were no longer an inadmissible "hotchpotch of words," to quote Antonin Artaud in his *Lettre aux médecins-chefs des asiles de fous* (1925): "How many of you are there who actually look on the dreams of schizophrenics and the images which prey on them as anything more than a hotchpotch of words?"

They were indeed few in number, but the works of Réja, Prinzhorn and Morgenthaler had opened up a way from which there was no return. It was followed up in the 1960s by the Compagnie de l'Art Brut which published and exhibited the fruits of its research on the initiative of Jean Dubuffet, painter and writer, the author of, among other books, *Asphyxiante culture* (1968). Indeed one of the Company's first publications was a French translation of Morgenthaler's book on Adolf Wölfli.

On the question of madness and creation, it is interesting to note that Tristan Tzara felt it necessary to dissociate himself from the new aesthetic

category which seemed inevitably to be forming at the period. He did so in a few incidental lines in an essay in the catalogue of the Dada Salon: "I detest madness and its platonic form, which is the absurd and poetry. 'I detest' no longer has the disagreeable savor it once had; today it simply means that I smoke a cigarette." ("L'art et la chasse," Galerie Montaigne, Paris, June 1921).

It is obvious that Tzara never shared the Surrealists' infatuation with madness and paranormal phenomena, because he saw only too clearly the kind of romantic idealizations they might inspire when literary men full of psychological theories took off into the "intense inane." Dada took the quite different attitude that creative art is a fully conscious, imaginative and well thought out action. In Russia Malevich and Khlebnikov were similarly motivated when, starting from a deliberate disregard of conventional·logic, they developed the procedure known as "transrational realism" during the years 1910-1914.

Such attitudes were all the more pertinent because of the reappearance now of a comparison often made (beginning with Lombroso, an Italian criminologist of the nineteenth century) between genius and madness (in the Middle Ages communications with higher spiritual powers were often attributed to "madmen"). This was a comparison not without danger, because in combination with other ingredients such as the nationalism engendered by the First World War and the rejection of modern art, it could be stood on its head. Then the institutionalized literary or artistic establishment would no longer be poring over the extraordinary lexical richness of certain works by the inmates of asylums, which "confront us with an insoluble and unbearable question to which they are nevertheless the paradoxical answer" (Frédéric Baal). On the contrary, the works of modern artists would then be explained in terms of mental pathology. This kind of reasoning, current in reactionary right-wing circles in France after the First World War, later took a disturbing turn in Nazi Germany (see Chapter 8) when the "degenerate art" exhibitions were organized.

Cover of Jedermann sein eigner Fussball, *Berlin, February 1919*

Newspaper advertisement for the First
International Dada Fair, Berlin, 1920:
"Athlete wanted."

The most important manifestation of Berlin Dada after the soirées of January and April 1918, the First International Dada Fair opened on June 24, 1920 in the two small rooms of the gallery of Dr. Otto Burchard, art historian and art dealer, at 13 Lützow-Ufer. If we are to believe an advertisement in the press, it appears that the organizers, half in jest and half in earnest, were looking for an athlete as doorman. The advertisement specified that he was to carry out his duties in "professional dress." This detail did not pass unnoticed by the Parisian Dadaists who turned it into an amusing, apparently inexplicable quotation on the cover of the catalogue of the Dada Salon (June 1921) in the Galerie Montaigne: "Athletes wanted."

Organized by Marshal Grosz, Dadasopher Raoul Hausmann and Monteurdada John Heartfield, the Dada Fair concluded a tour of Dada manifestations which had taken Baader, Hausmann and Huelsenbeck all over Germany. It revealed both the essence and scope of the German contribution to the Dada Movement, most importantly the photomontages and collages of Raoul Hausmann and Hannah Höch, as well as the most accomplished works of Grosz, a large polymaterial construction by Johannes Baader and several other skilfully devised works.

The poster for the exhibition was also its catalogue. One large sheet folded at the center forming a program of four oblong pages showed, as a colored background, a simultaneous collage with an urban atmosphere, the work of Heartfield, treated typographically in red, ochre and yellow (*Leben*

First International Dada Fair of 1920

Catalogue-poster for the First
International Dada Fair, Berlin,
1920

und Treiben in Universal-City, 12 Uhr 5 mittags), a background collage on which some items of practical information were overprinted in black, as well as, upside down at the foot of the cover, a programmatic declaration by Hausmann: "Dada man is the radical enemy of exploitation, the sense of exploitation produces nothing but fools and Dada man hates folly and loves nonsense! So Dada man reveals himself as genuinely real as opposed to the stinking sham of the family man and capitalist croaking in his armchair."

The two inside pages contained only two reproductions in black and white, a "corrected Picasso" and a Douanier Rousseau presented as a "corrected masterpiece." The expression *Vollendete Kunst* figures on the Picasso, an oil on canvas and *papier collé* (*Head of Young Girl*, 1913) and means something more like finished, accomplished, perfected art.

While endorsing the formal severity of Picasso's Cubist composition, Grosz and Heartfield extended it and gave it an acceleration, a new field of tensions. Parallel to the oblique incision in the center of the canvas, they inserted a black secant, which had the almost Suprematist effect of forming a new plane in relation to the volume, to the frame of the work, and energizing the ensemble. This movement was continued by the overlaying of photographs, word groups and printed texts which also gave it a new graphic intensity (and sound undertones), and a bantering narrative appearance which the iconoclastic and mocking nature of the gesture did nothing to contradict.

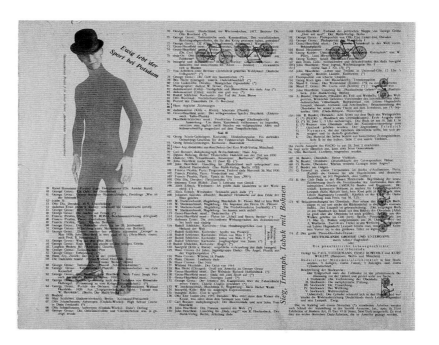

Back of the catalogue-poster of the First International Dada Fair, Berlin, 1920, with the Obermusikdada Gerhard Preisz dancing

George Grosz and **John Heartfield:**
La Vie heureuse ("Picasso corrected"), 1920

George Grosz and **John Heartfield:**
A Masterpiece Corrected (the Douanier Rousseau's Myself, Portrait-Landscape*), 1920*

From the Douanier Rousseau's well-known painting, *Myself, Portrait-Landscape* (1890), Grosz and Heartfield borrowed its anecdotal and naïve character and added to it a paper garland and an Eiffel Tower. They also improved on its "Sunday" peacefulness by inserting recent buildings instead of trees and landscapes, a neon advertisement for improbable Leibniz cakes and a da/da pennon at the top of a mast already decked out with charming flags by the Douanier. Rousseau's face was replaced by Raoul Hausmann's: the author of *New Material in Painting* inherited the brush and palette, central elements of the canvas whose pomp he punctured, transforming them into implements that were ridiculous and embarrassing in the context of the new urban reality.

Although very much in the minority, painting was not entirely absent from the Dada Fair, in spite of the lack of space in Dr. Burchard's gallery and the obvious bias of the Berliners in favor of collage and photomontage. In addition to the works mentioned and an important canvas by Grosz, *Deutschland, ein Wintermärchen* (*Germany, a Winter's Tale*, 1917), later destroyed by the Nazis, and a small canvas by Max Ernst (*Stamens and Marseillaise of Dada Arp*, 1919), there were two Verist painters belonging to the Neue Sachlichkeit movement, Georg Scholz (*Bauernbild*) and Otto Dix (*45% Erwerbsfähig*, "45% fit for active service," reproduced in the Entartete Kunst catalogue before being destroyed). Scholz and Dix were very much in sympathy with Grosz's themes of social satire, and by the

Hannah Höch: *Construction in Red, 1919*

virulence of their caricatural subjects, they contributed a supplementary note of sarcasm to the biting wit of the Dadaists, although they never actually joined the movement.

The arrangement of the works on the gallery walls produced a lively sense of packed and crowded variety. Instead of hanging the works in the modern way, displaying them one by one facing the spectator, as was done even before the war at the Brücke exhibition (Dresden, 1910) and the Sonderbund exhibition (Cologne, 1912), the Dada Club returned to the old-fashioned hanging system (still used by the Blaue Reiter at Munich in 1912 and at the Armory Show in New York in 1913) to accentuate cumulative effect by a profusion of very different works.

Like a page of Dada typography, the way the things were hung never gave the eye of the spectator a minute's rest, for it was constantly attracted by extremely dense compositions, by posters and photographs, even by suspended figures such as the *Prussian Archangel* described in the catalogue as a "ceiling sculpture." This grey-greenish dummy, an effigy devised by Heartfield and Schlichter of a German officer with a pig's head topped by a cap, hovered over the room; according to some sources, it had a placard around its neck saying "Hanged by the Revolution," although it did not appear in contemporary photographs. But there is no doubt that the half-porcine, half-military effigy bore a label, tied on with string, saying: "To understand this work of art, you would have to drill for twelve hours a day on the Tempelhof parade ground, carrying a heavily loaded haversack."

In such a context, as eventful and sharply contrasting as a street demonstration, libertarian claims arose on all sides. The exhibits at the Dada Fair were not presented as works of art, thus precluding any purely contemplative interpretation (felt by the Dadaists to be incompatible with the urgency of the moment) of works which, by their extreme novelty, could easily have lent themselves to it. This determined attitude deepened the rift

First room of the International Dada Fair, Burchard Gallery, Berlin, 1920

between the Dada Club and the more advanced circles of modern art in Berlin, especially Herwarth Walden's Sturm Gallery, one of whose artists, Kurt Schwitters, was significantly absent from the exhibition.

So that there should be no mistake, the show even included a provocative statement with a double meaning, "Dada is political," and quite unexpectedly, but with no repercussions, to be sure, a poster for the Deutsche Volkspartei.

Above and between the works were some twenty colored panels of great graphic intensity, proclaiming, like so many streamers: "Dada for everybody!", "Dada is against the art swindle of the Expressionists!", "Dilettantes, rise up against art!", "Dada is the opposite of the inexperience of life!", "Dada sides with the revolutionary proletariat!", "Throw open your mind at last to the needs of the times", "Down with art! Down with bourgeois mentality!", "Dada is the voluntary decay of the world of bourgeois concepts", together with a quotation from the Symbolist painter Wiertz: "One day photography will supplant and replace the whole of pictorial art."

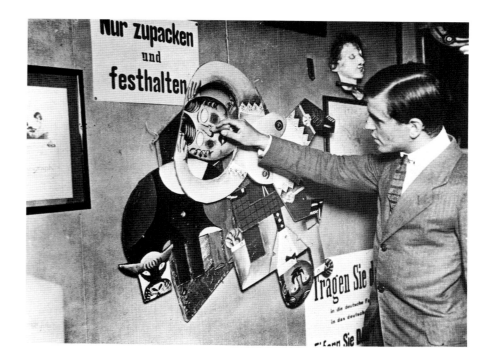

Otto Dix in front of his rotary picture, Berlin Dada Fair, 1920

Raoul Hausmann and Hannah Höch at the First International Dada Fair, Berlin, 1920

George Grosz and John Heartfield with their panel "Art is dead" in front of their sculpture Rabid Bourgeois, Berlin Dada Fair, 1920

First International Dada Fair, Dr. Otto Burchard Gallery, Berlin, June 1920. Left to right: Raoul Hausmann, Hannah Höch (seated), Dr. Burchard, Johannes Baader, Wieland Herzfelde and his wife, Otto Schmalhausen (seated), George Grosz, John Heartfield. Hanging from the ceiling: the Prussian Archangel, *a dummy of a German officer with the head of a pig, made by Heartfield and Rudolf Schlichter. Left wall, Dix's* 45% Erwerbsfähig; *right wall, Grosz's* Deutschland, ein Wintermärchen.

By a sorry reversal of history, one of these declarations, "Take Dada seriously, it's worth your while," was taken over unchanged by the organizers of the Nazi "degenerate art" exhibition in 1937, and so assumed a cruel twist by a simple change of context, with the regime making use of it to justify its persecution of artists.

The cumulative effect was sometimes pushed so far that some works overlapped with each other. For example, certain parts of Dix's large canvas being considered as empty spaces, two works by Grosz were superimposed on them. These were the celebrated montage *Remember Uncle August, the Unhappy Inventor* and the fan made for the cover of the one and only number of *Jedermann sein eigner Fussball* (Every one his own football), both executed the year before.

Hung in the middle of the largest wall in the first room, Dix's canvas split up two groups of works. On the left were some of the most important photomontages and collages by Raoul Hausmann (*Le critique d'art, Dada siegt, Tatlin at Home*) and some satirical/mechanical drawings (*Der eiserne Hindenburg, Deutsche Freiheit*), whose spatial composition, taken from Chirico and Carrà, and the outline in Indian ink may have influenced Baargeld in Cologne.

Hausmann's mechanical linework and his photomontage *Tatlin at Home* seemed to be echoed by the panel placed above them: "Art is dead/Long live Tatlin's machine art." The panel remained in the annals of Berlin Dada through a photograph (published a few weeks later in the *Dada Almanac*) showing Grosz and Heartfield, panel in hand, in front of their *Rabid Bourgeois*, an "electro-mechanical Tatlinian sculpture," a strange and very fine, yet disturbing composition, a pre-punk dummy, the head made of an illuminated light-bulb, the left leg amputated at the knee. Instead of genitals, it had a shell-fish or set of teeth, half-way between nostril and plexus a card with the cut out number 27, and instead of the left epaulet a small door bell on its little wooden board, as well as a fork at the level of the heart; and lastly a prestigious decoration hanging around the neck and a revolver in the place of the right arm, acting as an armpit.

Below the dummy by Grosz and Heartfield, lit by the bulb, could be made out a mechanical drawing by Max Ernst, *Erectio sine qua non*, the only work representing the Cologne group, together with a photomontage *Self-Portrait* by Johannes Baargeld, grafting a photograph of his head on to the bust of the Venus of Milo.

Mixed up with Raoul Hausmann's photomontages were some typographical works, such as the cover of *Der Dada 1* designed by Baader and Hausmann, printed in black on a pink ground, bearing the words (among others) "Jahr 1 des Weltfriedens. Avis dada." Other typographical works were exhibited: some prototypes of the page setting by Hausmann and Heartfield of the anthology *Dadaco*, a project undertaken with the publisher Kurt Wolff which never materialized. Among them, one page reproduced the sound poem *Karawane* recited by Hugo Ball at Zurich in 1916, in a colored typographical interpretation due to the Berlin Dadaists.

To the right of Dix's picture were watercolors by Grosz and his celebrated montage *The Monteur John Heartfield. After Franz Jung's attempt to put him on his feet*, together with a *Tatlinesque Sketch of the Chambers of Horrors*. In the midst of Grosz's works, there was an almost unexpected Parisian exhibit, the pink cover of *391* designed by Picabia and a few drawings by Arp, the only examples of the work of the original Zurich group.

George Grosz: Remember Uncle August, the Unhappy Inventor, 1919

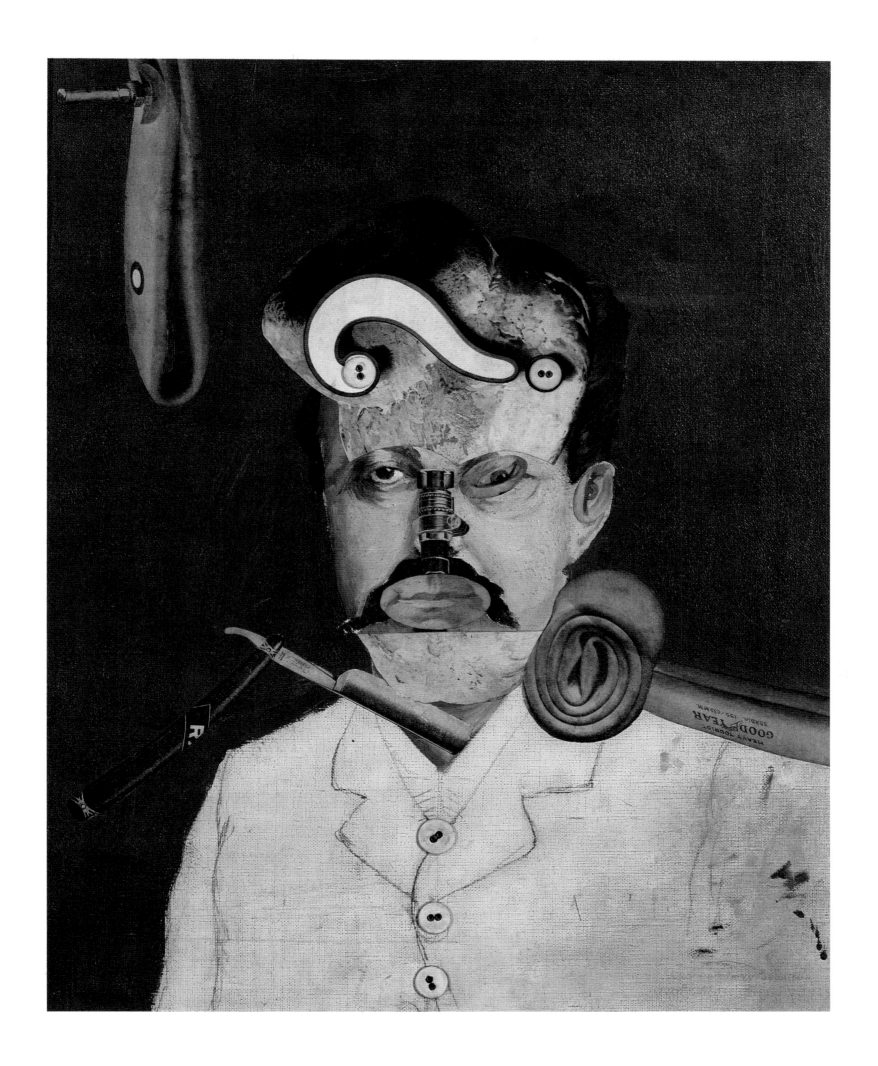

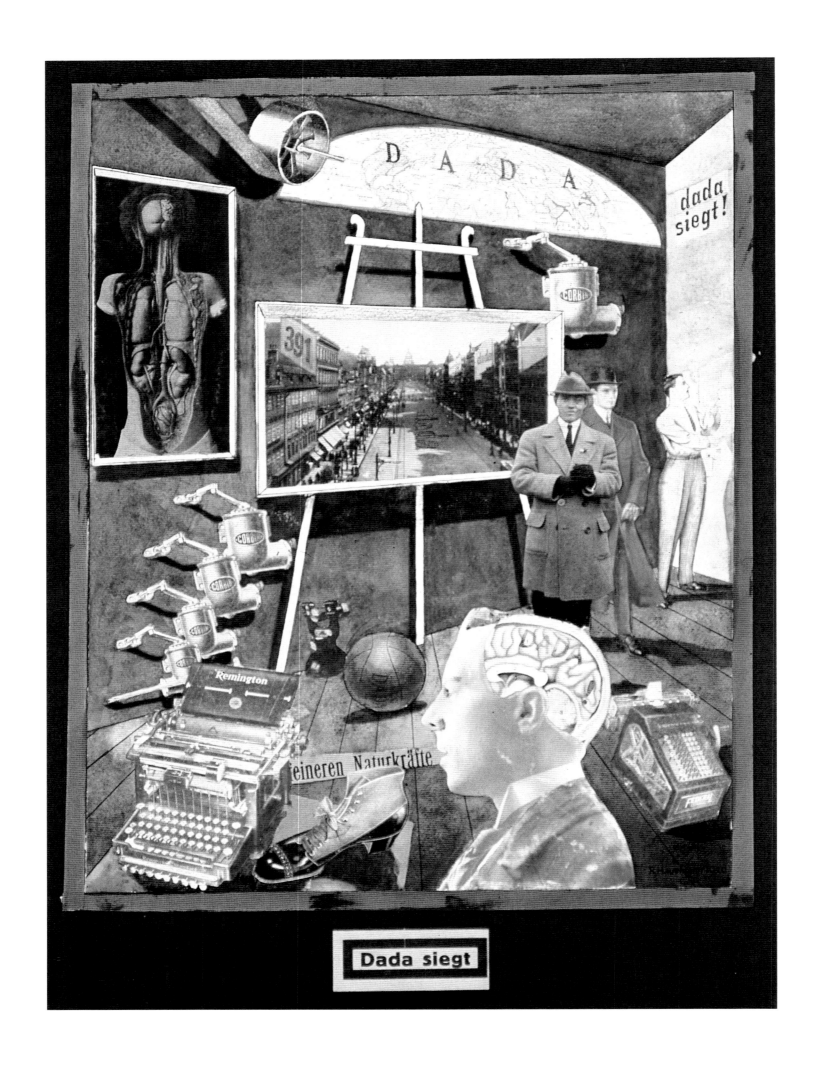

Raoul Hausmann: *Dada wins, 1920*

several years), because he was responsible for the first zoological gardens without bars (at Stellingen near Hamburg) where wild animals in captivity could enjoy the greatest possible freedom in extensive grounds, among rocks and artificial streams. Had the Oberdada dreamed of animal freedom for Dadaists, unburdened by the constraints of human life in society? Or did he wish to give his friends a space where, though apparently captive, they would actually, by this strange reversal of roles, be protected from the authorities who looked on them as wild animals? Baader had always dreamt of a free space, of universal temples and world periodicals freed from the contingencies and constraints of a cramped reality (see the only published number of *Freiland Dada*). He himself, the Dadaist and Christ-like subverter, made use of his own madness against repression. He carried on him, like a safe-conduct, the certificate issued by the German military authorities stating that he was not responsible for his acts! The President of the League of Intertelluric Superdadaist Nations was in the position of a monarch standing beyond the reach of civil liability!

Johannes Baader beside his assemblage Greatness and Downfall of Germany *at the First International Dada Fair, Berlin, 1920*

The even smaller second room of Dr. Burchard's gallery was almost entirely given over to the Oberdada Johannes Baader, although a contemporary photograph of it also shows Otto Dix in front of an unidentified detachable rotatory relief. Some people have looked on Baader simply as an unbalanced fantasist (his contribution as such would have been by no means negligible), but in fact the Oberdada took a keen interest in the technique of photomontage worked out before him by Hausmann and Hannah Höch, so much so that he plunged into an intense creative activity before Heartfield himself began to use the same medium in 1920. It is noteworthy, however, that Heartfield's Dada photomontages are rather few; it was only later, in his fight against the Nazi regime, that he produced them in large numbers.

Baader went out and tore down posters in the streets, classifying and assembling them carefully at home, mixing them with extracts from newspapers, color patches, letters and numbers. He stuck them in his *Manual of Superdadaism* (*Handbuch des Oberdadaismus*, abbreviated to HADO), sometimes called the *Book of the Last Judgement* (*Buch des Weltgerichts*), a notebook and personal diary. We know, because he recorded it in the catalogue of the Dada Fair, that he finished the first *Hado* on June 26, 1919 and another on June 28, 1920 and that he exhibited both of them.

In the center of the second room of the Dada Fair, Baader constructed an assemblage, the *Plasto-Dio-Dada Drama*, for which he personally drafted the "Instructions for gazing at it":

> The Great Plasto-Dio-Dada Drama
> Germany's Greatness and Downfall
> by Schoolmaster Hagendorf
> or
> The Fantastic Life Story of the Oberdada
> Monumental Dadaist architecture on five floors with three gardens, a tunnel, two lifts and a door shaped like a top hat. The ground floor or level is the fate predetermined before birth and has nothing to do with the story. Description of the floors: 1: The Preparation of the Oberdada. 2: The Metaphysical Ordeal. 3: Initiation. 4: The World War. 5: The World Revolution.

That was not all. Baader also exhibited a plan for an animal paradise in the Paris Zoological Gardens, with accommodations for all the German and French Dadaists. For had not Tristan Tzara written in his *Manifesto of Mr. Antipyrine*: "Dada remains within the European frame of weaknesses it's shit after all, but from now on we mean to shit in assorted colors and bedeck the artistic zoo with the flags of every consulate"?

At all events, Baader's project recalls one of his earlier achievements (an eminent architect, Baader had been head of a practice at Magdeburg for

Nevertheless, charges of "outrage against the armed forces of the Reich" were brought against Baader and some of the other participants in the Dada Fair, including George Grosz, the painter Rudolf Schlichter, Wieland Herzfelde and Otto Burchard, who had opened his gallery to them. Among the exhibits, the uniformed effigy of a Prussian officer with a pig's head hanging from the ceiling certainly had something to do with it, as did a portfolio by Grosz sold at the entrance, essentially consisting of caricatures of Prussian officers, published by Malik Verlag, entitled, complete with the ironic inverted commas, "Gott mit uns" (May God be with us!). The trial was held in the spring of 1921 and inspired some bitter pages by the writer Kurt Tucholsky (1890-1935), incidentally a great admirer of Grosz.

> The Dada exhibition had set up a couple of figures of fun aimed at the gods of Prussia, its officers. George Grosz in particular had produced a brilliant portfolio entitled *Gott mit uns* which showed caricatural faces of such unprecedented brutality that the German army and its members felt themselves insulted...
>
> The accused disappointed me. Five living creatures sat in the dock, and only one real man among them: Wieland Herzfelde. He was the only one to say what was necessary from time to time and not get rattled. Otherwise, the affair was like the Kapp Putsch: there was no leader. None of the lads present was the one who had smashed the windowpane...
>
> I don't know whether Grosz was ill, or whether the slackness of his defense was due to an inability to express himself. Not a word he said was equal to one stroke of his caricatures...
>
> The court condemned the draftsman Grosz to a fine of three hundred marks and the publisher Herzfelde to six hundred, which together amount roughly to the fine imposed in Germany for incitement to murder (of pacifists). (The assessment was based on the fact that the publisher had made a financial gain from the sale of the portfolio.) The comical dolls in the exhibition were regarded as practical jokes brought on by beer drinking. The lenient sentence was perhaps due to the opinion of Redslob, curator of the Reich Museum, who had supported Grosz energetically, while tactfully avoiding the political aspect of the affair. That made an impression: for the curator of the Reich Museum is subject to the Ministry of the Interior, and a Prussian judge always has respect for authority. For art, less so. (Addressing Grosz, one of the magistrates said: "You must be aware of this, since you wish to be a draftsman and artist.")

> What game are they up to here?
>
> It will be observed that these proceedings have nothing to do with justice. I have never understood why the accused is not forced to enter the courtroom and say: "My name is Grosz, arch-criminal," and the judge would say, "Pleased to meet you. Fined three hunded marks." That would save a lot of time and work. But given the political schooling and general education of our magistrates, one cannot expect them to view these matters as we would. We no longer have any confidence in the penal justice of the country. In all such cases what is punished is not crime. What is punished, knowingly and consciously, is opinion.

Baader declared at the beginning of the hearing that Dadaism had "a duty to act against the formation of sediments harmful to culture" and added that "humor" was "the best means," even if "the Germans were singularly lacking in it." He incurred no penalty, because the Public Prosecutor felt that Baader's participation in the exhibition could not be proved, although his name and the pages of HADO had appeared in the printed catalogue leaflet. But the court, after also acquitting Burchard and Schlichter in respect of whom fines had been called for, did not comply with the Public Prosecutor's demand for six months' imprisonment for Grosz and Herzfelde. As for Grosz, he was defended in glowing terms not only by the curator of the Reich Museum, but also by the director of the Dresden collections, called in as an expert, who considered him to be one of the most important and talented artists in Germany. The court ordered the confiscation or destruction of the plates used for printing the caricatures, and the sheets and publishing rights were awarded to the Ministry of the Armed Forces of the Reich.

Cover of Kurt Tucholsky's book Deutschland, Deutschland über alles, *with a photomontage by John Heartfield, 1929*

Raoul Hausmann: *The Iron Hindenburg, 1920*

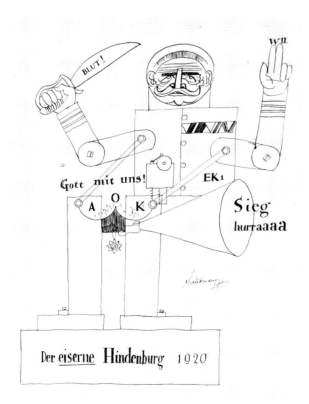

Cover of the reissue of Richard Huelsenbeck's "Fantastic Prayers," with a drawing by George Grosz, Berlin, 1920

Cover of "Dada Almanach" edited by Richard Huelsenbeck, Berlin, 1920, with Beethoven's death mask overprinted by Otto Schmalhausen, the Oz Dada

Cover by John Heartfield for Richard Huelsenbeck's "Dada Wins! A Balance-Sheet of Dadaism," Berlin, 1920

Huelsenbeck and the *Dada Almanach*

The *Dada Almanach*, the first attempt to give an account of the movement's international activities, at least in Europe, appeared in the autumn of 1920, a few weeks after the Dada exhibition closed. Published on the initiative of Huelsenbeck, who was absent from the exhibition, it consisted of a collective but selective volume, marking the first Dadaist dissension. Although he collaborated on the almanac, Baader was taken to task in it. In addition Huelsenbeck castigated Schwitters in the introduction.

Nevertheless it contained important articles on the theory of Dadaism by Daimonides (the pseudonym of Dr. Carl Doehmann, composer, Dada pianist and contributor to the periodical *Die Aktion*), as well as valuable statements by the Dada Club and some pages by less well-known Dadaists, such as Walter Mehring ("You banana-eaters and Kayak people!"), sound and letter poems by Adon Lacroix, Man Ray's companion in New York, not to mention a highly ironical letter by the Dutch Dadaist Paul Citroën, dissuading his Dadaist partners from going to Holland. The volume was also distinguished by the French participation of Picabia, Ribemont-Dessaignes and Soupault, quite unexpected in Berlin; their contributions were presumably collected and sent on from Paris by Tristan Tzara. The latter, living in Paris with the Picabias since early January 1920, gave in the *Dada Almanach* a scrupulous and electrifying account of the doings and publications of the Zurich Dadaists.

Tzara's personal contribution to the almanac was a twenty-page essay in French, entitled *Chronique zurichoise* (Zurich Chronicle), one of the most dizzying documents in the history of the movement. The chronological overview of events, mostly concerned with the boisterous Dada evenings at the Cabaret Voltaire, unfolds at a breathless pace, heightened by the typographical layout and the telegraphic nouns summing up the succession of events. The use of insets (like small advertisements) makes these pages something of a novelty in both journalism and prose—a prose enriched with the latest poetic resources of simultaneity.

About this time Huelsenbeck moved away from the group, no doubt to continue his medical studies. But he also wrote about it, in almost historical terms. In 1920 he reissued his *Phantastische Gebete* of the Zurich period, illustrated now by Grosz, and also published the following: *En avant Dada, Die Geschichte des Dadaismus* and *Dada siegt, Deutschland muss untergehen* (Dada wins, Germany must perish). Not only interesting witness accounts, they were Huelsenbeck's way of saying goodbye after the last soirée he had organized, with Max Reinhardt as entertainer, at the Cabaret Schall und Rausch (December 1919), which he described in the *Dada Almanach* under the pen name Alexis.

Kurt Schwitters in Hanover: the Merz dissidence

When we approach the plastic and literary work of Kurt Schwitters, we are struck by the contrast and alliance that come into play between his apparently random approach and his strict handling of form. His texts and manifestoes have the same broad scope as his paintings, collages and sculptures. Schwitters wrote little stories full of imagination and sensitive anecdotes, endowed with a touch of nonsense worthy of Lewis Carroll or Edward Lear, as well as theoretical reflections on the highest level and demanding works such as his abstract-concrete poems, his poems with words ("Cigarren"), numbers ("Gedicht 25") and letters.

The visual, rhythmic and almost musical qualities of these poems reached their peak in his *Ursonate*, Kurt Schwitters' most accomplished "verbi-voco-visual" work, a masterpiece of sound poetry. When he published it in 1932, in the form of a twenty-nine page pamphlet set by the celebrated typographer Jan Tschichold, accompanied by a gramophone recording, the whole forming the last number of his review *Merz*, he had been working on it for more than ten years; if not since 1919, at least since September 1921 at the end of an anti-Dada Merz evening in Prague with Hannah Höch and Raoul Hausmann. The first part appeared in 1928 in the Constructivist review *i10* published in Amsterdam from 1927 to 1929 by Arthur Lehning, an important figure in anarchist circles and founder in 1935 of the International Institute of Social History.

For his *Ursonate*, Schwitters borrowed from Raoul Hausmann's abstract phonetic poems of 1918 the opening motif "fmsbwtözäu," which he extended by repeating it fifty times and adding to it the scherzo "lanke trr gll." He admitted this quite openly in a letter of 1947 to Hausmann: "Merz made the *Ursonate* in a symphonic form after your Dada poem."

Friendship between the two men began at the Café des Westens in Berlin, one night in October 1918. On that particular night Schwitters asked if he could join the Dada Club, but Huelsenbeck turned him away. In his view, Schwitters was artistically compromised because he had exhibited in Herwarth Walden's Sturm gallery and contributed to its magazine, and his poetry was still considered to be expressionist. In the *Dada Almanach* published by Huelsenbeck, Schwitters was singled out for attack in the introduction: "Dada rejects, in principle and energetically, works like the famous *Anna Blume* by Kurt Schwitters."

With regard to *Der Sturm*, Hausmann shared Huelsenbeck's animosity. Hausmann looked on Walden as a "Hohenzollern collaborator," the man who had published a "Song of Songs of Prussianism" ("something we found revolting," he recalled in *Courrier Dada* in 1958). Hausmann and the Dadaists preferred to collaborate sporadically with *Die Aktion*, Franz Pfemfert's review, open to writers and painters alongside purely political authors, even though the policy of the review was not very clear, rather than contribute to the genuinely modern art magazine *Der Sturm*. Another

Raoul Hausmann: *fmsbw..., poster poem, 1918*

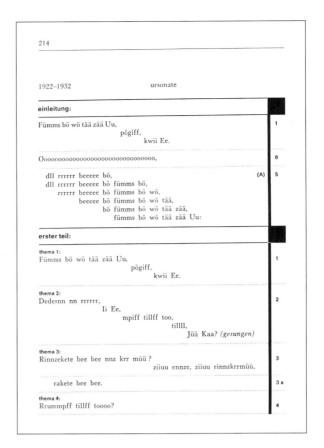

The Ursonate *of Kurt Schwitters, typography by Jan Tschichold, 1932*

Photograph of Kurt Schwitters, c. 1920

Cover of Kurt Schwitters' set of lithographs
Die Kathedrale, *Hanover, 1920*

collaborator with *Die Aktion* was Franz Jung, whose acquaintance Hausmann made before the creation of *Die Freie Strasse*.

This divergence helps to explain why Schwitters was rejected by the Dada Club. He did not utter a word of protest. He cut one out. A combination of method and event that produced "merz," the verbal cut-out on which he founded his own dissident movement: Merz. He cut these four letters out of an advertisement containing the words "Kommerz und Privatbank" when he was making a collage. After removing the syllable "Kom" the remaining fragment "merz" appeared in his picture. (The same word division occurs in Raoul Hausmann's famous collage of 1919-1920, *Le critique d'art:* coincidence or a wink at Schwitters?) Originally created playfully as a word or label on its own, it later gave historical confirmation to Schwitters' private brand of art as an expression of dissidence, the Merz secant cutting into the randomness of Dada. The concept of Merz, a synonym for the process of transformation, allowed Schwitters to enter the different artistic disciplines transversally and reactivate them from within.

A semantic and verbal clone of Dada, Merz became a generic term covering all Kurt Schwitters' artistic activities from 1919 until his death in 1948: Merzbau, Merzbild, Merzzeichnung, Merzbühne and Merzdichtung. Like Dada, Merz was the symbol of the new "transmutation," indeed the word even became substantive or verb ("merzen") and sometimes the twin patronymic of Schwitters, depending on the context; it signified the operation of transformation in painting, construction, collage, theater and poetry.

Kurt Schwitters: Merz 448. Moscow, 1922

The Sonata consists of four movements, of an overture and a finale, and seventhly, of a cadenza in the fourth movement. The first movement is a rondo with four main themes, designated as such in the text of the Sonata. You yourself will certainly feel the rhythm, slack or strong, high or low, taut or loose. To explain in detail the variations and compositions of the themes would be tiresome in the end and detrimental to the pleasure of reading and listening, and after all I'm not a professor.
In the first movement I draw your attention to the word for word repeats of the themes before each variation, to the explosive beginning of the first movement, to the pure lyricism of the sung "Jüü-Kaa," to the military severity of the rhythm of the quite masculine third theme next to the fourth theme which is tremulous and mild as a lamb, and lastly to the accusing finale of the first movement, with the question "tää?"...
The fourth movement, long-running and quick, comes as a good exercise for the reader's lungs, in particular because the endless repeats, if they are not to seem too uniform, require the voice to be seriously raised most of the time. In the finale I draw your attention to the deliberate return of the alphabet up to a. You feel it coming and expect the a impatiently. But twice over it stops painfully on the b . . .
I do no more than offer a possibility for a solo voice with maybe not much imagination. I myself give a different cadenza each time and, since I recite it entirely by heart, I thereby get the cadenza to produce a very lively effect, forming a sharp contrast with the rest of the Sonata which is quite rigid. There.

Kurt Schwitters, 1927

Kurt Schwitters: *The Heart Goes from Sugar to Coffee, 1919*

Let me explain: Dada is the big root of all the little roots. Secret telewireless undermine eagerness [from behind]. — Dada is the little rootlet, the little thread line of sublime grace [I write this as an illuminee]. Dada is the great sacred wave going from Dada to Dada. To Dada Dada floats riverlike around Dada. Around Dada dadate dadating Dada [let it be said for all who don't know yet]. — To Dada Dada Dada Dada Dada Dada Dada Dada Dada Dada. To Dadadadadadadadadadadadadadadadadadadadadadadadadadadadadadadadadadadadadada-dadadadadadadada.

Kurt Schwitters, 1921

Schwitters reciting the Ursonate, *London, 1944*

He was also the inventor of the Merz pliers which kept art and errantry close together. The cobblers of poetry, stitching their leather together with pointless diligence, were as different from him as a songbird from an elephant. With an irresistible eagerness he would sing, trill, murmur, and warble his "pre-syllabic Sonata," till he drew his listeners out of their grey skins. His Merz pictures are full of secrets and sagacity. With them, Schwitters has taught us to see life and beauty in the slightest things, in a tram ticket thrown aside, in a scrap of paper. He shared the opinion of Heraclitus that the sun is no bigger in reality than it seems to us.

Hans Arp, 1949

Kurt Schwitters: *fec. 1920, 1920*

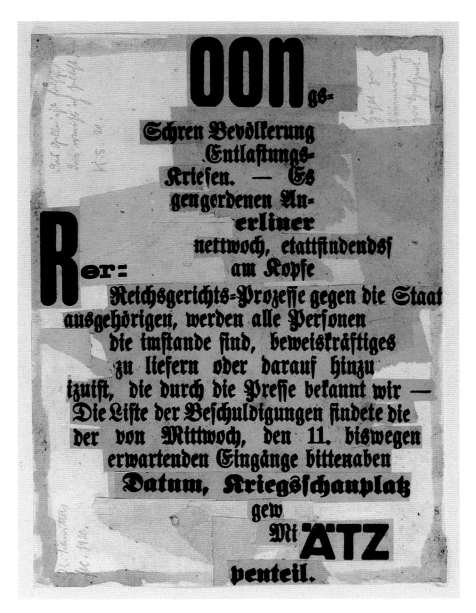

Kurt Schwitters: *Axial Drawing, 1917*

Inheriting from Cubism the use of added materials in the picture, Schwitters developed the process until he was working directly with litter, oddments and debris picked up in the streets of Berlin, where he lived and exhibited at the Sturm gallery during the early post-war period. "As the country was ruined," he wrote, "for the sake of economy I took whatever came to hand. One can even create out of rubbish and this is what I did, nailing and gluing it together."

In Cubism the object added to the picture or the external element pasted on to it are integrated into the composition, and so we remain in the realm of painting. Not so with Schwitters. With him the object becomes the real protagonist of the work.

The use of materials picked up in the streets (Schwitters had sacks full of refuse) enabled him to reduce to a minimum the gap between intuition and "visualization of the artistic concept." Merz, being direct contact with "fragments of nature," meant that plastic creation included the recognition of rhythm throughout nature. "Greater knowledge is required," he explained, "to cut a work of art out of nature, which from an artistic point of view is only formed to construct a work of art based on its own artistic rules."

Kurt Schwitters' individualistic attitude completely modified the problem that the fabrication of a plastic proposition sets the new artist. His wayward outlook led Merz to a theory and practice which were quite separate from those of the autonomous development of art. It certainly involved transforming rational material logic and producing an internal logic peculiar to the work of art, notably by the prominence given to each element, to each material pregnant with its own content and history (the nostalgia and memories clinging to derelict objects that are found and saved). But it also meant that the naturalistic work of art now took shape in a new way: unlike the old imitative painting, it was closer to nature insofar as it did not copy it, but shaped itself as nature herself does. Here Merz showed a complicity with reality which is worth emphasizing.

Thus, in an article written in 1926, Schwitters was able to weigh creation as it is found in nature against ordering artistic creation: "There you will find clearly demonstrated (in *Merz*, no. 8/9: *Nasci*, see Chapter 7) the essential likeness of a drawing by Lissitzky to a crystal, of a building by Mies van der Rohe to the strict economical construction of the upper thighbone; you will recognize the Constructivist tendency in the position of leaves on a stem, you will take a photograph of the surface of Mars for an abstract picture, by Kandinsky for example, simply because it is surrounded by a black frame. You will see in my *i* picture that nature or chance, whichever you prefer, often combines elements that resemble in themselves what we call rhythm. The artist's one activity lies there: in recognizing and delimiting... For even if the crystal has a structure like that of a Lissitzky drawing, it is still a crystal and not a work of art, whereas the Lissitzky drawing is a work of art and not a crystal. But knowing how to recognize a work of art is an innate ability, the result of an innate desire for a creative and ordering artistic activity."

Apart from the fact that this position recalls the readymade (the artist recognizes, chooses, delimits), it quite significantly crosses the dividing line which is supposed to separate Dadaist "eccentric sensoriality" (the title of a book by Raoul Hausmann in 1969) from the constructed austerity of pure plastic art. The relation between Merz and fragments of nature, odds and ends recovered and used in new ways, led Schwitters to look on himself as an assembler and shaper: "The word Merz," he wrote in 1920, "had no precise meaning when I formed it. Now it has the meaning that I gradually give it. The meaning of the concept Merz changes according to the knowledge and insight of those who continue to work with it. Merz aims at liberation from all fetters, for the sake of *shaping* things artistically. Freedom does not mean unbridled licence, it is the outcome of strict artistic discipline... An artist should have the right, for example, to make a picture merely by assembling blotting paper, provided he knows how to *shape* things... I am interested in other art forms, like poetry. The elements of poetry are letters, syllables, words, phrases. Poetry arises from the interaction of these elements. Meaning is only important if it is employed as one such factor."

Kurt Schwitters: *Merz Picture with Green Ring, 1926*

Merz pictures are abstract works of art. Essentially the word Merz means the assemblage for artistic purposes of all imaginable materials; technically, as a matter of principle, it means that each of these materials has the same value. Merz painting, then, makes use not only of color and canvas, brush and palette, but of all materials visible to the eye and of all necessary tools. It does not matter whether the materials used were already designed for some other purpose or not. The artist creates by choosing, arranging and deforming the materials.

The deforming of the materials may already come about through their arrangement on the picture surface. It may further be emphasized by breaking them up, twisting them, covering them over, or painting them over.

Merz painting aims at immediate expression by shortening the way from the intuition of the work of art to its visualization.

Kurt Schwitters, 1919

Kurt Schwitters: *Der Weihnachtsmann (Santa Claus), 1922*

Such a declaration announced a profound revolution with regard to meaning as conventionally produced and asserted, even more than the manifesto of Elementary Art (Chapter 7), a theoretical position that initiated creative dynamics of the elementary type. Schwitters lays emphasis on the shaping growth of materials and the relations that develop between them, as well as the fact that the form of a work is never completed. For Merz, as for Dada, a form never *is* completed: it remains constantly moving, growing, it is a *work in progress*.

This statement also foreshadows the prominent part that concrete (also called elementary) poetry would play in Schwitters' work throughout his life, beginning with *Cigarren* (1921), the *Ursonate* (1924-1932) and ending with *Ribble Bobble Pimlico* (1946), *Rackedika* (1946) and *In grr grwrie* (1945-1947).

During the anti-Dada Merz evening organized in Prague on September 1, 1921 with Raoul Hausmann and Hannah Höch, Schwitters recited his *Alphabet read backwards*, the poem *Cigars* (composed solely of the eight letters in the German word Cigarren), the story *Revolution in Revon* (Revon standing for Hanover) and *Anna Blume* (Anna Flower), a major poem in the volume of the same name which made him famous within a few weeks in 1919 and was republished several times. *Anna Blume* obviously retained traces of the old poetic feeling and this probably had something to do with the hostility to Schwitters shown by Huelsenbeck, who after the Zurich days was committed to pure abstract poetry.

As a poet, however, Schwitters was to follow a line of development hardly hinted at in *Anna Blume*. For he became, with Raoul Hausmann, the leading poet of the concrete persuasion, of which he remains to this day the unrivaled forerunner. The *Ursonate*, although it is the best known and most important of his poems, should not be allowed to eclipse the rest of Schwitters' large poetic output. The rhythms of the *Ursonate* give us an idea of the full scope of this new music, whose like is only to be found again in the writings of Gertrude Stein.

The rhythmic patterns of the *Ursonate* form a bridge between his elementary poems and the construction of the Merzbau (Chapter 7). The typography demanded by the visualization of the rhythm on the page prepares the way for a rhythmical construction in the field of architecture.

Kurt Schwitters: *Merz 316. ish yellow, 1921*

Cover of Kurt Schwitters' book of verse Anna Blume, *Hanover, 1919*

TO EVE BLOSSOM (''An Anna Blume'')

O, thou beloved of my twenty-seven senses, I love thine!
Thou thee thee thine, I thine, thou mine. – We? –
That belongs (by the way) not here.
Who art thou, uncounted woman?
Thou art – art thou? –
The people say thou werst. –
Let them say. They don't know how the church-tower stands.
Thou wearest thy hat on thy feet and walkest about on thy hands,
on thy hands walkest thou.
Hallo! Thy red dress, shredded into white folds.
Red I love, Eve Blossom, red I love thine!
Thou thee thee thine, I thine, thou mine. – We? –
That belongs (by the way) in the cold fire.
Red Blossom, red Eve Blossom, what do the people say?...

Thou simple maiden in everyday-dress, thou sweet green beast,
I love thine! –

Thou thee thee thine, I thine, thou mine. – We? –
That belongs (by the way) in the fire-grate.
Eve Blossom! Eve, E-v-e, I drip thy name.
Thy name drips like soft candle-wax.
Doest thou know, Eve, doest thou already know it?
One can also read thee from behind, and thou, thou most glorious of all,
Thou art from the back as from the front: ''E-v-e.''
Candle-wax drips caressing over my back.
Eve Blossom, thou drippy beast, I love thine!

Kurt Schwitters, 1922

Kurt Schwitters: *Merz. ELIKAN, c. 1925*

In any case, Merz rhythmic and plastic intensity stamps the whole of Schwitters' work. In the collage of cut out pieces of paper (*Merz*, c. 1925), which takes the pasted paper revolution launched by the Cubists to its peak, different rhythms are simultaneously set up by the accumulation and overlay of scraps of paper and, almost incidentally and briefly, by the repetition of the letters ELIKAN in the center of the composition (the same letters reappear in a 1937 collage, *Ramberg*), as well as by the interplay of colors (the juxtaposition and gradations of warm creamy tonalities with blue grey cobalt azure) and by interwoven shapes (the contrast between carefully snipped parallelepipeds and more hastily arranged triangles, trapezia and zigzags). As reminders of the reality external to the abstraction of the work, a few press cuttings have been slipped in, mainly for the iconic quality of the Gothic lettering.

This is one of Schwitters' particularly clean compositions. Consisting essentially of pre-colored pieces of paper, it does away with brushes and tubes of paint, whereas the thinness of the material, while accentuating its tactile sensuality, confers on it an unusual flatness, with no trace of the roughness and relief characteristic of the works he made from rubbish and other scrap materials.

An example of the latter is *Merz 316. Ische gelb* (*Merz 316. ish yellow*, 1921), typical of the simultaneous use of various fragments presumably picked up at random when Schwitters was out walking. The printed letter also has a high value in it, accentuating, as a cut out, the bursting of vocal and visual discourse and, by the neatness of its design, the raw beauty of the laceration and of the apparent disorder of the collage.

After the decline of Dada in Berlin, Hausmann and Schwitters drew closer again through their collaboration on the two periodicals edited by the Dutch painter and theorist Theo van Doesburg: the major and influential Constructivist review *De Stijl*; and *Mecano*, the prototype of the little Dadaist magazine, consisting of one large folded sheet, published by Van Doesburg under the pseudonym I.K. Bonset, which he used for the Dada side of his personality (see Chapter 7).

Early spring in Cologne: Max Ernst and Johannes Baargeld

Max Ernst: *Self-Portrait (The Punching Ball or The Immortality of Buonarroti), 1920*

As the third platform of Dada in Germany, the Cologne group was just as much marked by political activism as the Berlin group. On the aesthetic level its leading figure was Max Ernst, who became one of the masters of collage. In him one finds great virtuosity in the arrangement of narrative sequences, a poetry inspired by the natural sciences (sediments, animals, leaves, stamens, sandworms) and often akin to that of his friend Arp, a delicate palette, a deft handling of watercolors, a metaphorical richness in his picture titles (*The Gramineous Bicycle*, *The Fall of an Angel*, *The Chinese Nightingale*, *Wet-Nurse of the Stars*). The dramatic power of his collage novels and the combination therein of realities from very different sources are like the pictorial transposition of imagery à la Maldoror. These qualities, after his Dada phase in Cologne, gave him a leading place in the ranks of French Surrealism.

Max Ernst (also known as Dadamax) made contact with the Paris group in the winter of 1920, when he proposed to Tzara to send some of his pictures to Paris. They were exhibited there in the spring of 1921. Although it was expressly a Dada exhibition, he was already close to the circle around the periodical *Littérature*, to Breton in particular who had organized it and now numbered Ernst as one of his group.

The Cologne group, consisting essentially of Max Ernst and Johannes Baargeld, stood halfway between the joint influence of Zurich and Paris. It arose under the auspices of Arp on his return from Zurich and was stimulated by the first signs of Parisian Dadaism after Max Ernst's discharge from the army. Ernst had been a member of the German occupation forces which had mutinied in Brussels at the urging of Carl Einstein, and he had shaken hands with him after one of Einstein's rousing speeches in the Grand Place.

Max Ernst: *Lithograph from* Fiat Modes. Pereat Ars, *1919*

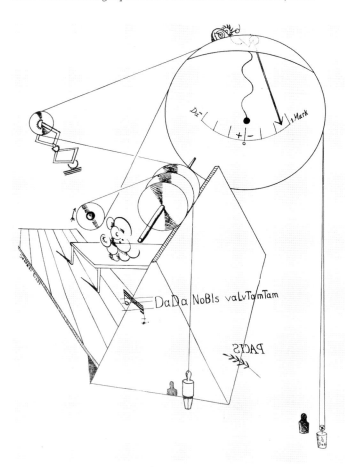

Together with a few photomontages (like *The Punching Ball or The Immortality of Buonarroti*, also known as *Dadafex maximus*), Max Ernst's paintings, collages (so different from those of his friend Arp) and frottages (around 1925) made the Cologne Dadaist one of the pioneers of the narrative procedures of Surrealism. The elementary deconstruction/construction techniques worked out in Zurich and Berlin held no appeal for him.

Significantly, Max Ernst shared the Parisian group's enthusiasm for the so-called metaphysical painting of Giorgio de Chirico, which he discovered in a special Chirico number of the review *Valori plastici*. Just after the war, he came under the influence of the Italian artist. It is particularly noticeable in the spatial conception, the perspectives, the vanishing lines and the dummies of *Fiat Modes (Pereat Ars)*, a set of eight lithographs published in Cologne in 1919.

Max Ernst was comparatively isolated. Admittedly, Cologne had housed the important Sonderbund exhibition (1912) and in Cologne Ernst did meet August Macke, one of the most talented painters in the Munich Blaue Reiter group. Himself a native of Cologne, Macke introduced Ernst to modern art during his return visits to the Rhineland city. A visit to Paul Klee was also decisive. Ernst was especially attracted to the painting of Emil Nolde and James Ensor. During a stay in Paris in 1912, he made the chance acquaintance of the painter Jules Pascin at the Café du Dôme in Montparnasse. Although it led to nothing, it already showed Max Ernst's predilection for Paris (as attested by the strong French participation in *Die Schammade*, the Cologne Dada review) and his desire for exile, prepared by his epistolary links with Breton and Eluard soon after the end of the war, in 1919, and his first exhibition at the Au Sans Pareil bookshop (see Chapter 6).

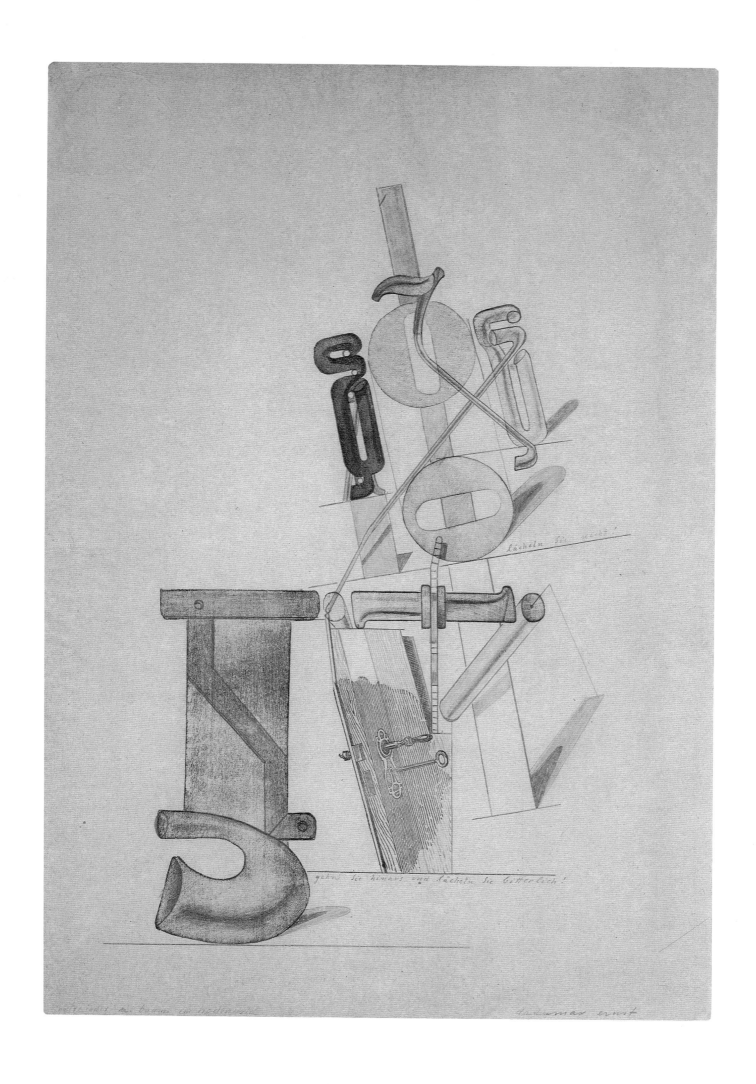

Max Ernst: *Do not smile!, 1919*

● ● BULLETIN D ●

. . . . . schlagt das warme Ei aus der Hand!" . . . . .

Ahehe: Cézanne ist chewing-gum. Der Grunewald verdaut van Goghs gelbes Gebiss.
Van Gogh roch aus dem Mund und ist tot. Eljen dada!

Behehe: Die Phallustrade der Expressionisten erschöpft den Lezithinvorrat der gesamten bebauten wie
bekannten Bauchrinde. Die Bauchbinde der Patti ist beigesetzt. Die Leichenbeschauer Dr. Rudolf
Steiners traten der internationalen Assoziation DADA (iadede) bei. Eviva dada!

Cehehe: incasso cassa picasso. Citoyen pablo picasso verteilt sein abgeschlossenes oeuvre an die Witwen
Madrids. Nunmehr sind die Witwen in der Lage, einen Kursus in schwedischer Massage zu
nehmen, um da . . . . picasso Umdada?

Dehehe: Der Zahnrat war ein Weib. Der Expressionismus ist eine Hautbinde mit Nabelschnurcharakter.
Meldung: Bindehaut intakt.

Ehehe: Es kann deshalb Prof. Oskar Kokoschka heutzutag mit Sicherheit als Erfinder des automecha-
nischen Blutegels „Selbsthilfe" angesprochen werden. Et Propopo, et Propopos!

Fehehe: Hasenclevert in weißer Tennishose! Hasenclevers, vereinigt euch! Da, ut dem dada.

Gehehe: Am Unterleib der Gesellschaft wächst die Kunst. Die Kunst wächst in den Unterleib. Das Geheimnis
des Oberleibes ist sein unterer Leib. Die Kunst ist revolutionär bis zum Unterleib. Die Gesellschaft
hat sich den Expressionismus eingeführt. a = o = expr = unterleib = hämorrhoidalsuppositorium.

Hahehe: Die expressionistischen Dichter dichten, weil die expressionistischen Nichtdichter nicht schweigen.
Himmel Höll und Kloßkapöll — Dreifach lyrisches Gebröll — Däublerbrillatine sternt — Licht-
schachtwerfel ganz entfernt — Becher erdrubinern lernt, dada.

Ihehe: Der Waldenismus autosezessioniert unter Aufrechterhaltung der amerikanischen Buchführung aus
dem jeweiligen Präwaldenismus. Seine Stilkunde steht auf der dritten Seite des Generalkatalogs
der Grands Magasins des Quatre Saisons für das Jahr 1920 und finden Beiträge nur unter Bei-
legung des vollen Jahresabonnements in Briefmarken Beachtung.

Kahehe: Balter ropft Dada
Aniunde in Tomatenbecken
Waldas Toria aus Verzähen glecken
Koloman Psilander Hodenberg Rockdada.

Lehehe: Menschenfreunde! Ce qu'on dom ist Dostojewski. Die rechte Seite des piperdämons ist noch
0,879 dada von der Biscaya entfernt (quer durch Europa). Die internationale Assoziation Dada
beschloß auf ihrer letzten Konferenz auf die Biscaya einen Abtritt-deckel zu malen. dada.

Mehehe: Es gibt keine „aktivistische" Kunst. Der Künstler ist ein Teil des Lebens, das er zerstört.
Aktivismus ist Merkmal alles Lebenden. Das Geschwätz vom Aktivismus zeigt uns an, daß die
Sprengung des Schoßes Lebensfrage wird für das Neue. Der beengende Aktivismus des
Schoßes findet unsern Aktivismus bereit. . . . . . Das Alte deckt sich und nennt sich „Leben
schlechthin". Leben lebt nur sich aus (l'expressionisme pour l'expressionisme). Egozentric act:
ein Herr . . . . . keine Dame. Das „Leben schlechthin" ist zum Fraß des Neuen da. Das Alte
verfällt der Materiatur seines Antichrist. Kyrie eleison Antichriste!!

Nehehe: Idionopolis brennt. Niemals brennt Idionopolis. Einstein ist eine Zigarre und schneidet sich ab.
Eljen Karolyi! Nieder Idionopolis! Nieder die idionome Kunst. kr krr krrr rasierter . . . .
un . . . wollen wir manet ausstopfen, wollen wollen. Die Malerei ist wert keinen Hasenknopf.
Dada = Hasenknopf. Franz Marc ist der Begründer des cul de Berlin und wird von Damen
vor dem Schoße getragen. Verhindern, Hintern. Lest die Manifeste Dada. 0,000001 dada = chemisch
rein. Hoch die iadede! caracho! cocha bamba!!!   Johannes Theodor Baargeld.

Cover of Johannes Baargeld's review Bulletin D, *Cologne, 1919*

Johannes Baargeld: *Venus in the Game of Kings, 1920*

Yet Max Ernst did not ignore the Berlin art world. In 1913 he exhibited two canvases at the first German Autumn Salon organized by Herwarth Walden at the Sturm gallery. While on leave in 1916 he exhibited there again and on that occasion met George Grosz and Wieland Herzfelde. Although they sympathized with its aim, Grosz and Herzfelde did not join the Dada Club when it was founded two years later, and they were the butt, like the rest of the Berlin Dada group, of Ernst's mockery. Repeatedly Max Ernst made fun not only of Grosz whom he called a "prominent idiot," but also of the Berlin Dada group which he regarded as a "counterfeit." In spite of that, several of his works were exhibited at the First International Dada Fair in Berlin in June 1920.

Johannes Baargeld (actually Alfred Gruenwald), painter and poet, founded the Rhineland section of the German Communist Party. Son of the general manager of the Rhineland Reinsurance Company, he combined an artistic and political life, without subordinating one to the other. Schwitters wrote of him: "One of the most capable artists and Dadaists was Baargeld. He came like a girl from the south, and glittered and shone for only a few minutes like the Queen of the Night."

With Max Ernst, Baargeld edited (and presumably financed) the Communist review *Der Ventilator*, with a print-run at times of twenty thousand copies. It was sold in the streets, barracks and factories before being banned, so it seems, by the British military authorities who occupied the left bank of the Rhine at the time, up to 1926, under the terms of the Armistice.

To us [Max Ernst told Patrick Waldberg in 1958], Dada was above all a moral reaction. We were going to sabotage the performances of the *Young King*, a patriotic monarchist play of insulting stupidity. My friend Baargeld and I used to distribute our review *Der Ventilator* at factory gates. Our rage aimed at total subversion. A horrible futile war had robbed us of five years of our existence. We had experienced the collapse into ridicule and shame of everything represented to us as just, true and beautiful. My works of that period were not meant to attract but to make people scream.

Max Ernst's main link with Dada went back to his pre-war friendship with Arp, when the latter was employed in an avant-garde gallery in Cologne. "Arp," Max Ernst later told Edouard Roditi, "was still a rather precious young man, affecting the behavior and manners of a dandy of the Oscar Wilde period, but already very well informed about everything that was going on in art and literature, although with little inclination to take part in political activities, as I was already doing. It was only later, during the war, that the Zurich Dadaists managed to make him take a stand, as a pacifist refugee in Switzerland, and participate actively in their manifestations."

A declaration vouching for the divided purposes of the Cologne Dadaists. While at first the group was keen on politics, Arp's return apparently brought about a withdrawal from it in favor of purely Dada activities.

Max Ernst: *Health through Sport, c. 1920*

In February 1917 the painter Max Ernst and myself were at the front, barely a kilometer away from each other. The German artilleryman Max Ernst was shelling the trenches where I, a French infantryman, was mounting guard. Three years later we were the best friends in the world, and since then we have struggled together eagerly in the same cause: the total emancipation of man.

Paul Eluard, 1936

Illustration for Dilettanten W/3
by Johannes Baargeld, 1920

*DADA siegt! (Dada wins!), poster for the reopening of the Dada Early Spring
exhibition, Cologne, 1920, after it had been closed down by the police*

The Cologne group then set about organizing two exhibitions and publishing the reviews *Die Schammade* and *Bulletin D,* activities carried on in the oppressive climate of the censorship exercised by the British occupation forces.

The first Dada exhibition in Cologne took place in premises devoted to new trends by a recently created Society of Arts, welcomed for the occasion by the Kunstverein in November 1919. Invited to exhibit by the organizers, Baargeld and Ernst met with a refusal when they brought their works along. The management of the Kunstverein settled the differences between the organizing committee and Baargeld and Ernst by separating the exhibitions and dividing them between two rooms. On entering, the Dada room was on the left, the Society of Arts room on the right. Separate posters and catalogues avoided any possibility of confusion (which no doubt explained their confiscation by the British), while Baargeld and Ernst posted up this notice at the entrance:

> By special request of the Society of Arts
> No connection exists between Dada and the Society of Arts.
> Dada has nothing in common with the amateurism of the aforesaid society.
> signed J.T. Baargeld, Max Ernst
> ... this way to Dada ⟵——⟶ this way to the Society of Arts

It had the effect of attracting the public to the Dada room and leaving the other one empty.

Otto Freundlich, Heinrich Hörle and Franz Seiwert also took part in this exhibition. Freundlich went on to become a well-known abstract painter in the twenties and thirties. The other two withdrew their works at the last minute, because through a sudden U-turn of a political nature they felt that Dada was a "bourgeois undertaking," to use Seiwert's words. The Dada exhibition also included works by the mentally ill, naïve painters and dilettantes. By a happy coincidence, testifying to the international network now being created in support of the movement, Katherine Dreier was visiting Cologne and looked in during the hanging of wire constructions and found objects. She offered to put on the exhibition in her New Haven gallery. Ernst and Baargeld accepted enthusiastically, but the British authorities refused an export license for this "scandalous exhibition" (Ernst).

A second show was held a few months later in April 1920 in the entrance hall of the Museum of Applied Arts after Arp's return to Cologne. Arp,

Max Ernst: *"Plans of attack on the Dada stronghold detected just in time,"* 1919

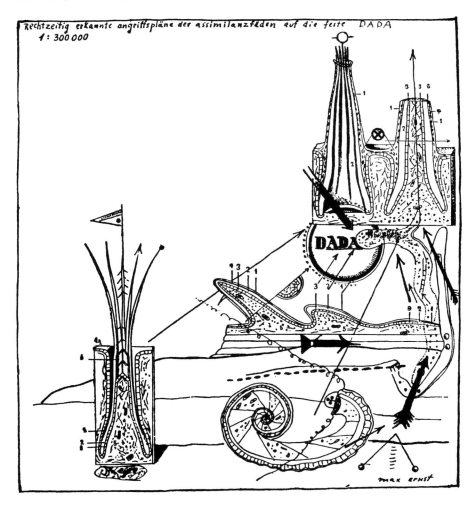

What the newspapers blame me for is untrue. I have never used the reflections of the lower belly to heighten the lighting effect of my pictures. I confine myself to merely using rhinocerized belching pincers.

Max Ernst, 1920

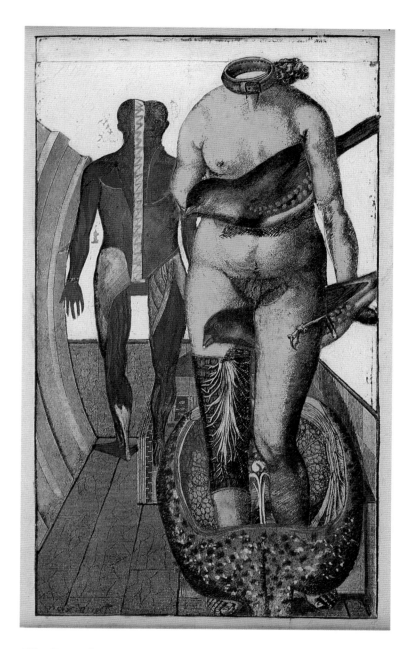

Max Ernst: *Speech or The Bird Woman, 1920*

Baargeld and Ernst suggested a name for it: Central W/3 (three because there were three of them, W for west). In spite of the free participation offered by the organizers, the Cologne Artists' Union (which had promised a juryless exhibition), the entries of Baargeld and Ernst caused an unfavorable reaction. They were immediately removed by the director of the Museum on the fallacious pretext that the works had to go before a selection committee.

Dadamax and Baargeld at once rented the little glass-roofed court behind the Brauhaus Winter in the Schildergasse, which could only be reached through a men's lavatory (Duchamp's urinal again!). Their showing there was interpreted as a provocation. They were charged with outrage against public morals and the exhibition was closed. The police claimed to have discovered a pornographic work by Max Ernst, a collaged gouache entitled *Speech or The Bird Woman* (1920), which later went to illustrate *Répétitions*, one of the two books he brought out with Paul Eluard in 1922, the other being *Les Malheurs des immortels.*

When the artists were summoned to appear, it turned out that in his collage Ernst had borrowed an *Eve* of 1504 by Albrecht Dürer. In point of fact he had interspersed it with birds and balanced it with an anatomical figure. Significantly enough, the police were paying more attention here to the established order of speech than to morality. The liberty taken by Ernst in fabricating images suddenly "revealed" a hackneyed conventional nude, lost from sight until then. Far more than an alleged obscenity, Max Ernst disclosed the mechanism of the narrative and its representation. An artist at the pivotal point between Cologne Dadaism and nascent Surrealism in Paris, Ernst was Dada when he took these mechanisms to pieces and Surrealist when, taking up the cause of the poetic image, he charted out the perspectives of a "surreality" of which he was one of the forerunners.

After withdrawal of the "obscene" print, the exhibition was authorized again. As a sign of victory, Baargeld and Ernst published a poster whose words could be given a double meaning: "Dada wins! Reopening of the exhibition closed by the police. Dada stands for calm and order." There was an ironic twist to this statement, because the infuriated visitors destroyed the works on show which were immediately replaced with others by their creators. But this poster too had to be withdrawn after a telephone call from the chief of police to Baargeld.

Thus German Dada is a staccato record, if not of dissensions, anyhow of sudden outcroppings: Huelsenbeck founding the Dada Club as a projection of the Zurich group; Baader rallying to Dada without being a member of the Club, yet feeling the need to found what he called the Club of the Blue Milky Way; Hausmann drawing away while proclaiming that Dada was more than Dada and declaring himself a Presentist; Schwitters, blackballed by Huelsenbeck, launching Merz and involving Hausmann and Hannah Höch in his anti-Dada Merz soirées, while gaining the support of Tzara in Zurich; Ernst in Cologne viewing the Berlin group as a counterfeit and setting up his own Dada faction linked with Zurich and, in due course, with Paris; Huelsenbeck on his side publishing a *Dada Almanach*, frowning on Baader and Schwitters, and belittling the part played by Ball in Zurich and Hausmann in Berlin.

But such was the nature of a movement whose every member was Chairman in his own right. No one would step down from the heights. Every tendency had its own life and luster without courting anyone's authority, backing or blessing.

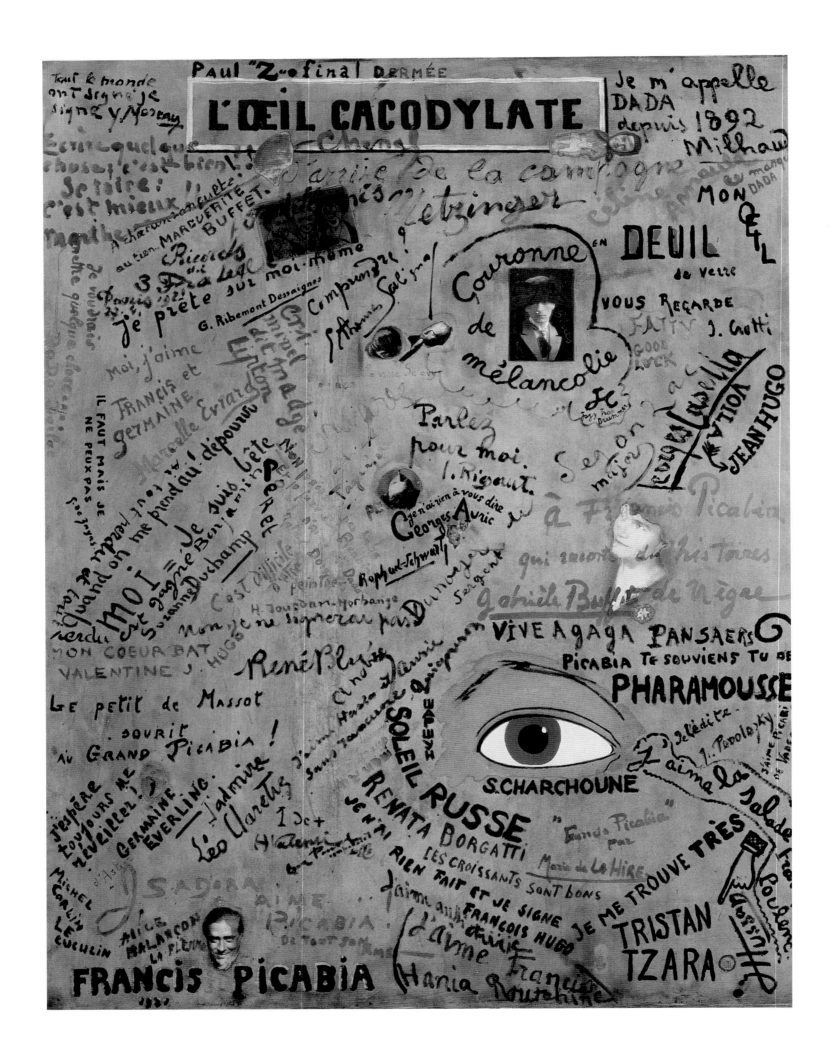

Chapter 6

Paris: Recognition to Dada

The first echoes of Dada activity in Zurich reached Paris by way of letters exchanged between Tristan Tzara and Guillaume Apollinaire at the end of 1916. Nevertheless we have to wait until 1919 before relations were established first between Tzara and Picabia, and then between Tzara and Breton. These relations augured well for the future, since Dada found its anchorage in Paris from 1920 to 1923, beginning with Tzara's arrival there in January 1920.

The movement in Paris was characterized by intense activity: manifestations, reviews, books, various actions, protests and interventions, mainly in 1920 and 1921. The haphazard outcome of encounters and initiatives, friendships and alliances were formed, broken up and re-formed. By turns, the protagonists were united or divided, shared or disputed the initiative as to attitudes and methods of action. The aim of these young writers and artists was simultaneously to dissociate themselves from the new Cubist academicism, counter the so-called advance of Futurism, make the most lively and creative protests in the language of art itself in the face of a hostile environment and lastly, for some of them at least, to oppose the onset of Surrealism.

The issue was to go beyond the question of art alone in the name of life itself, to reshape not only its form and meaning, but also, the primordial question, to decide on the use to be made of it, even down to affecting the course of history. "We searched for an elementary art," wrote Hans Arp in 1948, "that would, we thought, save mankind from the furious folly of these times."

Questioning art each in his own way, taking the mechanisms of representation to bits and putting them together again, each of the Parisian protagonists of Dada adopted an individual attitude beyond the positions common to all. The aesthetic choices, the offers made by magazine editors, always on the look out for youthful talents (the Dadaists were undoubtedly the most brilliant of them) and the fundamental difficulty of escaping from the state of general alienation which made itself felt in every possible way, did the rest.

The rise of the movement—initially represented in Paris by Tzara and Picabia, before it spread—was fostered by a set of circumstances which occurred throughout 1919 and changed the Parisian context, making it particularly favorable to future Dada seasons. The first of these circumstances goes back to the summer of 1918, when Picabia, on a rest cure in Switzerland, received a letter addressed to him in Paris by Tzara and then forwarded. The two men started to correspond, but they did not meet. The death of Apollinaire in November 1918 affected both of them. Tzara had never met the poet, but had exchanged several letters with him. Picabia and his wife Gabrielle Buffet had been close friends of his.

Apollinaire was only thirty-eight. His death on Armistice day, resulting from his war wounds and the trepanning he had undergone, was mourned by all the avant-garde painters and writers whom he had befriended and championed. Born in Rome of an Italian father and a Polish mother, he had become the best-loved poet in France, a warm and generous man, "lyricism in person" (as Breton described him in 1952) with "the cortege of Orpheus following in his steps."

Tristan Tzara and André Breton about 1920

First meeting of Picabia and Tzara in Zurich

Tzara's *Dada Manifesto 1918* was published in *Dada 3* (December 1918). When he read it, Picabia was bowled over. It was this, apparently, that took him to Zurich in January 1919 for the express purpose of making Tzara's acquaintance. Arp describes the occasion:

> I got acquainted with Francis Picabia during his visit . . . to Zurich. He came as an emissary of the American Dadaists to greet his colleagues in Zurich. Curious and moved, Tristan Tzara and I went to his hotel. We found him busily occupied in pulling an alarm clock to pieces. It made me think of Rembrandt's *Anatomy Lesson* in the Amsterdam Museum. At least a good step forward had been made toward abstraction.
>
> He stripped his alarm clock remorselessly, right down to the spring which he pulled out triumphantly. He stopped work to greet us, and without further ado, using the wheels, springs, hands and other secret parts of the clock, immediately impressed them on paper. He connected these imprints by lines and accompanied the action of drawing by remarks of unusual wit far removed from the world of mechanical stupidity. At this period he delighted in wheels, screws, motors, cylinders and electrical wiring. Making use of these forms, he drew and painted machines with unconscious secrets. He created any number of these fanciful machines. *The Girl Born Without a Mother*, a slim volume of poetry that overwhelmed us, was written at the time. In this book there was no longer the slightest trace of the dried up sponges of rhetoric, nor any glittering phases, nor any trompe-l'œil in a bra.

At the time when Arp and Tristan Tzara met Picabia, and chose his *Alarm Clock* for the cover of the forthcoming number of *Dada 4-5*, André

Francis Picabia: *Flirt, 1920*

Cover of Dada 4-5, *Zurich, May 15, 1919, with Picabia's "Alarm Clock" drawing*

Breton in Paris, carried away by the *Dada Manifesto 1918* and heartbroken by the death of his friend Jacques Vaché, wrote to Tzara: "I've really gone into raptures over your manifesto; I no longer knew from whom to expect such courage as you show. Today my eyes are turned in your direction alone. (You don't know much about me. I am twenty-two. I believe in the genius of Rimbaud, Lautréamont and Jarry; I greatly loved Guillaume Apollinaire, I have a profound tenderness for Reverdy. My favorite painters are Ingres and Derain; I am very sensitive to Chirico's art.) I'm not so naïve as I look."

1919, the year that preceded Tzara's welcome to Paris, was a year of transition. It saw a transmission of powers on the literary scene. As a result of Apollinaire's death, the poet Pierre Reverdy gave up editing his review *Nord-Sud*. Although Apollinaire certainly played a predominant part in it, the review (partly financed by the Chilean creationist poet Huidobro) also published the early writings of the younger generation of writers, among them Louis Aragon, André Breton, Paul Dermée, Vicente Huidobro himself, Philippe Soupault and Tristan Tzara.

It was the void left by *Nord-Sud* which, about three weeks later, inspired three of these young writers, Aragon, Breton and Soupault, known as "the three musketeers," to found their own review *Littérature*, so christened on Paul Valéry's advice, the underlining of the title being meant to suggest that it should be taken with a pinch of salt. (At the height of the Dada Period, Picabia suggested calling it "Antilittérature.") Together with *Dada*, Tzara's review, and Picabia's *391*, it was one of the three active organs of Dada in Paris.

On closer examination, however, *Littérature* can only be connected with Dada to the extent that it followed in the latter's footsteps, the path having been trodden first by Tzara (*Dada*) and Picabia (*391*). *Littérature* announced its commitment to the movement, while remaining somewhat aloof, a faithful reflection of the successive enthusiasms and apprehensions of its leading lights. Moreover, their typographical inventiveness, the spatial arrangement of texts on the page and the colors used for printing, sometimes differing from one title to another, distinguished the specifically Dadaist reviews, *Dada* and *391*, from *Littérature*, whose neutral appearance recalled Apollinaire's *Les Soirées de Paris* in many respects.

Reception in Paris of the Zurich *Dada Manifesto 1918*

Left to right, André Breton, René Hilsum, Louis Aragon, and
Paul Eluard, all disguised, reading Dada 3, 1919

André Breton with Picabia's poster for the Dada Festival,
Salle Gaveau, Paris, May 1920. It reads: "You are incapable
of liking anything unless you've seen and heard it for a
long time, you bunch of fools."

Beginnings of the periodical Littérature

There was at that time in Paris a periodical very much alive, called
Nord-Sud, and we were quite certain, however fond we were of its
editor Pierre Reverdy, that never in Nord-Sud would Reverdy admit
the new trend. And we did not want a cage, however fine. Among us
were some common favorites, Lautréamont, Jarry, Rimbaud. The man
closest to us, Reverdy himself, we found too offhand with Rimbaud,
always careful as he was to reduce things to the right proportions
(Rimbaud is not Jesus Christ, etc.), and for the others no need to waste
one's breath.
Paul Valéry when consulted suggested we replace it by Littérature: this
word meant derisively by us, but taken generally as calling for what
Verlaine disdained ("And all the rest is literature") was accepted at
once for what it conveyed of provocative, disagreeable, pretentious,
skeletal. On the whole it was not liked, by Reverdy in particular who
suggested we call our periodical Carte Blanche. After some hesitation
this title was rejected; there was too much Picasso in it or too much
Reverdy, it was too cubist. I underscore these last two words because of
the vulgarity of this statement which at the time we would have
shrugged off, but which no doubt is the true reason why we declined a
charming title evocative of what we then liked best. For what marked
the birth of Littérature was indeed the birth of a still obscure opposition
to cubist taste, a defense against that renewal of grace which Lhote and
company were soon to extoll, and whose success has now meant a
revival of the Pompadour style in poetry and painting.
I have already implied that by putting well-tried names on our contents
page we were seeking less to strengthen our hand than to compromise
them: and also to place all literary values on a plane we were familiar
with, one where we could impose on them a slight and by no means
ordinary revision. I won't deny that between Soupault, Breton and
myself there was something of a plot, still undefined, but soon to shape
up. We moved very cautiously: the choice of books for review in that
first issue (Reverdy's Jockeys camouflés, Tzara's 25 Poèmes) was just
barely enough perhaps to make the reader prick up his ears.

Louis Aragon, about 1923

ERUTARETTIL (Littérature spelled backwards), spread in
Littérature, No. 11-12, Paris, October 1923

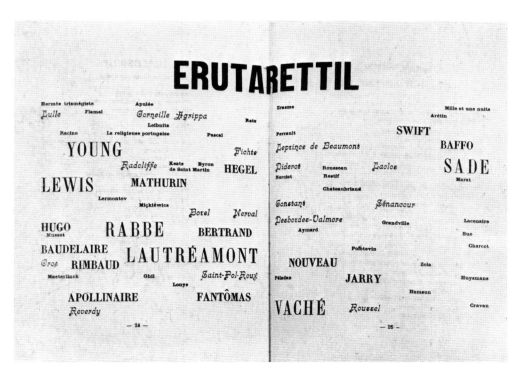

Man Ray: *Tristan Tzara, October 1921, photograph overprinted on another of Madeleine Turban*

Les Champs magnétiques

The conventional layout and the rather innocuous articles, with André Gide, Paul Valéry, Jean Paulhan, Léon-Paul Fargue, Paul Morand, Mallarmé and Jules Romains appearing side by side with the new writers who animated the review and others such as Tzara, Blaise Cendrars, Ramón Gómez de la Serna, Drieu La Rochelle and Raymond Radiguet, had little to do with asserting *Littérature*'s personal editorial outlook. This was primarily conveyed by the prominence given to Lautréamont and Rimbaud, those symbolic figures, and subsequently by the publication of *Les Champs magnétiques* (The Magnetic Fields).

In April or May 1919, impressed by the verbal agility of Tristan Tzara which they had discovered, if not in the books he had already published at that date (*La Première Aventure céleste de M. Antipyrine* and *Vingt-cinq poèmes*), at least in his poems published in *Dada* ("total circuit by the moon and by color"), André Breton and Philippe Soupault embarked on the writing of *Les Champs magnétiques* which, in a letter to Tzara in July 1919, Breton still referred to as "a hundred or so pages of prose and verse." Illustrations by the Douanier Rousseau were even envisaged for their publication in 1920.

Three years later, in November 1922, the period of the first hypnotic trance sessions, a year after his meeting with Freud, just as he was moving

LES CHAMPS
MAGNÉTIQUES

par ANDRÉ BRETON et PHILIPPE SOUPAULT

A PARIS, AU SANS PAREIL

Cover of Les Champs magnétiques *(The Magnetic Fields) by Breton and Soupault, Paris, 1920*

away from Dada, Breton presented those pages as being the product of psychic automatism: "In 1919," he wrote in *Entrée des médiums*, "my attention was focused on the more or less fragmentary sentences, which in complete solitude, on the approach of sleep, become perceptible to the mind without it being possible to discover any previous motivation for them. These sentences, full of remarkable imagery and with an impeccable syntax, struck me as being poetic elements of the first order . . . It was later that Soupault and I thought of deliberately reproducing in ourselves the state in which they had taken shape."

The experiments which Breton and Soupault carried out (for six to eight days according to the former, for a fortnight according to the latter) for eight or ten hours at a time, possibly more, daily and separately, differed from the procedures worked out by Tzara in Zurich.

Tzara and his friends, painters, sculptors, photographers and filmmakers, had intervened actively, cutting up, mounting and pasting things together physically and concretely (down to the crude and deliberately spectacular method of picking words out of a hat), and thereby attained a level of abstraction verging, to use Picasso's famous expression, "on the highest pitch of reality." André Breton, for his part, was intent on suggesting the existence of an unconscious infra-language, whose "impeccable syntax" amazed him and from which he elicited "the poetic images of the first order" concealed within it.

To the "exploration of the night and unfathomed depths . . . where terrors and wonders would have turned the head of a lone man and sent him reeling

into the abyss" (Aragon on *Les Champs magnétiques*), to this fascination due to the resolutely literary preferences of the young Parisian poets, the Dada groups in Zurich, Berlin and Hanover opposed in broad daylight, by way of the materiality of actual picture making, their bold manipulation of a reality whose syntax, "impeccable" or not, seemed to them quite arbitrary and certainly less convincing than those which they recreated and opposed to it.

The young writers of *Littérature*, still under the spell of Valéry and Barrès, had not acquired the determination and liberty that the painters were used to. As poets, they were more attracted by the interweaving of visual and narrative sequences, a metaphorical process as practised by Max Ernst (whose works they welcomed to Paris in the spring of 1921), than they ever would be by the work of Picabia or the German and American Dadaists. Echoes of these Dadaists' activities did reach them, but only in a muffled and sporadic way, probably because they were not really interested in them.

In this context, the satisfying results of *Les Champs magnétiques* acted as a creative liberating experience and freed its authors from the stock procedures on which, as writers, they had formerly been dependent. When the moment of Surrealism came, Breton and Soupault justly used this experience as an argument to claim a distinct approach of their own antedating the Dada activities into which they had thereafter thrown themselves under the influence of Tristan Tzara.

The creation of the review *Littérature* in March 1919 (by Breton at the Hôtel des Grands Hommes) and the writing of the *Champs* marked off a new area in the literary world of Paris in which the various artistic tendencies present since Tristan Tzara's arrival were now to confront each other.

The adventure of Dada in Paris was enacted from the outset in the field of literature, and in the polemics, always decisive in the French capital, which sprang up between the Dadaists and the literary establishment. Disagreements with the *Nouvelle Revue Française*, with Gide (remember the apocryphal Gide-Cravan conversations), with Jacques Rivière (the *Open Letter to Jacques Rivière* sent from Zurich by Tzara before his arrival), the Barrès "trial" organized by Dada, the plays by Georges Ribemont-Dessaignes (*L'Empereur de Chine*), the questionnaires ("Why do you write?"), the opposition to the Futurist Marinetti, the manifestoes and clarifying or challenging statements: all this punctuated a sustained poetic effervescence throughout these years.

André Breton, Paul Eluard, Tristan Tzara, and Benjamin Péret at the time they were editing the periodical Littérature, *1922*

In the space of a few months appeared works by Tzara (*Cinéma calendrier du cœur abstrait. Maisons, Le Cœur à gaz*), Ribemont-Dessaignes (*L'Empereur de Chine, Le Serin muet*), Picabia (*Pensées sans langage, Unique Eunuque, Jésus-Christ Rastaquouère*), Aragon (*Feu de joie, Le Mouvement perpétuel*), André Breton (*Mont de Piété, Les Champs magnétiques, S'il vous plaît*), Philippe Soupault (*Rose des vents, Westwego*), Clément Pansaers (*Bar Nicanor*), Paul Eluard (*Les Animaux et leurs Hommes, Les Malheurs des immortels*), Benjamin Péret (*Le Passager du Transatlantique*), Serge Charchoune (*Foule immobile*), Paul Dermée (*Films, Le Volant d'Artimon*) and Céline Arnauld (*Poèmes à claires-voies, Point de mire, Guêpier de diamants*). They profoundly transformed French poetry, sweeping it up and recasting it in both aesthetic and ideological terms.

Tzara-Dada headquarters at Picabia's:
for action, against literature and art

As soon as Tzara arrived in the early days of January 1920, Picabia's flat in the Rue Emile-Augier became Dada headquarters. As Picabia's guest, Tzara soon set things moving. With Breton, he at once transformed an already planned meeting of *Littérature* (January) into a Dada matinée. He improvised a Dada evening at the Salon des Indépendants in the Grand Palais des Champs-Elysées (February). In March the first Dada plays were put on at the Théâtre de l'Œuvre (under the management of Lugné-Poe), beginning with a performance of *Le Serin muet* by Georges Ribemont-Dessaignes.

After that, one thing followed another throughout 1920. In April, a Picabia exhibition at the Au Sans Pareil gallery, where he showed some twenty works without attracting much attention (including *Very Rare Picture on Earth*); and the appearance, on Picabia's initiative, of the review *Cannibale* ("with the collaboration of all the Dadaists in the world"). In May, the Dada Festival at the Salle Gaveau, the wildest of the Dada manifestations in Paris, unleashed a wave of general protest.

Things slowed down as summer approached. In August Tristan Tzara went on a trip which took him first to the scene of the "original sin" in Zurich, then to Bucharest, Athens, Istanbul, Naples and finally back to Zurich. The end of 1920 was marked by another Paris exhibition of Picabia's work at Povolozky's gallery La Cible, during which Tzara read two scintillating manifestoes, *Manifesto on Feeble Love and Bitter Love* and *How I became charming, delightful and delicious.*

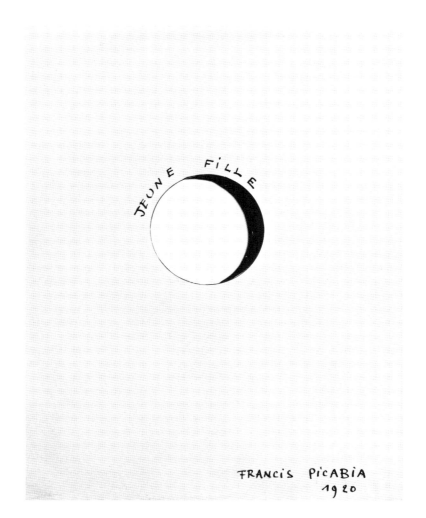

Francis Picabia: *Young Girl, 1920*

Some of the contributors to 391, *Paris, 1921.*
In front, left to right: Tristan Tzara, Céline Arnauld, Francis Picabia, André Breton (with glasses). Behind, left to right: Louis Aragon, Paul Dermée, Théodore Fraenkel, Philippe Soupault, Paul Eluard, Georges Ribemont-Dessaignes, Clément Pansaers

The door of the next room opened and in came a small dark-haired man who took three brisk steps forward, then stopped, and we realized that he was short-sighted. It was Tzara I had come to see, but never having imagined him in this shape, a young Japanese with eyeglasses, I faltered for a moment and so did he. Here he is, then, this agitator whom we have called to Paris, the man who in his photograph with leather gloves looked like Jacques Vaché, the man whose poetry was commonly likened to that of Rimbaud (and that was saying a lot). His elbows held to his body, his delicate hands half-open at the end of horizontal forearms, he had something of the air of a night bird frightened by daylight with his lock of dark hair falling over his eyes. A very pretty fellow, one thinks at first, but after two minutes' talk his burst of laughter disfigures him, shaking down from the parting a tuft of hair cleaving the face. How ugly he is! A certain stupor after laughing restores that Oriental finesse to the deathly pale face, whose whole flame has withdrawn into the dark and very fine gaze. At that time, on his arrival in Paris, he spoke French rather slowly, rather incorrectly, with a very pronounced Rumanian accent: I remember that he said Dàdà, the two a's very short, and that it was Théodore Fraenkel who taught him to say Dada as we do here.

Louis Aragon, about 1923

RAHAT-LOUKOUMS

I've got troubles,
The downward path is steep and bare,
The rebounds look petticoatless over the sea
To hug me voluptuously like a bouquet
It puts to sleep my little opium tears
Infinite science, mandarin moon man
There's my kite-like garment of frozen honey.
I wrote it on the converted bed of the summer months
That to coddle one's breasts several times over
In the closed museum
Under bunched up clothes
Turns into makeup on a clock.
The cross of alcohol with blue poetic chin
Reveals a fence of lanterns to me,
Redoubtable volte-face
Of the dancer on the platform floor
In the silent unexpectedness of an empty lane
I am on the mountain of women proudly
Sculptured up to the eyes.

Francis Picabia, 1918

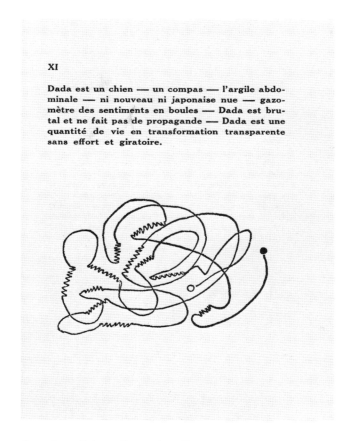

Page from Tristan Tzara's Manifesto on Feeble Love and Bitter Love, *with a Picabia drawing, 1920*

Francis Picabia: *St. Vitus' Dance (Tobacco-Rat), 1919*

With almost premonitory clairvoyance Tzara seized the opportunity of a forthcoming lecture by Marinetti to settle some old scores with the Italian Futurists, who were too often lumped together with Dada by journalists incapable of making any distinction:

> Is poetry necessary? I know that those who write most violently against it unconsciously desire to endow it with a comfortable perfection...; they call this hygienic future.

Here the allusion was obviously to Marinetti's manifesto (*War the world's one hygiene*). The "comfortable perfection" already refers to the armchair awaiting Marinetti in the Royal Italian Academy to be founded by Mussolini.

On January 12, 1921, the day of the lecture on tactile art given by Marinetti at the Théâtre de l'Œuvre, the Dada group published a tract entitled *Dada stirs up everything* to dissociate themselves yet again and quite unequivocally from the Futurist school and its leader. It will be remembered that Cravan, too, had warned critics who were tempted to confuse his review with a Futurist flourish. With the help of effective well-designed typography and giving the contents a lighter note through simplicity and irony, Dada totally rejected Marinetti's nationalism and drew up an inventory of the paraphernalia of Futurist *idées fixes* ("Italy, the Fatherland, sardines, Fiume, d'Annunzio, heroism, moustaches, lechery, the past, smells, genius genius genius, ladies' trousers"). For the benefit of the amused reader, in case he got lost in the labyrinth of arguments, the tract ended by stating frankly:

> One is presented today in pornographic form with a vulgar and baroque spirit which is not the pure idiocy called for by Dada, but dogmatism and pretentious imbecility!

On the day of Marinetti's lecture, the Dada group, delighted for once to find themselves in the role of a public called on to show its clamorous disapproval, turned up in full force at the Théâtre de l'Œuvre to disrupt, under the benevolent eyes of Lugné-Poe, the lecture given by the leader of the Futurists. Marinetti delivered it as best he could, an old campaigner even though upset by the agitation. He walked about placidly, puffing away at cigarettes during the interruptions. From time to time, not short of repartee or wit, he apostrophized the Dadaists and argued with them.

On the subject of his tactile tables made of rough, warm, prickly materials, or cool and smooth fabrics, Picabia published a warning against Marinetti in *Comoedia*, asserting that the invention of tactilism should be attributed to an American artist, Miss Clifford-Williams.

This series of spectacular manifestations characterized the movement in Paris from the first weeks of 1920, coming as the natural sequel to the antics of the Dada soirées in Zurich. Although the highly charged climate of wartime Zurich had had its day, it fell to Tzara alone, its exporter/instigator, to keep it going in Paris. There the intellectual climate was different because his new friends, the founders of *Littérature*, Aragon, Breton and Soupault, as well as Ribemont-Dessaignes and Eluard, were dependent on literary ideas from which they were only beginning to free themselves, in this quite unlike the Zurich Dadaists, radicalized by their close contacts with new pictorial practices and an unrivaled knowledge of abstract painting.

Kandinsky, *Der Sturm*, Arp, Van Rees and Segal were familiar to the Zurich Dadaists and not only gave writers the freedom to use daring poetic methods (such as the simultaneous, static, "bruitist" poems of Richard Huelsenbeck, the abstract sound poems of Hugo Ball, and Tzara's *poèmes nègres*), but also partially impressed their theoretical orientation on the Dada manifestoes issued in Zurich (Tzara, Serner) and Berlin (Huelsenbeck).

In Paris the cosmopolitan climate and attraction to artistic and literary innovations characteristic of the pre-war period, had been replaced by a conservative withdrawal and a sometimes overwrought hostility to moder-nity, from which Apollinaire, to mention only one artist, had suffered a great deal. This new context would go some way to explain Breton's attempt at the beginning of 1922 to organize an International Congress for the Determination of Directives and for the Defense of the Modern Spirit.

From then on, the Parisian manifestations acquired a different tone from the evenings at the Cabaret Voltaire in Zurich. They were less subversive on the artistic level, less pregnant with an immediate vital urgency, depending more on the literary scene. Their audacity was first asserted when it came to methods of provocation in the face of a reactionary environment, an attitude which foreshadowed the revolutionary problematics of the future Surrealist group (and also heralded the stock figure of the French left-wing intellectual of later years). The mock trial of Maurice Barrès significantly separated the original Dadaists from the members of *Littérature*.

For the time being, however, their public attitude obviously betrayed a common desire to prevent their works from being annexed, absorbed or diverted from their force of protest by way of a purely aesthetic interpretation or, at least, to put off such a fate as long as possible both by the writing itself and by the behavior of the author; and on this level the Dada manifestations proved very useful.

In front, left to right: Paul Eluard, Jacques Rigaut, Mick Soupault, Georges Ribemont-Dessaignes; behind, left to right, Paul Chadourne, Tristan Tzara, Philippe Soupault, Serge Charchoune, photographed by Man Ray, Paris, 1921

Georges Ribemont-Dessaignes: *The Oceanic Spirit, 1918*

Poster for the Dada Festival, Gaveau Hall, Paris, May 26, 1920

"We are at the Dada Festival," a journalist wrote. "The eyes of all these people are gleaming impatiently and their feet are tapping nervously. They are expecting a treat, and a tasty one." In the audience were Gide, Romains, Vildrac, Duhamel, Allard, Valéry, Rivière and Copeau representing the *NRF*; Rachilde, Paul Léautaud and Fontainas representing the *Mercure de France*, as well as Barzun, Natalie Barney, Gleizes, Metzinger, Léger, Dorgelès, Mercereau, Paul Souday, Poiret, Bernouard and Barthou. At the entrance, a certain Léon Brulot, attorney general at the Supreme Court of Appeal, tried in vain to get in and, when he got home, sent his card to Francis Picabia. "I had to give up elbowing my way through the crowd in the presence of ladies," he wrote, "and I withdrew full of respect for such well organized disorder. Was this obstruction also Dada?"

On the same occasion, Georges Ribemont-Dessaignes performed the "frontier dance" wrapped in a large cardboard funnel oscillating on its tip. Tzara's *Symphonic Vaseline* was played by twenty persons. "Its performance had been the cause of some inner group difficulties," Ribemont-Dessaignes wrote in *Déjà jadis.* "Unmusical as it was, it aroused the manifest wrath of André Breton, who hated music for one thing and for another was not very proud of being reduced to the role of an interpreter, in this case as an instrumentalist or member of the choir."

A sketch by Breton and Soupault, *Vous m'oublierez* (You Will Forget Me), a *Système DD* by Louis Aragon, and some acts put on by Picabia, Dermée, Arnauld and Eluard completed the session. A fashionable foxtrot, the Pelican, was played on the Salle Gaveau organs, which were more accustomed to the strains of Bach.

*Eluard (above), Soupault (on all fours), Breton (seated)
and Fraenkel during a performance of* You Will Forget Me,
*a vaudeville sketch by Breton and Soupault, at the
Dada Festival, Paris, 1920*

The Dada Festival

The Dada Festival, the main Parisian demonstration, was held at the Salle Gaveau, Rue La Boétie, on Wednesday, May 26, 1920. This event brought the movement widespread publicity within a few hours. Indeed, just as Dada was being violently attacked and mocked in the press, the group's audacity and humor won for it an intellectual and social success which cut a bright swathe through the drab post-war climate.

The universal stir that Dada created in Paris can only be understood when we remember that *Littérature* and *391* had at once aroused the attention, if not the envy, of the world of letters, which tried on several occasions to separate the good literary wheat from the Dadaist tares. Gide, and most of all Jacques Rivière in a full-dress essay ("Recognition to Dada") published in the *Nouvelle Revue Française* in August 1920, a few weeks after the Festival at the Salle Gaveau, awarded the good points.

On the occasion of the Festival, *Littérature* published a number containing the "Twenty-three Manifestoes of the Dada Movement." The authors included both the founding members from Zurich (Arp, Tzara, Serner) and the Parisian Dadaists (Aragon, Céline Arnauld, Breton, Dermée, Soupault, Eluard), as well as the para-Dadaist American collector Walter Arensberg, whose manifesto was entitled *Dada is American*.

Théodore Fraenkel: *The Death of the Pope in Ice-Skating Land, 1920*

Francis Picabia's Dada Cannibal Manifesto
as published in Dadaphone, *No. 7, Paris, March 1920*

MANIFESTE CANNIBALE DADA

Vous êtes tous accusés : levez-vous. L'orateur ne peut vous parler que si vous êtes debout.

Debout comme pour la Marseillaise,

debout comme pour l'hymne russe,

debout comme pour le God save the king,

debout comme devant le drapeau.

Enfin debout devant DADA qui représente la vie et qui vous accuse de tout aimer par snobisme. du moment que cela coûte cher.

Vous vous êtes tous rassis ? Tant mieux, comme cela vous allez m'écouter avec plus d'attention.

Que faites vous ici, parqués comme des huîtres sérieuses — car vous êtes sérieux n'est-ce pas ?

Sérieux, sérieux, sérieux jusqu'à la mort.

La mort est une chose sérieuse, hein ?

On meurt en héros, ou en idiot ce qui est la même chose. Le seul mot qui ne soit pas éphémère c'est le mot mort. Vous aimez la mort pour les autres.

A mort, à mort, à mort.

Il n'y a que l'argent qui ne meurt pas, il part seulement en voyage.

C'est le Dieu, celui que l'on respecte, le personnage sérieux — argent respect des familles. Honneur, honneur à l'argent ; l'homme qui a de l'argent est un homme honorable.

L'honneur s'achète et se vend comme le cul. Le cul, le cul représente la vie comme les pommes frites, et vous tous qui êtes sérieux, vous sentirez plus mauvais que la merde de vache.

DADA lui ne sent rien, il n'est rien, rien, rien.

Il est comme vos espoirs : rien.

comme vos paradis : rien

comme vos idoles : rien

comme vos hommes politiques : rien

comme vos héros : rien

comme vos artistes : rien

comme vos religions : rien

Sifflez, criez, cassez-moi la gueule et puis, et puis ? Je vous dirai encore que vous êtes tous des poires. Dans trois mois nous vous vendrons, mes amis et moi, nos tableaux pour quelques francs.

Francis PICABIA.

Dada and the press

The newspapers had a field day. The press involuntarily proved to be one of the active promoters of Dada, but the Dadaists, who had taken the initiative, kept one length ahead. From Zurich, Tzara had already written to Picabia: "I imagine that idiocy is the same everywhere since there are journalists everywhere." The Dadaists were amused by hostile criticisms. They used them, pulled them to pieces, even anticipated them by parodies, so ensuring for themselves an unprecedented polemical position.

The press played very much the same role as the public during manifestations or as the critics reacting to the works. The headlines reflect the incomprehension and mixed-up attitudes of the period: "Dada boche, the modern Trojan horse" (*Le Phare*, Nantes, April 26, 1920), "Dadaism, a gentle madness" (*L'Avenir du Puy-de-Dôme*, May 29), "Dada and suckers" (*La France*, May 27), "Dada or the triumph of nothing" (*L'Echo de Paris*, May 27, J.N. Faure-Biguet), "Wits and half-wits" (*La Liberté*, May 30), "The Gagas" (*L'Echo de Paris*, May 30, signed AB) and "Herr Dada" (*Les Nouvelles*, Bordeaux, May 30). *Le Petit Parisien*, annoyed at the goings-on, complained: "DADA. They bellowed, they miaowed, they barked, but they didn't have their hair cut." And *L'Eclair* added: "The Dadaists who undertook to have their hair cut while on stage, according to their poster, cynically broke their promise. We, however, were cut to the heart with boredom. The show began with a performance by a highly esteemed Dadaist, Philippe Soupault (the turn was called 'The Celebrated Illusionist'). He appeared on stage as a negro wearing a white smock and carrying an enormous knife. The doorman of the Salle Gaveau followed, with a trunk on his shoulder. We all know this set-up which nearly always accompanies circus turns, such as clowns or conjurers. Well, Philippe Soupault is neither; he's a literary man, so it seems. After opening the trunk, he took out five small red balloons which he released after baptising them with well-known names: Rachilde, Clemenceau, Pétain, Benedict XV and Jean Cocteau. But he burst the Cocteau balloon violently with his knife as a sign of contempt. For Jean Cocteau is said to be a renegade Dadaist, hence Philippe Soupault's great rage. Incidentally, the show was much more amusing in the hall than on the stage. People were laughing and singing; they interrupted the impassive Dadaists; they hurled various missiles at them such as peach stones, bread rolls and rotten eggs."

The Dadaists were also dismissed as facetious undertakers' mutes (*Le Carnet de la Semaine*, June 6, 1920), while the *New York Courier* (May 29, 1920) exclaimed: "This is madness! Will the world end up in a gigantic padded cell?"

A common tactic in Paris was to put the movement down as a plot hatched by the enemy, Germany, intended to undermine French culture from within. Even a prominent literary magazine like the *Mercure de France* followed this line. In March 1920 a certain Henri Albert had no qualms about writing in its columns: "Even though the Germans confess that they took the word Expressionism from France, while twisting its meaning, they can rightly claim that they fathered Dadaism, for it was devised in 1917 by German refugees in Zurich..." One might suppose that Germans who refused to bear arms against France and met in the name of Voltaire would have been congenial to an editor of the *Mercure*, but he went on: "...German refugees in Zurich intent on escaping the many annoyances of the war, unfit for military service or absentee conscripts, with shattered nerves, who hoped to restore their health by imitating the baby talk of early childhood. Apollinaire who was fond of mystification was amused by these eccentricities and lent his support."

Although the poet died as the result of his war wounds, Apollinaire's memory was not respected by the *Mercure*'s editors, Vallette and Rachilde. To them Apollinaire's friends were "dagos, Cubists, Bolshevists, Dadaists and other kinds of Boches." Rachilde, a popular woman-novelist, was not afraid of saying privately: "They bore us with their Apollinaire. As for me, when he died, that suited me. I said: so much the better. We're well rid of him."

At the same time, Rachilde had dreamt of doing away with Picabia: "It's very simple," she wrote to him on January 20, 1921, "I felt like killing you."

Georges Ribemont-Dessaignes in 1922

André Breton and Paul Eluard disguised, at the
Au Sans Pareil bookshop and gallery, Paris, early 1920s

André Breton in uniform, 1918

René Crevel, Tristan Tzara, and Jacques Baron, 1924

*We were a group of young men, I say young men rather than writers
and artists, although we were that too, roughly speaking, because there
were several among us who in our eyes owed their glory to the fact that
they did not write, or did not paint, or did not compose, as if that were
not the most widespread thing on earth. We were a group of young
men brought together chiefly by the love of excess in everything. It so
happened however that most of us did write or paint, as if from
weakness it would seem, one apologized for it, or one pleaded each
time that it was all for the sake of novelty, of raising the stakes, of
defiance, of scandal. It seemed at each occurrence that the thing had
been done for the last time. And we contrived to believe it. And yet we
very naturally took that weakness, that defiance, that scandal, as being
the purpose of that group, which denied having any purpose, and that
group would take as its cue or stalking-horse a book, a poem, a show, a
picture, and would defend them not only by speech and writing, but
also with their fists and canes.*

Louis Aragon, about 1942-1945

Louis Aragon in Dadaphone, *No. 7, Paris, March 1920*

Notebook of Dr. Serner in 391,
No. 11, Paris, February 1920

Paul Dermée in Dadaphone, *No. 7, Paris, March 1920*

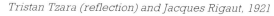

Tristan Tzara (reflection) and Jacques Rigaut, 1921

The Paris Dada Group in unknown circumstances, undated

The most decided hostility came from the Cubist painters, who before the war had already refused Marcel Duchamp's *Nude Descending a Staircase* (see Chapter 1). After inviting Dada to take part in a re-edition of the celebrated pre-war Section d'Or exhibition (October 1912, Galerie La Boétie), the Cubists hastened to exclude the Dadaists at a rowdy meeting held at the Closerie des Lilas café in February 1920. Albert Gleizes, a major figure in Cubist circles, stepped into the front line in "The Dada Affair," an article published by the review *Action*: "Sometimes even the pathological case suddenly becomes apparent. We constantly find their brains haunted by a sexsual (*sic*) delirium and a scatological appetite. The taint appears in all its amplitude... They are obsessed with the organs of reproduction."

Picabia, never shy or behindhand, replied: "It does not surprise us that he has written 'The Dada Affair.' Everything is affairs to this gentleman! During the war, while in Spain, he wanted to become a naturalized German, but it was his wife, more far-sighted, who advised him to wait... Today, a trumpery revolutionary socialist, he throws over his petty bourgeois family of Courbevoie, but finds it convenient enough to marry the great Dada Bourgeoisie with whom he is not even capable of having children!... His sexual apparatus, as he so elegantly calls it, what can he use it for? Doubtless to construct aquatic Cubism! You are a great constructor, Monsieur the Leader of Cubism, but your brain-stuffing antics only catch on with fools."

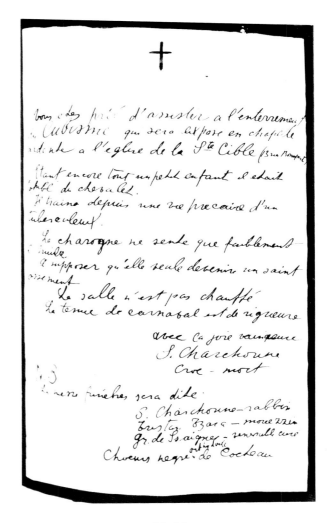

Invitation to the funeral of Cubism written by Serge Charchoune, 1920

Serge Charchoune: *Ornamental Cubism No. 26B, c. 1922*

" L'Affaire Dada "

Ça ne nous étonne pas qu'il ait écrit " l'Affaire Dada ". Tout est affaires pour ce Monsieur !

Pendant la guerre, étant en Espagne, il voulait se faire naturaliser Allemand, c'est sa femme, plus clairvoyante, qui lui donna le conseil d'attendre.....

Aujourd'hui, socialiste révolutionnaire à la mie de pain, il renie sa famille, petite bourgeoisie de Courbevoie, mais trouve assez commode d'avoir épousé la Grande bourgeoisie Dada, avec laquelle il n'est pas même capable de faire des enfants !

Son appareil sexuel, ainsi qu'il le nomme si élégamment, à quoi peut-il bien lui servir ? Sans nul doute à construire du cubisme aquatique !

Vous êtes un grand constructeur, Monsieur le chef du cubisme, ~~c'est une erreur, le laisser tel que~~, mais votre bourrage de crânes ne prend qu'auprès des imbéciles.

Francis PICABIA
l'intoxiqué

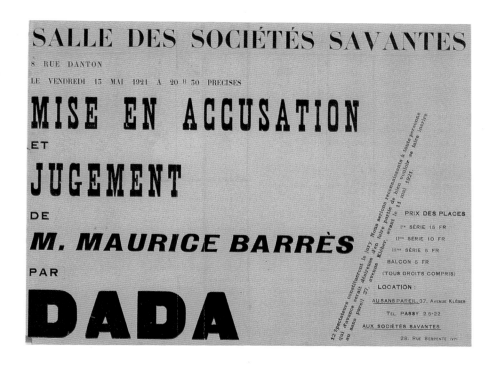

*Maurice Barrès as a member
of the Académie française*

*Invitation to the "Committal for Trial and Sentencing
of Mr. Maurice Barrès by Dada," Paris, 1921*

The trial of Maurice Barrès

Nothing testifies better to the tangle of contradictory feelings and to the hasty action provoked by Dada in the development of the *Littérature* group than the "trial" of Maurice Barrès in the spring of 1921, although even in 1919 Breton had asked him to write the preface to Jacques Vaché's *Lettres de guerre* (War Letters).

In the same year, 1921, when the German Dadaists were appearing in court in Berlin to defend their exhibition of the previous year, the Dada Movement in Paris was balancing things out by accusing Maurice Barrès of a "criminal attempt against the security of the spirit." Each in its own way, the two trials were a parody of justice. The first, an unintentional parody, was held quite legally by the German State. The second, on the other hand, was meant to be a mockery (notifications, posters, writing up of the record of the trial), while at times proceeding almost like an actual trial. It caused a split among the Dadaists.

Although ever fond of provocation, the "genuine" Dadaists such as Tzara, Picabia, Ribemont-Dessaignes, Satie and Pansaers were against the idea of a revolutionary tribunal. Breton, on the other hand, liked the idea. This difference of opinion deepened the cleavages now opening up, later to have far-reaching effects. The novelist Maurice Barrès (1862-1923), an anarcho-socialist in his youth, had turned into an ardent nationalist and royalist. His changes of political color preoccupied Breton who, as a young writer, saw him as a renegade betraying the revolutionary ideals. Tzara, however, could not see in Barrès the moral and aesthetic importance that Breton attached to him. This divergence between Tzara and Breton over the French cultural heritage became an open break in February 1922 over the question of the Paris Congress (never held). For the time being, differences were glossed over and the Dadaists entered into the spirit of the game, even though it disclosed their own contradictions.

For the actors, the mock trial of Barrès was both a courtroom stage play and a group psychodrama. Breton was cast as the judge, Ribemont-Dessaignes as a very singular public prosecutor; Aragon (who had had the idea of the trial) was counsel for the defense, together with Soupault. Witnesses: Serge Romoff, the Italian poet Giuseppe Ungaretti, Rachilde, Jacques Rigaut (who refused to be sworn in) and Pierre Drieu La Rochelle. To add to the fun, Benjamin Péret burst into the room as the unknown soldier wearing a gas mask (a reminiscence of the Dada Fair in Berlin?) and interrupted the hearing, speaking in German. The fact that he wore a German uniform added a sarcastic note to the polemics which had divided France a few weeks before over the question of interring an unknown soldier beneath the Arc de Triomphe.

The committal of Barrès was thus turned into a short masterpiece of shrewd Dada dialogue, an anthology piece of Dada humor and critical sagacity. Tzara outdid himself. Mischievously choosing the double-faced role of simple "witness," he electrified the hearing and, as later at the Weimar Constructivist Congress (September 1922), he kept things from getting too serious, thanks to a polemical virtuosity in which mockery vied with dialectical skill:

> I have no confidence in justice, even if the justice is done by Dada. You will agree with me, Your Honor, he said, addressing Breton, that we are all a bunch of scoundrels and that consequently minor differences —whether we're bigger or smaller scoundrels—don't much matter ...
> I declared at the beginning of my testimony that I knew nothing about Barrès, but I still possess the minimum of demagogy necessary to know that Barrès acted out of low-down demagogy. I wish to make it clear that I know absolutely nothing about what went on inside Barrès, but I consider that he is a good-natured chap and it is a great pleasure for me to state that, in spite of the defensible actions in his life, Monsieur Barrès is still the biggest swine of the century.

After a few exchanges during which Breton was losing control of the trial, he offered Tzara a last chance: "Is the witness trying to pass himself off as an utter fool or does he hope to get himself interned?" Tzara was unabashed: "Yes, I am trying to pass for an utter fool and I am not trying to escape from the lunatic asylum in which I spend my life."

At the very time when the court usher was stepping up to ask in a loud clear voice "Are you there, Barrès?", *Littérature* tells us that Barrès himself, the superpatriot, "was making a speech in Aix-en-Provence about the French soul during the war. A few young provincials were listening open-mouthed to the Academician and Deputy from Paris."

*Left to right: Aragon, unidentified man, Breton, Tzara, Soupault,
Fraenkel, Barrès (a dummy), Ribemont-Dessaignes, Péret,
Rigaut, Hilsum and Charchoune during the mock trial
of the nationalist writer Maurice Barrès, Paris, May 13, 1921*

Dada, its birth, life and death

ÇA IRA

DADA
SA NAISSANCE, SA VIE, SA MORT

COLLABORATIONS DE :

CÉLINE ARNAULD, PIERRE ALBERT BIROT,
CHRISTIAN, JEAN CROTTI, PAUL ELUARD, PIERRE
DE MASSOT, CLÉMENT PANSAERS, BENJAMIN PÉRET,
FRANCIS PICABIA, EZRA POUND, G. RIBEMONT-
DESSAIGNES, RENÉE DUNAN.

PRIX : 1 Fr. 50   N° 16

The Barrès trial only brought to light divergences that had already appeared in other circumstances, notably at the time of the "liquidation-questionnaire" conducted by *Littérature* a few weeks earlier, in March. It consisted in giving marks to about 190 celebrities, from Alcibiades to Zola, by way of the Dadaists, the members of the review, some politicians and the great names in Art and Letters (Berlioz, Chateaubriand, Dante, Dostoyevsky, Maeterlinck, Nietzsche, Sade, Saint-John Perse, Whitman). Although the questionnaire was preceded by a disclaimer ("We find this scholastic method rather ridiculous . . . we are not proposing a new order of values, our aim being, not to classify, but to declassify"), the review had established a scale of preferences, for all that. Conducted with a master's hand by Breton who won some authority as a result, this poll did in fact create a scale of values that was likely to be more acceptable because it was the product of the electoral process. Among the names that came out on top were Breton, Soupault, Charlie Chaplin, Rimbaud, Eluard, Ducasse, Aragon, Tzara, Jarry, Rigaut, Ribemont-Dessaignes, Apollinaire, Arp, Vaché, the writer of the Pink Pills advertisement and the Marquis de Sade.

Obviously the dynamic acceleration of cultural particles set off by Dada did not allow it to "acknowledge receipt" of historical culture en bloc and then proceed to such a classification of values, at least not for the reasons invoked by the members of *Littérature*. Dada kept integrating and

*Cover of Ça ira, Antwerp, 1921, featuring
"Dada, Its Birth, Life, and Death"*

Paul Joostens: *Propellor, c. 1919-1920*

disintegrating this cultural heritage. For Tzara, there was no point in choosing or evaluating and still less in handing out good or bad marks to a cultural past that he had rejected. Nevertheless, he did take part, generally adding a rider to his marks "with the greatest aversion" to show how inappropriate he found the process of assessment. The poll had also annoyed Picabia, who wanted no part in it and showed his disapproval at the Barrès trial by ostentatiously walking out of the room.

Lastly, the "liquidation-questionnaire," only too well named by the review, isolated Dada within the *Littérature* group. If we except Tzara himself, who was high up in the final classification, such outstanding Dada experimenters and inventors as Man Ray, or Picabia himself who embodied the first Dada generation, were visibly underestimated by the younger members of *Littérature*.

So the first dissensions became public and split the Dadaists into three groups, crystallized around Tzara, Picabia and Breton respectively.

Things were brought to a head by the "wallet affair" (a dispute over a wallet lost by a waiter at the Café Certà). As a result, Clément Pansaers broke with the group and went on to what he called "the assassination of Dada" in a special number of the Antwerp review *Ça ira* entitled "Dada, its birth, life and death" (November 1921).

This Antwerp magazine, and its editor in particular, Paul Neuhuys (*Le Zèbre handicapé*, 1923), had felt the influence of Paris Dada in its full force, chiefly by way of Pascal Pia and Pansaers himself. In Antwerp, too, working in isolation, Paul Joostens also looked to Dada for inspiration, without ever joining the movement. An exacting artist, he made collages (*Propellor*), paintings, and Constructivist-Dadaist reliefs (*Construction*). So it was that, through Clément Pansaers, it fell to the review *Ça ira* to record the passing of Dada in Paris.

Picabia for his part, irked by the Barrès trial and impressed by the freedom and spontaneity shown by Pansaers in standing up to Breton, followed his example and at once published an outspoken article in the Paris magazine *Comoedia*. In it he scoffed, not at Dada, but at what Aragon, Breton, Soupault and their friends were making of it: "Now Dada has a law court, lawyers and probably quite soon police and a Monsieur Deibler . . ." (Deibler was the name of the public executioner!)

Paul Joostens: *Construction, 1920*

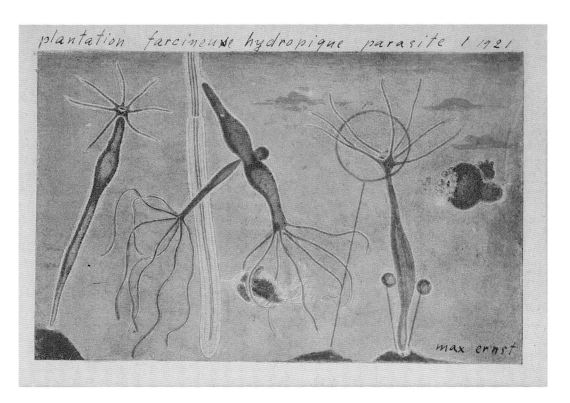

Max Ernst: *Farcied Hydropic Parasitic Plantation, 1921*

Cover of the review Proverbe, *Paris,*
February 1, 1920, edited by Paul Eluard

From the street, unaccountably, one could hear caterwauling, frenzied words, a distant barking, coming from the bookshop.
I go in. I come across little Tristan Tzara, his black shock of hair with the parting on the left, one lock falling over the right eye where gleamed the monocle of a Rumanian aesthete, with his stiff, broken-edged collar bereft of a tie, offering his white-gloved hands to everyone around him, and laughing! outbursts of laughter from that broad thick mouth of his. One Dada hidden in a closet insulted the guests as they arrived, calling them out by name. André Breton, solemn and priestly, was sucking matchsticks. The caterwauling got louder than ever, from mischievous little devils who popped up all of a sudden from the basement. Other Dadas were shaking hands and parting, only to seize each other's hands again and go on shaking and shaking them. An owl made itself heard, then several of them, hooting at André Gide who swallowed down his laugh of surprise, and stood there dazed; but pulling himself together he made a gesture of regal indulgence and came forward undismayed with his nephew Marc Allégret. Philippe Soupault, Breton and Tzara greeted him now, bowing down to his feet, then left him there to go off and play hide-and-seek.

Maurice Martin du Gard, 1957

Cover of the review Projecteur, *Paris,*
May 21, 1920, edited by Céline Arnauld

Dada Max Ernst in Paris

Max Ernst's first exhibition in Paris was held a few days after the Barrès trial. In the same way as many new Dada or Dada-inspired reviews were coming out on their own (*Proverbe, Projecteur, Z, Le Coq, Aventure*), without relying on any official or commercial support (publishing houses and collections), so the Dadaists never sought out, nor did they reject, the backing of artistic circles (exhibiting in a gallery). They exhibited in any premises they were allowed to use with freedom.

André Breton, Philippe Soupault, Jacques Rigaut, Benjamin Péret,
and Serge Charchoune outside the Au Sans Pareil bookshop,
Paris, during the Max Ernst exhibition, May-June 1921

René Hilsum, Benjamin Péret, Serge Charchoune, Philippe Soupault (top, with bicycle), Jacques Rigaut (upside down) and André Breton outside the Au Sans Pareil bookshop, Paris, during the Max Ernst exhibition, May-June 1921

Francis Picabia: *Rastadada Picture, 1920*

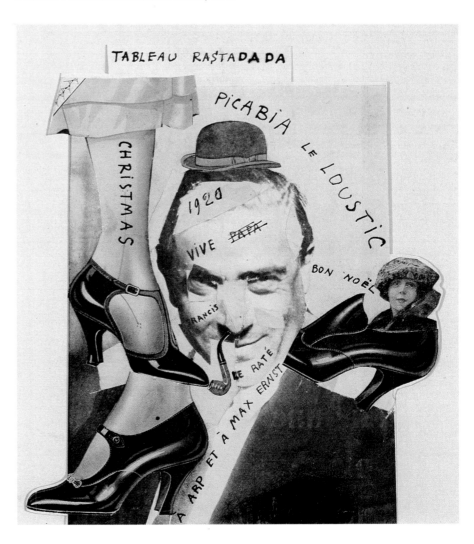

As a result, the Max Ernst Dada exhibition was held in the Au Sans Pareil bookshop in the spring of 1921, just as the Six bookshop would welcome Man Ray's works at the end of the year, shortly after his arrival in Paris.

In the exhibition, which Ernst himself called "La mise sous whisky marin" (Setting under Sea Whisky), figured such small-scale works as he was able to send in from Germany, numbered with bus tickets, among them 42 Painto-paintings, 8 drawings, including the *Plantation farcineuse hydropique parasite*, as well as 4 Fatagagas (abbreviation of "fabrication de tableaux garantis gazométriques") and a sculpture. The exhibition sparked off André Breton's first attempt at art criticism, with a title suggested by Ernst, and produced a "happening" improvised to pay homage to the painter in his absence. (He was held up in Germany owing to red-tape when applying for a visa.)

The private view at the Au Sans Pareil has left a few traces in the annals of the period. We are indebted for them to the pen of Maurice Martin du Gard and some photographs showing, before the austere shop front in the 16th arrondissement, Philippe Soupault perched on top of a ladder with a bicycle and holding the feet of Jacques Rigaut, who is upside down, surrounded by Breton (to the right, on the first rung) and on the left by René Hilsum (school-mate of Breton's at the Lycée Chaptal and founder of the small Au Sans Pareil publishing unit), Benjamin Péret and the Russian Dadaist Serge Charchoune.

The initiative behind the exhibition has sometimes been attributed to the *Littérature* group, in an attempt to counteract Picabia's supremacy as the only genuinely Dada painter in Paris, if we except the pictorial temptations Ribemont-Dessaignes sometimes happily yielded to (*The Oceanic Spirit*, 1918) and the activity of Jean Crotti (*Mystère acatène*, 1921) under the aegis of Tabu. In fact the initiative was taken by Tzara (at Ernst's own request), who naturally left its organization to Breton as *Littérature* had rooms at its disposal at Au Sans Pareil. Picabia had been exhibited by Ernst at the Brauhaus Winter in Cologne and kept up his friendship with Arp, sealed in Zurich. Picabia's *Rastadada Picture* is not only dedicated to Arp and Ernst, but its collage and photomontage technique, unique in Picabia's work, can be interpreted as a homage to the picture-making methods coming from Germany.

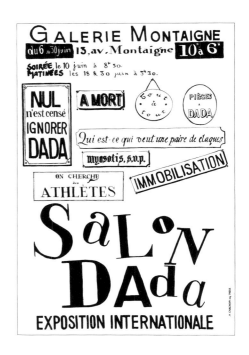

Three photographs of the Dada Salon, Montaigne Gallery, Paris, June 1921: dummy with a row of hanging neckties (above), Dada object-sculpture with a Max Ernst collage on the wall behind it (lower left), and Théodore Fraenkel's Procédé à fil *or Thread Process (lower right); under the table Ribemont-Dessaignes' glass tube entitled* Thinking, *and on the wall Julius Evola's* Picture N° 69.

Poster for the Dada Salon, 1921

In June 1921 the Dada Salon took up a challenge sent out by Tzara to his Parisian friends: by virtue of the creative logic displayed by many Dadaists, he asked the writers to show their mettle as picture makers.

Tzara rejected the notion of modern art for all that it implied of history and evolution: the time had come for a radical rethinking of creative procedures as such. The Dadas, then, were no longer "artists" but, as the Berliners declared, engineers, mounters, contrivers.

The Dada Salon, then, was a gamble or a fillip, and a provocation in the best sense of the word. Planned by Tzara and Picabia early in 1921 as a countermove to the Salon des Indépendants, it was held in June, organized by Tzara alone, after Picabia had bowed out, but he had the active and enthusiastic support of the *Littérature* group, except for Breton, who held aloof. The Dada Salon was held at the Studio des Champs-Elysées, coupled with three performances of Tzara's play *Le Cœur à gaz* (The Gas Heart), two of them being cancelled by the theater management.

The result was a host of bewildering, shortlived, spontaneous works, miles away from anything like pictorial craftsmanship. But they were unusual, they were surprising, and they came up to the expectations aroused

Philippe Soupault: *Portrait of a Fool, 1921*

Julius Evola: *Picture No. 69, 1921*

Louis Aragon: *Portrait of Jacques Vaché, 1921*

by Dada in Paris. All that remains of it are a few photographs. These pictures and object-sculptures "crafted" by writers are a mockery of the notion of art, and were meant to be. On a small stand set on a table was a ball of twine with a sponge on top of it, entitled *Thread Process*, probably by Fraenkel. Between floor and table stood a transparent glass cylinder: this was a sculpture by Ribemont-Dessaignes entitled *Thinking*.

Aragon exhibited a delicate *Portrait of Jacques Vaché*, made of paper cutouts and dead leaves, fragile and tender as the nostalgic memory of the friend who had died in 1919. Tzara and Ribemont concocted a weird sculpture of an "ex pin-headed murderer." From the ceiling hung a row of neckties. Conventions were short-circuited with irony. Soupault exhibited an eighteenth-century mirror (*Portrait of a Fool*, while an empty frame was entitled *Portrait of an Unknown*), together with a chunk of asphalt entitled *Cité du Retiro* (the place in Paris where it was torn up). The fun-loving Soupault attended the show got up as the President of Liberia and handed out matches in a parody of an official ceremony.

Man Ray in Paris: rayographs and abstract films

Man Ray, Paris, 1924

A few weeks later, in July 1921, Man Ray arrived in Paris and was welcomed by the Dadaists, except for Tzara, who was away. In December an exhibition was organized for him in the bookshop just opened by Philippe and Mick Soupault, near the Invalides (Avenue de Lowendal). Early in 1922 this bookshop, the Librairie Six, is mentioned as the publisher of *Les Champs délicieux*, Man Ray's first set of twelve rayograms, prefaced by Tzara. The title seems to be an echo of *Les Champs magnétiques*.

The rayographs or rayograms that Man Ray (a name he invented, meant to be taken in its literal sense) had discovered a few weeks earlier were based on a process (the photogram) which was not entirely new, because it was successively invented or discovered, quite independently, by Christian Schad (schadographs), Man Ray, Moholy-Nagy and Lissitzky. Rayographs are cameraless photographs, obtained directly on sensitized paper. Various items, usually objects or paper cutouts, were placed on a table in a darkroom. Then it only needed a source of light for the paper thus exposed to darken all over, allowing the negative imprint of the areas protected from the light by objects laid on the paper to appear. In his *Self-Portrait* (1963) Man Ray recounts the accidental discovery of the process:

Man Ray: *Rayogram from* Les Champs délicieux, *1921-1922*

I turned on the light; before my eyes an image began to form, not quite a simple silhouette of the objects as in a straight photograph, but distorted and refracted by the glass more or less in contact with the paper and standing out against a black background, the part directly exposed to the light. I remembered when I was a boy, placing fern leaves in a printing frame with proof paper, exposing it to sunlight, and obtaining a white negative of the leaves . . . This was the same idea, but with an added three-dimensional quality and tone graduation.

This technique, used by many artists in the twenties (Max Burchartz, Oskar Nerlinger, Kurt Schwitters), at once aroused Tzara's enthusiasm. "They are pure Dada creations," he told Man Ray, "and far superior to similar attempts—simple flat textural prints in black and white—made a few years earlier by Christian Schad, an early Dadaist." In his preface to *Les Champs délicieux*, an essay highly critical of modern painting in Paris, Tzara laid emphasis not only on the importance of the discovery of the material, but also on its beauty as a "physico-chemical" product.

The process opened a whole field of new experiments. Not only did the photogram reveal a fresh range of non-pictorial plastic possibilities, but it also recorded the appearance of a pure material, an energy: light.

Moholy-Nagy brought out all its instrumental importance in his writings (*Malerei Photographie Film*, 1925 and 1927) and in his work, mainly the *Lichtrequisit* (*Space-Light Modulator*, 1922-1930). Already present in the canvases of Impressionist painters where it dissolved contours and the identity of objects, light was also handled by the Italian Futurists, who broke it down into a multiplicity of colors (Balla's iridescent compenetrations), but even more by Robert Delaunay (see Chapter 2).

Man Ray: *Clock Wheels, 1925*

Man Ray's studio in New York, 1920

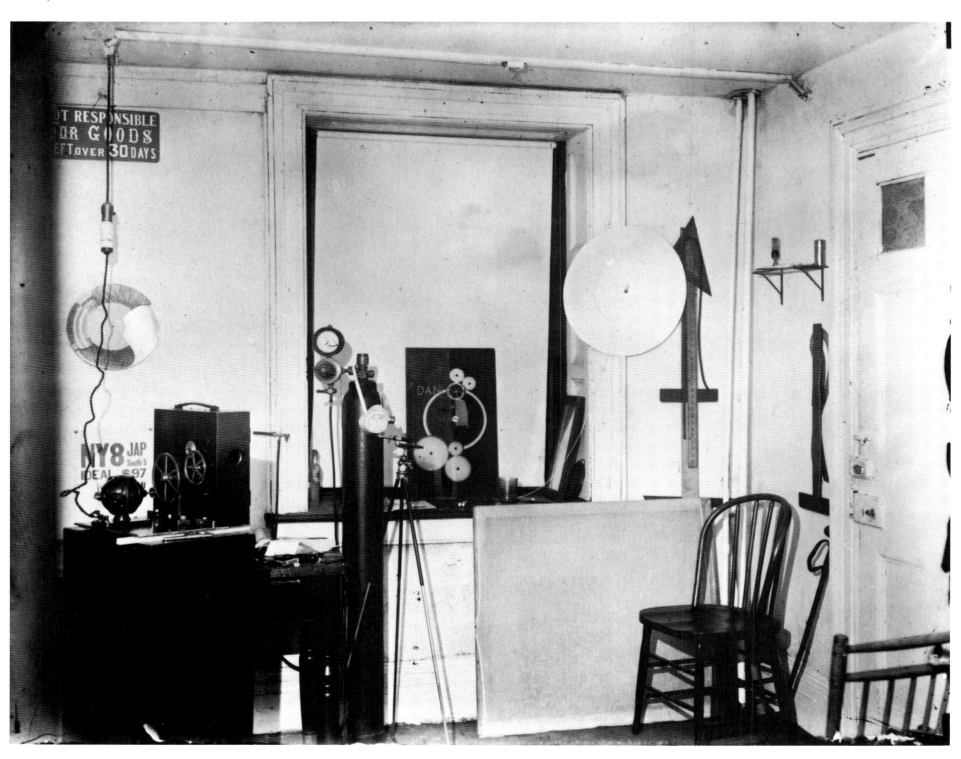

Man Ray: *Dancer Danger, 1920*

As an element opposable to pigment, and thus to every conception derived from the traditional picture, light was to become the object of a full artistic treatment in its own right. This was exemplified by an abstract film in which Moholy-Nagy made it the principal factor of the film, and by artists such as Nikolaus Braun, a pupil of Segal's in Berlin. So it is hardly surprising that Tzara's preface ("La photographie à l'envers") was translated into German by Walter Benjamin in *G*, a magazine mainly devoted to the purely abstract film (Chapter 7), edited by Hans Richter and Werner Graeff in Berlin.

For the moment, Man Ray, anxious to preserve his discovery, damped the enthusiasm of his friend Tzara who wanted to continue the experiments with other materials. But Tzara returned to the attack when he asked Man Ray to make a short film for the evening of the *Cœur à barbe* (Bearded Heart) next year, in July 1923.

Man Ray: *Rayogram, 1922*

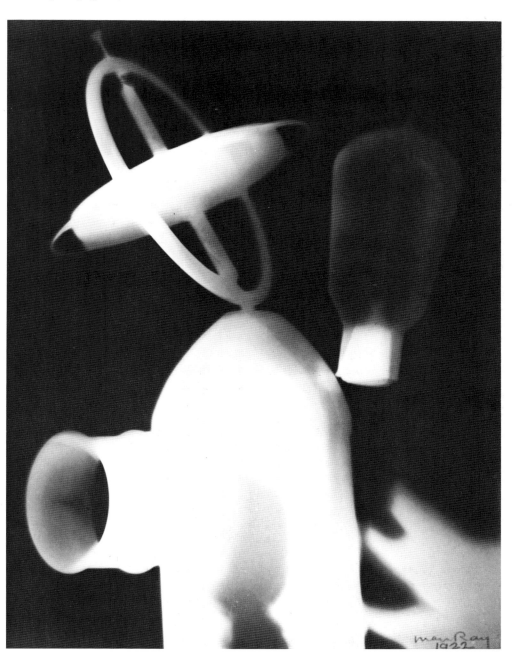

When everything that goes by the name of art was well overgrown with rheumatism, the photographer lit the thousands of candles in his lamp, and the sensitive paper gradually absorbed the black outlined by a few commonplace objects. He had invented the power of a fresh and tender lightning flash which exceeded in extent all the constellations intended for the pleasure of our eyes. The precise, unique and correct mechanical distortion is recorded, smoothly filtered out like a head of hair through a comb of light.

Tristan Tzara, 1922

Erik Satie in a scene from the René Clair film Entr'acte, *1924*

Poem by Louis Aragon, 1920

Failure of the Paris Congress. Dada victory

One can understand that the hopes some people set on Dada have been dashed. Did it not promise a revolution that never came? Yet, with all its might, it strove for that revolution. Nothing seemed to it more hateful than the molding of a new conventionalism. Breton's attempt to give Dada a fresh impetus by instituting the Paris Congress (for the determination of directives and the defense of the modern spirit, April 1922) seemed to me, as to several others among us, particularly dangerous. It was an attempt to objectify the position which Dada still meant to keep on the plane of subjectivity. To confront Dada with the trends of the so-called "modern" spirit, the latter looming up at the time chiefly in the stereotyped and sterilizing form represented by the periodical L'Esprit Nouveau, *would have meant challenging Dada's originality in relation to the other currents which it claimed to have outstripped. Dada, furthermore, asserted that it was not modern, and the advanced stage to which it had led that spirit permitted it to deny any modernity. Dada's refusal to take part in the systematic codification of its lack of system, was the last manifestation of Dada (*Le Cœur à Barbe, *April 1922).*

Tristan Tzara, 1931

The atmosphere had changed between Tzara's proposal and the projection of Man Ray's first abstract film at the *Cœur à barbe* evening. A difference of views, at once made public at the beginning of 1922, gave an irreversible turn to the now open clash separating Dada and its friends from the reformist line chosen by Breton.

Early in February the editor (i.e. Breton) of *Littérature* was preparing the Congress for the Determination of the Directives and the Defense of the Modern Spirit. He formed a highly eclectic committee, consisting of Léger, Ozenfant, Delaunay, Auric, Paulhan and Vitrac. Tzara was invited to join the committee but at once refused to have anything to do with it. He had stated his reservations at the start: "I consider," he wrote to Breton, "that the low ebb of things at present, resulting from the jumble of tendencies, the confusion of genres, and the substitution of groups for individuals, is more dangerous than reaction."

An irritated Breton issued a communiqué in *Comoedia* written by himself, but to his own name he added those of Léger, Delaunay, Auric, Ozenfant and Vitrac. Thinking he could thereby re-echo the vague accusations made against Tzara by Schad in a letter to Picabia, Breton "warned public opinion against the doings of a person known as the promoter of a 'movement' originating in Zurich" and against the "calculations of a publicity-hungry impostor."

In reply, Eluard, Ribemont-Dessaignes, Satie and Tzara summoned all the avant-garde to a meeting to mobilize against "the ridiculous bureaucratic preparations" for the Congress.

The protest meeting at the Closerie des Lilas on February 17, 1922 sided wholeheartedly with Tzara in a collective resolution. The forty-five artists who signed it withdrew their confidence from the original Congress committee, even though it had now disowned Breton and the abusive terms he had used. Among the signers were Satie (who henceforth referred to the members of *Littérature* as "bogus Dadaists"), Arp, Man Ray, Pansaers, Tzara, Zdanevich (Iliazd), Cocteau, Brancusi, Metzinger, Charchoune, Ribemont-Dessaignes, Eluard, Huidobro, Van Doesburg, Péret and Arland.

On his side, from Saint-Raphaël on the Riviera, Picabia published a one-off number of *La Pomme de pins* in which he warmed to the idea of the "Congress" and made a few hits at Tzara. It is true that in a letter Breton expressed his desire "to file away Dada much as Dada had filed away Cubism" and that Picabia, too, had turned over a new leaf, although it seems clear that he hoped to play a role at the Congress like that played by Tzara at the Barrès trial. Ironically, Tzara concluded: "The members of the Congress of Modernism, as the result of threats by some perfidious impostors, decided a few days ago to drop the excellent idea of moving about like dogs on a lead among the principles of celebrated theorists. The Congress is dying of chocolate nationalism, of vanilla-flavored vanity and the quasi-Swiss stupidity of some of our most punctilious fellow-citizens."

Jean Crotti: *Mystère acatène (Acatenian Mystery), 1921*

So the Paris context had changed when Man Ray, approached again by Tzara, set about making a film for him. Man Ray had a small automatic camera which held only about three feet of standard film, and now and then he used it to make quite unrelated shots, a field of daisies, a nude torso (that of his companion Kiki de Montparnasse) moving in front of a striped curtain with the sunlight coming through it, a suspended paper spiral (prototype of the celebrated *Lampshade*), an egg-crate carton dangling at the end of a piece of string. Whereas Man Ray was planning to make a film with a few subtitles lasting for ten to fifteen minutes (films at the time were still silent), Tzara asked him to make, almost overnight, a short reeler to be shown at the *Cœur à barbe* (Bearded Heart) evening being organized at the Théâtre Michel by a group of Russian artists from Montparnasse (July 1923). Man Ray remembers:

> I explained [to Tzara] that what I had would not last more than a minute; there was not sufficient time to add to it. Tzara insisted: what about my Rayographs . . . couldn't I do the same thing on movie film and have it ready for the performance? The idea struck me as possible and I promised to have something ready for the next day.
>
> Acquiring a roll of a hundred feet of film, I went into my darkroom and cut up the material into short lengths, pinning them down on the work table. On some strips I sprinkled salt and pepper, like a cook preparing a roast, on other strips I threw pins and thumbtacks at random; then turned on the white light for a second or two as I had done for my still Rayographs.

Man Ray joined up the images obtained in this way and, to make the film longer, added on the few sequences already shot with his camera. Then he barely had time to take it to the Théâtre Michel where the evening was in full swing, making it clear to Tzara that the film, with no subtitles, would need a few words of explanation.

Sonia Delaunay: *Mrs. Mouth and Mr. Eye, costume designs for Tzara's play* Le Cœur à gaz, *1923*

The evening at the Théâtre Michel, Rue des Mathurins, owing to the circumstances of the moment, took an unexpected turn in which the foreseeable break between Dada and the future Surrealists culminated in physical violence. The *Littérature* group were in the midst of their "hypnotic" sleep sessions. An article by Breton, *Entrée des médiums* published in *Littérature* in November 1922, aroused only sarcasm from the Dadaists because of its spiritualistic overtones, which Breton denied.

Simultaneously, in reply to Vitrac who had flung back at him his famous question "Why do you write?", Breton, trying to be more Dadaist than the Dadaists, took up an untenable position. He said he would give up writing, ignore magazines, books and newspapers, and withdraw from the editorship of *Littérature*, in this modeling his attitude on that of Marcel Duchamp, who was just then giving up all aesthetic activities, after having put the finishing touches to his *Large Glass*.

An actress as Mrs. Mouth and René Crevel as Mr. Eye in Tzara's play Le Cœur à gaz *(The Gas Heart) at the Théâtre Michel, Paris, July 6, 1923*

Zaum is a language with a Russian look whose words and onomatopoeias are such that they act as the framework for the meaning of several words of similar sound.

In Zaum each word therefore carries, more or less emphatically, several meanings of different orders and levels, concrete or abstract, particular or general. The listener's imaginative participation lies in keeping doors and windows open, for it is within him that the various evocative elements are awakened.

But one must not see it as having a creative role. The meanings evoked exist even beyond the author's control; he may not have wanted them and some may occur which were not invited. Once a word is formed, one is no longer the master of it. Thus God found himself exposed to the complaints of man as soon as man was created.

Georges Ribemont-Dessaignes, 1923

Still from Man Ray's film Retour à la raison *(Return to Reason), 1923: the torso of Kiki de Montparnasse streaked with light and shadow*

Typography by Ilya Zdanevich (Iliazd) for the cover of his book Easter Island, *Tiflis, 1919*

Tzara adopted a more playful position (see above his replies to Vitrac) and resumed the offensive. The opportunity was offered to him by a circle of Russian artists who had taken the name Tcherez (a Russian word meaning ''through'' or ''over,'' a bridge between the Russian and French cultures). The friendship linking two of them, Iliazd and Serge Romoff, with Tzara led them to organize a new performance of Tzara's play *Cœur à gaz*, which had already been staged at the Dada Salon in the Galerie Montaigne in June 1921. The actors represented the parts of the face: Jacques Baron the neck, René Crevel an eye, Pierre de Massot the nose; the mouth, eyebrow and ears were played by professionals from the Odéon in costumes by Sonia Delaunay.

For this same evening, Theo van Doesburg (who had settled in Paris in March 1923) designed settings for the dances by Lizica Codreano, who interpreted the Zaum poems of Ilya Zdanevich (Iliazd) in costumes by Sonia Delaunay. The sets for Tzara's play (unfortunately destroyed during the brawl which broke out on the stage) were by the non-objective Russian artist Granovski.

In addition, abstract films by Man Ray, Hans Richter (*Rhythm 21*) and Charles Sheeler (*Mana Hatta*, retitled in Paris *Les fumées de New York*) were shown; and Marcelle Meyer interpreted music by Georges Auric, Darius Milhaud (a shimmy called *Soft Caramel*), Erik Satie and Stravinsky. On many levels these performances provided a fresh international stimulus for the Dada Movement, thought by some to be played out (chiefly by Breton, to justify his desire to have done with Dada). A like concern with launching a second Dada wave had led in the previous fall to the project for the review *Bilboquet* which, under its editor Clément Pansaers, was to bring together Duchamp, Brancusi, Pound, Stravinsky and Cocteau.

But purely Parisian circumstances interfered with this new international orientation, in particular with Iliazd's Zaum language (dismissed as trivial by the *Littérature* group, and still unappreciated in France), and this soirée of July 1923 was sabotaged. For the organizers had reckoned without personal susceptibilities when they left the actors (Marcel Herrand, who in 1917 had played in *Les Mamelles de Tirésias* by Apollinaire, and Pierre Bertin) free to choose the poems they would recite (by Apollinaire, Baron, Cocteau, Eluard, Soupault and Tzara). The group had long flaunted its contempt for Cocteau, and Eluard took this as a pretext for refusing to write the preface he had promised for Iliazd's book of Zaum poems *Ledentu le Phare* (it was then written by Ribemont-Dessaignes); and Eluard declared he would do his utmost to prevent the reading of his own poems, since they were being put on the same footing as those of Cocteau, the bugbear of the future Surrealists.

The latter, moreover, frowned on Tzara's new friendships and artistic connections (Delaunay, Iliazd, Van Doesburg, Codreano); and they were alarmed at seeing their friend, the founder of Dada, break free, and move away on international lines, from the hold which they had on him as the first group to welcome him in Paris—this, just as their own limits were being shown up by the new orientation.

FRANCIS PICABIA

Francis Picabia: *The Holy Virgin, 1920*

Group photograph at the opening of the Jockey Club, Paris, November 1923. Seated, Tristan Tzara and Jean Cocteau. Standing, left to right, Man Ray, the painter Hilaire Hiler, Smith (a jockey), Ezra Pound, the pianist Les Copeland, Snow (owner of the club), and the photographer Curtis Moffat

The hall was packed on the night of the first performance. After a shimmy by Milhaud, Auric's foxtrot, the reading of poems and a "Dada address" ("Blow your nose") by Ribemont-Dessaignes, Pierre de Massot began a parody of a monument for the death of the great fighters of modern art and declaimed a litany for those dead on the field of honor, mentioning André Gide as well as Picasso, Picabia and Duchamp (the last-named being reported missing). The Dada position was quite clear. For them, the whole art world was tarred with the same brush. On the pretext of defending Picasso who was present in the audience, Breton jumped on to the stage, made a dash at Pierre de Massot, and with a sharp blow of his cane broke Massot's arm. At this the crowd went wild. In response to the public outcry (according to Jane Heap in *The Little Review*, and to Theo van Doesburg, who wrote in a huff, "They nearly killed Tzara"), the police were called in by a journalist named Gilbert Charles and ejected Breton, Desnos and Péret.

Calm was restored with difficulty. Tzara took the stage and announced the film "by that renowned artist, Man Ray, made in one of his lucid moments." The audience relaxed and sighed with relief.

The theater went dark and the screen lit up. It looked like a snowstorm, with the flakes flying in all directions instead of falling, then suddenly becoming a field of daisies as if the snow had crystallized into flowers. This was followed by another sequence of huge white pins criss-crossing and revolving in an epileptic dance, then again by a lone thumbtack making desperate efforts to leave the screen. There was some grumbling in the audience, punctuated by a whistle or two; but suddenly the film broke, due to my inexpert mounting ... The next image was of the light-striped nude torso, which called forth the applause of some connoisseurs, but when the spiral and the egg-crate carton began to revolve on the screen, there was a catcall, taken up by the audience, as always happens in a gathering. But again the film broke, plunging the theater into darkness. One spectator loudly vented his dissatisfaction, the man behind, evidently a sympathizer of the Dadaists, answered him; the dialogue became more personal; finally a loud slap was heard, followed by the scuffling of feet and shouting. A cry for the lights arose, the theater lit up, disclosing a group locked in a struggle preventing the participants from striking any blows.

Again the police intervened. The battle continued outside. Meanwhile the curtain went up on the first act of *Cœur à gaz* (The Gas Heart). The play was

*Handbill of the Transmental Ball in honor of
the Zaum poets Iliazd, Kruchenykh, and Terentiev
at the Salle Bullier, Paris, February 1923*

*Poster for a lecture by Ilya Zdanevich (Iliazd)
at the University of Degree 41, Paris, May 12, 1922*

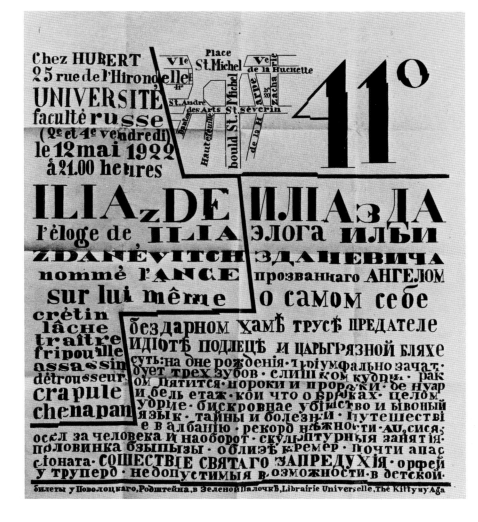

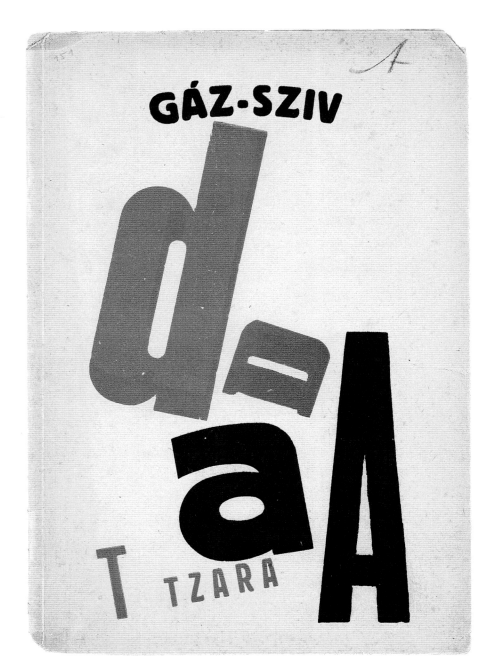

Cover by Lajos Kassák for a Hungarian translation of Tzara's play Le Cœur à gaz,
c. 1924

immediately interrupted by Eluard, his blood up, who challenged Tzara to explain Breton's expulsion. Some spectators came to blows. The author appeared on the stage. Eluard (who had already quarreled with Tzara at the beginning of the year over the preparations for the Transmental Fancy-Dress Ball) leapt on to the stage and struck Tzara and Crevel in the face. The actors took Tzara's side and tried to protect him from the attack by Eluard who was manhandled in his turn.

The management canceled the following night's performance. These incidents would probably have had no great "historical" echo if Breton had not claimed wrongly in *Nadja* in 1928 that there had been collusion between the police and Tristan Tzara. Nevertheless, Breton had to reconsider these accusations against the founder of Dada which were added to those for which the meeting at the Closerie des Lilas had unanimously withdrawn their confidence from Breton the year before. Did he not write in his own hand in Tzara's personal copy of *Nadja*: "I wish I hadn't written that. Perhaps I was mistaken. In any case, Tzara can boast of being my first great cause of despair. All the confidence of which I have ever been capable was at stake. This is my defense."

Thus the period of friendships and battles jointly conducted since Tzara's arrival in Paris ended in confusion. Tzara continued to be intensely active with an unfailing spontaneity and energy. In many respects, if it delighted his new friends and swept them beyond themselves, it also had the effect of preventing them from carrying out projects that were a bit too sensible in the eyes of Dada's originator. From the first Friday evening gathering of the *Littérature* group, Breton blamed himself for having led Picabia (who, incidentally, shrank from public demonstrations) into the rash adventures instigated by Tzara.

The wide free prospects opened up by Dada caused some alarm. During the summer of 1920, while Breton was publishing an article on Dada in the *Nouvelle Revue Française* and correcting the proofs of Marcel Proust's great work, the editorial director at Au Sans Pareil, dismayed by the manuscript of Picabia's *Jésus-Christ Rastaquouère*, refused to publish it unless he made some changes. As for Breton, he refused to write the preface.

The year 1924 marked the transition from the French version of Dada to Surrealism, with a few notable exceptions such as the performance of Tristan Tzara's *Mouchoir de nuages* at the Théâtre de la Cigale. Tzara brought together his manifestoes, hitherto scattered in various reviews, for publication. *Sept manifestes Dada et lampisteries* issued by Budry, later reprinted, remains to this day the only version available in French. The salvo of honor was fired.

Breton now gathered around him a new group which launched a new review in the fall, *La Révolution surréaliste* (editors: Pierre Naville and Benjamin Péret). In December he published the *Surrealist Manifesto*.

Picabia mockingly invented a new "ism" and devoted the last number of *391* to it, subtitled "Journal of Instantaneism." It came out on the occasion of the performance of his ballet *Relâche* by the Swedish Ballet. Incidentally, Erik Satie's music entitled *Obscene Ballet* was described as an "instantaneist ballet" with reference to this movement, which was as shortlived as its name suggests.

Before turning the Dada page, Picabia wrote for his "Journal of Instantaneism" an unanswerable article, "Opinions and Portraits," setting the record straight.

Francis Picabia: *Surrealism Crucified, c. 1924*

◁ *"Opinions and Portraits," a polemical article by Picabia against André Breton, published in 391, No. 19, Paris, October 1924*

Cover of *391*, No. 19, "Journal of Instantaneism," edited by Francis Picabia, Paris, October 1924

OPINIONS ET PORTRAITS

Vraiment on pourrait mourir de rire en lisant l'article de M. Maurice Martin du Gard, paru dans *Les Nouvelles Littéraires* — évidemment rire c'est quelque chose — mais, ou M. Maurice Martin du Gard n'est au courant de rien, ou cet article a été écrit par André Breton et c'est encore ce qui me semble le plus probable; le fait même d'y avoir accompagné mon nom du qualificatif d'artiste peintre, prouve que Breton cherche à faire oublier ce que j'ai écrit dans le *Camera Work* paru à New-York en 1914 : *Le Portrait de Stieglitz, La Fille née sans Mère* et *Rateliers platoniques* en 1917. Quant à Tzara, il écrivait en Suisse des œuvres extrêmement personnelles où Breton a puisé sans scrupules, pendant que d'autre part il se prosternait aux pieds de Gide et faisait des avances à Blaise Cendrars. L'affaire Dada il cherche à l'arranger de la façon la plus avantageuse pour lui et surtout le moins génante; Vaché est un grand homme mais il est mort... Les œuvres de Messieurs Breton et, comment dites-vous? Philippe Coupeaux, je crois, sont une pauvre imitation de Dada et leur surréalisme est exactement du même ordre.

André Breton me fait penser à Lucien Guitry jouant une pièce de Bernstein; il est certainement aussi bon acteur, mais plus démodé que Guitry.

Monsieur Maurice Martin du Gard, vous tenez André Breton pour un homme d'une classe supérieure à celle de Dermée et Birot, si vous aimez le théâtre, évidemment, je n'insiste pas, mais il me faut bien vous dire que Birot, par exemple, que je connais depuis longtemps, m'a souvent exprimé des idées nouvelles, et, qu'il a à son actif des inventions cinématographiques extrêmement curieuses ; quant à

Dermée il faut être moins superficiel que vous ne l'êtes pour s'apercevoir que ce n'est pas un acteur, mais un homme qui reste avec simplicité dans la vie, c'est ce qui m'intéresse le plus. Le surréalisme d'Yvan Goll se rapporte au cubisme, celui de Breton c'est tout simplement Dada travesti en ballon réclame pour la maison Breton et Cie.

Maurice Martin du Gard, André Breton plusieurs fois devant moi vous a traité d'idiot et déclarait que votre journal était imbécile. Il entre maintenant chez vous chapeau bas avec les plus belles phrases de politesse sur les lèvres, vous vous y êtes laissé prendre, c'est un grand service que vous avez rendu à tous les hommes qui pouvaient avoir quelques doutes sur Breton; Breton est un acteur qui veut tous les premiers rôles au théâtre des illusionnistes, et ce n'est qu'un Robert Houdin pour hôtels de province !

(À suivre si le besoin s'en fait sentir)

Francis PICABIA
Metteur en scène du surréalisme d'André BRETON.

DERNIÈRE HEURE :

Je viens de rencontrer Robert Desnos il m'a affirmé que Breton n'était pour rien dans l'article des *Nouvelles Littéraires*, je ne demande qu'à le croire et je publie ici une lettre adressée par Breton à Desnos à propos de cet article :

11 Octobre 1924.

Mon cher Robert Desnos,

Est-il besoin de vous dire que je suis tout-à-fait étranger, dans l'article des Nouvelles Littéraires, au premier membre de la phrase qui vous concerne? Qui a pu le suggérer à Martin du Gard? Si vous estimez qu'il y a lieu, en toute occasion je ne me suis pas exprimé nettement à ce sujet, je suis prêt à adresser quelques lignes de rectification.

Votre ami, André BRETON.

Des "œufs durs" sortent des poussins, je vous souhaite mon cher Breton de n'avoir pas trop de déception dans l'élevage de vos couvées.

DADAISME, INSTANTANÉISME **391**

Journal de l'Instantanéisme
POUR QUELQUE TEMPS

L'INSTANTANÉISTE EST UN ÊTRE EXCEPTIONNEL CYNIQUE ET INDÉCENT

L'INSTANTANÉISME : NE VEUT PAS D'HIER
L'INSTANTANÉISME : NE VEUT PAS DE DEMAIN.
L'INSTANTANÉISME : FAIT DES ENTRECHATS.
L'INSTANTANÉISME : FAIT DES AILES DE PIGEONS.
L'INSTANTANÉISME : NE VEUT PAS DE GRANDS HOMMES.
L'INSTANTANÉISME : NE CROIT QU'A AUJOURD'HUI.
L'INSTANTANÉISME : VEUT LA LIBERTÉ POUR TOUS.
L'INSTANTANÉISME : NE CROIT QU'A LA VIE.
L'INSTANTANÉISME : NE CROIT QU'AU MOUVEMENT PERPÉTUEL.

Francis Picabia: *Drawing for the ballet* Relâche, *1924*

Language, from the angle of human relations, was for Dada a problem and a constant concern. Through that tentacular and scattered activity which was Dada, poetry is harassed, insulted and despised. A certain poetry, to be specific, art-poetry based on the principle that beauty is static. To that Dada opposed a "state of mind" which, in spite of its fundamental antidogmatism, was able to demonstrate that everything is movement, a constant alignment on the flight of time. When in 1920, at the "Littérature" matinée, Picabia exhibited a drawing executed over a black picture which was wiped out in front of the public; when I myself, on the pretext of reading a poem, recited a newspaper article while an electric doorbell drowned out my voice; when a little later Aragon's poem "Suicide," consisting of nothing more than the alphabet, was published in Cannibale; when in the same magazine Breton published an extract from the telephone book under the title PSST (and many other examples could be cited)—are we not entitled to see in these manifestations the affirmation that the poetic work has no static value, that since the poem is not the aim of poetry, then the latter may just as well exist elsewhere?

Tristan Tzara, 1931

I.K. Bonset: *Matter Denaturalized (Destruction 2), c. 1921*

Chapter 7

Elementary Structuring

Theo van Doesburg in the Aubette cinema and dance hall, Strasbourg, 1927

While events as they unfolded in Paris led the French section of the movement to a literary conclusion, Dada enjoyed a new lease of life on the international scene, entering there into a wide range of fresh and stimulating alliances. For it would be a mistake to identify the role of Dada with that played by Tristan Tzara in Paris. He was based there of course, from 1920 on, but as founder and ringleader of the movement the task facing him after Zurich was cosmopolitan and he carried it out on a broad front, while the initiatives of the German and Zurich Dadaists continued (see previous chapters), sometimes very actively.

The Dada diaspora was now in full swing, spreading its "virgin microbes" in all directions, to Italy and Spain, even to Holland, Hungary, Poland and Yugoslavia. "There's only one movement, and that's perpetual movement" (Picabia, on the cover of *391*, *Journal of Instantaneism*, reproduced on page 159).

Dada now was more than ever spontaneous, shifting, checkered, manysided, international. At a Dada exhibition at the Casa d'arte Bragaglia in Rome, the poet and painter Julius Evola launched a Dada Collection and in it published two books of verse (*Arte Astratta*, 1920, and *La Parole obscure du paysage intérieur*, 1921); then, after organizing a Jazz Dada Ball (January 1921), Evola was invited by Tzara to take part in the Dada Salon in Paris in June 1921, which he did (see Chapter 6, pages 146-147).

In Spain, thanks to Guillermo de Torre, Dada was brought into relation with Ultraist circles there, in particular the reviews *Ultra* in Madrid (Cansinos Asséns, Gómez de la Serna, Borges) and *Grecia* in Seville (del Vando Villar). The Chilean creationist poet Huidobro lived for a time in Madrid and this was a determining factor. Borges published the manifesto *Ultraism* (in *Nosotros*, December 1921): its leaning toward Dada was made all the clearer by its criticism of Futurism ("the overwrought rhetoric and dynamist stew of the poets of Milan"). Jacques Edwards, editor in Madrid of the "Dadaist-Ultraist" review *Vertical* (1920), was appointed by Tzara "Dada's chargé d'affaires in Santiago, Chile."

Other little known Dadaists are worth mentioning. One was the photomontage artist Paul Citroën, a Dutchman born in Berlin. There he was intimate with Walter Mehring and the "Chaplinist Dada President Bloomfield" (Erwin Blumenfeld); he also saw much of Hausmann and the Herzfelde brothers. Back in Holland for his military service, Citroën set up the "Dada Cultural Panel in Holland." Another was the painter Hugo Dux, whom Huelsenbeck during a visit to Teplitz-Schönau appointed "Head of the Czech Dadaists." Noteworthy too is the Russian musician Jefim Golyscheff, who from 1919 organized Dada happenings in Berlin.

But it is the new collective positions that call for notice rather than these scattered elements. While strictly Dada activities marked time for a while, contacts were made between the Constructivists Van Doesburg, Lissitzky and Moholy-Nagy and the Dadaists Arp, Hausmann, Schwitters and of course Tzara himself. Little by little these contacts revealed common theoretical interests and bore fruit. Many artists emerged from their isolation and met together, with a new working basis to start from and new concepts in mind, as the congresses and manifestoes testify.

In this new phase Dada got its second wind. Its energies flowed openly into a creative process at once deconstructive and positive, at once destructive and constructive, in active polarity. Here Van Doesburg played with virtuosity an essential and significant dual role. Although wholly dedicated to the pure plasticism sponsored in Holland by himself and Mondrian, the periodical *De Stijl* (founded in May 1917) welcomed, in the spring of 1921, Raoul Hausmann's Dada manifestoes (*Dada is more than Dada, PREsentism*), the programmatic essays of Georges Ribemont-Dessaignes, and poems by Clément Pansaers. These publications were only the prelude to wider and deeper contacts between Dada and Constructivism.

In 1922 two major group meetings took place. The first, the Congress of International Progressive Artists at Düsseldorf in April, brought together Hans Richter, Werner Graeff, Raoul Hausmann, Hannah Höch, Otto Freundlich, Franz Seiwert, Theo and Nelly van Doesburg, Cornelius van Eesteren, El Lissitzky, Ruggero Vasari and Stanislas Kubicki. The second, the Constructivist Congress, was held at Weimar, headquarters of the Bauhaus, in September 1922, on the initiative of Van Doesburg; it included several events and lectures by Dadaists (Schwitters, Tzara).

With the open complicity of Arp and that of Van Doesburg behind the scenes, Tzara set the mark of Dada on the Weimar Congress from the start (his mere presence had the effect of stirring up dissension). This Congress sealed the virtual formation of an Artistic International.

In addition to Van Doesburg, participants included Kurt Schwitters, El Lissitzky (a regular contributor to *De Stijl* and *Merz*), the painter and photographer Max Burchartz, the Dutch architect Cornelius van Eesteren, the film-maker Werner Graeff, the painter and designer Karl-Peter Röhl, Moholy-Nagy (painter, photographer, co-editor of the review *MA* and professor at the Bauhaus a few months later) and three Dadaists from the original Zurich nucleus, Hans Arp, Tristan Tzara and Hans Richter:

> Arriving there [wrote Moholy-Nagy in *Vision in Motion*], to our great amazement we found also the Dadaists Hans Arp and Tristan Tzara. This

At the Congress of Progressive Artists, Düsseldorf, 1922, left to right: Werner Graeff, Raoul Hausmann, Theo van Doesburg, Cornelius van Eesteren, Hans Richter, Nelly van Doesburg, unidentified, El Lissitzky, Ruggero Vasari, Otto Freundlich, Hannah Höch, F. W. Seiwert, unidentified man seated

caused a rebellion against the host, Van Doesburg, because at that time we felt in Dadaism a destructive and obsolete force in comparison with the new outlook of the Constructivists.

Doesburg, a powerful personality, quieted the storm and the guests were accepted, to the dismay of the younger, purist members who slowly withdrew and let the congress turn into a Dadaist performance.

At that time, we did not realize that Doesburg himself was both a Constructivist and Dadaist, writing Dada poems under the pen name of I.K. Bonset.

That same year, 1922, the First Russian Exhibition was held in Berlin. It revealed non-objective Russian art to the European art scene. The works of Suprematist and Constructivist artists figured prominently in it: Malevich, Lissitzky, Kliun, Olga Rozanova, Nina Kogan, Alexander Rodchenko, Naum Gabo and Tatlin. But the Russian artists were already having difficulties with the commissars responsible for foreign trade, who were reluctant to allow their participation, so that the exhibition, instead of focusing on non-

At the Dada-Constructivist Congress, Weimar, 1922: center, Tristan Tzara kissing the hand of Nelly van Doesburg; between them, with paper hat, Theo van Doesburg; behind the latter, with cap and pipe, El Lissitzky; lying on his back, Hans Richter; front row, far right, Hans Arp; back row, right, László Moholy-Nagy

Cover of The Next Call, *Groningen, November 1926, edited by H.N. Werkman*

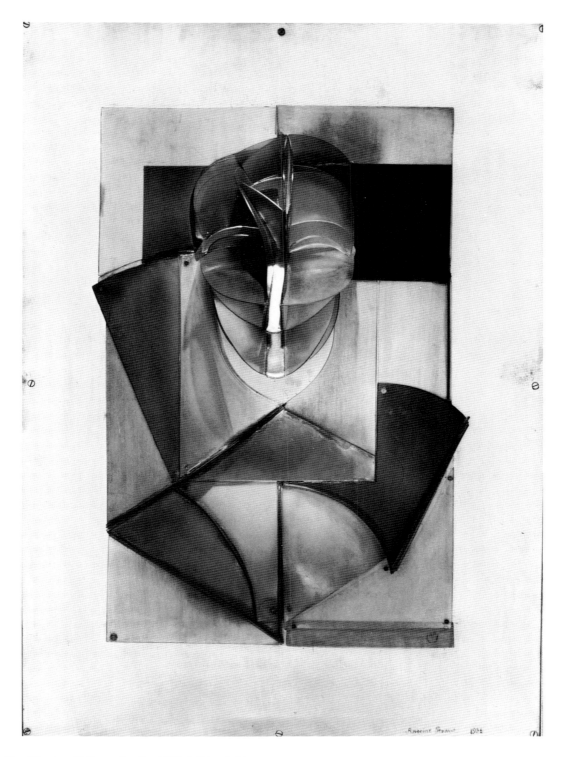

View of the First Russian Exhibition, Van Diemen Gallery, Berlin, 1922: left to right,
David Sterenberg, Maryanov, Nathan Altman, Naum Gabo, and Dr. Ludwig Lütz

objective art, became a compromise between various tendencies in Russian art.

The Russian exhibition then moved on to the Stedelijk Museum in Amsterdam early in 1923, while a De Stijl exhibition was held at the Léonce Rosenberg gallery in Paris in the autumn. That same year the Bauhaus presented its important (and only) exhibition at Weimar (July-September 1923). These interchanges and exhibitions, and the creation of the Dada-Constructivist reviews *Merz* (Schwitters) and *G* (Hans Richter, Werner Graeff, Lissitzky), in addition to the already existing *De Stijl* and *MA*, changed the landscape of the international avant-garde.

Common platforms were set up, in particular on the occasion of the *Proletarian Art Manifesto* (quoted in Chapter 5) signed by Van Doesburg, Schwitters, Spengemann (friend and interpreter of Schwitters at Hanover) and Tzara at the Hague in March 1923, when Schwitters and Van Doesburg were jointly embarking on a tour of Merz Dada evenings in Holland. Under the aegis of *De Stijl*, Van Doesburg published a booklet *Wat is Dada?* (What is Dada?): on the pretext of explaining Dada, it constituted a manifesto in itself. In the fall, acting on his own at Groningen, Hendrik Nikolaas Werkman published on his wooden press a hand-crafted review, *The Next Call*, in which Dada themes were combined with a Constructivist layout and page design.

Cover of Julius Evola's book of verse Arte Astratta, *Rome, 1920*

The elementary typographical layout consists in creating the logical and visual relation between the typefaces, words and phrases employed.
The organization of these elements is twofold: internal (ordering of the content) and external (interrelation of the typographical means). The elementary layout is never absolute or final in typography, for the very notion of elementary layout continually and necessarily changes according to the transformation of the elements in question (as a result of discoveries and the use of new elements of typographical layout).

Jan Tschichold, 1925

Handbill of a Dada lecture in Yugoslavia by Dragan Aleksić, 1922

Cover of the first number of the periodical Dada-Tank, *Zagreb, 1922, edited by Dragan Aleksić*

Theo van Doesburg and **Kurt Schwitters:** *Poster for their tour of Merz Dada evenings in Holland, 1923*

Hans Arp: *Abstract Composition, 1915*

Beyond the obvious novelty of the works, it was the creative process itself which underwent a profound transformation. If the freedom won by the artist within the Dada movement released him from the systems which governed the meaning of images, the Constructive sensibility also laid emphasis on the structures of representation and the constituents as such. With the help of this dual emancipation, by tackling on the one hand the organization of meaning, and on the other by acting on the pure constituents (words, images, sounds) which he could transform, permute, rectify or transpose at will, the new artist was able to produce unprecedented structurations, pictorial and verbal statements, which revolutionized the very framework of the "set forms" (Tzara) inherited from an order of culture now null and void.

Arp, Hausmann, Schwitters and Van Doesburg, simultaneously painters, poets, writers, typographers, publishers and stage designers, all followed the free yet rigorous road of "elementary art."

The word was not new. Recalling the Zurich period, Arp wrote in *Dadaland*: "We searched for an elementary art that would, we thought, save mankind from the furious folly of these times . . . We rejected everything that was copy or description, and allowed the elementary and spontaneous to react in full freedom." The term "elementary" took on a public and more formally programmatic meaning when Dadaists and Constructivists together drew up in October 1921 a *Call for Elementary Art*, signed by Raoul Hausmann, Hans Arp, Ivan Puni and Moholy-Nagy, published by Van Doesburg in *De Stijl*:

To the artists of the world!

In art we love bold invention and renewal. Art is the outcome of all the forces of a period. We live in the present. And so we call for the outcome of our time, an art which can only originate from us, which neither existed before us nor will exist after us. It is not a changing fashion, but stems from the knowledge that art is eternally new and does not come to a halt with the consequences of the past. We stand for elementary art. It is elementary because it does not philosophize, because it is built up of its own elements alone. To yield to the elements of form and design is to be an artist. The elements of art can only be found by the artist. They do not arise from his individual whim; the individual does not stand in isolation and the artist is only an exponent of the forces which give shape to the elements of the world. Artists, proclaim your solidarity with art!

Turn away from styles. We call for stylelessness in order to achieve *the* style!

Style is never plagiarism!

This manifesto is meant for action. Caught in the movement of our time, we proclaim with elementary art the renewal of our outlook, of our awareness of the ever interacting sources of energy which shape the spirit and form of a period and in it bring forth art as something pure, freed from utility and beauty, as something elementary in the individual.

We call for elementary art! Against reaction in art!

This elementary art, which had to be allowed to react in full freedom, was meant literally and in every sense of the word. It referred first of all to the element in the strict sense, the simple elementary constituent, paper, form,

Hannah Höch: *Rhythm, 1924*

color as such, light, sound, object, word, letter, phoneme, typeface, each considered as the elementary material unit, the starting element: the pure "spontaneous" element which had to be allowed "to react in full freedom." That is, without being subjected in the nascent work to the outworn mechanisms of a mimetic representation, to the old imitative techniques that rejected the physical reality of this elementary unit and the energy emanating from it as an autonomous element.

The simultaneously concrete and conceptual freedom which the Dadaists and Constructivists conferred on this element allotted it a manysided, interchangeable function. The elementary units, deploying a field of dynamic interrelations, developed an inner logic of elementary art (assemblages, constructions) once they were "manipulated" by the artist, who allowed them to act and grow. These original articulations and interactions gave rise to unprecedented pictorial, verbal, visual, musical and written statements, whose structuring abolished "language in its set conventional form" (Tzara) and constituted an epistemological break in itself.

It is not surprising that Mondrian's only contribution to *Mecano*, a quotation probably chosen on purpose by Van Doesburg, insisted on this reversal: "The strivings of the new plasticism are dominated by the old spirit so long as the new spirit is not conscious in man. Man uses his new creations in the old way. The true plasticism appears by *mutation* once *evolution* has done its work."

Hendrik N. Werkman: *a a a a,*
plate from his periodical
The Next Call, *Groningen, 1926*

DE STIJL MANIFESTO II, 1920

LITERATURE

contemporary literature still lives on the sentimentality of an enfeebled generation

THE WORD IS DEAD

the naturalistic clichés and dramatic word films
that the book makers offer us
by the yard and by weight
contain no inkling of the new bold strokes of our life

THE WORD IS POWERLESS

the asthmatic and sentimental poetry
the ''I'' and the ''him''

which is still current everywhere
and principally in Holland
is under the influence of a timorous individualism of space
fermented residue of bygone days

and fills us with disgust . . .

like the old view of life
books are based on
LENGTH on DURATION
they are
VOLUMINOUS
the new view of life lies in
DEPTH and INTENSITY
and so we want poetry

to build literarily the many events
around us and through us
it is necessary for the word to be reconstituted
according to both the SOUND and the IDEA

while in the old poetry
by the sway of relative and subjective feelings
the intrinsic meaning of the word is destroyed
we want by every means in our power
syntax
prosody
typography
arithmetic
spelling
to give new meaning to the word and new forcefulness to expression

Cover of Merz 1, *Hanover, January 1923,*
edited by Kurt Schwitters

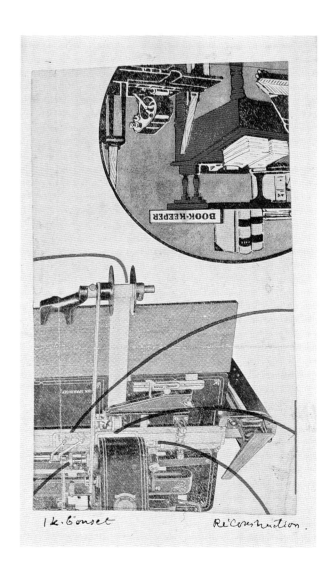

I.K. Bonset:
Reconstruction, 1921

Through the bonds of work and friendship formed between Dadaists and Constructivists, the two sides of this elementary sensibility found a particularly interesting expression in the dual artistic personality that Van Doesburg adopted on the one hand, and on the other in his shared activities with Kurt Schwitters and El Lissitzky: notably a tour of Dada evenings with the former in Holland and the publication of their respective reviews, *Mecano*, *Merz* and *Veshch/Objet/Gegenstand*. Van Doesburg secretly added a Dadaist side, for which he chose the pseudonym I.K. Bonset, to his activities as architect, painter, theorist and editor of *De Stijl*.

Under this pen name supposedly derived from the Dutch expression *''Ik ben sot''* (I'm crazy), he published in 1922-1923 a little Dadaist review *Mecano*, of which I.K. Bonset was the literary editor and Theo van Doesburg the ''picture mechanic.'' That was not his only pseudonym, for under the name Aldo Camini (sometimes mistaken for a Futurist because of the Italian name) Van Doesburg wrote several articles in *De Stijl*, while carefully keeping his borrowed identities a secret from his closest friends. (Doesburg itself was a pseudonym, his real name being Christian Emil Marie Küpper.)

So at the Weimar Congress Van Doesburg continued, even when conferring with so trustworthy a Dadaist as Tzara, to keep up the fiction of Bonset's separate identity. When Tzara hoped that the Dutch Dada poet would contribute to his *Dadaglobe* project, Van Doesburg told him: ''I expect he'll agree to take a hand in it . . . Bonset shares our ideas, but he's a queer fish and keeps out of sight.'' At Weimar, too, Doesburg let Arp and Tzara write a letter to Bonset (he may have put them up to it!), and on the back of it he added a word of his own, with sly humor: ''You see the increasing sympathy aroused by your reputation as an unseen personage'' (letter of September 27, 1922).

Tzara and Van Doesburg had got in touch with each other in the spring of 1920, but did not meet apparently until April 1921, when the Dutch artist and his third wife Nelly van Moorsel (Petro van Doesburg) paid a visit to Paris. In October Van Doesburg wrote to Tzara: ''I like the Dada spirit more and more. There is the same spirit of contrast in it that we have proclaimed as the modern spirit. Only the ways are different. It's a great pity that Mr. Picabia has backed out [see Chapter 6 on the withdrawal of Pansaers and Picabia in the spring of 1921]. I know the reason, but I believe in the possibility of a deeper contact (and combination) with Dada and the consequences of (serious-modern) art.''

Tristan Tzara: Cocoa-nut Portrait of
Theo van Doesburg, c. 1923

Van Doesburg and Schwitters: the same spirit of contrast

Kurt Schwitters: The Flag of Van Gogh, 1925

Theo and Nelly van Doesburg with Kurt and
Helma Schwitters, The Hague, 1923

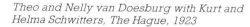

Although the surrealists emphasized such a goal, the new form of communication was not accomplished by them, but more by the dadaists and simultaneously even more by James Joyce. (This observation is not only valid in literature. It is significant that the revolutionary impulses and aims crystallized during the first quarter of the twentieth century have been diluted everywhere into an often inconsequential estheticism by the young generation.) . . . The dadaistic poem shows more freshness than the surrealist literature. Dada is more "poetic" and richer in its exciting perceptive potency. In comparison to it an Eluard poem is rationalized fantasy, fireworks of images taken from the dictionary, not the eruption of life encompassing intellect and emotion. Except for his experiments in the simulation of psychotic writings, one is at a loss to see why Eluard is called surrealist. He is an amiable, melodious poet but rather conservative when measured by the dadaists' achievement of a multidimensional language.

László Moholy-Nagy, 1947

Mecano and Merz Dada in Holland

*Theo and Nelly van Doesburg with the dancer Camares
in their studio at Clamart, near Paris, 1925*

Mecano, whose first number, ready in the fall of 1921, only came out in February 1922, was typical of the little Dada-Constructivist magazines and became the platform for Van Doesburg's Dada contacts. In it he welcomed Arp's poems, Charchoune's drawings, Man Ray's pictures, Hausmann's manifestoes and collages, poems and articles by Schwitters, articles by Tzara and Ribemont-Dessaignes; and, from the Constructivist circle, a sculpture by Georges Vantongerloo, reliefs by Moholy-Nagy, drawings by Röhl, and so on.

Since with *De Stijl* Van Doesburg already had a purely Constructivist review at his disposal, he now used *Mecano* to express the Dada side of his personality. Witness the tour of Dada evenings he made with Schwitters in Holland. In an article written as a tribute to Van Doesburg after the latter's untimely death in March 1931, Schwitters looked back:

> At the end of 1922, Theo van Doesburg invited the leading Dadaists to a Congress in Holland, which was to take place the following year. Unfortunately we underestimated the receptivity of the Dutch, and so, aside from Van Doesburg, I was the only Dadaist who appeared for the introductory evening at the Hague Kunstkring. Theo van Doesburg delivered an explanatory lecture about Dadaism and I was supposed to provide an example of Dadaism. But the truth is that Van Doesburg, as he appeared on the platform in his dinner jacket, distinguished black shirtfront and white tie, and on top of that, bemonocled, powdered all white, his severe features imprinted with an eerie solemnity, produced an effect that was quite adequately Dada; to cite his own aphorism: "Life is a wonderful invention."
>
> Since I didn't know a word of Dutch, we had agreed that I should demonstrate Dadaism as soon as he took a drink of water. Van Doesburg drank and I, sitting in the middle of the audience, to whom I was unknown, suddenly began to bark furiously. The barking netted us a second evening in Haarlem; as a matter of fact it was sold out, because everyone was curious to see Van Doesburg take a drink of water and then hear me suddenly and unexpectedly bark. At Van Doesburg's suggestion, I neglected to bark on this occasion. This brought us our third evening in Amsterdam; this time people were carried out of the hall in a faint, a woman was so convulsed with laughter that for fifteen minutes she held the public attention, and a fanatical gentleman in a homespun coat prophetically hurled the epithet "idiots" at the crowd...
>
> It was for me the finest of experiences when suddenly, in Utrecht, as I was proclaiming the great and glorious revolution [i.e. *The Revolution in Revon*] (Van Doesburg was in the dressing-room), several unknown, masked men appeared on the stage, presented me with an extraordinary bouquet and proceeded to take over the demonstration. The bouquet was some three yards high, mounted on an immense wooden frame. It consisted of rotted flowers and bones, over which towered an unfortunately unpotted calla lily. In addition, an enormous putrid laurel wreath and a faded silk bow from the Utrecht cemetery were laid at the feet of the bourgeoisie. One of the gentlemen sat down at my table and read something out of an immense Bible he had brought with him. Since I understood very little of his Dutch, I considered it my duty to summon Van Doesburg to exchange a few friendly words with the gentleman.
>
> But this is not quite what happened. Van Doesburg came and saw and conquered. He took one look at the man and did not hesitate for long but, without introducing himself, without any ceremony whatsoever he tipped the man with his Bible and gigantic bouquet over into the music pit. The success was unprecedented. The original invader was gone, to be sure, but the whole crowd stood up as one man. The police wept, the public fought furiously among themselves, everyone trying to save a little bit of the bouquet; on all sides the people felicitated us and each other with black eyes and bloody noses. It was an unparalleled Dadaist triumph.

*"Does at Mid-Lent,"
Van Doesburg at the Bauhaus fancy-dress ball, Weimar, 1922*

*Handbill for a Dada evening
by Kurt Schwitters at Drachten,
Holland, April 1923*

*I love the pure idiocy of soft idealists sexless morality
disciples cut off by the Marquis de Sade and Lautréamont
holy men tougher than the sex devils Tolstoy fried potatoes
and Jesus Christ
kermis of soap trinkets laconic fetishism hideous branch of
Italian tailor's dummies with no member little pasteboard
idols at the street corners a thousand pineapple gods
captain of the metal sky
straw mattress in orange ultramarine little corporal dismissed by me bonset no immense and talkative of the flat
country beside a sea of cold urine
concave country of small typhoid burghers with flat feet
suckling the journalistic breasts of Lucas Bols*

Theo van Doesburg, 1921

There is no doubt that for Van Doesburg, confined in his circle of friends from *De Stijl* who would certainly have disapproved of collaboration with Dada, this tour and the review *Mecano* created a new outlet for mockery and letting off steam, clearly perceptible in Bonset's *Manifesto 0.96013*. In these circumstances, the major accomplishment in Dada-Constructivist publishing from the standpoint of the new elementary consciousness fell not to *Mecano* but to *Merz*, when in January 1923 Kurt Schwitters published its first number entitled *Holland Dada* on the occasion of the tour organized by Van Doesburg. Although the review was based on Dada, Schwitters declared in 1924:

> I dedicated my Merz writings to Dada. Merz was to serve Dada, abstraction and construction. Latterly the constructivist shaping of life in Germany has become so interesting that we are venturing to publish the forthcoming *Merz* numbers 8/9, called *Nasci*, with Dada... With us in Germany Dada is no longer as necessary now as it was in 1918. Artists now are living and creating in the spirit of the time, the spirit of 1924. Dada prepared the ground for them and lends them assistance even today. Here I am thinking, to mention only a few names, of people like Lissitzky (Hanover, Ambri-Sotto), Burchartz (Bochum), Moholy, Gropius and Meier (Weimar), Mies van der Rohe and Richter (Berlin), Schwitters (Hanover) and many others. There exists a "young" Dadaism of 1924; in 1918 there was only the "old" one of 1918. At that time Dada was forced to fight against everything, mainly against Expressionism which was then suffering from chronic gastric flu.

So the elementary approach continued and widened, giving a fresh impetus to "the constructivist shaping of life." In a statement of 1927 Schwitters used the term in speaking of "elementary poetry" and "elementary knowledge in painting."

This concept also had the advantage of singling out the presence, from 1918 on, of these potentialities in Hausmann's poster poems in Berlin, as in Tzara's proclamations on art and Arp's reliefs and collages in Zurich. In spite of dismissive or negative interpretations of Dada, the concept of the elementary called attention to the analogies of structure that relate Dada to Constructivism, which was likewise disparaged, in its case as cold, empty, anti-pictorial abstraction, as reducing design to the straight line, etc.

The term elementary art, as proclaimed in Berlin in October 1921, then covered all the manysided experimentation being carried out by Hausmann, Schwitters, Van Doesburg and Lissitzky, who were at once poets, architects, typographers, magazine editors and men of the theater, because they carried out a single task on all fronts. The new elementary outlook transcended the old formalistic categories by virtue of a vital overall artistic purpose which also reflected an intense metaphysical aspiration compar-able to that of the first abstract artists, Kandinsky, Malevich and Mondrian.

Cover of the periodical De Stijl, *No. 12, Leiden, 1924-1925, edited by Theo van Doesburg*

This new impetus marked the apogee of Dada on the international scene. The "new typography" (title of a book by Jan Tschichold in 1928) brought out the similarity of the researches which were being conducted throughout Europe, especially in the East, and which were so many striking points of convergence between Dada and Constructivism.

Never can the international avant-garde movement have been so close to initiating a thorough renewal of all kinds of printed matter, the design of books, reviews, posters, as well as advertisements, newspapers and all documents of practical use (receipts, bills, handbills), a visual revolution whose benefits the contemporary book trade seems to have decided to ignore completely.

Thus Lajos Kassák, a Constructivist poet and painter first in Budapest, then in Vienna (after his review was banned in Hungary), welcomed many Dadaists in *MA* (1916-1925), a periodical comparable in importance with *De Stijl*, and introduced a wide variety of red and black typography on the covers of his review.

One of the chief contributors to *MA* was Moholy-Nagy. In his book *Malerei Photografie Film* (1925) he called on artists to make good use of a certain number of typographical signs (such as full stops and rules) and of the page make-up. He explained that it was a question of abandoning the old concentric order/balance for a new, dynamic but eccentric balance, a page design more interesting to the eye than the old centered reductive layout.

Thus we have in Poland the typographical compositions of Stazewski and Syrkus for the periodical *Praesens*, as well as those of the Unist painter and theorist Strzemiński for the New Art exhibition (1923).

In Holland a major and unusual contribution, on the fringe of *De Stijl* and *Merz*, was made by the large folded sheets that Hendrik Werkman published from 1923 to 1926 and which made up the nine numbers of his review *The Next Call* in Groningen. Using an old hand-press, Werkman printed the wood elements (*druksels*) of his composition one by one. By its exploitation of the sensitivity of wood and the effect of sensually evaluated pressure, his work combined in complete purity a Constructivist plastic art and a Dada content. His choice of inks (ochre, red, midnight blue) and cream paper naturally played a large part in the impact of the whole.

In 1928, the year when Tschichold's book on the new typography was published, the Berlin periodical *Der Sturm* devoted a special number to this subject, probably on the initiative of Schwitters, with contributions by Piet Zwart, Otto Goedecker, Jan Tschichold and Schwitters himself. Nevertheless, we are indebted to Raoul Hausmann for a statement that reflects the resonance of work on the visual sign in an article published in 1932:

> In typography the naturalistic vision reached its peak during the eighteenth and nineteenth centuries, while at the same time, on the physiological level, quick and easy communication by reading sank to a low ebb. The first steps away from the anarchy of naturalism were taken by the Futurists and Dadaists. This resulted apparently in a new anarchy, but one purely autophonetic this time, which became the basis of the new typography. Until then the absolute rule had required the page setting, especially the title pages, to be organized in relation to the central axis. The Futurists, and even more the Dadaists, understood that only optically could the reading or communication of sounds be made effective. It was in certain pages printed around 1919 that the physiological-optical principle was consistently applied for the first time. Not without reason was the purely phonetic poem only discovered then, and supported optically by a new kind of typography. The photomontage also put forth by the Dadaists served the same purpose: renewal and reinforcement of the physiological aspect of typography. During this period it had already been noticed that the growing need for the image, in other words, the redoubling of the text by a visual illustration, could not be satisfied by their simple juxtaposition, but called for an optical construction based on a conceptual linguistic foundation.

Phonetic poem by Til Brugman published in De Stijl, *Leiden, March-April 1923*

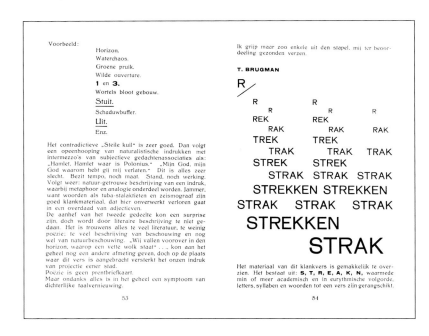

László Moholy-Nagy: *Light-Space Modulator, 1930, as reconstructed in 1970*

The elementary poems of Schwitters (*Bildgedicht*, *Gesetztes Bildgedicht*), like the "W" poems by the writer Anthony Kok, Bonset's *letterklankbeelden*, the *klankvers* by Til Brugman (the woman friend of Hannah Höch), the dactyloplastic or typoplastic works of Pietro Saga (pseudonym of Stefi Kiesler, wife of the New York architect and stage

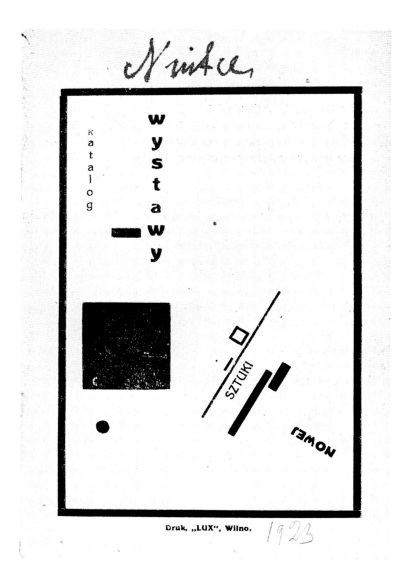

Cover of the catalogue of the New Art exhibition,
Wilno, Poland, 1923, with typography by Strzemiński

designer Frederick Kiesler), as well as the important work on ''bioscopic''
book design developed by Lissitzky, the typographic ventures of Iliazd (for
his Zaum writings) and Werkman, can all be read as the optical dimension of
an experiment on sound and rhythm at the meeting point of language and
music.

These experiments were devoid of the symbolical elements attaching
to the luxuriant transrational linguistic productions of Khlebnikov (see
Chapter 2), as also to Baargeld's *Bimmelresonanz* (rich in the legacy left by

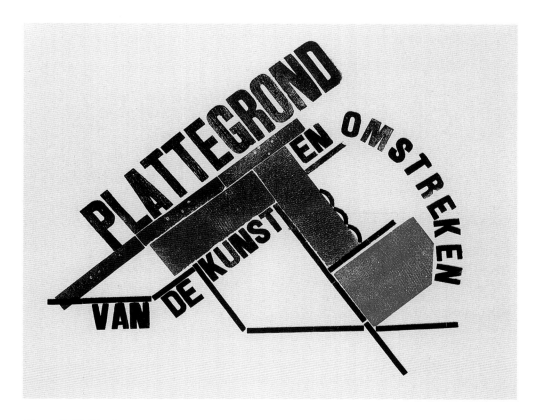

Hendrik N. Werkman: *Plattegrond, plate from* The Next Call, *1926*

Page from the art periodical De Stijl with a sound poem
(''Letterklankbeelden'') by I.K. Bonset, November 1921

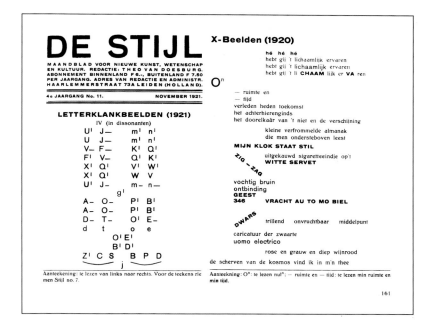

the Expressionist poets Stramm and Morgenstern). They should rather be
compared with Joyce's masterpiece, *Finnegans Wake*, written from 1922
to 1939. This last-named work, of major importance in the twentieth century,
was passionately analyzed, and rightly so, by Moholy-Nagy in *Vision in
Motion* (1947), because this book, testament of the Hungarian Constructivist
who headed the New Bauhaus in Chicago, was wholly dedicated to his theory
of perception, to the dynamics of vision and the need for a change of
biological, social and technological data permitting man to transform his life
and environment.

The typography in the above-mentioned poems (Kok, Brugman,
Van Doesburg-Bonset) resulted from the visual literary transcription of an
uttered sound, from which emanated a vibratory visual tension. So true is this
that Hausmann called his poems ''optophonetic'' (e.g. *kp'erioum*, 1920). It
also explains why, when publishing in July 1921 some elementary poems by
Kurt Schwitters consisting wholly of a pattern of numbers, the editors of *De
Stijl* reproduced, not the numbers, but their transliteration, in order to bring
out their sound value (*klankwaarde*), the last-named word evoking in Dutch
the title of poems made up of letters of different sizes published by Bonset
(*letterklankbeelden*): sound images of letters.

The Aubette cinema and dance hall, Strasbourg, 1926-1928,
designed by Hans Arp, Sophie Taeuber-Arp and Theo van Doesburg

Running parallel, not limited to purely forming and creative aesthetic purposes, but with much wider aims in view, these researches culminated, beyond the closely connected fields of typography and page and space layout, in a new and singularly bold architecture of space, stemming from earlier reliefs and assemblages: Kurt Schwitters' *Merzbau*, Lissitzky's *Proun* spaces and Cabinet of the Abstractionists, to which we should add the designing and installation of the Aubette restaurant complex in Strasbourg (1926-1928) by Hans Arp, Sophie Taeuber and Van Doesburg, together with the constructions and stage sets of Murayama, a Japanese artist trained in Berlin.

Little known in Europe, classified by Lissitzky under the heading Merz in *The Isms of Art*, Murayama, after his return to Japan early in 1923, championed what he called "conscious constructivism," devoting himself simultaneously to choreography, sculpture and stage design, notably for Kaiser's *From Morning to Midnight* in 1925. Murayama then became one of the founders of the Dada-Constructivist group Mavo (a name composed of letters chosen at random, often abbreviated to MV), whose review stood out for its typographical inventiveness.

Many achievements in the field of stage design attracted attention at the time. In particular, in 1923, the sets done in Leningrad by Tatlin for Khlebnikov's *Zanguezi* (a few months after the poet's death); and in Paris Fernand Léger's décor for *The Creation of the World*, staged by Rolf de Maré's Swedish Ballet with a libretto by Blaise Cendrars, music by Darius Milhaud and choreography by Jean Börlin. In their capacity as theater settings, these works, although verging on the abstract, were "functional" for all that. The important architectural project begun by Schwitters in the same year, 1923, acquired a different status.

Tomoyoshi Murayama: *Set design for Georg Kaiser's play* From Morning to Midnight, *1924-1925*

Cover of the Japanese periodical Mavo,
No. 5, June 1925

Vladimir Tatlin: *Set for Khlebnikov's* Zanguezi, *Leningrad, 1923*

Elementarized Architecture

A system of tension in free space.
Changing space into town-planning.
No groundwork, no wall.
Breaking loose from the earth,
Doing away with the static axis.
By creating new possibilities of living,
A new society is created.

Frederick Kiesler, 1927

Fernand Léger: *Set design for the ballet*
The Creation of the World, *Paris, 1922*

The Merzbau

The Merzbau (Merz building) was Kurt Schwitters' *magnum opus*, a metamorphosis of space of great plastic and rhythmic beauty. Fate saw to it that he had to construct it three times (along with the *Ursonate*, he looked on it as his masterpiece), although not a single original Merzbau has come down to us.

The first Merzbau at Hanover on which he worked from 1923 to 1936 was destroyed during air raids in 1943, long after he had left Germany. From photographs of it taken by Schwitters, a reconstruction (1988) was attempted at the Sprengel Museum in Hanover, which also houses the Kurt Schwitters archives.

Fleeing Nazi Germany, which had included his Merz pictures in the Degenerate Art exhibition, he undertook a second Merzbau after he had settled at Lysaker in Norway in 1937. It was destroyed by fire in 1951, three years after his death. Ahead of the advancing Germans, Schwitters reached England in 1940, where he was interned in various camps for seventeen months as an "enemy alien." After settling at Ambleside in the Lake District, he started a third Merzbau in 1947. This time he called it Merzbarn, partly because he built it in a barn and partly to show his rejection of the German language. His death at the beginning of 1948 prevented him from finishing it.

Kurt Schwitters: *View of the Hanover Merzbau, 1923-1936, destroyed in 1943*

Merzbau is the construction of an interior space by means of plastic forms and colors. In glassed-in grottoes Merz compositions form a cubic volume and join up with white cubic forms to make up the interior architecture. Each inner part acts as a hinge element for the next part. There are no details forming a unit in themselves or a partial composition. A great many different forms act as intermediaries between the cube and the undefined forms. Sometimes I have taken a form in nature, but usually I constructed the form in terms of the different parallel or crossing lines. In this way I found my most important form: the demi-helix.
I make a great difference between artistic logic and scientific logic, between constructing a new form and observing a form in nature. In constructing a new form, one creates an abstract and artistic work. In observing a form in nature, one makes no work of art, one only studies nature.

Kurt Schwitters, 1933

Kurt Schwitters: *Merz Composition, 1923*

The first Merzbau, $11\frac{1}{2}$ feet high, stood in Schwitters' house in the Waldhausenstrasse, Hanover (bombed out in 1943). It consisted of a column which ran through two storeys of the building, the house being "pierced from top to bottom with passages like mineshafts, crevasses artificially created through the storeys and spiral tunnels connecting the cellar with the roof" (Arp).

In the descriptions supplied by Schwitters, he called this Merzbau "the cathedral of erotic misery," a title which masked ironic and provocative commentaries, while possibly hinting at other associations. We should remember that in Zurich Hugo Ball had called abstraction "the cathedral of the future" and that in Paris Picabia dismissed Cubism as a "cathedral of shit." In Germany itself, in a leaflet issued during the first and only Bauhaus exhibition at Weimar in 1923, just as Schwitters was setting to work on the Merzbau, Oskar Schlemmer had spoken of building "the cathedral of socialism."

To crown it all, Schwitters declared that this name bore no relation to its content, "the fitting destiny," he remarked ironically, "for names."

Kurt Schwitters: *View of the Hanover Merzbau,*
1923-1936, destroyed in 1943

His house in Hanover was shot through with mine shafts from top to bottom. Openings in the floors made a system of tunnels connecting the roof with the ground floor. Obviously not a residence in the style of the Sun King. Working hard at it over a period of years, Schwitters succeeded in completely "Merzing" the house where he lived. The soaring Merz columns ingeniously constructed out of rusty old iron bars, mirrors, wheels, family portraits, bedsprings, newspapers, cement, paints, plaster, and glue—lots and lots of glue—forced their way upward through successive holes, gullies, abysses, and fissures.

Hans Arp, 1949

Kurt Schwitters: *View of the Hanover Merzbau, 1923-1936, destroyed in 1943*

The Merzbau was a "pure shaping" of autobiographical elements, these latter giving a Dadaistic literary background to the work. In the alveoles, called grottoes, the inventor had placed light bulbs which illuminated the whole. After a short-circuit he replaced them by candles which made it look like a Christmas tree (visitors could wind up an organ which played "Silent Night, Holy Night"). In the "sadistic grotto" reposed the mutilated body of a young girl "worthy of regrets," colored with tomato juice, surrounded by offerings. In another corner stood "the 10% disabled war veteran" with his headless daughter. This girl, called Mona Hausmann, actually turned out to be a reproduction of the Mona Lisa. The new face, that of his friend Raoul Hausmann, added Schwitters, took away "the stereotyped smile." Elsewhere could be found the treasure of the Nibelungen with a thousand glittering objects, a Goethean grotto with one of Goethe's legs by way of a relic, as well as "pencils worn down almost to the tip by poetry," a corner devoted to Luther and a brothel with a three-legged lady conceived by Hannah Höch . . .

The explanations given by Schwitters are all the more interesting because in many respects they are unexpected, considering the austerely constructed plastic aspect of the Merzbau which implies the absence of any anecdotal literary content. During the visit of Willi Pferdekamp, sent by his friend Michel Seuphor to find out about the Merzbau, Schwitters ceremoniously took out of a niche a box containing a doll and presented it as the tomb of St. Cecilia; from another recess he took a closed jar containing "the master's urine" in which everlasting flowers were dissolved. All things considered, behind the author's assertion that there was no relation between the title of the work and its contents, the shrewd visitor divined some duplicity, especially as many of the commentaries freely made by Schwitters were packed full of interpretative meaning. Seuphor goes on to say:

> Pferdekamp had been Schwitters' companion on a trip to Berlin. Gently but firmly Schwitters led him to the Potsdammerplatz in the evening to read the illuminated news flashes, among which, in between the political news items and announcements of various catastrophes, Pferdekamp was rather astonished to see the words *Kurt Schwitters ist in Berlin* (Kurt Schwitters is in Berlin). Only the Berlin readers of *Der Sturm* (and there were very few of them) knew the name of Kurt Schwitters at the time. But this authentic Dadaist had taken the precaution of announcing his visit to himself.

The Merzbau became consubstantial with its inventor. When the course of events in Europe drove him away from this "space in progress" so closely bound up with his very life (remember that the first Merzbau was created while Joyce was writing his own cathedral *Finnegans Wake*), Schwitters never stopped rebuilding it, as if it were as essential to him as the shell to the snail. This hardship was spared him with the *Ursonate* which this total artist had made into his sound environment. He gave a recital of it at leisure for himself and his intimates, photographed by Lissitzky and by his own son Ernst, "just as in himself eternity changes him."

Artists in the Unovis Free Workshops at Vitebsk, White Russia, c. 1919-1920

El Lissitzky: *Cover of the periodical* Broom, *February 1923*

After Lissitzky settled in Germany in the autumn of 1922, the relations he established during the Weimar Dada-Constructivist Congress with Van Doesburg, Arp and Schwitters were among the closest ever made between Dadaist and Constructivist circles.

Lissitzky was an active contributor to *De Stijl*. In the number for October 1922 he published his *Suprematist Story of Two Squares*. This children's story conceived at Vitebsk in 1920 is not a tale made up of abstract images, but a concrete book, bringing about a material transformation of reading, developing a different relation with the world and space. As a children's book, the *Suprematist Story of Two Squares* links up with Lissitzky's earlier books in the Jewish tradition (*The Legend of Prague, The Goat's Story*).

Lissitzky had explained his "bioscopic" conceptions of book design and typography, visually expressed in the *Suprematist Story of Two Squares*, in the first number of *Unovis*: "The ancient Bible was printed with letters alone. The new one will enter man's head through the eye. Books must be constructed as bodies launched into space and time, like a dynamic bas-relief, in which every page brings new forms. Waves of great speed and intensity will move about on their path."

A native of Smolensk in Russia, Lissitzky had studied architecture in Germany, at Darmstadt. (His matriculation at the Petrograd Academy of Arts had not been accepted because of the small number of places reserved for members of the Jewish community.) On his return to Russia he completed his studies under an architect, before teaching architecture and the graphic arts at the Free Workshops at Vitebsk. These Free Workshops, founded by Marc Chagall in the fall of 1918, subsequently called on Lissitzky, a former pupil, to take charge of the lithography workshop.

One of the future signatories of the *Call for an Elementary Art*, the painter Ivan Puni, was teaching there at the same time. His long-standing friendship with Malevich went back to the days before the advent of Suprematism and Malevich replaced him after his departure. Malevich's arrival marked an important date, because a working group called *Unovis* (short for Affirmation of the New Art) was immediately formed on his initiative.

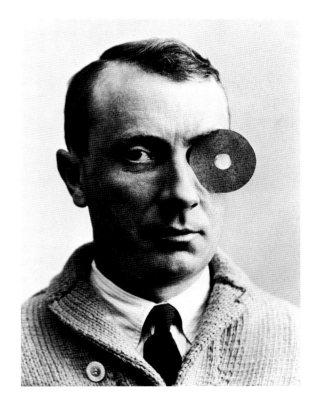

El Lissitzky:
Photograph of Hans Arp with Dada monocle, 1923

179

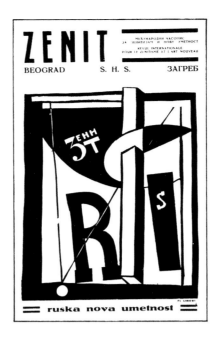

In this context, Lissitzky met Malevich and produced his *Proun* paintings (*proekt uverzhdenii a novago*, project for the affirmation of the new), which should not be looked on as pure painting. Owing much to their creator's training as architect and engineer, they set out installations and devices (especially rotatory ones) in the new non-objective space advocated by Malevich. In *Die Kunstismen* (The Isms of Art), Lissitzky himself defined Proun as "the interchange station between painting and architecture."

Lissitzky executed his first portfolio of Proun lithographs at Vitebsk in 1920 and supervised the publication of Malevich's first didactic work, *O novykh sistemakh v isskusstve* (On New Systems in Art) in 1919.

The work taken up by Lissitzky with Van Doesburg, Arp and Schwitters innovated chiefly in the field of book design and typography, in which the Zurich Dadaists had already experimented very freely in the workshop of the printer Heuberger. It was a field in which Lissitzky revealed a probably unsurpassed mastery. His principal successes consisted on the one hand in the cover designs for the review *Broom*, for example, and for booklets by Ehrenburg, Mayakovsky and Vkhutemas (Higher Artistic and Technical Workshops), but also and above all in the overall design of Mayakovsky's book of verse *Dlya golosa* (For the Voice) published in Russian in Berlin in 1922, comprising sixty-two plates in red and black.

Lissitzky also designed the cover of the catalogue of the *Erste russische Ausstellung* (First Russian Exhibition) at the Van Diemen gallery in Berlin (October 1922), a decisive exhibition for the diffusion of Russian non-object-ive art in the West. It seems that the organizing role played by Lissitzky was vital to its success, not forgetting the help given by the poet Ilya Ehrenburg.

Title page of Insel Almanach *with a photogram by Jan Tschichold, 1929*

El Lissitzky: *Cover of* Merz 8-9, *special* Nasci *number, Hanover, April-July 1924*

Marking the high point of the Schwitters–Lissitzky collaboration, the celebrated *Nasci* number of the review *Merz* (April-July 1924) bore on its blue and red cover by Lissitzky the declaration: "Nature, from the Latin Nasci, means being born, becoming, that is to say everything which, by its own force, develops, forms and moves." It appears that Lissitzky chose the word as a symbolic formula, so that he could turn this number into a "museum of avant-gardes" and take stock of the artistic situation in a preface whose philosophical tone Schwitters corrected by stating clearly that the number represented neither a philosophy nor a system. The idea reappeared later in the book written by Lissitzky and Arp (*Die Kunstismen*, The Isms of Art) and in the creation of the "Cabinet of the Abstractionists."

Lissitzky was approached by Schwitters to compose the typography of the *Ursonate*, but this collaboration did not last, because, according to its author, Lissitzky proved to be more of a competitor than a friend in the undertaking. Finally, it was Jan Tschichold, an independent authority as author of *The New Typography* (1928), who carried out the task which Schwitters obviously wanted to delegate to a third party, perhaps owing to his rejection of a functional typography which he was already practicing because of professional obligations: Schwitters was co-founder in 1927 of the *Ring neuer Werbegestalter* (Association of New Advertising Artists), with Baumeister, Domela, Tschichold and Vordemberge-Gildewart.

As compared with the stricter design of a Lissitzky, Dadaist typography owes more to Mallarmé and Apollinaire than to any thinking along architectural lines. Indeed, it forms a contrast by its use of polysemic words, by the multitude of signs, by the intensity of contradictory, spontaneous, indeterminate impulses, deliberately irreducible to ordinary channels of writing and speech. Tristan Tzara had already proclaimed in the *Dada Manifesto 1918*: "Every page must explode, either by profound heavy seriousness, the whirlwind, poetic frenzy, the new, the eternal, the crushing joke, enthusiasm for principles, or by the way in which it is printed."

Nevertheless, in so far as elementary spontaneity found an outlet in the explosion of speech in letters, i.e. in typographical characters and signs, much typography in the twenties clearly reveals a combination of two apparently contradictory conceptions. Thus Schwitters declared in the Berlin periodical *G* that "the associations of ideas and words are not elementary, but the letters are" and that in fact he himself wrote "poems made of letters."

At all events, in this area where two sensibilities met, the great typographical innovations of the twenties were made, such as those of Lajos Kassák, painter and editor of the review *MA*, or those of the Polish painter Strzemiński, theorist of Unism (1928), for the books of verse by his friend, the poet Julian Przyboś.

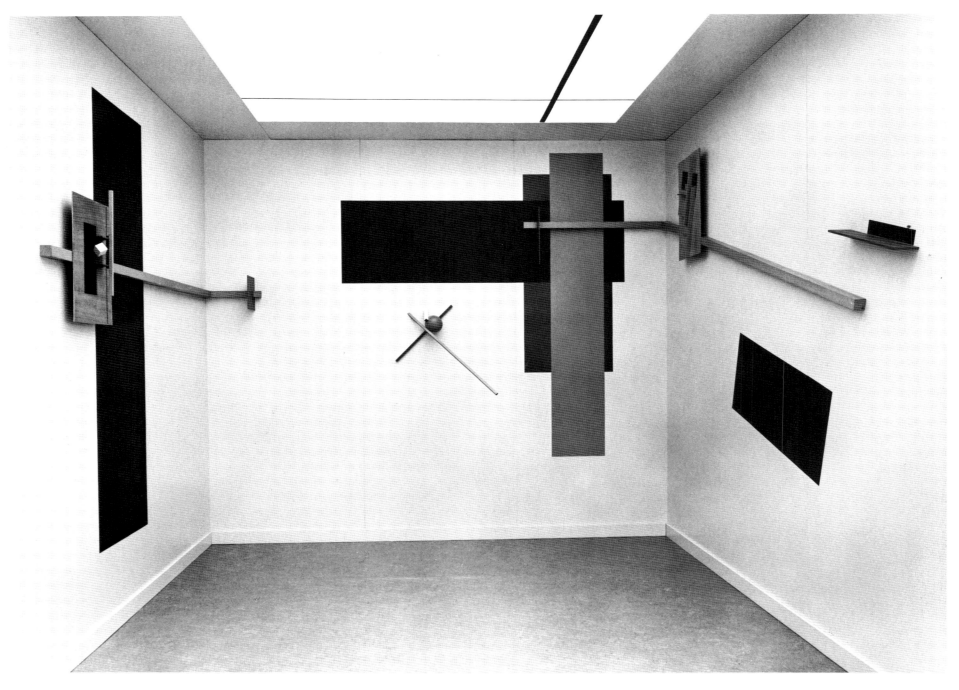

El Lissitzky: Proun Space, 1923, as reconstructed in 1965

The new Proun space

The Proun spaces (*Prounenräume*) worked out by Lissitzky just as Schwitters was beginning his Merzbau confirmed the interchangeability of concepts and realizations in the elementary approach. Lissitzky constructed three Proun spaces in Germany from 1923 to 1927. They consisted of small rooms housed in museums for which he was wholly responsible. The first Proun space was created in Berlin in 1923 in the rooms of the *Grosse Berliner Kunstausstellung*. Reproduced in the first number of *G*, it was rebuilt in Holland in 1965 by the Van Abbe Museum at Eindhoven. It had absolutely no functional purpose and consisted basically of the integration of Proun reliefs into a cabinet whose conception formed a new work in itself, a new Proun expressed in terms of volume.

The second Proun space was constructed in Dresden in 1926. As a last stage, Lissitzky constructed in 1927 in the Hanover Landesmuseum a "Cabinet of the Abstractionists" in which he incorporated a selection of abstract Constructivist works (Moholy-Nagy, Buchheister) with his own work on the surfaces of the walls. Destroyed by the Nazis in 1936, the Cabinet of the Abstractionists was rebuilt in 1979 by the Sprengel Museum in Hanover.

Cover of the book by Hans Arp and *El Lissitzky*, Kunstism 1914-1924: Die Kunstismen. Les ismes de l'art. The Isms of Art, *Zurich-Munich-Leipzig, 1925*

The review *G* and the abstract film

Lastly we should mention the active part played by Lissitzky in the review *G* (for *Gestaltung*: design, shaping), founded in Berlin by Hans Richter, member of the first Dada nucleus in Zurich, with Werner Graeff and Lissitzky, and financed by Mies van der Rohe. Six issues appeared from July 1923 to April 1926. Presented in the form of a newspaper at first, *G* later adopted the genuine aspect of a review, while the typographical conception, by its painstaking precision, stood out from other works which combined Dada and Constructivist trends in the new elementary impetus (*"Es lebe die elementare Gestaltung,"* Long live elementary design, proclaimed Werner Graeff).

Highly attentive to problems of habitat and construction, especially in the industrial field, under the influence of Mies van der Rohe, the review *G* had various Dadaist collaborators (George Grosz, Arp, Tzara) who enlivened the austerity of the typographical design (e.g. the imprint in Toyen's lipstick sending "wireless kisses"). Raoul Hausmann, known as something of a dandy, appeared in it as a mannequin, asserting that "fashion is not mere nonsense, but an external expression of the body."

The review was also the only one to draw attention to the photograms by Man Ray (*Champs délicieux*) and Lissitzky, the abstract films by Hans Richter (*Rhythm 21*), Viking Eggeling (*Diagonal Symphony*) and Walter Ruttmann (*Opus*), also the films of Fernand Léger and Dudley Murphy (*Ballet mécanique*, with music by George Antheil) and René Clair (*Entr'acte*).

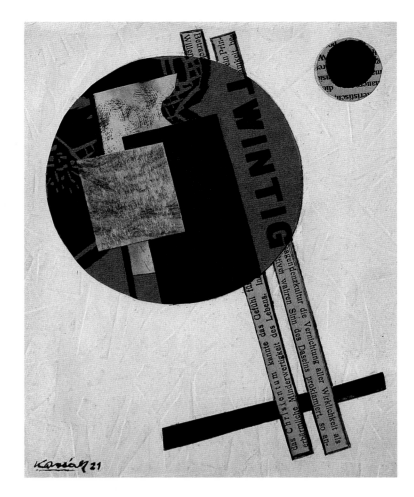

Lajos Kassák: *Untitled, 1921*

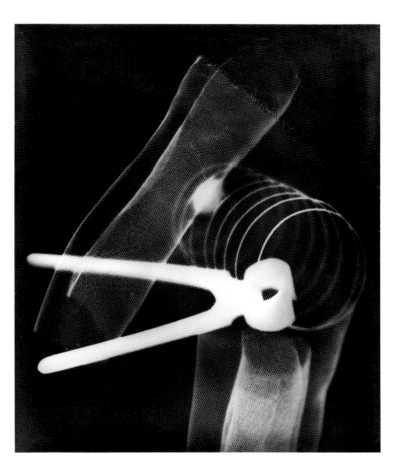

El Lissitzky: *Composition with Pliers and Spirals, before 1929*

The isms of art

In 1925 Lissitzky, together with Arp, published a short recapitulative essay, illustrating modern tendencies: *Die Kunstismen*. It is not without interest, at the end of this chapter on the history of the avant-gardes, to list the names of the movements, and those of the artists representing them, as they appeared in the inventory made by Arp and Lissitzky from 1925 to 1914, going backwards in time.

They singled out the following categories: abstract film (Eggeling, Richter), Constructivism (Tatlin, Obmokhu, Ladowski Workshop, Gabo), Verism (Grosz, Dix), Proun (Lissitzky and Lissitzky Workshop), Compressionism (Baumeister, Schlemmer), Merz (Schwitters, Murayama), Neo-Plasticism (Mondrian, Huszar, Rietveld, Van Doesburg, Vantongerloo), Purism (Ozenfant, Jeanneret), Dada (Picabia, Hausmann, Ernst, Arp, Man Ray, Hannah Höch, Sophie Taeuber), Simultaneism (Robert and Sonia Delaunay), Suprematism (Malevich, Unovis, Rozanova, Kliun), Metaphysical Painting (Chirico, Carrà), Abstraction (Kandinsky, Rodchenko, Miturich, Altman, Popova, Moholy-Nagy, Péri, Arp, Segal, Molzahn), Cubism (Picasso, Braque, Léger, Gleizes, Gris, Feininger, Archipenko, Lipchitz), Futurism (Boccioni, Severini, Balla, Russolo), and Expressionism (Chagall, Klee, Marc) in 1914. This slim volume, through its format and typography due to Lissitzky, recalls the series of Bauhausbücher (Bauhaus books); and by its system of classification ("the isms of art"), it stands out as the prototype of the many histories of modern art which have since been published during the twentieth century. By its historical and anthological conclusion, it heralds the coming end of the heyday of the avant-gardes, whose decline began with the approach of the thirties.

Chapter 8

The Dadaists After Dada

Tristan Tzara playing chess, Paris, c. 1960

The advent of Surrealism, a writers' movement which drew artists in its wake, heralded the decline of those forces that had pioneered the new modes of representation. Pictorial Surrealism retained some aspects of Dada —its provocative stance, its innovative approach to narration and poetry— but it nevertheless fell into a rut: it became a genre. The specific representational modes that Dada had privileged—and the novel, aleatory, playful and elementary creative procedures—were virtually discarded. Painting lost its autonomy. In the hands of the Surrealists provocativeness, which had been an essential ingredient of the Dadaists' creative freedom, became a genre in its own right, a set of "literary" themes that prefigured the group's flirtation with the ideology of revolution.

All those fields (typography, film, the abstract poetry of "unknown words") which had achieved independence under the Dadaists were again subordinated to literary preoccupations. André Breton expressed the Surrealists' attitude in a nutshell by dismissing the optical experiments of Dadaist poetry as mere "coquetry." He declared baldly that "though it was undermined by the Dada spirit, the review *Littérature* nevertheless remained relatively faithful to its original presentation. The typographical artifices that were the principal coquetry of *Dada* and *391* played no part in it." And he added, forgetting that the Dada microbe was "virgin": "Collaboration with elements that were, if not hostile to the new spirit, at least immune to its contagion—Valéry, Gide or Max Jacob, Cendrars, Morand— continued up until February 1920" (*Entretiens*, 1952).

Except for the "action" against the performance of *Cœur à gaz* in Paris (see Chapter 6) and Tzara's statement to Ilarie Voronca about personally renouncing Dada, that international movement disintegrated in much the same way it was born, almost randomly. Nevertheless most of its members, apart from those who joined the Surrealist ranks, continued to proclaim their allegiance to Dada for the rest of their lives. Such was the strength of this movement which was presided at once by no one and everyone. Each artist and writer, however isolated, continued to embody the Dada spirit and perpetuate all of its energy and creativity singlehandedly.

Kurt Schwitters, for example, not only carried on his Dada œuvre (like Duchamp, Picabia, Arp and Hausmann), but continued to publish his review *Merz* until 1932. The last number was a recording of the *Ursonate*. And it is surely fitting that Merz survived until long after the demise of Dada as an international movement.

And yet, as the social and political climate in Europe became increasingly troubled towards the end of the twenties, the power of the avant-garde innovators declined. The destiny of Schwitters and his Merzbau is exemplary in this regard; it shows us how hostile was the environment surrounding some of the major artists of the twentieth century. Time and again in the course of a life checkered with difficulties and exile Schwitters had to rebuild his Merzbau (which he had begun in 1923, see Chapter 7).

The regression in the arts that set in even before the thirties isolated the avant-garde all the more completely in that it went hand in hand with the rise of totalitarian régimes. How these avant-garde movements contributed unwittingly to the backlash that fostered the ideology of these antidemocratic systems is a topic well worth pursuing.

Contrary to the false report being spread about, to the effect that Dada's death is due to the withdrawal of a few individuals, the fact is I killed Dada myself, deliberately, because I considered that a state of individual freedom had in the end become a collective state and because the different "presidents" were beginning to think and feel in the same way. Now nothing is more repugnant to me than the lazy-mindedness which annihilates individual movements, even if these are akin to madness and contrary to the general interest. What I dislike about Surrealism today is in the same line of thought. The followers, who cannot be dispensed with, have assumed the command. Mediocrity has leveled everything down, and slackness and stupidity keep these men's feet in the mud from which they don't know how to extricate themselves. Their hypocritical dissimulation of mind gives an outward impression of discipline and unanimity, while inside them there is nothing but poverty and repression.

Tristan Tzara, 1925

Kurt Schwitters: *The Cult Pump (Merz 30, 54), 1930*

But first one must distinguish Italian Futurism (or more precisely Marinettian Futurism, to distinguish it from dissident Futurists like Palazzeschi) and its involvement with Fascism in the early twenties. Nothing similar occurred with Dada.

The first of the avant-gardes that overlapped during and immediately after World War One, Italian Futurism, with its carefully prepared social "actions," gave more weight to ideological issues than to purely creative ones. Worse, Mussolini adopted some aspects of the Futurists' program, in particular their rejection of uncertainty (in contrast to the Dadaists who celebrated and even dramatized polemics and contradictions) and their theoretical justification of violence.

Though it would be wrong to lump together Italian Futurism and Fascism, it is nevertheless impossible to overlook the numerous Futurist elements that helped to shape the Fascist ideology. These include Marinetti's concept of catharsis, his hostility to any kind of reform, his advocacy of violence as a means of settling arguments, his will to fuse the collective and the individual, his confusion of frustrated sexuality and religious feeling ("We despise women. We are convinced that love as a feeling and a wantonness is the least natural thing in the world. It is only the propagation of the species that is natural. When the sensual life is reduced to the strictly self-propagating

George Grosz: *Germania ohne Hemd, 1919*

Schulzens Seele

186

Hitler visiting the Nazi exhibition of "Degenerate Art",
Munich, July 1937

function we will have taken a great step forward in mankind's progress towards a grander stature'').

The dramaturgy of Fascism (parodied in Charlie Chaplin's *The Great Dictator*) was modelled on the histrionics of Italian Futurism whose leader, F.T. Marinetti, had proclaimed as early as 1911: "The word Italy must predominate over the word liberty."

The example of Italian Futurism has cast discredit on the very concept of the avant-garde. There is a recent theory based on the history of Marinetti's Futurism that modern art and the various avant-garde movements, as well as the different varieties of "progressive" thought in our century, are tainted because they embraced the myths of the "new man" and social progress, and because in their fervor the artists and theorists belonging to them contributed in the end, willingly or unwittingly, to the growth of totalitarianism.

There is a certain truth to this in the Italian context, but the theory is not borne out elsewhere, as shown by the Dadaists' permanent opposition to the Futurists and their ideas. This is clear from the manifestoes and proclamations issued by the Dadaists around this time, beginning with those of Tzara and the *Proletarian Art Manifesto* (1923, see Chapter 5); they are extraordinarily severe—more so than any other early twentieth century documents—as regards any form of ideological commitment, any attempt to legislate unity or to impose a general order (as Balla and Depero did when they called for the "Futurist reconstruction of the universe" in 1915).

The example of Schwitters who fled Germany after some of his works were shown in the "degenerate art" exhibitions organized by the Nazis, or that of Malevich and other avant-garde artists who were faced with execution or imprisonment in Russia, obviously calls for an analysis of the way the authoritarian conservative reaction used modern art to give itself a semblance of legitimacy.

In Germany the campaign against modern art culminated in the *Entartete Kunst* (degenerate art) exhibitions of 1937. But even before that date there were numerous attacks against the avant-garde, particularly Dadaism (whose works were described as the "extravagances of madmen or decadents"). In *Mein Kampf*, which Hitler wrote in jail in 1924 after the failure of the Beer Hall Putsch in Munich, we read the following: "Sixty years ago an exhibition of the testimonies of the so-called Dadaists would have seemed quite simply impossible and its organizers would have been confined in a madhouse, while today they preside over groups of artists. This epidemic could not have occurred, for public opinion would not have stood for it and the State would not have looked on without intervening. It was up to the government to see that the nation was not pushed into the arms of an intellectual folly. An end had to be put to a development like this. For if the day came when this form of art really corresponded to the general state of mind, then an upheaval big with consequences would have taken place among mankind. The wrong-headed development of the human brain would thus have begun . . . One trembles at the thought of how it might end." (*sic*)

Hannah Höch and her dolls, 1920

It is difficult to sum up the innumerable expressions of hostility to Dadaism in a few words. Nevertheless, at the risk of one more misunderstanding, we shall attempt a brief formulation; the misunderstanding from which Dadaism suffered is a chronic disease that still poisons the world. In its essence it can be defined as the inability of a rationalized epoch and of rationalized men to see the positive side of an irrational movement ... If this positive element has always been disregarded, any innate nastiness in Dadaism is less to blame than the generally negative, critical and cynical attitude of our time, which drives people to project their own vileness into persons, things and opinions around them. In other words, we believe that the neurotic conflict of our time, that manifests itself in a generally negative, unspiritual, and brutal attitude, discovered a whipping boy in Dadaism.

Richard Huelsenbeck, 1949

In such circumstances, the Dadaists had no choice but to leave Germany. Schwitters fled to Norway in 1936 when thirteen of his works were withdrawn from German museums. The following year four of them were exhibited as examples of "degenerate art." Walter Serner traveled frequently to other European countries and wrote several books (including the novel *Die Tigerin*) which are now being rediscovered in Germany; they were banned by the Nazi régime and he himself was arrested. He was last heard of in August 1942, when he was shipped with other deportees from Prague to Theresienstadt, a notorious concentration camp.

George Grosz did sets for Erwin Piscator and other German theater directors. He left the Communist Party in 1923 and stopped contributing to Communist periodicals, but frequently got into trouble with the German authorities (he was arrested for "blasphemy" in 1928). He then began a more realistic period, working in a simpler graphic style and in a less overtly controversial manner, laying down a few thick black lines with a brush to suggest themes that were nevertheless still engaged. He narrowly escaped being arrested and fled to the United States in 1932. Upon his arrival in New York, where he immediately founded an art school, he learned that he had been stripped of his German citizenship. His works were shown in American museums and the Guggenheim awarded him a grant. He became fascinated with Manhattan and took many photographs of New York's inner city.

Raoul Hausmann left Nazi Germany in 1933, studied the local architecture in the Balearic Islands, photographed nudes (some of which were published in Man Ray's album *Nudes* in 1935) and lived in Paris, then in Czechoslovakia.

Self-Portrait of Raoul Hausmann, 1930

Hans Richter: *Portrait of Walter Serner, 1917*

Photograph of Man Ray by David Bailey

During World War Two he returned to France, seeking refuge at Peyrat-le-Château and settled finally at Limoges. Hannah Höch, who was active in Holland on the fringe of the De Stijl group from 1926 to 1929, spent the war years in hiding in the caretaker's lodge of an abandoned airport at Heiligensee north of Berlin.

Richard Huelsenbeck signed up as ship's doctor in 1925 and journeyed to Japan, Burma, Formosa, Sumatra and the Philippines. Meanwhile he continued to contribute to journals like the *Berliner Illustrierte* and the *Münchner Illustrierte* (which sent him to Russia, China and Manchuria as their correspondent). Between 1926 and 1933 he wrote a series of articles on Dada —and a play—which were later collected and published by Robert Motherwell. He was expelled from the German Writers' Union in 1933 and forbidden to write. Perpetually in danger of being arrested, he spent three years vainly trying to get a visa for the United States. Finally, he shipped on a boat bound for India and eventually reached New York in 1935, where he practiced psychiatry under the name Charles R. Hulbeck. His writings were published in the sixties under the title *Memoirs of a Dada Drummer*. The *Dada Almanach* he had published in Berlin in 1920 was reissued in a facsimile edition by Dick Higgins, the publisher of composer John Cage and concrete poet Emmett Williams, at Something Else Press, a publishing house in the Fluxus spirit.

Far from the upheavals in Europe, the situation in America was very different. The Dadaists' creations had a place here. Ever since the Armory Show (1913), Mutt-Duchamp's *Fountain* (1917) and the founding of the Société

Anonyme (see Chapter 1), Dada was part of the history of the visual arts in the United States. The important exhibition of the Société Anonyme collection that Katherine Dreier organized at the Brooklyn Museum in 1926 was followed, and in a sense continued, by Alfred H. Barr's shows at the Museum of Modern Art, with their substantial catalogues (especially *Cubism and Abstract Art*, 1936).

Robert Motherwell began to bring out his Documents of Modern Art series in 1944. The first volume was a translation of Apollinaire's *Méditations esthétiques*; then came selected writings of Piet Mondrian, Wassily Kandinsky, Jean (Hans) Arp (*On My Way*), László Moholy-Nagy (*The New Vision*) and Richard Huelsenbeck (*Memoirs of a Dada Drummer*). Motherwell himself compiled an international Dada anthology, *The Dada Painters and Poets* (1951), that remains unrivaled in any language.

Concurrently, Motherwell's publisher (Wittenborn, Schultz) issued Huelsenbeck's *Dada Manifesto 1949* as a separate broadside. Motherwell had wanted to include it in his book, but Tzara had objected strongly, no doubt because in it Huelsenbeck again claims to have "found" the word Dada. Marcel Duchamp had then tactfully offered to translate Tzara's *An Introduction to Dada*, which was published as a separate broadside too. To add a footnote to the debate over the origin of the word Dada, it is significant that, following Tzara's objection, none of the Dadaists would co-sign Huelsenbeck's manifesto, even though the "Dada drummer" compares the attacks against modern art in the late forties to the Nazi campaign against the Dada Movement. "The closer we look," he writes, "the clearer it becomes that the creative principle that developed in Dadaism is identical with the very principle of modern art."

In 1953 a small exhibition was held at the Sidney Janis Gallery in New York, *Dada 1916-1923*. The catalogue, designed by Marcel Duchamp and printed on a large sheet originally distributed as a crumpled ball of paper, contained statements by Arp, Hulbeck (i.e. Huelsenbeck) and Tzara. Sidney Janis also organized two Schwitters shows in 1952 and 1956. (Schwitters had died in England in 1948.)

On the other side of the Atlantic, a rapprochement between the Dadaists and the Surrealists took place in May 1924 when Tzara's play *Mouchoir de nuages* was performed in Paris. And yet, though the founder of Dada fraternized with André Breton and his circle, who admired his play, there is a perceptible coolness, if not outright hostility, towards Surrealism in Tzara's last interviews, in particular in his rather mordant comments about the Surrealists' flirtation with parapsychology.

For the attitude of André Breton's group was that, whenever it looked like Dada might steal the limelight from Surrealism, it had to be upstaged. As a result, during the twenties the fact that the theoretical positions of Dada and Constructivism were interwoven at the heart of the international artistic avant-garde from 1916 to 1923 tended to be overlooked.

And so the critical commonplace that the Dada Movement was merely an extended adolescent caper, an exuberant but nihilistic and scandalous provocation in the spirit of Alfred Jarry's *Ubu*, gradually acquired the status of a historical verity. Had it not been for Aragon, Breton and Soupault, who gave it a less negative sequel when they published *Littérature*, the official version goes, Dada would never have led anywhere; it would have had no artistic epilogue. This judgment is based solely on the history of Paris Dada, yet it is not totally groundless. The Dadaists were skeptical about art,

Marcel Duchamp:
Fresh Widow (back view), 1920

Sophie Taeuber-Arp: *Triptych, 1918*

Hans Arp: *The Umbilical Bottle, c. 1918*

particularly modern art. However they knew for their part how much was lost through the Surrealists' diversion of their movement. They knew too that the Surrealists' reading of art history overlooks the potential of a truly international cooperation of writers and artists (Iliazd's Zaum, Delaunay and Van Doesburg's sets for Tzara's *Cœur à gaz*), not to mention the contribution of those isolated Constructivists who were active in Paris in the early twenties (Mondrian and Van Doesburg) and the example of that most elementary of all artists, Kurt Schwitters (see Chapters 5 and 7).

The Paris Dadaists took part sporadically and singly in the activities organized in the early twenties by the *Littérature* group and later by the Surrealists.

From 1929 to 1931 Georges Ribemont-Dessaignes edited an outstanding literary review, *Bifur*, which published poetry and prose by Henri Michaux, Isaac Babel, Tristan Tzara, William Carlos Williams, Ramón Gómez de la Serna, Michel Leiris, Ernest Hemingway, James Joyce, the Russian Formalist Shklovsky, Kafka, Arp, Roger Gilbert-Lecomte, as well as statements by Buster Keaton, some of Hölderlin's later "mad" poetry, excerpts from Giorgio de Chirico's *Hebdomeros* and documents relating to Mayakovsky's suicide.

In 1931 Tzara wrote an *Essai sur la situation de la poésie* and published a book-length poem, *L'Homme approximatif*. Attacked by the collaborationist press during the war, hunted by both the Gestapo and the Vichy police, he went into hiding at Souillac in southwestern France and wrote for the Resistance papers while continuing to produce poetry (*Grains et issues*) and criticism (*Le Pouvoir des images* and *Les Ecluses de la poésie*).

Tzara was invited to lecture at the Sorbonne in 1947, not on Dadaism but on Surrealism and the post-war period. This did not prevent him from slipping in numerous asides about Dada. Meanwhile Jean-Paul Sartre, then at the peak of his career as an Existentialist philosopher and writer, proclaimed himself the "new Dada" (if we are to believe Huelsenbeck).

Memoirs, autobiographies and first-hand accounts by Dadaists, and the first extensive interviews with them, began to appear immediately after World War Two, their value enhanced by the fact that some of the original Dadaists had already died. Besides Walter Serner who had disappeared in 1942 (see above), Sophie Taeuber-Arp had died in Zurich in 1943, poisoned by fumes from a leaky stove. She was recognized posthumously as one of the major exponents of pure plasticism. The last of her activities in this field had been to co-found the review *Plastique* (1937-1939) with Arp, César Domela, Otto Freundlich (who died en route to a Nazi concentration camp in 1943) and the critics Carola Giedion and Herta Wescher. The first number was a tribute to Kasimir Malevich (who died in the spring of 1935); in general, the review was a forum for plasticists and artists who remained true to the Dada sensibility.

Arp gave voice to his grief at Sophie Taeuber's death in a series of elegiac poems ("Sophie dreamt Sophie painted Sophie danced") and in a number of his later pictorial works (*Flower Shed for a Dead Lady*, *Despairing Man's Constellation*). He dedicated the first complete edition of his French poems to her (*Le Siège de l'air*, 1945) and devoted several poems to her memory (*Ecritures d'ange*, 1952). Later, Arp insisted regularly that her work be shown with his.

Accused by the German occupation forces in Holland of printing nonconformist works, Werkman was executed at Groningen in 1945. The Dadaist and Creationist Vicente Huidobro died at his home in Cartagena, Chile, in 1948, two years after the publication of *Three Exemplary Stories* which he wrote jointly with Arp at Arcachon in 1931. 1948 was also the year Kurt Schwitters died at Kendal, in the Lake District of northern England, at the age of sixty, only a few months after starting work on his third and last Merzbau (*Merzbarn*, which was left unfinished).

Woodcut by Hans Arp, from a drawing by Sophie Taeuber-Arp, and poems by Hugo Ball in Poésies de mots inconnus, *edited by Iliazd, Paris, 1949*

During the war László Moholy-Nagy, who was by then the director of the Chicago Bauhaus, communicated Schwitters' address to Raoul Hausmann living in isolation at Limoges, and was thus instrumental in getting the two exiled friends to start up a correspondence and to publish jointly a new periodical, PIN. The preface reads like a manifesto.

> A fancy
> A thing of fan
> The right thing of Phan
> World needs new tendencies in poeting and paintry
> Old stuff is not able to lead further on
> Muses ought to be whisked, when mankind will survive
> In the very war creative whisky is fallen very dry
> We will develop whisky spirit, because we see with our ears
> and hear with our eyes
> Our phantic drsls and rlquars are full of whisked away
> formal life
> They overwhelm "modern poetry" by their new taste
> Their phantic contents are so direct that they are placed
> above the meanings of language at all
> Language is only a medium to understand and not to
> understand
> You prefer the language when you understand by it
> things which everybody knows by heart already. We
> prefer the language which provides you a new feeling
> for new whiskers to come
> Give up your human feelings and please go through our
> fan pin and you will know that it was worth while
> PIN
> The thing of phan——fan

Schwitters tried in vain to get the London Gallery to publish this review. In a letter to Hausmann, dated March 1947, he complained: "I am very sad, but despite all my efforts Mr. Mesens does not want to publish PIN. Even when I told him that we did not want any money he laughed and said that we would have to pay him to publish it, which he had no intention of doing. He read it carefully but didn't like it. He says that it would have been more topical twenty-five years ago, and that now we would not be understood. And there is something else: there are imitators, for example the 'Lettristes' in Paris who are copying the *Ursonate* by Hausmann and myself and not even acknowledging us, we who made it twenty-five years before them and for better reasons."

Directed by the Belgian Surrealist E.L.T. Mesens, who professed to be keenly interested in Dada, the London Gallery would not publish PIN but invited Schwitters to read his "Merzpoems." The BBC sound men who came to record him left in the middle of the *Ursonate*. It is worth noting in passing that, as a riposte to the *Lettristes*, Iliazd, the Zaum poet and typographer, published an anthology a few months later in Paris entitled *Poésie de mots inconnus* (The Poetry of Unknown Words), which combines work by leading verbal artists with experimental typography and engravings.

As for PIN, it was rescued by Schwitters' "English" friends—notably the Pole Stefan Themerson (1910-1988)—who published it in a bilingual

Kurt Schwitters: *Monument to the Artist's Father, 1922-1923*

"Anything, but not Picabia": such has been the bargain offered to innovating art over these last twenty years. And the bargain has been accepted pretty generally, although it is a most shameful one, and from it Picabia will be seen to emerge all the greater. Held up to an uncommon execration, he has systematically done just the opposite of what was necessary to ward it off.

André Breton, 1940

Birdiness:

Oiseautal

Pitsu puit puittituttsu uttititi ittitaan
pièt pièt pieteit tenteit tuu uit
ti ti tinax troi troi toi to
Iti iti loi loi loioutiouto!
turulu tureli tur luititi
Gou-guiqu gou-guiqu
Psuit psouit psui uitti It
Loitiioito!
Prrn prrn qurr nttpruin
tiou-tiou-iou Oui o'
Oui-oui lii lii lo'
Psuiti tipsru!
Troi ti ti loinax

Raoul Hausmann, 1946-1947

French-English edition in 1962. The editors had banned German from the venture (Schwitters corresponded with Hausmann in English). On the other hand, an edition of Schwitters' collected writings began to appear in Germany in 1973. It runs to more than 1,700 pages.

Paul Dermée, the "Cartesian Dadaist," died in 1951. A year later he was followed by his wife Céline Arnauld, whose book of verse *Guêpier de diamants* (1923) had been hailed by Antonin Artaud.

Then, in 1953, Picabia died. For most of his life he had lived in Cannes, producing a body of paintings that challenged the artistic mainstream of his times, a pictorial "anti-œuvre" that is still little known today. Gabrielle Buffet-Picabia wrote about him in *Aires abstraites* (1957), as did Germaine Everling in *L'Anneau de Saturne* (1970), but Picabia himself has left us no autobiography or memoirs, no personal statement other than a few passages in his letters to a young artist friend (*Lettres à Christine*, 1945-1951), such as the following penned in 1946: "Ever since my life began, the public has passed its sentence on me: 'he's making fun of us.' I have always been amused by this; the public knows me but doesn't know itself."

Picabia's last painting, completed a few days before his death in November 1953, is entitled *The World is Round*, which re-echoes one of Gertrude Stein's last books (*The World is Round*, 1939). Picabia had met Stein in Paris on his return from the Armory Show in 1913, but it was only in the thirties that their friendship was cemented over their mutual mental reservations about the then ubiquitous Surrealist movement. In *The Autobiography of Alice B. Toklas* (1933) Stein relates a conversation she once had with Picabia. To her statement that all modern art owed a debt to Cézanne, he replied, "Yes, except mine." And Stein remarks with amusement that there was truth in this.

Johannes Baader, the "Oberdada," died in 1955 in a castle that had been converted into a home for the elderly. 1958, the year that Marcel Duchamp's collected writings in French and English, *Marchand du sel*, were published in Paris, was also the year of Jean Crotti's death. Then, in 1959, two weeks after returning to live in Berlin, after twenty-five years' exile in America, George Grosz died. Tzara's death came in 1963, one month after his *Seven Dada Manifestoes* were reissued for the first time since 1924. At his funeral at the Montparnasse cemetery in Paris the Lettrist group caused a small disturbance by reading a declaration.

In 1966 the City of Zurich celebrated the fiftieth anniversary of the founding of Dada. A large Dada retrospective was mounted at the Kunsthaus and at the Musée National d'Art Moderne in Paris, and Jean Arp was invited to Zurich to unveil a white marble relief inlaid with a golden belly button (symbol in Alsace of birth and growth) on the façade of the Cabaret Voltaire. He died a few weeks later in Basel, and not long after his book *Jours effeuillés* was published in Paris.

Marcel Janco: *Rhythm, 1922*

In 1968 John Heartfield died in Berlin, and in October of that year Marcel Duchamp died in the Paris suburb of Neuilly, leaving some recorded talks (*Entretiens*) made the year before. Raoul Hausmann died at Limoges in 1971. Towards the end of his life, the "Dadasopher" had called himself a *Spontanéiste* rather than a Dadaist; he had become something of a recluse, declining to see any visitors except for a few young artists (like Villeglé, Paul-Armand Gette, Claude Viallat), yet active to the end as a plastic artist, photographer and photo-collagist. He had even taken up painting again in his seventies, and had capped his career with a brilliant series of torn and pasted papers.

Georges Ribemont-Dessaignes died on the Riviera in 1974, followed by Richard Huelsenbeck who had returned to Switzerland, the scene of his first Dada activities. Serge Charchoune, editor of the only Dada periodical in Russian, *Perevoz Dada*, died in 1975. A year later he was followed by two Dada film-makers: Man Ray in Paris and Hans Richter at Locarno. Hannah Höch died in 1978, in the house near Berlin where she had hidden during World War Two. Marcel Janco, who in 1953 had founded the artists' community of Ein Hod in Israel, died in 1984.

When *Les Champs magnétiques* was reprinted in 1968, Louis Aragon (who died in 1982) wrote *L'Homme coupé en deux*, a memoir published in *Les Lettres Françaises* which reveals the author's genuine warmth for Dada, behind the façade of his image as the poet laureate of the French Communist Party. Indeed he had already paid tribute to the Dadaists as early as 1929 in *L'Introduction à 1930*. What is more, Aragon is unusually respectful of his Dada friends in some of his as yet unpublished texts, notably in his *Contributions à une histoire littéraire contemporaine*, which he rather maliciously claimed to have destroyed or never to have written in the first place. He is the only contemporary of the Dadaists to have sketched literary portraits of all the movement's protagonists; some of his judgments are rather harsh, but when they are eventually published they will correct some of the errors perpetuated by historians of the Paris Dada group. They will make it clear in particular that the author of *Persiennes* and *Suicide* was in the front rank of the French Dada scene.

André Breton died in 1966. His *Entretiens* had been recorded in 1952. The first volume of his collected writings was published in Gallimard's prestigious Pléiade series in 1988. Philippe Soupault, the other co-author of *Les Champs magnétiques*, is now in his nineties. In his book *Profils perdus* (1963) he reminisces about his friends Guillaume Apollinaire, René Crevel,

The surréalistes are the vulgarization of Picabia as Delaunay and his followers and the futurists were the vulgarization of Picasso. Picabia had conceived and is struggling with the problem that a line should have the vibration of a musical sound and that this vibration should be the result of conceiving the human form and the human face in so tenuous a fashion that it would induce such vibration in the line forming it. It is his way of achieving the disembodied ... The surréalistes taking the manner for the matter as is the way of the vulgarizers, accept the line as having become vibrant and as therefore able in itself to inspire them to higher flights.

Gertrude Stein, 1933

Marcel Proust and James Joyce (Soupault had collaborated on the famous collective translation into French of *Anna Livia Plurabelle* under Joyce's supervision). He has recently completed the third volume of his autobiography, *Mémoires de l'oubli*.

In the United States, as we have seen, the Dada Movement was viewed as one of the leading trends of pictorial abstraction, but in Paris it is still regarded as a sort of libertarian, essentially literary prelude to Surrealism. Yet as a consequence of the student revolt of May 1968 and its artistic sequels, editions of the complete works of Georges Ribemont-Dessaignes (1974), Francis Picabia (1975), Tristan Tzara (1975), Vicente Huidobro (1976), Erik Satie (1977), Clément Pansaers (1986) and Arthur Cravan (1987) have been published in France.

Arthur Cravan, the first of the Dadaists to leave the scene—the reader will recall that he vanished mysteriously in 1918—preceded Clément Pansaers (who died in 1922), Erik Satie (1925), Hugo Ball (1927), Jacques Rigaut (1929) and Theo van Doesburg (1931). The latter's wife, the pianist Nelly van Doesburg (1899-1975), who was the first to play Satie's music in Holland (1923), once declared: "My belief is that art has come to the end of its rope. If Van Doesburg were still alive he would be fighting against pollution. He would concern himself with mankind's future. To think that two-thirds of humanity is living in squalor, while we're living in comfort like a lot of bourgeois! What future have they got? We used to say: the mind comes first. Art, that kind of thing. And we were sure that it all led somewhere. But what has it brought us? Something horrendous. Doesburg always said: machines will make us free. I wish he could come back and see what is happening. We have become the slaves of machines. That is the only reason why I want to go on living: to see a change, an improvement."

In contrast to this statement is the thesis, very alluring for art critics, that a direct line of descent can be drawn between the Dadaists and the so-called Neo Dada activities of American artists like Rauschenberg, Jasper Johns and Andy Warhol or the French New Realists like Hains, Villeglé, Dufrêne, Christo—or, more convincingly, the artists of the Fluxus group. There is indeed an obvious affinity between the formal vocabulary of Picabia's machine-style works, for example his "object portrait" of a young American girl as a spark plug drawn with the dryness and linear precision of a vignette in a manufacturer's catalogue, and that of Andy Warhol's *Campbell Soup Cans*. Warhol's stance during the heyday of American Abstract Expressionism recalls Picabia's anti-pictorial provocations and entails a similar rejection of anything like a personal *facture*. We know, moreover, that Warhol owned two Picabias, one of 1934, the other of 1946, and also a Man Ray (*Feminine Painting*) of whom he made a portrait in 1975. The dilemma that faced Warhol as an artist is summed up neatly in the famous anecdote of the two Coke bottles he showed to Emile de Antonio in 1962, one of them painted in the eminently pictorial style of Abstract Expressionism and the other in a cold mechanical style that affirms the power of readymade objects.

And yet such parallels rest solely on the kind of formal and aesthetic issues (the appearance of manufactured objects in an Arman "accumulation," a Jasper Johns flag, a Rauschenberg collage, a Villeglé "lacerated" poster) that Tzara always refused to privilege. They leave out the insurrectional context of Dada which, while it explains on one level the militant tone of Surrealism, seems totally lacking in the post-war art scene in America, with a few exceptions, like the writer William S. Burroughs.

William S. Burroughs: *Two pages from his* Scrapbook 3, *c. 1966-1971*

Marcel Duchamp between Carolyn Brown and Merce Cunningham, after a performance of the ballet Walkaround Time, *with sets by Jasper Johns based on Duchamp's* Large Glass, *Buffalo, N.Y., 1968*

I wish to say that I have never much cared for surrealist works. The critics make no mistake when in general they connect my activities with Dadaism. But I have had occasion to note that Dada in 1920 had a much more virulent need to break with the past, to make a clean sweep, than Dada in 1950 ... If I were compelled to choose between surrealism and Dada, naturally I would opt for Dada. And if I had to prefer one Dadaist to all the others, I would keep Duchamp. After that, of course, I would free myself from Dada.

John Cage, 1972

Teeny Duchamp, Marcel Duchamp and John Cage playing chess during Reunion, *a musical performance organized by John Cage, Toronto, 1968*

Interestingly, the exemplary detachment of John Cage, an avid chess player, a great admirer of Erik Satie and a close friend of Marcel Duchamp's, seems to owe as much to Zen Buddhism as to Dada, to the divinatory method of the *I Ching* as to the Dadaist cultivation of chance. It so happens that Tzara himself almost succumbed to the appeal of Zen, witness the following little noticed passage from his "Lecture on Dada," delivered at Weimar and Jena in September 1922, in which his own unorthodox position is made clear:

> Dada isn't modern at all, it is a return to a quasi-Buddhist religion of detachment. Dada gives things an artificial sweetness, a snow flurry of butterflies escaping from a magician's skull. Dada is immobility and does not comprehend the passions. This, you will say, is a paradox, since Dada manifests itself through violent actions. True, the reactions of individuals contaminated by *destruction* are fairly violent, but once they are spent, overwhelmed by the satanic insistence of a continual, increasing "What's the point?", what remains uppermost is *indifference*. For that matter, I could state the opposite with equal conviction. I admit that my friends do not share this point of view.

So we see in Tzara himself an ambivalence arising from the conflict between action and the non-action of pure thought, and this precisely at the time—a point worth emphasizing—when he was facing the intellectual challenge of pure plasticism (embodied by Mondrian, who was a Theosophist) and when one of the leading exponents of Purism, Theo van Doesburg, was moving towards Dada. That Tzara manifested an interest in

Far Eastern philosophy did not escape the notice of Tomoyoshi Murayama, founder of the Japanese Dada-Constructivist group Mavo in Tokyo.

However, the position that Tzara summarizes above does not in the least imply an acceptance of art as a means of "getting everyone to agree." If there was only one single thing about Dada to survive, apart from the creative effervescence always so highly characteristic of it, it would be the idea that the libertarian behavior expressed in an art work pertains mainly to the artist himself. As Tzara noted, Dada "requires that logic be reduced to a personal minimum and that literature be addressed first and foremost to the writer himself ... What interests a Dadaist is his own way of life."

Far from being vague or wavering, Tzara's views on the relation of art —even modern art—to life were a kind of *idée fixe*, a passionate commitment. We encounter them again in the "Lecture on Dada" cited above, and note that this was written in 1922, six years after the founding of Dada:

> What we want now is *spontaneity*. Not because it is better or more beautiful than anything else. But because we are represented by all that flows freely from us without the interference of speculative thought. We must speed up this life quantity that spends itself easily in every corner. Art is not the most precious manifestation of life. Art does not have that celestial and universal value that people are pleased to give to it. Life is a great deal more interesting. Dada boasts that it knows the right measure to give to art; with subtle and perfidious means it intrudes it into the acts of daily fantasy. And reciprocally.

The dialectic of Dada makes it virtually impossible to separate the demands of art from those of life itself. *And reciprocally*. This being so, there are legitimate grounds for making a connection between Dada and contemporary art only for those artists of today who are free enough, individual enough to repeat both the electrifying precision and the extreme diversity of behavior displayed by the members of that tremendously real yet purely whimsical movement.

Dada remains ephemeral, a moment, a dazzling shock, and all its participants felt nostalgia for it for the rest of their lives.

Few art works since then have had the same density of meaning, the same vitality and tension, the same rebelliousness or, in retrospect, the same historical relevance. However, it might be said (*pace* Nelly van Doesburg) that the Dadaists' social criticism is echoed on the contemporary scene by some of the statements made by authors who sympathize with the ideas of the Situationist International.

Among the active heirs of Dada in France must be numbered the leading members of this Situationist International. Back in the fifties they published an information bulletin called *Potlatch* (1954-1957) which began as the organ of the *Internationale Lettriste*, a leftist splinter group that split the Lettrist movement in 1952. The goal of the latter was, in 1954, to "give an absorbing structure to life... to create *appealing* situations by experimenting with ways of behaving, types of decoration, architecture, urban design and communication."

In an "intelligent survey of the avant-garde at the end of 1955," the editors of *Potlatch* declared that "all abstract painting since Malevich has addressed itself to problems that don't exist." As for poetry, they went on, "the almost complete disappearance of this activity, in the form under which it has been known since its beginning, a disappearance clearly linked to the continual withering away of aesthetics, is one of the most significant phenomena to occur before our eyes today." Concurrently, the recent "onomatopoeic poetry and neo-classical poetry have gone to demonstrate the total decline of this product."

A survey was made by the Belgian Surrealist review *Lèvres nues*, whose contributors included Debord, Fillon and Wolman (*Mode d'emploi du détournement, Théorie de la dérive*). The question asked was: "What is your goal in life and what are you doing to attain it?" Speaking for the Internationale Lettriste, Michèle Bernstein and Mohamed Dahou replied that "pressed to specify a goal for their exemplary lives, they see none save a permanent Situationist revolution."

The Situationists were practically the only ones at the time to carry on the Dada protest and to develop a critical and theoretical sequel to it, first with their review *Internationale situationniste* (1958-1969), then with Raoul Vaneigem's essay *Traité de savoir-vivre à l'usage des jeunes générations* (1967) and Guy Debord's *La Société du spectacle* (1967). Yet though they were well informed about the artistic experiments of the historical avant-garde and intent on maintaining the latter's insurrectional potential, and though sympathizing with the contemporary research of Asger Jorn, the Cobra group and Reflex, they never extended their manifold, extremely inventive activities to "works of art" (except for a few experimental works by Asger Jorn and Guy Debord).

In a preface to a reprint of *Potlatch* in 1985, Debord wrote: "The views of *Potlatch* concerning the death of modern art seemed extreme in the intellectual climate of 1954." But since 1954, he went on to say, "we have not seen a single genuinely interesting artist anywhere. We are aware too that no one outside of the Situationist International has gone to the trouble of formulating a *central critique* of our society, though it is *collapsing* all around us. While its disastrous failures crash down like avalanches it heaps up new ones ever more feverishly."

The following statement by Georges Ribemont-Dessaignes, made towards the end of his life, even sounds like the opening lines of Debord's Situationist book, *La Société du spectacle*: "The entire life of societies governed by the modern conditions of production appears to be a tremendous accumulation of *shows*. Everything that was experienced at first hand has moved off into a performance."

Everything has been turned into a show. Culture is a show lit up with plenty of spotlights and flashy colors, and explained by the blare of loudspeakers... The meaning of art has been changed, the art show has itself become an art, and all that's left is a universal Academy of False Arts cut off from life. We've come to the point of wondering whether life itself is not a shady business stealing along the path that leads to war, simply in order to restore Order, and what an Order!

Georges Ribemont-Dessaignes, 1958

George Brecht: *Piece for Violins at the Fluxus Festival, Nice, 1963, interpreted by Robert Bozzi, George Maciunas and Ben Vautier*

Breaks within the system

Meanwhile the artistic procedures developed by the Dadaists were re-employed in some of the rigorous recent avant-garde creations, notably in abstract (or sound) poetry, the "actions" and happenings staged by the Fluxus group, the choreography of Merce Cunningham and musical compositions of John Cage (specifically, their joint performances where music and dance unfold freely in space, independently of each other). All of these creations are artistic events of signal importance, having their due place in the uncompromising tradition of avant-garde art.

For example, Cunningham's 1968 ballet, *Walkaround Time*, was based on Marcel Duchamp's *Large Glass*. The décors consisted of Duchampian motifs reproduced, under Jasper Johns' supervision, on transparent plastic sheets and cloth panels. Another example is the Polish dramatist Tadeusz Kantor's Cricot theater which harks back openly to Picabia and, with *The Death Class*, to Schwitters' *Ursonate*.

In literature, the "cut-up" (or textual collage) can be compared to the Arpian method of the "laws of chance" or, better yet, to Schwitters' discovery of the word *Merz*, the first cut-up in the history of art (see Chapter 5). Discovered by the painter and writer Brion Gysin, who used a cutter to "cut up" a series of gouaches placed over his manuscripts, it has largely become associated with the American author William Burroughs. Just as, in Zurich, Arp dropped bits of torn paper onto colored sheets and Tzara composed poems by randomly drawing words cut out of newspapers from a top hat, the creative procedure developed by Burroughs and Gysin uses an artist's *trouvaille* to extend a writer's inspiration.

In his book *Nova Express* (1964), Burroughs has given the best definition so far of photomontage, as well as a particularly acute analysis of what he calls the "control mechanism." His observations on how language, sounds and images serve as instruments of creative manipulation seem to continue some of Tzara's remarks in his *Dada Manifesto 1918* (such as "I destroy the drawers of the brain and of social organization..."):

> Look at a photomontage—It makes a statement in flexible picture language—Let us call the statement made by a given photomontage X —We can use X words X colors X odors X images and so forth to define the various aspects of X—Now we feed X into the calculating machine and X scans out related colors, juxtapositions, affect-charged images and so forth we can attenuate or concentrate X by taking out or adding elements and feeding back into the machine factors we wish to concentrate—A Technician learns to think and write in association blocks which can then be manipulated according to the laws of association and juxtaposition —The basic law of association and conditioning is known to college students even in America: Any object, feeling, odor, word, image in juxtaposition with any other object, feeling, odor, word or image will be associated with it—Our technicians learn to read newspapers and magazines for juxtaposition statements rather than alleged content—We express these statements in Juxtaposition Formulae—The Formulae of course control populations of the world—Yes it is fairly easy to predict what people will think see feel and hear a thousand years from now if you write the Juxtaposition Formulae to be used in that period.

In the early sixties Tzara asked Brion Gysin: "Why are you and your friends doing over again what we did forty years ago?" Gysin replied: "Because you didn't do it well enough, because you did not explore the true significance of the problem. The Dada methods are valid only as long as the economic, political and social structures remain unchanged. What we are operating is a system of breaks within the system, so as to jam the workings of the media."

Increasing the human

Aside from these solid analogies, a number of more anecdotal parallels between Dada and the contemporary scene can be drawn as well. Worth mentioning are the Neo Dada Organizers in Japan (Shinohara, Yoshimura, Akasegawa, Kazakura, Arakawa) founded in 1960, and, in the United States, the poetry of LeRoi Jones, in particular "Black Dada Nihilismus" (1970) which voiced the revolt of the Blacks in Dada terms and was performed by the New York Art Quartet (a group formed on the initiative of John Tchicai and Roswell Rudd).

In its album *Fear of Music* (EMI & Sire Records, 1979), produced by Brian Eno, the New York group Talking Heads gives a musical performance of "I Zimbra," one of the sound poems that Hugo Ball had recited at the Cabaret Voltaire. In 1972 a teenage group at Sheffield in the North of England actually adopted the name of this famous café where Dada was born. Asked why they had chosen it, the musicians of the English Cabaret Voltaire, Stephen Mallinder and Richard Kirk, told the New York review SPIN: "It came from the original Cabaret Voltaire in Zurich [where the founders of Dada gathered during the First World War]. We were just interested in it, partly because we had art inclinations, but also, their attitude was very funny, because it was so antiestablishment, but also very humorous at the same time. The Dadaists were the ultimate pranksters, really."

In Tzara's final declaration on the state of culture, the founder of Dada pointed one last time to the difficult rapport between society and art, made particularly ambiguous when a society shows, as ours does, a keen interest in cultural values. In the long run that interest leads to a divorce between the arts and reality, for it means that in the social process the art object will be reduced to a functional purpose: it becomes the object of leisure activities, of consumer appetites.

Now at the end of his life in Paris, just as much as in early days at the Cabaret Voltaire in Zurich, Tzara set himself against that divorce between the arts and reality. In 1963, when his manifestoes were reissued by the publisher Jean-Jacques Pauvert, he was interviewed for the French weekly *L'Express* by Madeleine Chapsal. To her he said: "I believe in some kind of progress and I would not want to be unfair to the present day. But I sometimes wonder whether this multiplication always has good results. Nowadays everything is being multiplied: books, readers, exhibitions, pictures. You have to queue up in the museums. Mind you, I'm not complaining. Thanks to that I've seen some wonderful things, which I would never have seen without long and expensive journeys: the exhibitions of these last few years, for example, on the arts of Mexico, of Spain, of Italy... Only I can't help wondering about it. What is the use of this popularization? Are we sure that it is really beneficial? Does it answer the purpose of art which after all is to increase the human?... An infatuation leading nowhere, kept going by publicity slogans. Artists are put in the limelight. Does art benefit from it in any way? And what about the human? Where in all this do you find any increase of human values?... Dada had a human purpose, an extremely well marked ethical purpose! The writer made no concession to the situation, to opinion, to money. We were abused by the press, by society, and we let them do their worst. That showed that we had made no compromises with them. In short we were very revolutionary and very intransigent. Dada was not only the absurd, not only a joke. Dada was the expression of a deep-seated woe in the hearts of young men, brought on by the war of 1914 and the suffering that attended it. What we wanted was to make a clean sweep of the current values, but we did so precisely on behalf of the highest human values."

Fernand Léger: *Tristan Tzara, 1948*

Hans Arp: *Untitled, c. 1930*

Dear Mr. Brzekowski

You ask me what I think of painting and sculpture and particularly of neoplasticism and surrealism.
To answer that question I have to start with Dada which Tzara and I gave birth to with great joy. Dada is the staple of all art. Dada stands for no sense which doesn't mean nonsense. Dada like nature has no sense. Dada is for nature and against ''art.'' Dada like nature is direct and sets out to give each thing its essential place. Dada stands for infinite sense and definite means.
The goal of art is life. Art may misunderstand its means and do no more than aim at life instead of creating it. Then the means are illusionistic descriptive academic. I exhibited with the surrealists because their rebellious attitude to ''art'' and their direct attitude to life was wise as Dada is. Latterly the surrealist painters have employed illusionistic descriptive academic means which would give much pleasure to Rops.
Neoplasticism is direct but exclusively visual. What is lacking is the connection with the other human faculties.
But in the end I feel that man is neither a parasol nor a para-la-si-do nor a paramount for he consists of two carnivorous cylinders one of which says white when the other says black.
Believe me Sir yours fruitfully

Hans Arp

Sources of the Quotations and Acknowledgments

Chapter 1

Page 11

The quotation from Henri-Pierre Roché is from his "Souvenirs sur Marcel Duchamp," in Robert Lebel, *Marcel Duchamp*, with texts by André Breton and H.-P. Roché, 1959, Bibl. 85.

Page 12

Jules Laforgue's poem "Encore à cet astre" was first published in Jules Laforgue, *Œuvres complètes*, vol. II, Paris, Mercure de France, 1902.

Page 13

The insert quotation from Marcel Duchamp is from *Dialogues with Marcel Duchamp* by Pierre Cabanne, translated by Ron Padgett, Thames and Hudson, London, and The Viking Press, New York, 1971, by courtesy of Viking Penguin, a division of Penguin Books USA Inc.

Pages 14-15

The text quotation from Marcel Duchamp is from his interview with James Johnson Sweeney in *The Bulletin of the Museum of Modern Art*, New York, vol. XIII, nos. 4-5, 1946, pp. 19-21, by courtesy of the Museum of Modern Art.

Page 15

The quotation from Gaston de Pawlowski is from the beginning of his *Voyage au pays de la quatrième dimension*, Paris, Fasquelle, 1912.

Page 18

The Picabia quotation in the text is from his article "Ne riez pas, c'est de la peinture et ça représente une jeune Américaine" in *Le Matin*, Paris, December 1, 1913, reprinted in Francis Picabia, *Écrits*, I, Paris, Belfond, 1975, p. 26.

The insert quotation is from the interview with Picabia entitled "Why New York is the Only Cubist City in the World" in *The New York American*, March 30, 1913.

Chapter 2

Pages 21 ff.

On Italian Futurism see *Archivi del Futurismo*, edited by M. Drudi Gambillo and T. Fiori, Rome, De Luca, 1958, 2 vols., and *Futurist Manifestoes* edited by Umbro Apollonio, London, Thames and Hudson, 1973.

Pages 22 ff.

Most of the Russian Futurist publications are listed in Vladimir Markov, *Russian Futurism: A History*, 1968, Bibl. 691. See also Susan Compton, *The World Backwards: Russian Futurist Books 1912-1916*, 1978, Bibl. 656.

Page 23

The manifesto "A Slap in the Face of Public Taste" was originally published as a booklet, Moscow, December 1912-January 1913.

The poem *Zaklyatie Smiekhom* (The Laughter Plot) was published in 1910 in *Impressionist Studio*. The original Russian text will be found in Velimir Khlebnikov, *Tvoreniya*, Moscow, Sovietskii Pissatiel, 1986.

Page 24

Tristan Tzara, "Some Memoirs of Dadaism" in *Vanity Fair*, New York, July 1922, reprinted in Edmund Wilson, *Axel's Castle, A Study on the Imaginative Literature of 1870-1930*, 1931, Bibl. 448.

Page 25

The insert quotation is from Velimir Khlebnikov, prologue to *Victory over the Sun*, 1913.

Page 27

The Blaise Cendrars poem *Crépitements*, dated September 1913, appeared in May 1916 in the magazine *Cabaret Voltaire*, Zurich. It is the ninth of the *Dix-neuf poèmes élastiques*, Paris, Au Sans Pareil, 1919; reprinted in Blaise Cendrars, *Du monde entier*, Paris, Gallimard, 1967, a volume containing Cendrars' poems of 1912-1924. His complete poetry was published in 1944 by Denoël, Paris, then in the first (*Du monde entier au cœur du monde*) of the eight volumes of his *Œuvres complètes*, Paris, Denoël, 1961-1964. See also Miriam Cendrars, *Blaise Cendrars*, Paris, Balland, 1984.

Page 28

The quotation from Paul Morand is from his 1967 preface to Blaise Cendrars, *Du monde entier* (complete poems 1912-1924), Paris, Gallimard, 1967.

Page 29

Blaise Cendrars, *Les Pâques à New York*, last stanza of the poem, dated April 1912, published in Paris that same year.

Page 30

The quotation from Walter Arensberg is from his manifesto "Dada is American" published in the special number of *Littérature*, "Vingt-trois manifestes du mouvement Dada," no. 13, Paris, May 1920. Reprinted in Rothenberg, *Revolution of the Word*, Bibl. 701. The writings of Mina Loy have been collected in Mina Loy, *The Last Lunar Baedecker*, Highlands, The Jargon Society, 1982.

Page 31

William Carlos Williams, *Autobiography*, New York, New Directions, paperback edition, 1967, by permission of New Directions Publishing Corporation, Copyright © 1948, 1949, 1951 by William Carlos Williams.

The statements by Arthur Cravan were published in his periodical *Maintenant* (Paris, 1912-1915).

Chapter 3

Page 34

The Arp quotation is from his essay "Dadaland," published in Jean (Hans) Arp, *On My Way*, essays and poems 1912-1947, edited by Robert Motherwell, Bibl. 18.

Pages 34-35

The Tzara quotation is from "Tristan Tzara va cultiver ses vices" in *Le Journal du Peuple*, Paris, April 14, 1923, one of a series of interviews conducted by Roger Vitrac. A long passage from this Tzara interview appeared in *Merz*, no. 4, Hanover, July 1923.

Pages 35 ff.

The Hugo Ball quotation is from Hugo Ball, *Flight Out of Time*, edited by John Elderfield, translated by Ann Raimes, New York, Copyright © 1974 by The Viking Press, Inc., Bibl. 42. All rights reserved. Reprinted by permission of Viking Penguin, a division of Penguin Books USA Inc. Originally published in Hugo Ball, *Die Flucht aus der Zeit*, Munich-Leipzig, Duncker & Humblot, 1927, Bibl. 40.

Page 36

Arp statement from *Dada au grand air*, the eighth number of the periodical *Dada*, Tarrenz bei Imst, Tyrol, summer 1921.

Page 37

Quotation from Tristan Tzara's *Dada Manifesto 1918*, first published in *Dada 3*, Zurich, December 1918.

Page 38

The letter from Apollinaire (December 14, 1916) to Tristan Tzara was published in the special Guillaume Apollinaire number of *La Revue des Lettres modernes*, nos. 104-107, Paris, Minard, 1964.

The Alberto Savinio quotation is from the magazine *La Ronda*, Rome, November-December 1921.

The *Example* from Tzara's *Manifesto on Feeble Love and Bitter Love* is Ralph Manheim's translation in *The Dada Painters and Poets*, Bibl. 505.

Page 40

"L'Amiral cherche une maison à louer," simultaneous poem by Huelsenbeck, Janco and Tzara, published in *Cabaret Voltaire*, Zurich, May 15, 1916.

The Tzara quotation is from Tristan Tzara, "Note 18 sur l'art" published in *Dada 1*, Zurich, July 1917.

Page 41

Tzara, letter to Jacques Doucet, October 30, 1922, printed in Tristan Tzara, *Œuvres complètes*, I, Paris, Flammarion, 1975, p. 642.

Page 42

Press notice quoted by Hugo Ball in *Die Flucht aus der Zeit*, Bibl. 40, and *Flight Out of Time*, Bibl. 42, copyright © 1974 by The Viking Press, Inc.

Arp, passage from "Dadaland," first published in Jean (Hans) Arp, *On My Way*, Bibl. 18.

"Dégoût dadaïste," extract from Tzara's *Dada Manifesto 1918*, published in *Dada 3*, Zurich, December 1918.

Page 43

The text quotation is from Hugo Ball, *Flight Out of Time*, Bibl. 42, copyright © 1974 by The Viking Press, Inc. Originally published in Hugo Ball, *Die Flucht aus der Zeit*, Munich-Leipzig, Duncker & Humblot, 1927.

The insert quotation is from Hans Richter, *Dada: Kunst und Antikunst*, 1965, Bibl. 352.

Page 45

The Arp quotation on Janco, translated by Ralph Manheim, is from Jean (Hans) Arp, *On My Way*, Bibl. 18.

Page 47

Kurt Schwitters, *manifesto i*. Original German text in the *i* number of *Merz*, 2, Hanover, April 1923.

Insert quotation from Tristan Tzara, *Dada Manifesto 1918*, in *Dada 3*, Zurich, December 1918. This quotation translated by Michael Taylor.

Page 51

The Arp statement to Marcel Jean is quoted by the latter in his preface to *Arp on Arp*, Bibl. 20.

Page 57

The Janco quotation in the text is from his article in French, "TSF Dialogue entre le bourgeois mort et l'apôtre de la vie nouvelle," in the magazine *Punct*, 11, Bucharest, February 1925.

The insert quotation is from an undated letter from Marcel Janco to Michel Seuphor.

Page 58

The insert quotation is a Dada review of Richard Huelsenbeck's book *Verwandlungen* by Arp, Serner, and Tzara published in the German edition of *Dada 4-5*, Zurich, May 1919.

Page 60

The Arp quotation is from "Dadaland" in *On My Way*, Bibl. 18.

Page 61

The telegram from the Paris Dadas was published in the Geneva daily, *Tribune de Genève*, March 5, 1920.

Chapter 4

Page 64

Picabia's poem "Magic City" was published in *391*, no. 4, Barcelona, March 1917.

Page 71

The Man Ray quotation is from his *Self Portrait*, Boston, 1963, by courtesy of Little, Brown and Company, Bibl. 264.

Page 73

From Marcel Duchamp's lecture at the Museum of Modern Art, New York, October 19, 1961, published in *Art and Artists*, London, July 1966, p. 47.

Page 74

The Marcel Duchamp quotation is from his interview with James Johnson Sweeney in *The Bulletin of the Museum of Modern Art*, New York, vol. XIII, nos. 4-5, 1946.

Page 79

Cravan's letter (January 1916) to André Level was published in Arthur Cravan, *Œuvres*, Bibl. 69.

Page 80

Picabia's note on *291* was published in *391*, 1, Barcelona, January 1917.

Page 81

The Gabrielle Buffet-Picabia quotation is from her book *Aires abstraites*, 1957, Bibl. 58 and 59.

The insert quotation is from *Victor*, a novel written in 1957 by Henri-Pierre Roché and published in the catalogue *Duchamp*, Musée national d'art moderne, Paris, 1977. Bibl. 112.

Page 83

The Duchamp quotation was made by Fernand Léger in a talk published in *Cahiers d'Art*, 1954, II, pp. 133-172 (June 1955), repeated in Dora Vallier: *L'intérieur de l'art*, Paris, Seuil, 1982, p. 53.

Chapter 5

Page 91

The "Dada notice" by Raoul Hausmann appeared on the cover of *Der Dada*, 1, Berlin, June 1919.

Page 92

The *Proletarian Art Manifesto* was originally published in German in *Merz*, 2, Hanover, April 1923.

Page 94

Quotation from Raoul Hausmann, *Courrier Dada*, 1958, Bibl. 164.

Page 96

The Raoul Hausmann quotation is from the chapter "Poème phonétique" in his *Courrier Dada*, Paris, 1958.

The quotation from Vera Broido-Cohn is from an interview with Andrei Nakov published in the magazine *Apeiros*, 6, special number, "Raoul Hausmann et Dada à Berlin," Vaduz-Paris, Spring 1974, p. 73.

Page 97

The insert quotation is from Raoul Hausmann, *Courrier Dada*, 1958, Bibl. 164.

Page 98

Hausmann quotation from his *Pamphlet gegen die weimarische Lebensauffassung*, 1919, reprinted in the author's own French translation in Raoul Hausmann, *Courrier Dada*, Bibl. 164.

Page 100

Otto Gross quotations from Otto Gross, *Révolution sur le divan*, translated by Jeanne Etoré, preface by Jacques Le Rider, Paris, Solin, 1988.

Page 109

Johannes Baader, *Plasto-Dio-Dada-Drama*: quotation from *Dada Almanach*, edited by Richard Huelsenbeck, 1920, Bibl. 463.

Page 110

Kurt Tucholsky's article on the Dada trial appeared in *Die Weltbühne* 17, 1921, p. 454. Reprinted in Kurt Tucholsky, *Gesammelte Werke*, Bibl. 709.

Page 113

Kurt Schwitters, "Meine Sonate in Urlauten" in the magazine *i 10*, no. 11, Amsterdam, November 1927.

Page 115

Final paragraph of a text by Schwitters on "The Great Dada Eagerness. Funeral March," of which only Roland Schacht's French version remains, the German original having been lost. Translation published in *Anna Blume Dichtungen*, reprinted in *Das literarische Werk*, Bibl. 390, vol. 1.

Essay by Arp on Schwitters published in the periodical *K*, "Hommage à Schwitters," no. 3, Paris, May 1949.

Page 116

The text quotation from Kurt Schwitters is from an article called "Art and Time" written at Hanover in March 1926 and published in Czech in the almanac *Fronta*, 1927. Original text "Kunst und Zeiten" in Kurt Schwitters, *Das literarische Werk*, Bibl. 390, vol. 5, p. 236.

Insert quotation from Schwitters' article "Die Merzmalerei" in *Der Zweemann*, no. 1, November 1919, and in *Der Sturm*, no. 4, July 1919.

Page 118

English version of Schwitters' poem *An Anna Blume* by Myrttle Klein, published in *Transition*, 3, June 1927.

Page 122

The text quotation from Schwitters, referring to Baargeld, is from his article "Der Dadaismus" written at Hanover in 1924 and published as "Dadaizm" in the Polish periodical *Blok*, Warsaw, 1924-1925; reprinted in Kurt Schwitters, *Das literarische Werk*, Bibl. 390, vol. 5.

The statement by Max Ernst, made to Patrick Waldberg at Huismes (Indre-et-Loire) in August 1958, was published in the exhibition catalogue *Dada, Dokumente einer Bewegung*, 1958, Bibl. 576.

Max Ernst's statement on Arp will be found in Edouard Roditi, *Propos sur l'art*, Paris, José Corti, 1987.

Page 123

Paul Eluard quoted by Max Ernst, *Ecritures*, 1970, Bibl. 126, p. 25.

Page 125

Insert quotation from Max Ernst published in *Dada Ausstellung*, Cologne, 1920.

Chapter 6

Page 128

Arp's account of his first meeting with Picabia will be found in *Art d'Aujourd'hui*, no. 6, Paris, January 1950; reprinted in *Arp on Arp*, Bibl. 20.

André Breton's letter (January 22, 1919) to Tristan Tzara is quoted in Michel Sanouillet, *Dada à Paris*, 1965, Bibl. 552, p. 440.

Page 129

The passage from Louis Aragon comes from an unpublished manuscript, *Contributions à une histoire littéraire contemporaine*, 1923, Bibl 3. Quoted by courtesy of Jean Ristat and Marc Dachy.

Page 131

André Breton, "Entrée des médiums" in *Littérature*, new series, no. 6, Paris, November 1922; reprinted in André Breton, *Les Pas perdus*, Paris, 1924.

Page 132

The passage from Louis Aragon comes from an unpublished manuscript, *Contributions à une histoire littéraire contemporaine*, 1923, Bibl. 3.

Page 133

The Picabia poem "Rahat-Loukoums" ("Turkish Delights") was published in Francis Picabia, *Poèmes et dessins de la Fille née sans mère*, 1918.

Page 136

The card of Léon Brulot, Procureur Général at the Cour de Cassation, addressed to Picabia, is preserved in the Dossiers Picabia, Bibliothèque littéraire Jacques Doucet, Paris.

Page 137

Scene described by Paul Léautaud under date of October 6, 1921, in his *Journal littéraire*, I, Paris, Mercure de France, 1986, p. 1154.

The letter from Rachilde to Picabia (January 20, 1921) is in the Dossiers Picabia, Bibliothèque littéraire Jacques Doucet, Paris.

Picabia's *Manifeste Cannibale Dada* appeared in *Dadaphone*, no. 7, Paris, March 1920.

Page 138

The quotation is from Louis Aragon, *Pour expliquer ce que j'étais*, Paris, Gallimard, 1989.

Page 140

"L'Affaire Dada," pamphlet by Francis Picabia, published in *Cannibale*, no. 1, Paris, April 1920.

Pages 141 ff.

The quotation from Tristan Tzara at the mock trial of Maurice Barrès, together with other quotations from the trial and several of the adjoining illustrations, are from *L'Affaire Barrès*, Bibl. 482.

Page 144

The quotation from Maurice Martin du Gard is from the chapter "Saison Dada" in his *Les Mémorables 1918-1923*, 1957, Bibl. 692.

Page 148

The Man Ray quotation is from his *Self Portrait*, 1963, Bibl. 264, by courtesy of Little, Brown and Company, Boston.

Page 151

The insert quotation is from Tristan Tzara, "La photographie à l'envers, Man Ray," preface to Man Ray, *Les Champs délicieux*, 1922, Bibl. 257.

Page 152

Quotation from Tristan Tzara, "Essai sur la situation de la poésie" in *Le Surréalisme au service de la révolution*, 4, Paris, December 1931.

The poem "Persiennes" by Louis Aragon was published in *Proverbe*, 5, Paris, May 1920.

Pages 154 and 156

The Man Ray quotations are from his *Self Portrait*, 1963, Bibl. 264, by courtesy of Little, Brown and Company, Boston.

Page 155

The insert quotation is from Georges Ribemont-Dessaignes, preface to *Ledentu le Phare, poème dramatique en zaoum* by Ilya Zdanevich (Iliazd), Paris, Editions du Degré 41, 1923.

Page 158

"Opinions et Portraits," pamphlet by Francis Picabia published in *391, Journal de l'Instantanéisme*, Paris, 1924.

Chapter 7

Page 162

Text quotation from László Moholy-Nagy, *Vision in Motion*, Chicago, Paul Theobald and Co., 1947.

Page 164

Insert quotation from Jan Tschichold, "Typographie élémentaire" in *Communications typographiques*, 1925.

Page 166

"Call for Elementary Art," originally published as *Aufruf zur Elementaren Kunst* in *De Stijl*, October 1921, p. 156.

Page 168

Passages from "De Stijl Manifesto II," 1920, originally published in Dutch, German, and French in *De Stijl*, 6, April 1920, and signed by Theo van Doesburg, Piet Mondrian, and Antony Kok.

Page 169

The Moholy-Nagy quotation is from his *Vision in Motion*, Chicago, Paul Theobald and Co., 1947.

Page 170

Passage from Kurt Schwitters' article in memory of Theo van Doesburg, died March 1931, published in *De Stijl*, January 1932.

Page 171

The text quotation from Schwitters is from his article "Der Dadaismus" published in the Polish periodical *Blok*, Warsaw, 1924-1925; reprinted in Kurt Schwitters, *Das literarische Werk*, Bibl. 390, vol. 5.

Insert quotation from "Manifeste métallique de shampooing néerlandais" by I.K. Bonset (alias Theo van Doesburg), written in French in June 1921, first published in 1975 in *Nieuwe Woordbeeldingen*, Bibl. 48.

Page 172

Text quotation from Raoul Hausmann, "Typographie" in *Qualität*, 10. Jahrgang, 1932, no. 34.

Page 175

Statement by Frederick Kiesler in *De Stijl*, special tenth anniversary issue, nos. 79-84, p. 101.

Page 176

Statement by Kurt Schwitters accompanying two photographs published in *Abstraction-Création, art non figuratif 1933*, cahier no. 2, Paris, 1933.

Page 178

Insert quotation from Arp's essay on Schwitters published in the periodical *K*, "Hommage à Schwitters," no. 3, Paris, May 1949.

The text quotation from Michel Seuphor, on Schwitters, is from his article "Dadakoll" in *XXᵉ Siècle*, 1956, Bibl. 643.

Chapter 8

Page 185

The quotation from André Breton is from his *Entretiens*, 1952, Bibl. 54, p. 55.

Page 186

Statement by Tristan Tzara to Ilarie Voronca, "Marchez au pas," published in French in the periodical *Integral*, Bucharest, no. 12, 1925.

Page 188

The Richard Huelsenbeck quotation is from his *Dada Manifesto 1949*, written in March 1949 and published in the form of a yellow broadsheet ($22 \times 8\frac{1}{2}$ inches) by Wittenborn, Schultz, Inc., New York, 1951.

Page 190

The *Dada Manifesto 1949* by Richard Huelsenbeck (Dr. Charles R. Hulbeck) was issued by Wittenborn to coincide with the publication of *The Dada Painters and Poets: An Anthology*, 1951, Bibl. 505.

Page 192

The quotation from the preface to the periodical PIN is from Jasia Reichardt, *Kurt Schwitters and Raoul Hausmann, PIN and the Story of PIN*, Bibl. 395. The letter from Schwitters to Hausmann (March 29, 1947) is quoted in part by Asger Jorn in his article "La création ouverte et ses ennemis" in *Internationale Situationniste*, no. 5, December 1960, p. 32 (reprinted by Champ Libre, Paris, 1975). The letter was printed in full by Raoul Hausmann, *Courrier Dada*, Bibl. 164, p. 128.

Page 193

Picabia's reply, "Yes, except mine," is quoted by Gertrude Stein, *The Autobiography of Alice B. Toklas*, New York, Harcourt, Brace, 1933. Picabia is referred to several times in the book. See also Gertrude Stein, *The World is Round*, New York, W.R. Scott, and London, B.T. Batsford, 1939.

Raoul Hausmann's poem "Oiseautl" was published in the periodical *PIN*, Bibl. 395.

The André Breton quotation is from his introductory note to the Picabia texts published in Breton's *Anthologie de l'humour noir*, 1940, Bibl. 53.

Page 194

The French translation, referred to here, of James Joyce's *Anna Livia Plurabelle* was made in 1930 under Joyce's supervision by Samuel Beckett, Alfred Perron, Ivan Goll, Eugene Jolas, Paul Léon, Adrienne Monnier, and Philippe Soupault. Of this translation, Soupault gave a public reading in Adrienne Monnier's bookshop, "La Maison des Amis des Livres," rue de l'Odéon, Paris, on March 26, 1931. It was reprinted with a prefatory note by Soupault in James Joyce, *Finnegans Wake* (Fragments), followed by *Anna Livia Plurabelle*, Paris, Gallimard, 1962.

The insert quotation is from Gertrude Stein, *The Autobiography of Alice B. Toklas*, New York, Harcourt, Brace, 1933, p. 258, by courtesy of Random House Inc., New York.

Page 196

The insert quotation is from John Cage, *Pour les oiseaux: entretiens avec Daniel Charles*, Paris, Belfond, 1976. See also John Cage, *Silence. Lectures and Writings*, Cambridge, Mass., M.I.T. Press, 1966, and London, Calder and Boyars, 1968; and Richard Kostelanetz, *Conversing with John Cage*, New York, Limelight, 1988.

Page 197

The quotation from *Potlatch* is from no. 24 of November 24, 1955, reprinted in *Potlatch (1954-1957)*, Paris, Gérard Lebovici, p. 181.

The reply of Michèle Bernstein and Mohamed Dahou appeared in *Les Lèvres nues*, collection complète (1954-1958), Paris, Plasma, 1978.

The quotation from Guy Debord opens *The Society of the Spectacle*, Bibl. 660.

The statement by Georges Ribemont-Dessaignes, handwritten and entitled "Jadis Dada à Paris," appeared in facsimile in the exhibition catalogue *Dada, Dokumente einer Bewegung*, 1958, Bibl. 576.

Page 198

Quotation from William S. Burroughs, *Nova Express*, New York, Grove Press, Inc., 1964, pp. 93-94, Copyright © 1964 by William S. Burroughs, Bibl. 654.

The quotation from Brion Gysin is from "Rub out the Words," an interview with Gérard-Georges Lemaire in Paris in November 1974, published in *La Revue d'Esthétique*, "Il y a des poètes partout," Paris, Union Générale d'Editions, 10/18, nos. 3/4, October 1975, pp. 184-204.

The quotation from the Cabaret Voltaire musicians is from *Spin*, New York, vol. 3, no. 9, February 1988, p. 68.

Page 198

Statements by Tristan Tzara made in his Paris apartment, rue de Lille, November 12, 1963, to Madeleine Chapsal and published in *L'Express*, Paris. Reprinted in Madeleine Chapsal, *Les Ecrivains en personne*, Paris, Union Générale d'Editions, 10/18, 1973, and again in Madeleine Chapsal, *Envoyez la petite musique*, Paris, Le Livre de poche, Biblio Essais, 1987, p. 325.

Page 199

The letter from Hans Arp, dated 1929, appeared in the Franco-Polish periodical *L'Art contemporain*, no. 3, 1930, published in Paris by Jan Brzekowski. Reprinted in *Arp on Arp*, Bibl. 20.

Chronology
by Marc Dachy

1909

JANUARY
Paris: Marinetti's *Futurist Manifesto* published in the leading Paris daily *Le Figaro*. The avant-garde sees its ideas about art as an integral part of modern life.

1910

Russia: Khlebnikov's transrational Zaum poem *Zaklyatie Smiekhom* (The Laughter Plot) published in *Studio Impressionistov* (Impressionist Studio). In December, first exhibition of the painters of the Jack of Diamonds group in Moscow.

1911

Paris: Marcel Duchamp and Francis Picabia meet in Paris: they will be instrumental in creating the Dada spirit in New York, Barcelona, and Paris.

NOVEMBER
Paris: Prompted and financed by Marinetti, the Milanese group of Futurist painters comes to Paris, where their eyes are opened to Cubism. They visit the studios of Picasso and Archipenko, among others.

DECEMBER
Russia: Meeting of David Burliuk and Benedikt Livchits. The three Burliuk brothers and Livchits found the Hylaea group, soon joined by Khlebnikov, Mayakovsky, and Kruchenykh. This group will be the spearhead of Futurist poetry and the chief propagator of Cubist painting in Russia.

In Paris, Cubism gains public recognition at the Salon des Indépendants (spring) and the Salon d'Automne (September).

1912

JANUARY
Moscow: Second Jack of Diamonds exhibition, with many Western participants. It gives rise to public discussion marked by a violent clash of ideas between the avant-garde artists (Malevich, Larionov, Burliuk) and the modernist establishment.

FEBRUARY
Paris: Marcel Duchamp meets the Italian Futurist painters Boccioni and Severini at the Futurist exhibition, Bernheim-Jeune Gallery. This exhibition is subsequently shown in Berlin, Brussels, and London.

Munich: Arp, Larionov, and Malevich take part in the second Blaue Reiter exhibition. The Blue Rider group is keenly interested in non-European primitive art, and this exhibition includes a series of *lubki* (Russian folk pictures).

Moscow: A public discussion of Cubism organized by Larionov and Burliuk. Analytical approach and premises for a theoretical transcending of French Cubism.

MARCH
Paris: Marcel Duchamp's painting *Nude Descending a Staircase* creates a scandal and is withdrawn from the exhibition at the Salon des Indépendants.

Moscow: Exhibition of the Donkey's Tail group: Larionov, Ledentu, Malevich, Matveis (V. Markov), Morgunov, Shevchenko, Tatlin, Chagall. The show is temporarily closed because of some religious pictures by Goncharova; it is considered sacrilegious to exhibit them with a group bearing such a name. True to his conception of a free-wheeling, non-established avant-garde, Larionov dissolves the group after the exhibition.

APRIL
Paris: Arthur Cravan, poet and boxer, publishes the first issue of *Maintenant*, a "literary review" which he hawks in the streets (five numbers up to April 1915). With it, he is already working out the strategy of scandal later developed by Dada.

Milan: Boccioni publishes the *Technical Manifesto of Futurist Sculpture*, a theoretical affirmation of the use and indeed the need of many different materials for plastic purposes.

MAY
Paris: Duchamp, Gabrielle Buffet, Picabia, and Apollinaire attend a performance of the stage version of Raymond Roussel's *Impressions d'Afrique* (Théâtre Antoine).

JUNE
Moscow: Larionov writes the Rayonist manifesto, not published till April 1913. For the first time in Russia, it sets forth the theory of autonomous painting. During this year, collaboration between Larionov and the transrational poet Alexei Kruchenykh (booklets of 1913).

SUMMER
Moscow: *Starinnaya Lyubov* (Old-Time Love), a book of verse by Kruchenykh, illustrated with Larionov's first Rayonist lithographs.

SUMMER–FALL
Paris: First Cubist collages by Braque and Picasso. Materials become the subject matter of painting.

OCTOBER
Paris: At the prompting of Picabia, dissident Section d'Or exhibition (name chosen by Duchamp and Metzinger) at the Floury Gallery. Though intended as a theoretical systematization of Cubism, it includes such unorthodox Cubists as Archipenko and Exter, among others.

DECEMBER
Moscow: Publication of Khlebnikov and Kruchenykh's book of verse *Mirskontsa* (Worldbackwards) with illustrations by Goncharova, Larionov, Rogovin, and Tatlin in a half-abstract, half-primitivist style. Publication of the anthology *A Slap in the Face of Public Taste*, containing the manifesto of the same name (not diffused till January 1913), signed by Burliuk, Kruchenykh, Mayakovsky, and Khlebnikov. Affirmation of the "New Future Beauty of the Self-Sufficient Word."

Poème et Drame, a Paris review edited by Henri Barzun. First statement of the theory of simultaneous poetry.

1913

JANUARY

New York: Francis Picabia's first visit to New York on the occasion of the Armory Show. Series of canvases entitled *New York*. Friendship with the photographer Alfred Stieglitz, who runs the 291 Gallery at 291 Fifth Avenue, from which the future Dada group of New York originates. Success of Duchamp's *Nude Descending a Staircase* at the Armory Show.

MARCH

New York: Dinner at Healy's offered by the artists to the critics after the Armory Show.

Milan: Publication of Marinetti's manifesto *Immaginazione senza fili: Parole in libertà*. Luigi Russolo publishes his Futurist manifesto *The Art of Noises*: the cultural realm of music is thus extended to all sounds (noises).

Paris: Apollinaire: *Les Peintres cubistes, Méditations esthétiques*.

JUNE

Paris: Apollinaire signs the synthesis-manifesto *L'Antitradition futuriste*, in support of Marinetti. Exhibition of multimaterial sculptures by Boccioni, La Boétie Gallery.

SUMMER

Paris: Tatlin visits the studios of Picasso and Archipenko. Picasso's Cubist constructions are the inspiration behind the reliefs made by Tatlin on his return to Moscow.

OCTOBER

Paris: Blaise Cendrars and Sonia Delaunay collaborate on the book *La Prose du Transsibérien et de la petite Jehanne de France*, a continuous sequence of simultaneous color images and text in the form of a scroll unfolding over a height of some six feet.

NOVEMBER

Moscow: Ilya Zdanevich and Ledentu set forth Everythingism, an aesthetic shared with Larionov and Goncharova. It consists in "utilizing and combining all known forms of art of the past."

DECEMBER

St. Petersburg: Première at the Luna Park Theater of Kruchenykh and Matiushin's Futurist opera *Pobeda nad solntsem* (Victory over the Sun), with sets and costumes by Malevich, prologue by Khlebnikov. Malevich's "black square" here appears for the first time.

In Paris, creation of Stravinsky's *Sacre du printemps* by the Russian Ballet. Duchamp's first Readymades.

1914

FEBRUARY

Russia: Malevich and Tatlin break with the Union of Youth. Malevich draws away from his Futurist friends, including Burliuk. Unlike these latter, he sided with Marinetti during the latter's visit to Russia in January. His work moves along the lines of "transrational realism" (Zaum). With a wooden spoon in their buttonhole, Malevich and Morgunov demonstrate in the streets of Moscow and intervene in public discussions (against the "modernist" critic Tugendhold).

MARCH

New York: First issue of *The Little Review*.

JUNE

London: First issue of *Blast* (Wyndham Lewis, Ezra Pound, Ford Maddox Hueffer, Edward Wadsworth, Gaudier-Brzeska), a review setting forth the ideas of the English Vorticist movement.

Paris: Opening of the Paul Guillaume Gallery with a Larionov–Goncharova exhibition. Catalogue preface by Apollinaire, extolling Larionov's Rayonism. In the review *Les Soirées de Paris* Apollinaire publishes photographs of Archipenko's multimaterial constructions.

AUGUST

Paris: Germany declares war on France. To avoid service in the German army, Arp comes to Paris where he meets Max Jacob, Cravan, Picasso, Modigliani, Eggeling, Apollinaire, and the Delaunays. His first collages, deriving from Synthetic Cubism.

DECEMBER

Paris: Having volunteered, Apollinaire is assigned to the 38th Artillery Regiment of the French army at Nîmes.

Arp and Ernst become acquainted at Cologne in an art gallery.
Assassination of the French socialist leader Jean Jaurès (July 31).
In August, outbreak of the First World War. The intense international collaboration between modern artists is halted for the next few years. The name St. Petersburg is Russianized to Petrograd ("City of Peter the Great"); it will be changed to Leningrad in 1924.

Francis Picabia: Portrait of Stieglitz, 1915

1915

FEBRUARY

Switzerland: Arrival of Walter Serner from Germany.

MARCH

New York: First number of Stieglitz's review *291*, featuring Apollinaire, Haviland, Marius de Zayas, Steichen, Picabia. It is the forerunner of the avant-garde reviews and, with *Maintenant*, prefigures the Dada periodicals soon to come. Twelve issues up to February 1916. The one and only issue of *The Ridgefield Gazook*, written and illustrated by Man Ray while living at Ridgefield, New Jersey.

Milan: Balla and Depero publish their manifesto *Futurist Reconstruction of the World*, calling for the construction of plastic complexes, multimaterial and mechanical. Birth of the kinetic work of art.

MAY

Zurich: Marcel Janco a student at the Zurich Polytechnic. Arrival of Arp. Interviewed by the German consular authorities, he simulates insanity to avoid military service. Joins the Rumanian painter Arthur Segal and the painters Otto and Adya van Rees at Ascona (Monte Verità) in Italian Switzerland.

Paris: Picabia leaves for New York, sent on a mission to Cuba by the French military authorities.

Moscow: The "Year 1915" exhibition: several Futurist assemblages with a pre-Dada flavor by Kamensky, Larionov and Mayakovsky; one work includes an electric fan in action.

JUNE

Moscow: During a lecture Mayakovsky officially announces the death of Russian Futurism.

JULY

London: Second issue of the magazine *Blast*.

Russia: Malevich's first Suprematist canvases. They will be exhibited in December at the "Last Futurist Exhibition: 0.10."

AUGUST

New York: Arrival of Duchamp, staying with the Arensbergs. He left Paris because, though pronounced unfit for military service, he had encountered too much hostility.

OCTOBER

New York: Gabrielle Buffet joins Picabia, intending to go on to Cuba with him. Arrival from Barcelona of the newly weds Albert and Juliette Gleizes. On the 7th, opening of the Modern Gallery, 500 Fifth Avenue.

Zurich: Hugo Ball and the singer and dancer Emmy Hennings leave Berlin for Zurich. First issue of the Expressionist review *Sirius* edited by Christian Schad and Walter Serner.

NOVEMBER

Zurich: Arp exhibits with Otto and Adya van Rees at the Tanner Gallery. He shows some abstract collages.

Budapest: The painter and writer Lajos Kassák launches the review *A Tett* (Action).

DECEMBER

New York: Arrival of the French composer Edgar Varèse, a friend of Juliette Gleizes.

Petrograd: "Last Futurist Exhibition: 0.10" organized by Ivan Puni at the Dobychina Gallery. First showing of Malevich's Suprematist pictures and publication in January 1916 of his essay *Ot kubizma i futurizma k suprematizmu. Novyi zhivopisnyi realizm* (From Cubism and Futurism to Suprematism. The New Pictorial Realism). His *Quadrilateral*, simplified by critics to Black Square, creates a scandal. Tatlin exhibits non-objective reliefs and issues a personal folder. Rozanova, Puni and Kliun exhibit non-objective works, including multimaterial sculptures and assemblages.

———

Publication in Leipzig of Carl Einstein's book on African Negro sculpture (*Negerplastik*).
Raoul Hausmann and Hannah Höch become acquainted.

1916

JANUARY
Russia: First book of abstract collages: *Vselenskaya Voina* (Universal War) by Kruchenykh with collages by Rozanova.

Barcelona: Arthur Cravan is boxing coach at the Real Club Marítimo, where he joins his brother and sister-in-law, Olga Sakharov. On February 3 he referees a match between A. Cuchet and F. Hoche in the Iris Park. During this year Serge Charchoune meets Cravan's brother Otho Lloyd, then Cravan himself (whose real name is Fabian Lloyd). With Ricciotto Canudo, Charchoune devises some abstract films. With his lady friend Hélène Grunhoff he exhibits at the Dalmau Gallery, and both contribute to the review *Troços*.

France: André Breton, a medical student in a hospital at Nantes, there meets Jacques Vaché, who is being treated for a leg wound. In Paris, first number of the review *SIC* (Sounds Ideas Colors Forms) edited by Pierre Albert-Birot; though moderate in tone, it is the first of its kind in France and as such attracts some attention abroad.

New York: Picabia exhibition at the Modern Gallery, run by the Mexican caricaturist Marius de Zayas.

FEBRUARY
Zurich: On the 5th, at the Meierei in the Spiegelgasse, Hugo Ball founds the Cabaret Voltaire with Emmy Hennings (dancer), Hans Arp (Alsatian refugee), Sophie Taeuber (Swiss artist), the painter Marcel Janco and the poet Tristan Tzara, both Rumanians. Discovery and adoption of the word Dada. Exchange of letters between Max Jacob (Paris) and Tristan Tzara (Zurich). Huelsenbeck arrives from Berlin. This group forms the first Dada nucleus.

The Spiegelgasse, Zurich:
the Cabaret Voltaire was at No. 1, lower right

Hans Richter: Drawing for *Der Freie Verlag*, 1917

MARCH
Zurich: At the Cabaret Voltaire, singing of Negro songs to the beat of a drum and simultaneous poem *The Admiral's in Search of a House to Rent* by Huelsenbeck, Janco, and Tzara.

APRIL
Barcelona: Boxing match between the black champion Jack Johnson and Arthur Cravan, the latter being the challenger. Cravan knocked out after six rounds. Albert and Juliette Gleizes leave New York for Barcelona.

MAY
Zurich: Appearance in two editions (French and German) of the one number of the review *Cabaret Voltaire*, first publication of the Dada Movement, launched by Hugo Ball, with contributions by Apollinaire (his poem *The Tree*, reprinted without his permission), Cangiullo, Cendrars, Hennings, Huelsenbeck, Kandinsky, Marinetti, Modigliani, Picasso, Van Rees, Tzara. In his editorial Hugo Ball announces the forthcoming review *Dada*. Van Rees and his wife return to Ascona.

Cover of the monthly *SIC*,
Paris, January 1916,
edited by Pierre Albert-Birot

JUNE
Paris: The review *SIC* publishes a very short manifesto on "Nunism" (from the Greek *nun*, now).

New York: In a state of dejection, Picabia leaves for Barcelona.

Zurich: Huelsenbeck prepares a manifesto. Hugo Ball recites his sound poem *Karawane* at the Cabaret Voltaire.

Buenos Aires: Lecture at the Ateneo by the Chilean poet Vicente Huidobro, who from now on describes himself as a Creationist.

Barcelona: Boxing match between Cravan and Hoche.

JULY
Zurich: At the end of the month, Hugo Ball leaves for the mountains of the Ticino (Italian Switzerland) after a disagreement with his friends. Dada evening at the Zur Waag hall with music, dances, statements, manifestoes, poems, pictures, fancy dress, masks. First volume of the Dada series: *La Première Aventure céleste de M. Antipyrine* (The First Celestial Adventure of Mr. Antipyrine) by Tzara with colored woodcuts by Marcel Janco.

AUGUST
Budapest: An international number of *A Tett* is confiscated.
Zurich: Arrival of Hans Richter.

SEPTEMBER
Zurich: Second volume of the Dada series: *Phantastische Gebete* (Fantastic Prayers) by Richard Huelsenbeck, with seven woodcuts by Arp. "Literary Party" at Sophie Taeuber-Arp's, Magnolienstrasse 6 IV.

OCTOBER
Zurich: Third volume of the Dada series: *Schalaben schalomai schalamezomai* by Huelsenbeck with drawings by Arp. Poems of abstract sounds. Huelsenbeck decides to return to Germany and resume his medical studies at Greifswald University.

New York: Brancusi exhibition at the Modern Gallery.

Berlin: Johannes Baader writes a letter to Prince Friedrich Wilhelm of Prussia, calling on him to put an immediate stop to the war. From now on, the authorities apparently regard him as a lunatic.

NOVEMBER
Buenos Aires: Vicente Huidobro's lecture on Creationism, before he leaves for Paris (early 1917).

Geneva: Christian Schad settles in Geneva.

Budapest: *A Tett* is again confiscated (issue of September 20). Lajos Kassák then publishes the first number of *MA* (Today).

New York: From Zurich Tzara sends ten copies of *The First Celestial Adventure of Mr. Antipyrine* to Marius de Zayas, thus establishing relations between Zurich Dada and New York. Duchamp meets Henri-Pierre Roché.

DECEMBER
New York: Robert Coady publishes the magazine *The Soil*.

Paris: Lecture by Paul Dermée on Max Jacob ("Literary Cubism"), under the auspices of the "Lyre et Palette" association.

Budapest: Lecture by Lajos Kassák on modernity in literature at the Galileo Circle.

Moscow: A Suprematist group forms around Malevich during the winter of 1916-1917.

Zurich: Tzara destroys his first book of verse *Mpala Garoo*, which was to have appeared before *The First Celestial Adventure of Mr. Antipyrine*; only a set of proof sheets survives. On the 14th, letter from Apollinaire to

Barcelona:
Tzara who had been trying to contact him since April 1916 (when Apollinaire was hospitalized with war wounds).
Cravan leaves for Seville, then for New York.

Seventh issue of *391*. Leaving New York ("Goodbye, New York, I'm just passing through"), Cravan travels north to Connecticut, Boston, Maine, Nova Scotia, and Newfoundland.

1917

JANUARY
New York:
Arrival of Arthur Cravan. Man Ray and Adon Lacroix write their poem *Visual words, sounds seen thoughts, felt feelings thought.*

Zurich:
First Dada exhibition, with Arp, Van Rees, Helbig, Lüthy, Richter, and Negro art, at the Corray Gallery. Posters by Janco and Richter. Three lectures by Tzara.

Barcelona:
First number of *391* by Francis Picabia, now doing machine-style pictures.

FEBRUARY
New York:
Readymade by Marcel Duchamp: a urinal purchased from Mott and Co., entitled *Fountain*, signed R. Mutt, and submitted to the Independents exhibition, where it is rejected.

MARCH
Berlin:
Wieland Herzfelde founds Malik Verlag, a small extreme left-wing publishing house.

Paris:
First number of *Nord-Sud*, edited by Pierre Reverdy, with Apollinaire, Max Jacob, and Paul Dermée. Sixteen issues till October 1918.

Zurich:
Exhibition at the Dada Gallery: Campendonck, Kandinsky, Klee, Mense. Lectures by Tzara on Expressionism, Abstract Art, and Art Nouveau.

New York:
During this spring, Cravan meets Mina Loy at Walter Arensberg's.

APRIL
New York:
Arrival of Gabrielle and Francis Picabia with the four issues of *391* published in Barcelona. Exhibition of the Society of Independent Artists Inc. First number of *The Blind Man*, "Independents' Number." *Rogue* magazine ball.

Zurich:
Lecture by Hugo Ball on Kandinsky. "Sturm Soirée" at the Dada Gallery: introduction by Tzara, texts by Marinetti (on Futurist literature) and Kandinsky read by Ball, text by Apollinaire read by F. Glauser. "New Art" evening at the Dada Gallery: music by Schoenberg and Von Laban, texts by Léon Bloy, Hugo Ball (*Grand Hotel Metaphysik*, fancy-dress prose), Marcel Janco, Emmy Hennings, Hugo Ball, Tristan Tzara.

Moscow:
Khlebnikov: Manifesto of the Presidents of the Terrestrial Globe.

Paris:
From Zurich Tzara contributes to Reverdy's review *Nord-Sud* through Apollinaire.

MAY
Zurich:
Dada Gallery: exhibition of prints, embroideries, reliefs, children's drawings, with Negro music and dances. On this show, Tzara writes his *Note 18 on Art* in the first issue of *Dada*. "Alte und Neue Kunst" evening, with Negro poems read and translated by Tzara. After a sharp disagreement with Tzara, Hugo Ball breaks temporarily with Zurich Dada; in late May or early June he leaves Zurich for the summer.

New York:
Second number of *The Blind Man*, with several pages on the "Richard Mutt case," i.e. the rejection of Duchamp's *Fountain* at the Independents exhibition. Competition between the magazines *391* and *The Blind Man* leads to a chess duel between Picabia (*391*) and Henri-Pierre Roché (*The Blind Man*). Picabia wins and *The Blind Man* ceases to appear, being replaced by *Rongwrong*. *Blind Man* ball.

JUNE
New York:
Lecture by Arthur Cravan: drunk, he starts undressing on the platform; arrested, he is bailed out by Arensberg after a week in jail. A considerable scandal. Cravan travels to Philadelphia, Baltimore, and Annapolis.

Paris:
Performance of Apollinaire's "surrealist drama" *Les Mamelles de Tirésias* at the Théâtre Maubel, Montmartre. Philippe Soupault acts as prompter. There Breton joins Vaché. Annoyed by "the lyrical tone and the hackneyed Cubist sets and costumes," Vaché, wearing a British officer's uniform, brandishes his pistol. No. 18 of the review *SIC* is devoted to Apollinaire's play.

Hanover:
Schwitters takes part in the Young Artists exhibition at the Kestnergesellschaft.

JULY
New York:
Sole issue of *Rongwrong* by Duchamp, Roché, and Beatrice Wood. Tactile work (*Plaster to Touch at Marius de Zayas's*) by Miss Clifford-Williams.

Zurich:
First issue of *Dada*, "literary and artistic paper," from the press of the anarchist printer Julius Heuberger. Articles by Tristan Tzara, Francesco Meriano, Alberto Savinio, Nicola Moscardelli. Works by Arp, Janco, Lüthy, Prampolini.

Marie Laurencin: Portrait of Guillaume Apollinaire, 1917

OCTOBER
Moscow:
Russian première of Oscar Wilde's *Salome*, produced by Tairov with Suprematist sets by Alexandra Exter.

Barcelona:
Publication of *Cinquante-deux miroirs* (Fifty-two Mirrors, poems 1914-1917) by Francis Picabia.

Paris:
Louis Aragon and André Breton become acquainted.

Leiden:
First issue of *De Stijl*, edited by Theo van Doesburg, with Piet Mondrian, Antony Kok, J.J.P. Oud, and Bart van der Leck.

NOVEMBER
Tiflis:
Creation of the University of Degree 41, a new school of poetry, by Alexei Kruchenykh, Igor Terentiev, and Ilya and Kiril Zdanevich.

DECEMBER
Zurich:
Dada 2 appears. Letter from Apollinaire to Tzara: "I have sent you no copy because the position of this periodical with respect to Germany does not seem clear enough to me."

Paris:
Huidobro publishes *Square Horizon*.

———

Tristan Tzara and Daniel-Henry Kahnweiler meet in Bern.

1918

JANUARY
Berlin:
On the 22nd, first outburst of Dada in Germany: Dada propaganda evening organized by Huelsenbeck, back from Zurich, in Neumann's Graphisches Kabinett.

South America:
From Mexico City Cravan asks the English poetess Mina Loy to join him there. They get married and travel to Rio de Janeiro and Lima. Back in Mexico City, Cravan is boxing instructor in the physical culture school.

Tiflis:
On the 19th, lecture by Ilya Zdanevich ("Zaum Poetry and Poetry in General") at the Little Fantastic Cabaret, where the members of Degree 41 meet.

Paris:
Breton, still a medical student, prepares a lecture on Alfred Jarry and for this purpose consults Valéry, Rachilde, and Léon-Paul Fargue. Announced at the Théâtre du Vieux-Colombier, the lecture is canceled, the German bombardment of Paris having forced the theater to close. Aragon discovers Lautréamont.

Zurich:
Early in 1918, arrival of Viking Eggeling.

FEBRUARY
Berlin:
Johannes Baader "sits in the saddle of the white horse Dada" and proclaims himself President of the League of Intertelluric Superdadaist Nations.

Lausanne:	Picabia treated by the nerve specialist Dr. Brunschwiller.

MARCH

Berlin:	Huelsenbeck founds the Berlin Dada Club. Baader and Hausmann become acquainted. Publication of *Club Dada*, seventh issue of the review *Die Freie Strasse*, which opens its pages to the Berlin Dadaists.
Lugano:	Walter Serner draws up his *Letzte Lockerung* manifesto.
Moscow:	Seven articles by Malevich in the anarchist review *Anarkhia*.

APRIL

Berlin:	Huelsenbeck writes his *Dada Manifesto*. On the 12th, big Dada evening organized by Huelsenbeck, Hausmann, and Grosz in the hall of the Berlin Secession: *Der Dadaismus im Leben und in der Kunst* (Huelsenbeck), *Futuristische und dadaistische Verse* (Else Hadwiger), *Sincopations, eigene Verse* (Grosz), *Das neue Material in der Malerei* (Hausmann). Raoul Hausmann states (in *Courrier Dada*): "Huelsenbeck disappeared for a time [after that evening], and it was left to Baader and myself alone to carry on the Dada movement for the next nine months."
Paris:	Apollinaire publishes *Calligrammes* (poems, 1913-1918).

MAY

Paris:	Paul Dermée and Pierre Reverdy part company. Pretext: Dermée's lecture at the Rosenberg Gallery on Apollinaire and Jacob in which he

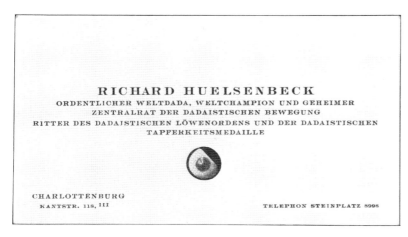

Visiting card of Richard Huelsenbeck

draws a parallel between poetry and insanity, with reference to Marcel Réja's book *L'Art chez les fous* published by the Mercure de France (1907).
Marriage of Apollinaire on the 22nd.

Tiflis:	On the 18th, lecture by Iliazd (i.e. Ilya Zdanevich), Kruchenykh, and Terentiev on "Zaum Theater and Donkey for Rent."

JUNE

Zurich:	"Studio party with art events" at Marcel Janco's.
Berlin:	On the 6th, Dada matinée organized by Baader and Hausmann at the Café Austria, Potsdamerstrasse: exhibition of montages and Hausmann recites his first phonetic poems. Schwitters' first one-man show at the Der Sturm Gallery, run by Herwarth Walden.

JULY

Zurich:	Tzara publishes *Vingt-cinq poèmes* (Twenty-five Poems) with ten woodcuts by Arp, in the Dada series. At the Zur Meise hall, Tzara reads some of his works, together with his *Dada Manifesto 1918*, the decisive text for the existence and influence of Dada, and one of wide theoretical scope. This manifesto will earn Tzara an international reputation and bring many adherents to the movement.
Berlin:	Baader proclaims and publishes his *Acht Weltsätze* (Eight World Theses), and he issues a statement on the Unpaid Workers' Council and the new Dada calendar.

SUMMER

Germany:	Hausmann discovers the technique of photomontage.
New York:	Marcel Duchamp sails for Buenos Aires on the *Crofton Hall*.
Zurich:	Tzara gets in touch with Picabia through a circular which he has sent him and which is forwarded to Picabia in Switzerland, at Bex near Lausanne, where he is now living. In August, performance of Carlo Gozzi's eighteenth century fairy tale play *The Deer King*, with puppets and sets by Sophie Taeuber.

SEPTEMBER

Zurich:	Exhibition of Arp, Richter, McCouch, Baumann, Janco, and others at the Wolfsberg Gallery.

Visiting card of John Heartfield

Mexico City:	Cravan is knocked out in a boxing match with Jim Smith (Black Diamond). Cravan and Mina Loy leave Mexico City.

OCTOBER

Paris:	Last number of Reverdy's review *Nord-Sud*, which had regularly published writings by Apollinaire, Max Jacob, Paul Dermée, André Breton, Philippe Soupault, Aragon, Tzara. Its disappearance will lead Aragon, Breton, and Soupault to found a periodical of their own, *Littérature*. Death of Raymond Duchamp-Villon, elder brother of Marcel.
Berlin:	At the Café des Westens Schwitters meets Raoul Hausmann and asks to become a member of the Dada Club; Huelsenbeck turns down his request. Schwitters creates his own art form: MERZ (said to be a cut-up from the word Kommerzbank, commercial bank), his one-man movement, an outgrowth of Dada. Huelsenbeck refuses to admit him to the Dada Club because of Schwitters' ties with *Der Sturm*, Herwarth Walden's gallery and Expressionist review. Friendship between Raoul Hausmann and Kurt Schwitters.

FALL

Madrid:	Huidobro settles in Madrid, where his Creationism influences the future Ultraist group.
Lausanne:	Publication of Picabia's *Poèmes et dessins de la fille née sans mère* (Poems and Sketches of the Girl Born without a Mother).
Mexico:	Arthur Cravan disappears at sea, never to be heard of again.

Page from *Dada*, 4-5, Zurich, May 1919, with woodcut by Raoul Hausmann

NOVEMBER

Berlin:
Two publications by Raoul Hausmann: *Material der Malerei, Skulptur und Architektur* (Material of Painting, Sculpture and Architecture), one of the earliest examples of semi-automatic writing, and *Synthetisches Cino der Malerei* (Synthetic Cinema of Painting). On the 17th, Johannes Baader interrupts a mass in Berlin Cathedral, upbraiding the priest and calling for greater respect for the teaching of Christ: "Einen Augenblick! Ich frage Sie, was ist Ihnen Jesus Christus? Er ist Ihnen Wurst . . ." ("Just a minute! I'm asking you what Jesus Christ means to you. You don't care a damn about him . . .").

Holland:
First manifesto of the art periodical *De Stijl*.

Paris:
Weakened by his war wounds, Guillaume Apollinaire dies of the Spanish flu.

Brussels:
Carl Einstein, as their uncompromising spokesman, plays a key part in the uprising of German soldiers and workers against their superiors in occupied Brussels. At his side, Pansaers takes an active part in this Spartacist insurrection.

DECEMBER

Lausanne:
Publication at Begnins, near Lausanne, of Picabia's poem in five cantos *L'Athlète des Pompes funèbres* (The Athlete of the Funeral Parlor); and at Lausanne, of Picabia's book of verse *Râteliers platoniques* (Platonic False Teeth).

Berlin:
Spartacist street demonstration.

Petrograd:
Creation of the weekly *Isskustvo Kommuny* (Art of the Commune), mouthpiece of the avant-garde movement, reflecting various trends. The official editor is Mayakovsky; the real editor is Nikolai Punin.

Zurich:
Tzara's *Dada Manifesto 1918* appears in *Dada 3*. On the cover, a quotation from Descartes: "Je ne veux même pas savoir s'il y a eu des hommes avant moi" (I don't even care to know whether there were any men before me). In it, writings by Reverdy, Picabia, Albert-Birot, Soupault, Camillo Sbarbaro, Tzara, Paul Dermée, Savinio, Huidobro; works by Janco, Arp, Prampolini, Segal, Richter, Picabia.

Brussels:
Jacques Vaché writes to André Breton: "Here I am in Brussels, once again in my dear atmosphere of 3 a.m. tango and wonderful industries, in front of some monstrous double-straw cocktail and some bloody smile."

Hausmann: creation of the poster poem and the phonetic poem. Amédée Ozenfant and C.E. Jeanneret (Le Corbusier): *Après le cubisme* (After Cubism), the first Purist manifesto.
End of the First World War.

1919

JANUARY

Zurich:
At the Kunsthaus, exhibition of Arp, Baumann, Augusto Giacometti, Janco, Picabia, Ricklin, Bailly, Lüthy, Morach. Lectures by Flake, Tzara, and Janco.
Picabia and Tzara meet for the first time.
Breton and Tzara begin corresponding.

France:
Death in a hotel room at Nantes, with two other young men, of Jacques Vaché, aged 23, from an overdose of opium. Breton puts it down as suicide, writing: "The admirable thing about his death is that it looks accidental. He absorbed, I believe, forty grams of opium, although it is thought that he was not an experienced addict. On the other hand, it is quite possible that his unfortunate companions were unacquainted with the use of opium, and that in dying he wished to commit at their expense one last *funny piece of roguery*" (Breton, *La Confession dédaigneuse*, 1924).
Michel Leiris saw it as an accident: "The corpse of André Breton makes me sick because it's the corpse of someone who himself has always lived off corpses. Vaché's accidental death (disguised as 'willful homicide' to give this episode, quite simple and all the more striking, a romantic cast which literature could turn to account), the recent suicide of Rigaut . . ., the internment of Nadja . . ., these are dramas from which the aesthete . . . will have known how to profit" (Leiris, in the Surrealist tract against Breton entitled *Un Cadavre*, January 15, 1930).

Germany:
Spartacist street fighting in Berlin, Stuttgart, Nuremberg, Bremen, Düsseldorf. After questioning, while in the hands of the police, the Spartacist leaders Rosa Luxemburg and Karl Liebknecht are shot down in Berlin, and the murderers are covered by the minister Noske. Thrown into the Landwehrkanal, the body of Rosa Luxemburg will only be recovered months later.

Zurich:
On the 16th, in conjunction with the exhibition at the Kunsthaus, lecture by Tzara on abstract art, with projections. After reading Picabia's books of verse, Tzara invites Picabia to come and see him: they meet on the 22nd.

FEBRUARY

Berlin:
Baader, the self-proclaimed President of the Universe, at the Kaisersaal des Rheingold. Pamphlet *Jedermann sein eigner Fussball* (Everyone his own football) by Wieland Herzfelde with Grosz, Mynona, Mehring, and a photomontage by Heartfield.

Cologne:
First number of the review *Der Ventilator* (five numbers, one double, from February to March), edited by Max Ernst and Johannes Baargeld (who helps to finance it), a mouthpiece of the political struggle. Arp (back from Zurich) and Ernst meet again in Cologne. New Dada phase, less directly political.
Provocation: interruption of the play *The Young King* at the Schauspielhaus.

Zurich:
Publication of *391*, No. 8, the "traveling review": it marks the New York–Paris–Zurich–Barcelona axis. On the 22nd, arrival of Walter Serner.

Lausanne:
Publication of Picabia's book of verse *Poésie Ron-Ron*.

Tiflis:
Ilya Zdanevich (Iliazd) founds Degree 41 Editions, which he keeps going for the rest of his life, and publishes *Easter Island*.

MARCH

New York:
Single number of *TNT* ("explosive review") by Man Ray, with Adon Lacroix, Soupault, Arensberg, Sheeler, Dawson. Marcel Duchamp: "He did it with a sculptor, Adolf Wolff, who was imprisoned as an anarchist" (*Dialogues with Marcel Duchamp*).

Berlin:
Baader founds the Club of the Blue Milky Way. First number of the satirical review *Die Pleite* (Bankruptcy), edited by Wieland Herzfelde; last number in 1924.

Paris:
First number of the review *Littérature*, edited by Aragon, Breton, and Soupault. At the suggestion of Jean Paulhan, Breton gets in touch with Paul Eluard.
Picabia returns to Paris, moving in with Germaine Everling.

Zurich:
Dances by Mary Wigman at the Pfauentheater.

Iliazd: *Degree 41*, No. 1, Tiflis, 1919

APRIL

Zurich:
Tzara quarrels with Janco because the latter has signed the progressive manifesto of the Neues Leben group (published in the *Neue Zürcher Zeitung* of May 4).
Hans Richter and Viking Eggeling leave for Berlin, where they collaborate on films.
Alice Bailly exhibition at the Kunsthaus. Eighth Dada evening at the Zur Kaufleuten hall: "Producer: Serner. Acrobat tamer: Tzara".

Paris:
Jean Crotti marries Suzanne Duchamp. As a wedding present Marcel Duchamp sends his sister an *Unhappy Readymade* consisting of a geometry textbook to be hung from the balcony by a thread.

Berlin:
In the periodical *Der Einzige* (The Unique) Raoul Hausmann publishes his manifesto *Gegen die Weimarische Lebensauffassung* (Against the Weimar View of Life). A Berlin daily announces Baader's death on April 1st and his resurrection on the 2nd. Proclamation of the Dada Republic of Nikolassee on April 1st. On the 30th, big Dada evening for the opening in May of the first Dada exhibition at Neumann's Graphisches Kabinett: Huelsenbeck ("Dada Proclamation"), Hausmann ("Soul Automobile"), and Golyscheff ("Antisymphony in Three Parts").

Budapest:
Béla Kun denounces the periodical *MA* as "bourgeois and decadent."

Paris:
Tzara's first contribution to *Littérature*, the poem "maison flake."

MAY

Paris:
Opening of the Au Sans Pareil bookshop in Avenue Kléber by René Hilsum, friend and schoolmate of Breton's at the Collège Chaptal just before the war, where he edited the school magazine which published Breton's first writings. To launch the series of *Littérature* publications, Au Sans Pareil issues an unpublished Rimbaud poem, *Les mains de Jeanne-Marie*, obtained through Patterne Berrichon.

Zurich:
Dada 4-5: Dada Anthology. The German edition contains Serner's manifesto *Letzte Lockerung* (Last Loosening).

Berlin:
Rosa Luxemburg's body is retrieved.

Moscow:
First exhibition of the Young Painters Association stemming from the Free Studios. The social activism of the most forward-looking among them is akin to certain Dada practices. Among the participants are several future Constructivists: the brothers Vladimir and Georghi Stenberg, the sculptors Yoganson and Medunetzky, and Naumov.

Johannes Baader: Tract on "War Guilt," Berlin, 1918

JUNE

Zurich: Fictive duel between Arp and Tzara (announced in the press) "to celebrate a bluish private victory."

Berlin: First issue of *Der Dada*, edited by Hausmann with Baader, containing a text by Tzara. On the 29th, opening at the Der Sturm Gallery of the first exhibition of Schwitters' Merz pictures.

Paris: André Breton: *Mont de Piété*, with two drawings by Derain, published by Au Sans Pareil. Breton and Soupault write *Les Champs magnétiques* (or already in April-May according to some sources).

Budapest: Firm reply of Lajos Kassák in his *Letter to Béla Kun in the Name of Art*: "Is all our history supposed to be no more than the ecstatic convulsion of a bourgeois decadence? If you are unaware of it, dear Comrade Kun, I must tell you that, while you were wasting your energy in the struggle alongside our Russian brothers, we were already militating . . . in favor of Communism . . . The new art . . . modulates all that is deepest in the human soul and . . . gives a synthesis of the dynamics of the world."

JULY

Budapest: The government forces the periodical *MA* to cease publication, on pretext of a paper shortage.

Berlin: Copies of Baader's tract *The Green Corpse* handed out to members of the Weimar parliament. Schwitters' manifesto on Merz painting published in *Der Sturm*, the term Merz here appearing for the first time.

AUGUST

Berlin: Schwitters' poem *Anna Blume* appears in *Der Sturm*. Huelsenbeck signs a contract with the publisher Kurt Wolff for the publication of a Dada world atlas called *Dadaco*; the project is never carried out.

Paris: Jacques Vaché: *Lettres de guerre* (War Letters). Cendrars: *Dix-neuf poèmes élastiques* (Nineteen Elastic Poems). Soupault: *Rose des vents* (Wind Rose). Picabia: *Pensées sans langage* (Thoughts without Language).

SEPTEMBER

Zurich: Ninth Dada evening.

Berlin: First number of *Der Blutige Ernst* (Sanguinary Earnestness), with contributions by Höxter, Firn, Haase, Huelsenbeck, Hausmann, Mehring.

Munich: Passing through, Max Ernst calls on Paul Klee, and will show two of Klee's pictures at the Bulletin D exhibition in Cologne.

OCTOBER

Paris: Paul Morand: *Lampes à arc*.

Zurich: According to Tzara in *Dada Almanach*, 8,590 articles on Dada have by now appeared in the newspapers of the world. Appearance of the sole number of *Der Zeltweg*, edited by Otto Flake, Walter Serner, and Tristan Tzara (the last Dada periodical in Zurich).

NOVEMBER

Cologne: Dada exhibition at the Kunstverein and publication of *Bulletin D* by Baargeld, Ernst, Otto Freundlich, Heinrich Hörle, and Franz Seiwert, together forming the "W5 Central Office," also called Stupid Group or Dada W5 Central Office. The Bulletin D exhibition will also be shown in Düsseldorf in February 1920.

Belgrade: First number of *Zenit* edited by Lyubomir Mitzich (eight numbers till summer 1920).

DECEMBER

Berlin: Second issue of *Der Dada* edited by Hausmann. Huelsenbeck organizes two Dada evenings at the Schall und Rauch cabaret. The first, on the 7th, is so successful that the manager proposes another on the 13th; Huelsenbeck accepts and causes the second to end in an unrestrained uproar.

Hanover: Kurt Schwitters sends a copy of *Anna Blume* to Tristan Tzara.

Paris: Breton writes to Picabia inviting him to contribute to *Littérature*. Breton envisages a demonstration to protest against the arrest of the Italian Futurist Marinetti. The latter, a member of the Fascist central committee, had stood for the Italian parliamentary elections, second on the list presented by Mussolini. After losing (on November 18), Marinetti, together with Mussolini, Vecchi and fifteen others, had been arrested and imprisoned for three weeks on a charge of organizing armed gangs and endangering the security of the State.
Aragon: *Feu de joie*, illustrated by Picasso.
Picabia informs Tzara that the latter has been elected a member of the Section d'Or group in Paris.

Zurich: Tzara leaves for Paris.

La Logique assassine (Logic is murderous), broadsheet by Adon Lacroix, typography by Man Ray.
Hugo Ball: *Zur Kritik der deutschen Intelligenz* (Critique of German Intelligence) published by Der Freie Verlag, Bern.

1920

JANUARY

Paris: Tristan Tzara settles in Paris, staying with Picabia. First get-togethers of Breton, Picabia, and Tzara at Picabia's. Au Sans Pareil publishes *Les Animaux et leurs Hommes* by Paul Eluard, illustrated by Lhote. First Littérature matinée at the Palais des Fêtes, program as follows: André Salmon (*La crise du change*); poems by Jacob, Salmon, Reverdy, Cendrars, Raynal; pictures by Juan Gris, Ribemont-Dessaignes, Léger, Picabia, Lipchitz; poems by Picabia, Aragon, Tzara, Breton, Cocteau; music by Satie, Auric, Milhaud, Poulenc, Cliquet; ending with poems by Ribemont-Dessaignes, Soupault, Drieu La Rochelle, Eluard, Radiguet, Dermée, Albert-Birot.

Vienna: Kassák, imprisoned after the collapse of the Hungarian Soviet Republic, is released and moves from Budapest to Vienna.

New York: The issue of *The Little Review* containing the Cyclops episode from James Joyce's *Ulysses* is confiscated and burned by the American postal authorities, and the magazine is prosecuted for obscenity.

Germany: Baader, Hausmann, and Huelsenbeck go on a Dada tour to Dresden and Hamburg.

Berlin: The periodical *Die Pleite* (Bankruptcy) is banned as subversive.

FEBRUARY

Germany: The Dada tour of Baader, Hausmann, and Huelsenbeck goes on to Leipzig (February 24), Teplitz-Schönau (February 26), Prague (March 1-2) and Karlsbad (March 5).

Düsseldorf: Bulletin D exhibition.

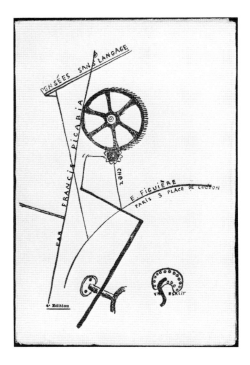

Francis Picabia:
Cover of *Pensées sans langage*, Paris, 1919

Berlin: New enlarged edition of Huelsenbeck's book of verse *Phantastische Gebete* (Fantastic Prayers), illustrated by George Grosz, published by Malik Verlag.

Paris: First of the six numbers of Paul Eluard's monthly sheet *Proverbe*, with texts by Apollinaire, Paulhan, Tzara, Soupault, Sade, Picabia, Breton, Raynal. Au Sans Pareil publishes Picabia's *Unique Eunuque*, preface by Tzara. Dada Movement matinée at the Salon des Indépendants in the Grand Palais of the Champs-Elysées. The four-page program constitutes the *Dada Bulletin*, forming the sixth issue of the review *Dada*. Press notice by Tzara announcing the presence of Charlie Chaplin and the conversion to Dada of Bergson, d'Annunzio, and the Prince of Monaco. The same program is presented at the Club du Faubourg (director Léo Poldès) in the disused chapel at Puteaux, in the west suburbs of Paris; and again on the 19th at the Université Populaire of the Faubourg Saint-Antoine. During a rowdy meeting held at the Closerie des Lilas café, the Dadas are excluded by the Cubists from the Section d'Or group headed by Gleizes.
Arp in Paris on a short stay.

Geneva: Dada exhibition of reliefs by Christian Schad and works by Gustave Buchet, organized by Walter Serner at the Salon Néri.

MARCH

Paris: *Dadaphone* no. 7 appears. Sole number of *Z*, a small magazine edited by Paul Dermée, the "Cartesian Dadaist." Performance of Ribemont-Dessaignes' play *Le Serin muet* (Théâtre de l'Œuvre) during the fourth manifestation of the Dada Movement, the first Dada show in Paris. Tzara prepares a project similar to *Dadaco*, which he calls *Dadaglobe*; it, too, fails to appear. Breton gives up medicine and obtains a post with the Gallimard publishing firm; one of his first jobs is reading aloud to Marcel Proust the proofs of his *A la recherche du temps perdu* (Remembrance of Things Past).

New York: In a letter dated the 2nd, Gabrielle Buffet-Picabia requests Tzara's permission for Stieglitz to open a Dada branch in New York.

Geneva: Grand Dada Ball organized by Walter Serner.

APRIL

Cologne: First number of *Die Schammade*, edited by Max Ernst and Johannes Baargeld. The Dada exhibition organized in the entrance hall of the Museum of Applied Arts in the Hansa-Ring is called off at the last moment by the museum director. Ernst and Baargeld transfer it at once to the backroom of the Brauhaus Winter. Improvised there, and called

Cover of *Der Dada 3*, Berlin, 1920, with photomontage by John Heartfield

Dada-Vorfrühling (Dada Early Spring), it provokes the ire of the public, who even destroy certain works. Closed by the police, the exhibition is reopened after some works have been withdrawn.

Berlin: *Der Dada 3* published by Malik Verlag, with contributions by Grosz, Heartfield, and Hausmann.

Hanover: Schwitters plans a film.

Munich: George Grosz exhibition at the Galerie Neue Kunst, run by Hans Goltz.

Leiden: De Stijl Manifesto II published by Van Doesburg, Kok, and Mondrian.

Paris: Picabia exhibition at Au Sans Pareil. First of two issues of Picabia's monthly *Cannibale*, published "with the collaboration of all the Dadaists in the world."

Geneva: Picabia and Ribemont-Dessaignes Dada exhibition organized by Walter Serner at the Salon Néri.

Poland: Bruno Jasieński's *Manifesto to the Polish People on the Immediate Futurization of Life*.

New York: Katherine Dreier, Marcel Duchamp, and Man Ray found the Société Anonyme. The name, equivalent to Inc., is suggested by Man Ray.

MAY

Vienna: Reappearance of the Budapest review *MA* edited by Lajos Kassák, with Béla Uitz and Sandor Barta. Russian *MA* evening, with projection of works by Kandinsky, Malevich, Rodchenko, Stepanova, Udaltzova, Tatlin.

Brussels: Publication of *Pan-Pan au cul du Nu Nègre* by Clément Pansaers.

Paris: Special issue of *Littérature* devoted to "Twenty-three Manifestoes of the Dada Movement." Quarrel between Picabia and Tzara. Dada Festival, Salle Gaveau, Rue La Boétie, the most important of the Dada shows. Extensive program of nineteen items, including *Le Nombril interlope* (Ribemont-Dessaignes), *Festival manifeste presbyte* (Picabia), *Vous m'oublierez* (Breton and Soupault), and *Vaseline symphonique* (Tzara, with twenty performers). Ribemont-Dessaignes exhibition at Au Sans Pareil, entitled *Cours d'élevage de cigarettes micro-cardiaques et d'alpinisme électrique* ("Course in Microcardiac Cigarette Breeding and Electrical Alpinism"). Au Sans Pareil publishes *Les Champs Magnétiques* by Breton and Soupault.

Leiden: First appearance in the periodical *De Stijl* of a Dada poet named I.K. Bonset (pseudonym of Theo van Doesburg).

JUNE

Paris: Independently, but under the Collection Dada imprint, Tzara publishes his book of verse *Cinéma calendrier du cœur abstrait. Maisons*, with nineteen woodcuts by Hans Arp.

Mantua: First issue of *Bleu*, edited by Julius Evola with Gino Cantarelli and Aldo Fiozzi (these last two previously with the review *Procellaria*).

Berlin: Erste Internationale Dada Messe (First International Dada Fair) at the Kunsthandlung Dr. Otto Burchard, Lützow-Ufer 13, from June 30 to August 25. With 27 exhibitors and 174 works, the show is organized by Grosz, Hausmann, and Heartfield. The catalogue, consisting of a broadsheet, is published two weeks after the opening. The exhibition gives rise to several indictments (trial in May 1921).

AUGUST

Paris: Tzara sets out on a journey that will take him to Zurich, Bucharest, Athens, Istanbul, Naples, and back to Zurich.

Paris: Au Sans Pareil hesitates to publish Picabia's *Jésus-Christ Rastaquouère* unless changes are made, even though all the books issued by this bookshop are published at the author's expense; and Breton declines to write the preface he had promised Picabia. The *Nouvelle Revue Française*, the Gallimard literary monthly, publishes an article by Breton (*Pour Dada*) and a short essay (*Reconnaissance à Dada*) by the editor, Jacques Rivière.

Hanover: Serner's Dada manifesto *Letzte Lockerung* (Last Loosening) published by Paul Steegemann.

OCTOBER

Paris: Short visit of Serner, who has come to see Breton and leaves him a wrong address. Tzara again staying in Picabia's apartment. Appearance of the first number of *L'Esprit Nouveau* (The New Spirit), an International Review of Aesthetics, edited by Paul Dermée with Amédée Ozenfant and C.E. Jeanneret (Le Corbusier).

Berlin: Arrival of Hans Arp, coming from Zurich.

NOVEMBER

Hanover: Schwitters plans an *Amerz* volume for *Der Sturm* in Berlin.

Brussels: A Dada demonstration planned by Pansaers, and discussed with Picabia, fails to materialize, owing chiefly to Tzara's absence during the summer of 1920.

Paris: Arrival of Jacques Rigaut.

DECEMBER

Madrid: The first number of *Reflector*, edited by the Ultraist Guillermo de Torre, publishes the *Vertical Manifesto* by Jorge Luis Borges.

Vitebsk: Malevich publishes his book *Suprematism, 34 Drawings*.

Paris: Picabia exhibition at the gallery La Cible, run by the Russian Povolozky: here Tzara reads his *Manifesto on Feeble Love and Bitter

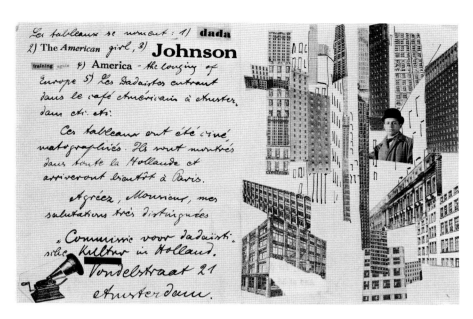

Letter to Picabia from Paul Citroën, Amsterdam, 1920

excursions includes a visit to the church of Saint-Julien-le-Pauvre in the Latin Quarter.

On the 25th, the Wallet Affair, a dispute at the Certa Bar over a waiter's wallet, found or forgotten. In course of argument Clément Pansaers proceeds to "assassinate" Dada, in opposition to Breton. Pansaers is backed up and followed a few days later by Picabia.

Letter to Picabia from Christian Schad, claiming that his friend Walter Serner originated the ideas expressed by Tzara in the *Dada Manifesto 1918*, and that the word Dada originated with Huelsenbeck and Ball. On this controversy, cf. above, February 1916.

New York: Sole number of *New York Dada*, edited by Marcel Duchamp and Man Ray.

Berlin: On the 20th, hearing of four Dadaists and Dr. Otto Burchard (the gallery owner) charged with insulting the German army during the First International Dada Fair in July-August 1920. The four are: Baader, Grosz (who made the set of prints *Gott mit uns!*), Wieland Herzfelde (who published them at the Malik Verlag), and Rudolf Schlichter. The court condemns Grosz to pay a fine of 300 marks, and Herzfelde a fine of 600 marks; the other two are acquitted.

LE 14 AVRIL 1921

OUVERTURE

DE LA

GRANDE SAISON

DADA

VISITES · SALON DADA · CONGRÈS ·
COMMÉMORATIONS · OPÉRAS ·
PLÉBICISTES · RÉQUISITIONS ·
MISES EN ACCUSATION ET JUGEMENTS

Se faire inscrire au SANS PAREIL

Opening of the Great Dada Season, Au Sans Pareil bookshop, Paris, April 14, 1921

Love and its supplement entitled *How I became charming delightful and delicious*.

Cologne: Max Ernst writes to Tzara proposing some of his works for an Ernst exhibition in Paris: it will be held at Au Sans Pareil in May 1921.

Dada Almanach, edited by Richard Huelsenbeck, published in Berlin.
Otto Flake: *Ja und Nein* (Fischer Verlag, Berlin).
Piet Mondrian: *Neo-Plasticism* (Rosenberg, Paris). Mondrian transforms his Paris studio and home into a Neoplastic environment.

1921

JANUARY

Paris: On the 12th, broadsheet *Dada soulève tout* against the lecture on Tactilism given by the Italian Futurist leader Marinetti at the Théâtre de l'Œuvre. Picabia protests in *Comoedia*: "Tactile art was invented in New York in 1916 by Miss Clifford-Williams . . . It is quite impossible for Marinetti to have been unaware of this new line of research . . . He plumes himself on having fathered everything, but I fear they were only imaginary pregnancies." Cf. above: *Rongwrong* (July 1917).

Berlin: *Maikäfer fliegt! Manifest von allem Möglichen* (May-bug flies! Manifesto on Everything Possible) by Raoul Hausmann. On the 20th, Faschings Dada Ball (i.e. Carnival Dada Ball) by Baader at the Marmorsaal am Zoo. Van Doesburg, visiting Berlin, meets Eggeling and Richter.

FEBRUARY

Berlin: Raoul Hausmann draws up his manifesto *PREsentismus, gegen den Puffkeismus der deutschen Seele* (PREsentism, against the Puffkism of the German Soul): it is read on the 8th by Mynona (S. Friedländer), Hannah Höch, and Hausmann at the Berlin Secession, 232 Kurfürstendamm ("Grotesken") and published in *De Stijl*, September 1921.

Dresden: Reading by Schwitters on the 19th.

Brussels: Clément Pansaers publishes *Bar Nicanor*.

MARCH

Paris: In the Collection Dada at Au Sans Pareil: *L'Empereur de Chine* (followed by *Le Serin muet*) by Ribemont-Dessaignes. Gallimard publishes *Anicet ou le Panorama, roman* by Aragon (dated March 1921, actually issued in the last quarter of 1920). *Littérature* publishes its Liquidation Survey (*Enquête-liquidation*).

Leiden: *De Stijl* publishes Raoul Hausmann's article *Dada ist mehr als Dada* (Dada is more than Dada). Leaving Holland, Van Doesburg stays in Paris, travels in Italy, settles in Germany.

APRIL

Madrid: Huidobro founds the review *Creación*, two issues subsequently appearing in Paris: texts by Radiguet, Dermée, Wolff, Goll, Schoenberg, Settimelli, Juliette Roche, and works by Gris, Gleizes, Picasso, Braque, Lipchitz.

Moscow: Manifesto *Long live the world's last Dada Internationale* issued by the Creative Office of the Nichevokis, a shortlived group consisting of Riurik Rok, Suzanne Mar, Sergei Sadikov, Oleg Ertsberg, and the painter Zemenkov.

Paris: Broadsheet announcing the opening of the Great Dada Season, with "visits, Dada exhibition, congress, commemoration, operas, plebiscites, requisitions, trials and convictions." The cycle of Dada

MAY

Madrid: *Anatomy of My Ultra* by Jorge Luis Borges in the review *Grecia*.

Paris: Arrival of Duchamp from New York. Opening of the Dada Max Ernst exhibition at Au Sans Pareil. Article by Picabia in *Comoedia*: *Picabia parts with the Dadas*. Organized by André Breton, mock trial and sentencing of the nationalist writer Maurice Barrès by Dada at the Salle des Sociétés Savantes, Rue Danton. Appearing as a witness, Tzara heaps ridicule on the proceedings and saves the trial from the serious anti-Dada character Breton had hoped to give it. Performance at the Théâtre Michel of Erik Satie's *Piège de Méduse*.

Weimar: Theo van Doesburg settles in Weimar (till the fall of 1922), hoping to obtain a teaching post at the Bauhaus (he fails). In 1925 the Bauhaus will publish his book *Grundbegriffe der neuen Gestaltenden Kunst*.

Rome: Dada lecture by Julius Evola at the University of Rome and reading of Tzara's *Dada Manifesto 1918*.

JUNE

Paris: Dada Salon at the Montaigne Gallery (located over the Théâtre des Champs-Elysées). Works by Arp, Aragon, Baargeld, Cantarelli, Charchoune, Eluard, Ernst, Evola, Fiozzi, Fraenkel, Man Ray, Mehring, Péret, Ribemont-Dessaignes, Ribemont and Tzara, Rigaut, Soupault, Stella, Tzara, Vaché, Gala and Paul Eluard, and "a friend from Saint-Brice." A sixteen-page catalogue is published with contributions from Soupault, Eluard, "Stanislas Margarine," Man Ray (a typographic poem), Rigaut, Ribemont-Dessaignes, Tzara, Péret, Aragon, Arp, Evola. Invited to take part, Marcel Duchamp sends (to Jean Crotti) a one-word telegram: "Podebal." Evening of Dada operas at the Salon, performance of Tzara's *Cœur à gaz* (Gas Heart) with costumes by Sonia Delaunay. The gallery management, however, frowns on the proceedings and without notice closes the Dada Salon before the matinée planned for the 18th.

Holland: Van Doesburg writes in French the *Manifeste métallique de shampooing néerlandais SLaM PANG* (unpublished at the time).

Antwerp: Appearance on the 15th of the Constructivist and Dada periodical *Het Overzicht*, edited by Seuphor and Pijnenburg.

JULY

Potsdam: Sole number of *Freiland Dada*, edited by Baader.

Jena: Reading by Schwitters on the 4th.

Paris: *Le Passager du Transatlantique* by Benjamin Péret. Special issue of *391* entitled *Le Pilhaou-Thibaou*. Man Ray arrives from New York and settles in Paris. Tzara gives up his *Dadaglobe* project for lack of funds.

Postcard to Paul Eluard from Arp,
Ernst and Tzara in the Tyrol, 1921

AUGUST

Tyrol: Summer vacation in Austria of Arp, Breton, Ernst, Eluard, and Tzara. Before Breton's arrival, Arp, Ernst, and Tzara compose a special issue of *Dada au grand air*.

Leiden: De Stijl Manifesto III, *Towards a New Shaping of the World*, published in *De Stijl*.

SEPTEMBER

Cologne: Ernst announces in a Cologne daily, the *Kölner Tagblatt*, that a Swiss mountain has just been named after Arp (and apparently there is a peak of that name near Mont Blanc).

Vienna: Poetry evening of the review *MA*, reading of works by Tzara, Sandor Barta, and Lajos Kassák.

Prague: On the 1st, Anti-Dada Merz evening with Schwitters, Hausmann, and Hannah Höch. Hausmann's reading of his poem *fmsbw* will inspire Schwitters to write his *Ursonate*. Schwitters recites his *Alphabet Read Backwards*, his poem *Cigarren* (composed around that one word, Cigars), *Anna Blume*, and *Revolution in Revon*. He writes *Auguste Bolte* during the journey.

OCTOBER

Berlin: Raoul Hausmann, Hans Arp, Ivan Puni (Jean Pougny), and László Moholy-Nagy sign a *Call for Elementary Art* published in the October issue of *De Stijl*.

Paris: Tabu manifesto issued by Jean Crotti and Suzanne Duchamp. Broadsheet-manifesto of Picabia-Funny Guy brought out to coincide with the opening of the Salon d'Automne.

Vienna: André Breton calls on Freud.

NOVEMBER

Paris: First number of the periodical *Aventure*, edited by René Crevel, with texts by Baron, Limbour, Vitrac, a survey entitled "Has humor failed us?" and drawings by Flouquet. Having left Russia, Iliazd settles in Paris, staying with Larionov; he meets the Dadaists, Robert and Sonia Delaunay, and Picasso. On the 27th, lecture by Iliazd on the new schools of Russian poetry, given in the studio of the singer Marie Olénine d'Alheim. Iliazd sets up his University of Degree 41 in the Café Caméléon.

Antwerp: Pansaers edits a special number of the periodical *Ça Ira* devoted to "Dada, its Birth, Life, and Death."

Vienna: Third MA evening with reading of Dada poems.

DECEMBER

Paris: Man Ray exhibition at the Librairie Six, Avenue de Lowendal (the bookshop run by Philippe and Mick Soupault). Drawing by Jean Dubuffet in the second issue of Crevel's review *Aventure*. Chameleon Evening organized by Serge Charchoune at the Café Caméléon.

Jorge Luis Borges publishes his manifesto *Ultraism* in the Spanish periodical *Nosotros*.
Hans Prinzhorn: *Bildnerei der Geisteskranken* (Artistry of the Mentally Ill).
Serge Charchoune: *Foule immobile* (Paris).

1922

JANUARY

Paris: Broadsheet-manifesto by Picabia against the selection committee of the Société des Artistes Indépendants, protesting against the rejection of two of his canvases by Paul Signac, chairman of the Salon des Indépendants. Marcel Duchamp leaves for New York.

FEBRUARY

Vienna: Issue of *MA* devoted to Ivan Puni (Jean Pougny). Opposed to Kassák's open-minded, internationalist views, Béla Uitz leaves *MA* to found another periodical with a Hungarian communist writer.

Holland: First issue of the periodical *Mecano* "jointly" edited by Theo van Doesburg and his alter ego I.K. Bonset. Four numbers (1922-1923).

Paris: Failure of Breton's projected Congress for the Determination of Directives and Defense of the Modern Spirit. Invited to join the planning board, Tzara refuses to have anything to do with it. On the 17th, at the Closerie des Lilas café, Breton is unanimously condemned and breaks with the Dadaists.

MARCH

Saint-Raphaël: Picabia and Herbiet issue their tract *Plus de cubisme* (No More Cubism) from Paris and Saint-Raphaël (Riviera).

New York: *The Little Review* brings out a special Picabia number.

Paris: New series of *Littérature* edited by Breton and Soupault, with some new contributors (René Crevel, Robert Desnos, Max Morise, Roger Vitrac). While the periodical seems to move away from Dada, yet it welcomes anything from Picabia (with the result that Soupault, hostile to Picabia, withdraws in September, leaving the editorship to Breton alone). From August, *Littérature* will receive a monthly subsidy from Jacques Doucet and will be distributed by Gaston Gallimard.

Weimar: At the Bauhaus Ball, on the 4th, Van Doesburg appears in a black dress-coat, his face covered with a long cardboard mask bearing the figure 13, holding in his hand the tricolor French flag.

APRIL

Paris: Tzara publishes *Le Cœur à barbe* (The Bearded Heart), a transparent journal on colored paper.

MAY

Düsseldorf: International Congress of Progressive Artists (May 29-31), in conjunction with the first international exhibition of a group of young artists. Participants: Werner Graeff, Raoul Hausmann, Van Doesburg, Van Eesteren, Hans Richter, Nelly van Doesburg, El Lissitzky, Ruggero Vasari, Otto Freundlich, Hannah Höch, F.W. Seiwert, S. Kubicki.

Berlin: First publication of Schwitters' "i poem." Two new periodicals appear: *Vesc/Objet/Gegenstand* edited by Lissitzky and Ehrenburg and *Perevoz Dada* edited by Serge Charchoune.

JUNE

Russia: On the 28th, death of Velimir Khlebnikov at Santalovo.

JULY

Lyons: First number of *Manomètre* edited by Emile Malespine (nine issues up to January 1928).

Imst: Tzara at Imst in the Tyrol with Matthew Josephson (about to edit the periodical *Broom*); he is later joined by Eluard, then by Arp.

SEPTEMBER

Rome: First issue of *Broom* (Rome, Berlin, New York), a Dada and Constructivist periodical.

Vienna: *Buch neuer Künstler* (Book of New Artists) by Lajos Kassák and László Moholy-Nagy, published in German and Hungarian (*Uj müvészek Könyve*).

Theo van Doesburg:
Simultaneous portrait of his wife Nelly-Petro
with dogs and cats, 1926

Cover of *Allgemeines Merz*,
edited by Kurt Schwitters, Hanover, 1921

Berlin: Invited by Hannah and Matthew Josephson (who after Paris and Rome now edit their periodical *Broom* from Berlin), Aragon spends September in Berlin, where Malik Verlag issues his pamphlet *Les Plaisirs de la capitale*, reprinted in *Le Libertinage* (NRF, 1924) under the title *Paris la nuit*.

Paris: First hypnotic sleep experiments in Breton's studio, Rue Fontaine, with Crevel, Péret, and Desnos.

Weimar: The Dada-Constructivist Congress opens on the 25th. Held on the initiative of Van Doesburg, it turns into a Dada meeting thanks to Arp and Tzara. Among the participants are Kurt Schwitters, El Lissitzky, Hans Richter, Max Burchartz, Alfréd Kemény. On the 23rd, lecture by Tzara at the Fürstenhof Hotel, with Arp reciting his *Cloud Pump* poems and Petro (Nelly) van Doesburg at the piano playing compositions by Vittorio Rieti.

Jena: On the 25th, Dada lecture by Tzara. On the 27th, Dada evening with Arp, Schwitters, and Nelly and Theo van Doesburg.
           Van Doesburg, together with El Lissitzky, Hans Richter, Karel Maes, and Max Burchartz, forms the planning committee of the I.C. or K.I. (International Union of Neoplastic Constructors), whose statement was published in *De Stijl* (August 1922).

Hanover: On the 30th, Arp, Schwitters, and Nelly and Theo van Doesburg put on a Dada-Revon evening at the Hannoversche Galerie v. Garvens.

Tokyo: First Dada poem in Japan by the poet Shinkichi Takahashi: *Dangen wa dadaisuto* (No Answer the Dadaist) in the periodical *Shukan Nippon*.

OCTOBER
Berlin: Erste Russische Ausstellung (First Russian Exhibition), Van Diemen Gallery.

Ticino: On the 20th, marriage of Sophie Taeuber and Hans Arp.

NOVEMBER
Barcelona: On the eve of the Picabia exhibition at the Dalmau Gallery, lecture by André Breton at the Ateneo: *Characteristics of the Modern Evolution and What Participates in Them*.

Berlin: Arrival of Kassák from Vienna.

Paris: On the 24th, formation of the Tcherez group of Russian artists, dedicated to the avant-garde theater (after a banquet in honor of Mayakovsky). On the 26th, lecture by Iliazd on Russian Dadaism, with the participation of Eluard, Soupault, and Tzara, in the studio of Marie Olénine d'Alheim. Aragon engaged by Hébertot to relaunch *Paris Journal* and turn it into a weekly competing with *Les Nouvelles Littéraires* which has just been founded (November 1). Aragon will leave *Paris Journal* in April 1923, because of unsparing criticism from his friends.

DECEMBER
New York: Jacques Villon exhibition at the Société Anonyme Gallery.

Paris: Man Ray's album of rayograms, *Les Champs délicieux*, with preface by Tzara entitled *Photography Upside Down*.

           ———

           Kurt Schwitters: enlarged reprint of *Die Blume Anna* (poems 1916-1922) and publication of *Memoiren Anna Blumes in Bleie* (Memoirs of Anna Blume in Lead).
           At the end of the year Van Doesburg leaves Weimar, having failed to obtain a teaching post at the Bauhaus.
           Mondrian retrospective at the Stedelijk Museum, Amsterdam.
           Serge Charchoune: *Dadaism*, sixteen-page booklet published in Berlin.
           Sole numbers of the Zagreb magazines *Dada-Jazz* edited by Dragan Aleksić, *Dada-Jok* by Virgil Poljanski and Lyubomir Mitzich, and *Dada-Tank* by Dragan Aleksić.
           Bulgaria (Jambol): the periodical *Crescendo* (Kiril Kristev, Teodor Dragonov, Ivan Milev).

In Brazil, the modernist periodical *Klaxon* at São Paulo (links with *L'Esprit Nouveau* in Paris).
Pierre de Massot: *De Mallarmé à 391* (Paris).
Gertrude Stein: *Geography and Plays*.

1923

JANUARY
Holland: The First Russian Exhibition, coming from Berlin, is shown at the Stedelijk Museum, Amsterdam.
           First number of the periodical *Merz* founded by Schwitters, entitled *Holland Dada*, to tie in with his tour of Dada-Merz manifestations organized in Holland with Theo and Nelly van Doesburg (periodical *De Stijl*) and Vilmos Huszár (the Hague on the 10th, Haarlem the 12th, Amsterdam the 16th, Diligentia Theater at the Hague the 28th, Utrecht the 29th, Rotterdam the 31st, Leiden February 14, Drachten April 13).

Tokyo: Tomoyoshi Murayama returns from Berlin.

FEBRUARY
Tokyo: *Dadaisuto Shinkichi no shi* (Poems of Shinkichi the Dadaist), edited and prefaced by Tsuji Jun, afterword by Sato Haruo, published by Chuo bijutsu-sha.

Paris: Great success of the fancy-dress Transmental Ball (in honor of the Zaum poets) at the Salle Bullier (for the benefit of the relief fund of the Union of Russian Artists). Quarrel between Tzara and Eluard on the occasion.

MARCH
The Hague: *Proletarian Art Manifesto* by Van Doesburg, Arp, Spengemann, Schwitters, and Tzara. Generally attributed to Schwitters, the manifesto is proclaimed at the Hague on March 6 and published in *Merz*, No. 2, April 1923.

Paris: Van Doesburg settles in Paris.
Brussels: Marcel Duchamp stays in the city until June.

APRIL
Paris: Aragon resigns from *Paris Journal* and leaves Paris until the fall, staying with Josephson at Giverny. On the 29th, during a soirée in honor of the poet Boris Bojnev, two works by Iliazd are interpreted: *Easter Island* is danced by Lizica Codreano to the rhythm of the text as read by the author; and *Donkey for Rent* is performed by puppets made by Granovski and Volovik.

MAY
Tokyo: First exhibition of works by Tomoyoshi Murayama. Works of "Conscious Constructivism" at the Bunpo-do.

Cracow: First number of the periodical *Zwrotnica*.

JULY
Paris: Tzara's book of early poems, *De nos oiseaux*, published by Kra. *Cœur à barbe* evening on the initiative of Tcherez which, as a tribute to the friendship between Iliazd and Tzara, asks the latter for a performance of his *Cœur à gaz* (Gas Heart) at the Théâtre Michel: the play is interpreted by Jacques Baron, René Crevel, and Pierre de Massot, with sets and costumes by Sonia Delaunay. On this occasion, showing of the films *Retour à la raison* by Man Ray and *Mana Hatta* (called in French *Les Fumées de New York*) by Charles Sheeler and Paul Strand. Violent outbreaks of the future Surrealists against the Dadas. Assault and battery. The police intervene.

MAVO Barber Shop, Tokyo, 1924

Marcel Duchamp and Man Ray playing chess, still from the René Clair film *Entr'acte*, Paris, 1924

Berlin:	The first number of *G*, a periodical edited by Hans Richter, together with Graeff and Lissitzky.
Tokyo:	Founding and exhibition of the Mavo group at the Denpo-in: Tomoyoshi Murayama, Masamu Yanase, Kamenosuke Ogata, Shuzo Ooura, Kunio Kadowaki, Iwane Sumiya, Michinao Takamizawa, Tokum Tokum, Osamu Shibuya, Shuichiro Kinoshita, Seicho Sawa.

SEPTEMBER

Groningen:	First number of H.N. Werkman's periodical *The Next Call*, hand-printed on a wooden press.
Paris:	Breton calls on the poet Saint-Pol Roux (1861-1940), one of the precursors of modern French poetry.

OCTOBER

Paris:	At the Gare du Nord Marcel Duchamp welcomes the Russian Constructivist Antoine Pevsner, who had been living in Berlin since the October Revolution and now settles in Paris.
	Iliazd: *Ledentu le Phare*, preface by Georges Ribemont-Dessaignes. The book is exhibited at the Paul Guillaume Gallery.
Japan:	"Anti-isms" exhibition in a cotton-spinning mill at Kami-Osaki.

NOVEMBER

Paris:	De Stijl exhibition at the Léonce Rosenberg Gallery.

DECEMBER

Hanover:	On the 30th, at the Tivoli, First Great Merz Matinée by Schwitters and Hausmann. They plan a periodical to be called *qngE*.

Kurt Schwitters begins work on his Hanover Merzbau (1923-1936, destroyed in 1943), in his house in the Waldhausenstrasse. During the summer, on the island of Rügen in the Baltic, Schwitters and Arp begin writing a novel, *Franz Müllers Drahtfrühling* (Franz Müller's Wired Springtime); it remains unfinished.
Theo van Doesburg: *Wat is Dada?* (De Stijl, The Hague).
Mina Loy: *Lunar Baedecker* (Contact Editions).

1924

FEBRUARY

Hanover:	On the 3rd, Merz evening. Another on the 5th in Magdeburg.

MARCH

Brazil:	Oswald De Andrade publishes his *Manifesto of Poetry Wood Brazil*.

MAY

Paris:	Performance of Tristan Tzara's *Mouchoir de nuages* (Cloud Handkerchief).

JULY

Paris:	Publication of Tristan Tzara's Seven Dada Manifestoes (*Sept manifestes Dada & lampisteries*).
Tokyo:	First of the seven numbers of the periodical *Mavo*.

OCTOBER

Paris:	Last number of Picabia's periodical *391*, entitled Journal of Instantaneism as a counterblast to nascent Surrealism.

NOVEMBER

Hanover:	On the 20th, Schwitters reads *Eigener Märchen* at the Kestnergesellschaft.
Milan:	First Italian Futurist Congress.

DECEMBER

Paris:	André Breton publishes his *Surrealist Manifesto*. First number of *La Révolution surréaliste*, edited by Pierre Naville and Benjamin Péret. Performance by Rolf de Maré's Swedish Ballet of *Relâche*, an instantaneist ballet in two acts by Picabia, with music by Erik Satie entitled *Obscene Ballet*, choreography by Jean Börlin and sets by Picabia. Shown during the intermission is *Entr'acte*, a film conceived by Picabia, adapted and produced by the film-maker René Clair, with music by Satie. This film sponsored by Rolf de Maré (who was to the Swedish ballet what Diaghilev was to the Russian Ballet) is rich in Dada sequences of the best vintage (in particular the funeral at Luna Park, with the hearse drawn by a dromedary). It remains one of the best-known Dada films thanks to its frenzied rhythm and burlesque character.
Tokyo:	Tomoyoshi Murayama publishes *Gendai no geijutsu to mirai no geijutsu* (Present Art and Future Art).
Weimar:	Closing of the Weimar Bauhaus. It will be reopened at Dessau in October 1925.

Arp and Lissitzky: *Die Kunstismen* (The Isms of Art).
Schwitters issues on a record the scherzo of the *Lautsonate* in *Merz 13*.
Tomoyoshi Murayama: sets for Georg Kaiser's play *From Morning to Midnight* at the Little Theater, Tsukiji, staged by Yoshi Hijikata.

Cover of Shinkishi Takahashi's novel *Dada*, Tokyo, 1924

Bibliography
by Marc Dachy

I.

LOUIS ARAGON (October 3, 1897 – Paris, December 24, 1982)

A. 1. Aragon, Louis. *Feu de joie.* Drawing by Picasso. Paris: Au Sans Pareil, coll. Littérature, December 1919. – 2. *Anicet ou le Panorama, roman.* Paris: NRF, February 1921. – 3. *Contributions à une histoire littéraire contemporaine.* Summary in *Littérature*, new series, no. 2, September 1922. Unpublished manuscript. – 4. *Une vague de rêves.* Paris: Hors commerce [1924]. – 5. *Les Collages.* Paris: Hermann, 1965. – 6. *La Défense de l'Infini* [1923-1927]. Extracts, and *Les Aventures de Jean-Foutre La Bite.* Drawings by André Masson. Introduction and notes by Edouard Ruiz, Paris: Messidor, 1986. – 7. *L'Œuvre poétique.* Tome 1, 1917-1926. Paris: Messidor, 1989.

CÉLINE ARNAULD (Nice, 1893 – Paris, 1952)

A. 8. Arnauld, Céline. *Tournevire.* Paris: L'Esprit Nouveau, May 1919. – 9. *Poèmes à claires-voies.* Paris: coll. litt. de L'Esprit Nouveau, March 1920. – 10. *Point de mire.* Paris: Povolozky, coll. Z, Dec. 1921. – 11. *Guêpier de diamants.* Antwerp: Ça Ira, 1923. – 12. Anthologie Céline Arnauld. Paris: Cahiers du Journal des Poètes, no. 3, February 1936.

JEAN ARP (Strasbourg, September 16, 1886 – Basel, June 7, 1966)

A. 13. Arp, Hans. *Der Vogel selbdritt.* Berlin: Otto von Holten, 1920. – 14. *Die Wolkenpumpe.* Hanover: Paul Steegemann, 1920. – 15. *Der Pyramidenrock.* Erlenbach-Zurich, Munich and Leipzig: Eugen Rentsch, 1924. – 16. Arp and El Lissitzky. *Kunstism 1924-1914 : Die Kunstismen, Les ismes de l'art, The Isms of Art.* Erlenbach-Zurich, Munich and Leipzig, Eugen Rentsch, 1925. – 17. Arp and Vicente Huidobro. *Tres novelas ejemplares.* Santiago: Zig-Zag, 1935. – 18. *On My Way.* Poetry and Essays 1912-1947. Trilingual volume (French, German, English). New York: Wittenborn, Schultz, Inc., 1948. – 19. *Unsern täglichen Traum... Erinnerungen und Dichtungen aus den Jahren 1914-1954.* Zurich: Peter Schifferli & Arche, 1955. – 20. *Arp on Arp* (Poems, Essays, Memories). Ed. by Marcel Jean, New York: Viking, The Documents of 20th-Century Art, 1972. – 21. *Gesammelte Gedichte* [Complete Poems]. Zurich: Arche and Wiesbaden: Limes. Three volumes already published : 1963, 1974 and 1984.

B. 22. SEUPHOR (Michel). *Arp. Sculpture.* Paris: Hazan, 1964. – 23. DÖHL (Reinhard). *Das literarische Werk Hans Arps, 1903-1930.* Introduction by F. Martini. Stuttgart: Metzler, 1967. – 24. READ (Herbert). *The Art of Jean Arp.* London: Thames and Hudson / New York: Abrams, 1968. – 25. LAST (Rex W.). *Arp: The Poet of Dadaism.* Chester Springs, Pennsylvania: Dufour & London: Oswald Wolff, 1969. – 26. HANS ARP. Die Reliefs. *Œuvre-Katalog.* Ed. by Bernd Rau. Introduction by Michel Seuphor. Stuttgart: Gerd Hatje, 1981.

C. 27. ARP. Museum of Modern Art, Ville de Paris, 1986. – 28. ARP. Curators: Jane Hancock and Stefanie Poley. Cambridge Univ., 1987. – 29. ARP (Hans). Ed. by Hans Bolliger, Guido Magnaguagno and Christian Witzig with an Introduction by Harriett Watts. Zurich: Kunsthaus, 1986.

D. 30. ARP. Poète plasticien. Actes du colloque de Strasbourg (Sept. 1986). *Mélusine*, Paris: L'Age d'Homme, 1988, no. IX.

E. 31. HUELSENBECK (Richard). "Arp and the Dada Movement" in: James Thrall Soby ed.: *Arp.* New York: Museum of Modern Art, 1958. Reprinted in *Memoirs of a Dada Drummer*, see Bibl. 222.

JOHANNES BAADER (Stuttgart, June 22, 1876 – Bavaria, January 15, 1955)

A. 32. Baader, Johannes. *Vierzehn Briefe Christi.* Berlin-Zehlendorf: Verlag der Tagebücher/ Architekt Baader, 1914. – 33. *Die acht Weltsätze.* Mühlheim an der Donau, 1919. [34. *The Eight World Theses.* Translated by Lerke Foster, typographical facsimile by The Center Press, Fine Arts Dada Archive, Univ. of Iowa,

1980] – 35. *Der Stern Erde und das Atomzeitalter.* Lindau, 1948 (300 copies printed by the author).

B. 36. *Johannes Baader, Oberdada.* Ed. with an Afterword by Hanne Bergius, Norbert Miller and Karl Riha. Lahn-Giessen: Anabas, 1977.

JOHANNES THEODOR BAARGELD (Stettin, October 9, 1892 – August 17 or 18, 1927)

A. 37. Baargeld, Johannes Theodor. *Dilettanten W x 3.* Cologne: Schloemilch, 1920.

B. VITT (Walter). 38. *Bagage de Baargeld.* Starnberg: Josef Keller, 1985.

HUGO BALL (Pirmasens, February 22, 1886 – Sant'Abbondio, September 14, 1927)

A. 39. Ball, Hugo. *Zur Kritik der deutschen Intelligenz.* Bern: Der Freie Verlag, 1919. – 40. *Die Flucht aus der Zeit.* Munich-Leipzig: Duncker & Humblot, 1927. – 41. Reissued in Luzern: Josef Stocker, 1946. – 42. American edition: *Flight Out of Time.* Ed. by John Elderfield. Transl. Ann Raimes. New York: Viking, 1974. – 43. *Gesammelte Gedichte.* Zurich: Die Arche, 1963. – 44. Ball & Emmy Hennings: *Damals in Zürich.* Briefe aus den Jahren 1915-1917. Zurich: Die Arche, 1978. – 45. *Briefe 1911-1927.* Ed. by Annemarie Schutt-Hennings. Einsiedeln-Cologne-Zurich: Benziger, 1957.

B. 46. STEINKE (Gerhardt Edward). *The Life and Work of Hugo Ball: Founder of Dadaism.* The Hague / Paris: Mouton, 1967.

C. 47. HUGO BALL. *Leben und Werk* (1886-1986). Ed. by Ernst Teubner. Wasgauhalle Pirmasens, Kunsthaus Zurich, Städtische Galerie Im Lenbachhaus, Munich, 1986.

BONSET (I.K.) alias Theo van Doesburg

A. 48. *Nieuwe Woordbeeldingen. De Gedichten van Theo van Doesburg.* Afterword by Karel Schippers. Amsterdam: Querido, 1975.

ANDRÉ BRETON (Tinchebray, February 18 or 19, 1896 – Paris, September 28, 1966)

A. 49. *Mont de Piété.* Paris: Au Sans Pareil, June 1919. – 50. *Les Champs magnétiques,* [with Philippe Soupault], Paris: Au Sans Pareil, May 1920. – 51. *Clair de Terre,* Paris: coll. Littérature, Nov. 1923. – 52. *Les Pas perdus.* Paris: NRF, Feb. 1924. – 53. *Anthologie de l'humour noir.* Paris: Le Sagittaire, 1940. – 54. *Entretiens.* Paris: Gallimard, 1952. – 55. *Œuvres complètes, I.* Ed. by Marguerite Bonnet. Paris: NRF Gallimard, La Pléiade, 1988.

B. 56. APOLLINAIRE (Guillaume) et les surréalistes. Letters to Tristan Tzara and André Breton. *Revue des lettres modernes.* Paris: 1964, no. 104-107. – 57. BONNET (Marguerite). *André Breton. Naissance de l'aventure surréaliste.* Paris: Corti, 1975. New edition 1988.

GABRIELLE BUFFET-PICABIA (Fontainebleau, November 21, 1881 – Paris, December 7, 1985)

A. 58. Buffet-Picabia, Gabrielle. *Aires abstraites.* Introduction by Jean Arp. Geneva: Cailler, 1957. [Reissued in 59. *Rencontres,* Paris: Belfond, 1977.]

SERGE CHARCHOUNE (Bougourouslan, August 4, 1888 – Villeneuve-Saint-Georges, November 24, 1975)

A. 60. Charchoune, Serge. *Foule immobile.* Twelve drawings by the author. Paris, Nov. 1921, 16 p. – 61. Reprinted in Vienna, 1922. – 62. *Dadaism.* Printed in Russian in Berlin: Ed. Europa Homeopathe, 1922, 16 p.

B. 63. CREUZE (Raymond). *Charchoune.* Paris: Creuze, 2 vol., 1975 and 1976. – 64. COPLEY (William & Noma). *Charchoune.* Chicago, [special issue of *Art News*], Copley Foundation, 1961.

C. 65. CHARCHOUNE. Contributions by Georges Hugnet, André Salmon, Philippe Soupault. Musée national d'art moderne, Paris, 1971. – 66. CHARCHOUNE. Text by Patricia Delettre. Paris: Guillon-Laffaille, 1988.

JEAN COCTEAU (Maisons-Laffitte, July 5, 1889 – Milly-la-Forêt, October 11, 1963)

A. 67. Cocteau, Jean. *Embarcadères.* [1917]. Montpellier: Fata Morgana, Bibl. artistique et littéraire, 1986.

B. 68. KING PETERS (Arthur). *Cocteau et son univers.* Introduction by François Weyergans. Paris: Le Chêne, 1987.

ARTHUR CRAVAN (Lausanne, May 22, 1887 – Gulf of Mexico, autumn 1918)

A. 69. Cravan, Arthur. *Œuvres, poèmes, articles, lettres.* Paris: Lebovici / Champ Libre, 1987. See: *Maintenant,* Bibl. 469.

B. 70. CARTANO (Tony). *Le bel Arturo.* Paris: Flammarion, 1989.

JEAN CROTTI (Bulle-lez-Fribourg, April 24, 1878 – Fribourg, January 30, 1958)

A. 71. Crotti, Jean. *Courants d'air sur le chemin de ma vie 1916-1921. Tabu-Dada.* Paris, 1941 (13 poems, 12 plates, 60 copies).

C. 72. TABU DADA. Jean Crotti & Suzanne Duchamp 1915-1922. Ed. by William Camfield & Jean-Hubert Martin. Paris: Musée national d'art moderne, Centre Pompidou, 1983.

PAUL DERMÉE (Liège, 1886 – December 27, 1951)

A. 73. Dermée, Paul. *Spirales.* Poems. Paris: Birault, October 1917. – 74. *Beautés de 1918.* Légende lyrique. Paris: L'Esprit Nouveau, March 1919. – 75. *Films.* Contes, Soliloques, Duodrames. Paris: L'Esprit Nouveau, November 1919. – 76. *Le Volant d'Artimon.* Poems. Paris: Povolozky, coll. Z, 1922.

THEO VAN DOESBURG (Utrecht, August 30, 1883 – Davos, March 7, 1931)

A. 77. Van Doesburg, Theo. *Wat is Dada ?* The Hague: De Stijl, 1923.

B. 78. BALJEU (Joost). *Theo van Doesburg.* London: Studio Vista, 1974. – 79. *Theo van Doesburg 1883-1931.* Een documentaire op basis van materiaal uit de schenking van Moorsel. Ed. by Evert van Straaten. Introduction by Wies van Moorsel and Jan Leering. Staatsuitgeverij, The Hague, 1983.

C. 80. *Projets pour l'Aubette.* Paris: Musée national d'art moderne, Centre Pompidou, Oct.-Dec. 1977.

MARCEL DUCHAMP (Blainville Crevon, July 28, 1887 – Paris, October 2, 1968)

A. 81. Duchamp, Marcel. *Salt Seller. The Writings of Marcel Duchamp.* Ed. by Michel Sanouillet and Elmer Peterson. New York: Oxford Univ., 1973 & London: Thames and Hudson, 1975. – 82. *Notes.* Introduction by Pontus Hulten. Presentation by Paul Matisse. Paris: Centre Pompidou, 1980. – 83. *Etant donnés* (Manuel of Instructions for). Philadelphia Museum of Art, 1987.

B. 84. CARROUGES (Michel). *Les Machines Célibataires.* Paris: Arcanes, 1954. – 85. LEBEL (Robert). *Marcel Duchamp.* Including texts by André Breton & Henri-Pierre Roché. Transl. George Heard Hamilton. New York, Paragraphic Press, 1959. – 86. CABANNE (Pierre). *Dialogues with Duchamp.* With an Appreciation by Jasper Johns. Transl. Ron Padgett. London: Thames and

Hudson, 1971. Reissued by Da Capo Paperback. – 87. PAZ (Octavio). *Marcel Duchamp or The Castle of Purity*. London: Cape Goliard, in association with New York: Grossman, 1970. – 88. PAZ (Octavio). *Marcel Duchamp: Appearance Stripped Bare*. [1970] New York: Viking, 1978. – 89. SCHWARZ (Arturo). *The Complete Works of Marcel Duchamp*. New York: Abrams, 1969. – 90. Augmented edition in 1970. – 91. GOLDING (John). *Marcel Duchamp: "The Bride Stripped Bare by Her Bachelors, Even."* New York: Viking, 1973. – 92. SUQUET (Jean). *Miroir de la mariée*. Paris: Flammarion, 1974. – 93. CLAIR (Jean). *Marcel Duchamp ou le grand fictif*. Paris: Galilée, 1975. – 94. DUCHAMP (Marcel) IN PERSPECTIVE. Ed. by J. Masheck. New Jersey: Prentice-Hall, A Spectrum Book, 1975. – 95. TOMKINS (Calvin). *The Bride and the Bachelors, Five Masters of the Avant-Garde: Duchamp, Tinguely, Cage, Rauschenberg, Cunningham*. New York: Expanded Edition, A Penguin Book, Art, 1976. – 96. LYOTARD (Jean-François). *Les TRANS formateurs Duchamp*. Paris: Galilée, 1977. – 97. ALEXANDRIAN (Sarane). *Marcel Duchamp*. Transl. Alice Sachs. New York: Crown, 1977. – 98. CLAIR (Jean). *Duchamp et la photographie*. Paris: Le Chêne, L'Œil absolu, 1977. – 99. THENOT (Jean-Paul). *Cent lectures de Marcel Duchamp*. Crisnée (Belgium): Yellow Now, 1978. – 100. DUCHAMP. Colloque de Cerisy. Contributors : Jindrich Chalupecky, Jacqueline Chénieux, Jean Clair, Hubert Damisch, John Dee, Thierry de Duve, Eliane Formentelli, André Gervais, Gilbert Lascault, René Micha, Jean Suquet. Paris: UGE, 10/18, 1979. – 101. MARQUIS (Alice Goldfarb). *Marcel Duchamp: Eros, c'est la vie: A Biography*. Troy, New York: Whitston, 1981. – 102. ADCOCK (Craig E.). *Marcel Duchamp's Notes from the Large Glass : An N-Dimensional Analysis*. Iowa: UMI Research, 1983. – 103. ARMAN (Yves). *Marcel Duchamp Plays and Wins*. Paris: Marval / New York: Yves Arman / Paris : Beaubourg Gallery / Geneva: Bonnier Gallery, 1984. – 104. DUVE (Thierry de). *Nominalisme pictural : Duchamp, la peinture et la modernité*. Paris: Minuit, 1984. – 105. BARUCHELLO (Gianfranco) & MARTIN (Henry). *Why Duchamp. An Essay on Aesthetic Impact*. New York: McPherson & Company, Documentext, 1985. – 106. SCHWARZ (Arturo). *Duchamp. La Sposa e i Readymade*. Milan: Electa, 1988. – 107. BONK (Ecke). *Marcel Duchamp : Box in a Valise*. New York: Rizzoli, 1989. – 108. CAMFIELD (William). *Marcel Duchamp: Fountain*. Houston: Fine Art Press / The Menil Collection, 1989. – 109. DUVE (Thierry de). *Résonances du readymade. Duchamp entre avant-garde et tradition*. Nîmes: Jacqueline Chambon, 1989.

C. 110. DUCHAMP. Ed. by A. d'Harnoncourt and K. McShine. New York: The Museum of Modern Art / Philadelphia Museum of Art / London: Thames and Hudson, 1973. – 111. Reissued in New York: The Museum of Modern Art, 1989. – 112. DUCHAMP. Four volumes : I. Biographie / Chronologie. II. Catalogue raisonné, sources et bibliographie. III. Abécédaire. Approches critiques. IV. *Victor*. Novel by Henri-Pierre Roché. Ed. by Jean Clair with Ulf Linde. Prepared in conjunction with the exhibition held in Paris: Musée national d'art moderne, Centre Georges Pompidou, January 1977. – 113. DUCHAMP. Exposición organizada por la Fundación Caja de Pensiones y la Fundació Joan Miró. Madrid, 1984. – 114. MARCEL DUCHAMP et ses frères. Paris: Dina Vierny, 1988.

D. 115. DUCHAMP ET APRES. *Opus International*. Paris, March 1974, no. 49.

VIKING EGGELING (Lund, October 21, 1880 – Berlin, May 3, 1925)

B. 116. O'KONOR (Louise). *Viking Eggeling, Life and Work*. Transl. Catherine G. Sundström and Anne Bibby. Stockholm Studies in History of Art, 23, Almqvist & Wiksell, 1971.

PAUL ÉLUARD (Saint-Denis, December 14, 1895 – Charenton, November 11, 1952)

A. 117. *Le Devoir et l'inquiétude*. Poèmes suivis de *Le Rire d'un autre*. Paris: Gonon, 1917. – 118. *Les Animaux et leurs hommes. Les Hommes et leurs animaux*. Five drawings by André Lhote. Paris: Au Sans Pareil, 1920. – 119. *Les Nécessités de la vie et les conséquences des rêves*. Note by Jean Paulhan. Paris: Au Sans Pareil, 1921. – 120. *Répétitions*. Drawings by Max Ernst. Paris: Au Sans Pareil, 1922. – 121. *Les Malheurs des immortels révélés par Paul Eluard et Max Ernst*. Paris: Librairie Six, 1922. – 122. *Mourir de ne pas mourir*. Paris: NRF, 1924.

B. 123. *Album Eluard*. Iconography ed. by René-Jean Ségalat. Paris: NRF, La Pléiade, 1968.

MAX ERNST (Brühl, April 2, 1891 – Paris, 1976)

A. 124. Ernst, Max. *Fiat Modes. Pereat ars*. Eight lithographs. Cologne: Schlömilch, 1919. – 125. *Les Malheurs des immortels, révélés par Paul Eluard et Max Ernst*. Paris: Librairie Six, 1922. – 126. *Ecritures*. Paris: Gallimard, 1970. – 127. "Some Data on the youth of M.E., as told by himself". In *View*, Max Ernst number, 2nd series, no. 1, New York, April 1942. – 128. Published too by: *New Roads*, London, 1943, pp. 200-203. – 129. "Souvenirs rhénans", *L'Œil*, Paris, no. 16, April 1956, pp. 8-12.

B. 130. RUSSELL (John). *Max Ernst, Life and Work*. New York: Abrams, 1967. – 131. MAX ERNST. *Œuvre-Katalog*. Ed. by Werner Spies. Werke 1906-1925. Menil Foundation, Houston, Texas and DuMont Schauberg, Cologne, 1975. – 132. SPIES (Werner). *Max Ernst. Collagen. Inventar und Widerspruch*. Cologne: DuMont, 1988.

C. 133. *Von Dadamax zum Grüngürtel. Köln in den 20er Jahren*. Cologne: Kölnischer Kunstverein, 1975. – 134. *Max Ernst in Köln: Die rheinische Kunstszene*. Ed. by Wulf Herzogenrath. Cologne: Rheinland, 1980.

OTTO FLAKE (1880-1963)

A. 135. Flake, Otto. *Nein und Ja*. Frankfurt, Fischer, 1920. Munich: Klaus Renner, 1982. – 136. *Es wird Abend*. Gütersloh: Siegbert Mon, 1960. – 137. *Werke in Einzelausgaben*. Frankfurt am Main: Fischer. Volume 1: *Erzählungen*. Nachwort von P. Härtling. 2. Aufl., 1977. Volume 2: *Fortunat*. Roman in zwei Büchern. Nachwort von M. Rychner. 1974. Volume 4: *Monthivermädchen*. 1982. Volume 5: *Freiheitsbaum und Guillotine*. 57 Essays aus sechs Jahrzehnten. Introduction by Kurt Tucholsky. Afterword by R. Hochhuth. 1976.

GEORGE GROSZ (Berlin, July 26, 1893 – West Berlin, July 6, 1959)

A. 138. Grosz, George. *Erste George Grosz Mappe*. Berlin: Heinz Barger, 1917. – 139. *Kleine Grosz Mappe*. Berlin: Malik, 1917 – 140. *Gott mit uns*. Nine lithographs. Berlin: Malik, 1920. – 141: *Mit Pinsel und Schere: 7 Materialisationen*. Berlin: Malik, 1922. – 142. *Ecce Homo*. Sixteen watercolors. Berlin: Malik, 1923. – 143. *A Little Yes and a Big No*. New York: The Dial, 1946. 144. Reissued : *An Autobiography*. New York: Imago Design Company, 1983. – 145. *Ein kleines Ja und ein grosses Nein*. Hamburg: Rowohlt, 1955. – 146. *Briefe 1913-1959*. Ed. by H. Knust. Reinbeck near Hamburg: Rowohlt, 1979.

B. WOLFRADT (Willi). 147. *George Grosz*. Leipzig: Von Klinkhard & Biermann, 1921. – 148. MYNONA. *George Grosz*. Dresden: Rudolf Kaemmerer, 1922. – 149. BAZALGETTE (Léon). *George Grosz, l'homme et l'œuvre*. Paris: Les Ecrivains réunis, 1926. – 150. AVERMAETE (Roger). *George Grosz*. Paris: Arts et Métiers graphiques, 1929. – 151. ANDERS (Günther). *George Grosz*. Zurich: Die Arche, 1961. – 152. SCHNEEDE (Uwe M.) & alii. *George Grosz. His Life and Work*. With contributions by Georg Bussmann and Marina Sczesny. Transl. Susanne Flatauer. London: Gordon Fraser, 1979. – 153. DÜCKERS (Alexander). *George Grosz. Das druckgraphische Werk*. Berlin and Vienna: Ullstein / Frankfurt am Main: Propyläen, 1979. – 154. DESHONG (Andrew). *The Theatrical Designs of George Grosz*. Iowa: UMI Research, 1982. – 155. KAY FLAVELL (M.). *George Grosz, A Biography*. New Haven and London: Yale Univ., 1988.

C. 156. GROSZ. *The Berlin Years*, Ed. by Serge Sabarsky. Contributors: Lothar Fischer, Marty Grosz, Uwe M. Schneede and Marina Sczesny. Transl. Christa Hartmann. New York: Mazzotta, 1985.

RAOUL HAUSMANN (Vienna, July 12, 1886 – Limoges, February 1, 1971)

A. 157. Hausmann, Raoul. Sound poem-bill [*fmsbw*, on green or brown paper], Berlin, 1918. – 158. Sound poem-bill [*OFFEA* on green or brown paper], Berlin, 1918. – 159. Sound poem-bill [*Kp'erioum* on pink Japan paper], Berlin, 1918. – 160. *Material der Malerei, Plastik, Architektur*. Berlin, 1918. – 161. *Synthetisches Cino der Malerei*. Manifesto. Berlin: April 1918. Transl. Mimi Wheeler in: Lippard, *Dadas on Art*, Bibl. 510. – 162. *Hurrah, Hurrah ! Hurrah !* Deutsche Satiren. Berlin: Malik, 1921 (Reissued: Anabas, Giessen, 1970). – 163. *Traité de questions sans solutions importantes*. Basel: Panderma, Bibliothèque intersidérale, 1957. – 164. *Courrier Dada*. Paris: Le Terrain Vague, 1958. – 165. *Siebensachen*. Stuttgart: Burkardt, 1961. – 166. *Poèmes et bois*. Paris: Iliazd, 1961. – 167. *Sprechspäne*. Flensburg / Glücksburg: Petersen Presse, 1962. – 168. *Mélanographie*. Paris: Sic, 1969. – 169. *Hyle, Ein Traumsein in Spanien*. Frankfurt am M.: Heinrich Heine, 1969. – 170. *Sensorialité excentrique*. Cambridge: Collection OU, 1970. – 171. *Am Anfang war Dada*. Ed. by Karl Riha and Günter Kämpf. Steinbach/Giessen: Anabas / Günter Kämpf, 1972. – 172. *Sagemorcim*. Brussels: Henry Fagne, 1971. – 173. *Je ne suis pas un photographe*. Paris: Chêne, 1975. – 174. *Bilanz der Feierlichkeit, Texte bis 1933*. Ed. by Michael Erlhoff, Volume 1, Munich: Frühe Texte der Moderne, Text + Kritik, 1982. – 175. *Sieg Triumph Tabak mit Bohnen, Texte bis 1933*. Ed. by Michael Erlhoff, Volume 2, Munich: Frühe Texte der Moderne, Text + Kritik, 1982.

B. 176. BORY (Jean-François). *Prolégomènes à une monographie de Raoul Hausmann*. Paris: L'Herne, 1972. – 177. BENSON (Timothy O.). *Raoul Hausmann and Berlin Dada*. Iowa: UMI Research, 1987. – 178. SCHEYING (Günther). *Die Dadaistischen Produktionen Raoul Hausmanns: Untersuchung ihrer Eigenart und theoretischen Fundierung*. Wissenschaftliche Hausarbeit in Rahmen der Ersten (Wissenschaftlichen) Staatsprüfung für das Amt des Studienrats, 1983. See REICHARDT (Jasia): Schwitters, Bibl. 395.

C. 179. Raoul Hausmann. Stockholm: Moderna Museet, 1967. – 180. L'Esprit de notre temps, Hausmann catalogue, Paris: Musée national d'art moderne, 1974. – 181. Raoul Hausmann. Malmö, no. 67, Konsthall, 1980. – 182. Raoul Hausmann. Rochechouart: Catalogue of the Musée départemental d'art contemporain in association with Mâcon: Ed. W, 1986. – 183. Les Peintures de 1959 à 1964. Fondation Cassan and Musée d'art moderne de Céret, 1986-1987. – 184. Hausmann : Ibiza. Musée départemental d'art contemporain de Rochechouart, Centre d'étude Hausmann, 1987. – 185. Raoul Hausmann. Fotografien 1927-1933 gegen den Kalten Blick der Welt. Ed. by H. Amanshauer and M. Faber with notes by Cornelia Frenkel-Le Chuiton and Andreas Haus. Österreichisches Fotoarchiv im Museum moderner Kunst, Vienna, 1986.

D. 186. HAUSMANN ET DADA A BERLIN (Raoul). Special critical issue edited by Roberto Altmann and Jean-François Bory. Review *Apeiros*. Vaduz, Liechtenstein, 1974, no. 6. – 187. HAUSMANN. Paris, review *F*, June 1974, no. 4.

JOHN HEARTFIELD (Berlin, June 19, 1891 – Berlin, April 26, 1968)

A. 188. Heartfield, John. *Photomontages of the Nazi Period*. New York: Universe Books, 1977. – 189. *Der Schnitt entlang der Zeit*. Ed. by R. März. With Gertrud Heartfield. Dresden: VEB, Verlag der Kunst, 1981.

B. 190. John Heartfield. Leben und Werk dargestellt von seinem Bruder Wieland Herzfelde. Dresden: Verlag der Kunst, 1962, 1971, 1976. – 191. SIEPMANN (Eckhard). *Montage: John Heartfield vom Club Dada zur Arbeiter-Illustrierten Zeitung*. Berlin: Elefanten, 1977. – 192. KAHN (Douglas). *John Heartfield: Art and Mass Media*. New York: Tanam, 1985.

C. 193. HEARTFIELD (John). 1918-1968. Institute of Contemporary Arts, London, 1969.

E. 194. Aragon, Louis. "John Heartfield et la beauté révolutionnaire". Lecture of May 2, 1935. In: *Les Collages*. Bibl. 5.

EMMY HENNINGS (Flensburg, January 17, 1885 – Magliaso, August 10, 1948)

A. 195. Hennings, Emmy. *Gefängnis*. Berlin: Erich Reiss, 1918. Reissued: Wetzlar: Büchse der Pandora, 1980. – 196. *Hugo Ball's Weg zu Gott*, 1931. – 197. *Ruf und Echo: Mein Leben mit Hugo Ball*, Einsiedeln: Benziger, 1952.

WIELAND HERZFELDE (Weggis [Switzerland], April 11, 1896 – Berlin, November 25, 1988)

A. 198. Herzfelde, Wieland. *Sulamith*. Berlin: Heinz Barger, 1917. – 199. *Tragigrotesken der Nacht. Träume*. Berlin: Malik, 1920. – 200. *Immergrün. Merkwürdige Erlebnisse und Erfahrungen eines fröhlichen Waisenknaben*. Berlin: Aufbau, Aurora Bücherei, 1949 and 1980.

HANNAH HÖCH (Gotha, Thüringen, November 1, 1889 – West Berlin, May 31, 1978)

B. 201. OHFF (Heinz). *Hannah Höch*. Berlin: Gebrüder Mann, Bildende Kunst in Berlin, 1968. – 202. ADRIANI (Götz). *Hannah Höch*. Cologne: DuMont, 1980.

C. 203. HANNAH HÖCH. Collages of the years 1916-1917. Academy of Arts, Berlin, 1971. – 204. Paris, ARC 2, Musée d'art moderne de la ville de Paris, 1976. – 205. Werke und Worte. Published as catalogue of the Remmert and Barth Gallery, Frölich & Kaufmann, 1982. – 206. *Collagen*. Institut für Auslandsbeziehungen, Stuttgart, 1984. – 207. HANNAH HÖCH: Eine Lebenscollage. Ed. by the Berlinische Galerie and Cornelia Thater-Schulz (Hannah-Höch-Archiv). Berlin: Argon, 1989.

D. 208. RODITI (Edouard). "Interview with Hannah Höch." New York: *Arts*, Dec. 1959.

RICHARD HUELSENBECK (Frankenau-Hesse, April 23, 1892 – Minusino, Ticino, April 20, 1974)

A. 209. Huelsenbeck, Richard. *Phantastische Gebete* . Poems with 7 Woodcuts by Arp. Zurich: coll. Dada, Sept. 1916. – 210. New edition : Berlin : Malik, Drawings by Grosz, 1920. Reissued in Zurich: Die Arche, 1960. – 211. *Schalaben schalamai schalamezomai*. Poems. With 4 drawings by Arp. Zurich: [third volume] coll. Dada, Oct. 1916. – 212. *Verwandlungen*. Novel. Munich: Roland, 1918. – 213. *Dadaistisches Manifest*. 25 copies, Berlin: April 1918. – 214. *Azteken oder die Knallbude*. Military novel. Berlin: Reuss & Pollak, 1918. – 215. *Deutschland muss untergehen. Erinnerungen eines alten dadaistischen Revolutionärs*. Two drawings by Grosz. Berlin: Malik, Abteilung Dada, 1920. – 216. *Dada siegt! Eine Bilanz und Geschichte des Dadaismus*. Berlin: Malik, 1920. – 217. *Doktor Billig am Ende*. Novel. Eight drawings by Grosz. Munich: Kurt Wolff, 1921. – 218. *En avant Dada, Die Geschichte des Dadaismus*. Hanover / Leipzig: Paul Steegemann, 1920. – 219. *Dada Manifesto 1949*. New York: Wittenborn, 1951. – 220. *Mit Witz, Licht und Grütze. Auf den Spuren des Dadaismus*. Wiesbaden: Limes, 1957. – 221. *Dada, Eine literarische Dokumentation*. Reinbeck bei Hamburg: Rowohlt, 1964. – 222. *Memoirs of a Dada Drummer*. Ed. by Hans J. Kleinschmidt. Transl. Joachim Neugroschel. New York: Viking, 1974. – 223. *Reise bis ans Ende der Freiheit*. Autobiographische Fragmente. Heidelberg: Lambert Schneider, 1984.

B. 224. SHEPPARD (Richard). *Huelsenbeck. Bibliography*. Ed. by Karin Füllner, Rolf Italiaander and Hans J. Kleinschmidt. Hamburg: Hans Christians, 1982. – 225. FÜLLNER (Karin). *Richard Huelsenbeck, Texte und Aktionen eines Dadaisten*. Heidelberg: Carl Winter Univ., 1983.

VICENTE HUIDOBRO (Santiago, Chile, January 10, 1883 – Cartagena, Chile, January 2, 1948)

A. 226. Huidobro, Vicente. In Spanish : *Ecos del alma*. Santiago de Chile, 1911. – 227. *Canciones en la noche*. Santiago de Chile, 1913. – 228. *La Gruta del silencio*. Santiago de Chile, 1913. – 229. *Pasando y pasando*. Santiago de Chile, 1914. – 230. *Las pagodas ocultas*. Santiago de Chile, 1914. – 231. *El espejo de agua*. Buenos Aires, 1916. – 232. *Ecuatorial*. Madrid, 1918. – 233. *Poemas árticos*. Madrid, 1918. In French: – 234. *Horizon carré*. Paris: Paul Birault, 1917. – 235. *Tour Eiffel*. Madrid: Imp. de Pueyo, 1918. – 236. *Hallali, poème de guerre*. Madrid: Imp. Lopez, 1918. – 237. *Saisons choisies*. Paris: La Cible, 1921. – 238. *Tout à coup*, Paris: Au Sans Pareil, 1925. – 239. *Manifestes*. Paris: Revue Mondiale, 1925. – 240. *Automne régulier*. Paris: Librairie de France, 1925. – 241. Arp and Huidobro. *Tres novelas ejemplares*. Santiago: Zig-Zag, 1935. – 242. *Obras poéticas selectas de V. Huidobro*. Ed. by Hugo Montes. Santiago de Chile: Pacífico, 1957.

B. 243. UNDURRAGA (Antonio de). *Vicente Huidobro, Poesía y Prosa – Antología*. Anthology with an Essay: *Teoría del Creacionismo*. Madrid: Aguilar, 1957. – 244. BAJARLIA (Juan-Jacobo). *La Polémica Reverdy-Huidobro: Origen del Ultraísmo*. Buenos Aires: Devenir, 1964. – 245. COSTA (René de). *Vicente Huidobro y el creacionismo*. Madrid: Taurus, 1975. – 246. WOOD (Cecil). *The Creacionismo of Vicente Huidobro*. Frederickton: York Press, 1978. – 247. BUSTO OGDEN (Estrella). *El creacionismo de Vicente Huidobro en sus relaciones con la estética cubista*. Madrid: Playor, 1983.

MARCEL JANCO (Bucharest, May 24, 1895 – Tel Aviv, April 22, 1984)

B. 248. MENDELSON (Marcel L.). *Marcel Janco*. Tel Aviv: Massadah, 1962. – 249. SEUPHOR (Michel). *Marcel Janco*. Amriswil (Switzerland), Bodensee Verlag Larese, 1963. – 250. *Marcel Janco*. Introd. by A. B. Joffe. Tel Aviv: Massadah Ltd, 1982.

C. 251. Marcel Janco. Paris: Denise René Gallery, 1963.

E. 252. JANCO (Marcel). "Dada à deux vitesses" in: *Dada*, bibl. 581. Transl. Margaret Lippard: "Dada at two speeds" in: *Dadas on art*, Bibl. 510. – 253. NAUMANN (Francis). "Janco / Dada: An Interview with Marcel Janco." New York: *Arts Magazine*, 5, no. 3, 1982.

LAJOS KASSÁK (Ersekujvár, Hungary, March 21, 1887 – Budapest, July 22, 1967)

A. 254. Kassák, Lajos (and Moholy-Nagy, László). *Uj müvészek Könyve*. [Book of New Artists] Vienna: Ma, 1922. – 255. German edition: *Buch Neuer Künstler*. *Ibid.*

MAN RAY (Philadelphia, August 27, 1890 – Paris, November 18, 1976)

A. 256. Man Ray. *A Book of Divers Writings by Adon Lacroix*. Designed and published by Man Ray at Ridgefield, New Jersey, January 1915 (20 copies). – 257. *Les Champs délicieux*. Twelve Rayographs. Foreword by Tzara. Paris, Dec. 1922, Hors commerce (40 copies numbered and signed, 37.2 x 28.2 cm). – 258. *Revolving Doors* 1916-1917 (10 plates reproducing collages from 1916-1917). Paris: Ed. Surréalistes, 1926 (105 copies numbered and signed, 57 x 39 cm). – 259. *Man Ray Photographs 1920-1934*. Paris: James Thrall Soby. – 260. *Facile* (with Paul Eluard). Paris: Guy Lévis-Mano, 1935. – 261. *La Photographie n'est pas l'art*. Paris: Guy Lévis-Mano, 1937. – 262. *Les Mains libres*. Drawings with poems of Paul Eluard. Paris: Jeanne Bucher, 1937. – 263. *Alphabet for Adults*. Beverley Hills, California, Copley Galleries, 1948. – 264. *Self Portrait* [1963]. Boston: A New York Graphic Society Book, Little Brown and Company, 1986. – 265. *Photographs PORTRAITS*. Introduced by L. F. Gruber. Commented by Man Ray. Gütersloh: Sigbert Mohn and Paris: Prisma, n.d. – 266. *I 50 volti di Juliet*. Milan: Mazzotta, n.d. – 267. Opera grafica. Vol. 1. Ed. by L. Anselmino, Turin, 1973. – Opera grafica. Vol. 2. Ed. by B. M. Pilat, Milan: Studio Marconi, 1984. – 268. *Les années Bazaar*. Paris: Adam Biro, 1989.

B. 269. RIBEMONT-DESSAIGNES (Georges). *Man Ray*. Paris: NRF, 1924. – 270. *Bonsoir Man Ray*. Dialogues with Pierre Bourgeade. Paris: Belfond, 1972. – 271. JANUS. *Man Ray*. Milan: Hachette-Fratelli Fabbri, 1973. – 272. SCHWARZ (Arturo). *Man Ray, the Rigour of Imagination*. London: Thames and Hudson, 1977. – 273. BRAMLY (Serge). *Man Ray*. Paris: Belfond, 1980. – 274. FORESTA (Merry A.). *Man Ray*. Paris, Centre national de la photographie, 1988. – 275. BALDWIN (Neil). *Man Ray, American Artist*. New York: Clarkson & Potter, 1988. – 276. BAUM (Timothy). *Man Ray's Paris Portraits: 1921-1939*. Washington: Middendorf Gallery Publications, 1989.

C. 277. Man Ray. By Jean Leymarie. Musée national d'art moderne, Paris, Jan.-Feb. 1972. – 278. Man Ray: Photographe. Introduced by Jean-Hubert Martin. Exhibition Dec. 1981-April 1982 at the Musée national d'art moderne. Paris: Philippe Sers, 1981. – 279. *Perpetual Motif : The Art of Man Ray*. Washington: National Museum of American Art, Smithsonian Institution, Washington, 1988.

PIERRE DE MASSOT [DE LAFOND] (Lyon, April 10, 1900 – Paris, January 3, 1969)

A. 280. Pierre de Massot. *De Mallarmé à 391*. Introduction by Christian. Saint-Raphaël: Au Bel Exemplaire, 1922. – 281. *Essai de critique théâtrale*. Foreword by Picabia. Portrait of the author by Picasso. Hors commerce, 1922. – 282. *Reflections on Rose Selavy*. The Wonderful Book, 1924. – 283. *Saint-Just ou le Divin bourreau*. Hors commerce, 1925. – 284. *Portrait d'un Bull-dog*. Photograph by Berenice Abbott. Hors commerce, 1926. – 285. *Francis Picabia*. Paris: Seghers, Poètes d'aujourd'hui, 1966.

WALTER MEHRING (Berlin, April 29, 1896 – Zurich, October 3, 1981)

A. 286. Mehring, Walter. *Berlin Dada*. Zurich: Die Arche, 1959.

CLEMENT PANSAERS (Neerwinden, May 1,1885 – Brussels, October 31, 1922)

A. 287. Pansaers, Clément. *Le Pan-Pan au Cul du Nu Nègre*. Brussels: Alde, coll. AIO, May 1920. – 288. *Bar Nicanor*. Brussels, London, Paris, New York, Madrid, Yokohama: AIO, Feb. 1921. – 289. *L'Apologie de la Paresse*. Antwerp: Ça Ira, August 1921. – 290. *Sur un aveugle mur blanc & autres textes*. Letters to Tzara, Picabia and Van Essche. Chronology and bibliography by Marc Dachy. Paris: Transédition, 1972. – 291. *Bar Nicanor & autres textes Dada*. Ed. by Marc Dachy. Paris: Lebovici / Champ Libre, 1985.

D. 292. DADA PANSAERS. Meeting pansaérien. Bassac: Review *Plein Chant*. Spring 1988, no. 39-40.

BENJAMIN PÉRET (Rézé, July 4, 1899 – Paris, September 18, 1959)

A. 293. Péret, Benjamin. *Et les seins mouraient*. Marseille: Les Cahiers du Sud, 1918. – 294. *Le Passager du Transatlantique*. Four drawings by Arp. Paris: [Coll. Dada], 1921. – 295. *Immortelle maladie*. Poem with a drawing by Man Ray. Paris: Coll. Littérature, 1924. See too *Oeuvres complètes*. Five volumes. Paris: Losfeld and Corti.

B. 296. BEDOUIN (Jean-Louis). *Benjamin Péret*. Paris: Seghers, Poètes d'aujourd'hui, 1961 and 1973. – 297. COURTOT (Claude). *Introduction à la lecture de Benjamin Péret*. Paris: Le Terrain Vague, 1965.

FRANCIS PICABIA (Paris, January 22, 1879 – Paris, November 30, 1953)

A. 298. *Cinquante-deux miroirs*. Barcelona, Oct. 1917. – 299. *Poèmes et dessins de la Fille née sans mère*. Lausanne: Imprimeries réunies, April 1918. – 300. *L'Ilot de Beau-Séjour dans le Canton de Nudité*. Lausanne, June 1918. – 301. *L'Athlète des Pompes funèbres*. Bégnins, Dec. 1918. – 302. *Râteliers platoniques*. Poem in two chapters. Lausanne, Dec. 1918. – 303. *Poésie ron-ron*. Lausanne, Feb. 1919. – 304. *Pensées sans langage*. Paris: Figuière, April 1919. – 305. *Unique Eunuque* Paris: Au Sans Pareil, Coll. Dada, Feb. 1920. – 306. *Jésus-Christ Rastaquouère*. Paris: Au Sans Pareil, Coll. Dada, Autumn 1920. – 307. *Manifeste du bon goût* [1923]. – 308. *Relâche* [1924]. – 309. *Entr'acte* [1924]. – 310. *Caravansérail* [1924]. Ed. by Luc-Henri Mercié, Paris: Belfond, 1975. – 311. *Lettres à Christine*. Ed. by Maria-Lluïsa Borràs and Jean Sireuil. Foreword and Chronology by Marc Dachy. Paris: Lebovici / Champ Libre, 1988. – 312. Picabia. *Ecrits*. Two volumes ed. by Olivier Revault d'Allonnes and Dominique Bouissou, Paris: Belfond, 1975 and 1978.

B. 313. LA HIRE (Marie de). *Francis Picabia*. Paris: La Cible, 1920. – 314. MASSOT (Pierre de). *De Mallarmé à 391*. Saint-Raphaël: Au Bel Exemplaire, 1922. – 315. SANOUILLET (Michel). *Picabia*. Paris: Ed. du Temps, Coll. L'Œil du temps, 1964. – 316. MASSOT (Pierre de). *Francis Picabia*. Paris: Seghers, Poètes d'aujourd'hui, 1966. – 317. SANOUILLET (Michel). *Francis Picabia et 391*. Paris: Losfeld, 1966. – 318. LE BOT (Marc). *Francis Picabia et la crise des valeurs figuratives*. Paris: Klincksieck, 1968. – 319. EVERLING-PICABIA (Germaine). *L'Anneau de Saturne*. Paris: Fayard, 1970. – 320. CAMFIELD (William). *Francis Picabia*. Paris: Losfeld, 1972. – 321. DOCUMENTS DADA. Ed. by Yves Poupard-Lieussou and Michel Sanouillet. Geneva: Weber, 1974. – 322. ALBUM PICABIA. Immagini della vita di Picabia raccolte da Olga Picabia-Mohler. Note by Maurizio Fagiolo. Turin: Stampatori-Notizie, 1975. – 323. CAMFIELD (William). *Francis Picabia: His Art, Life and Times*. Princeton: Univ. Press, 1979. – 324. BORRÀS (Maria-Lluïsa). *Picabia*. Transl. Kenneth Lyons. New York: Rizzoli, 1985.

C. 325. PICABIA. Städtisches Museum Leverkusen, 1967. – 326. Picabia. By William Camfield. The Solomon R. Guggenheim Museum, New York, 1970. – 327. Cat. by Jean-Hubert Martin and Hélène Seckel. Musée national d'art moderne, Galeries nationales du Grand Palais, Paris, January-March 1976. – 328. Paintings and Drawings 1913-1922. Rachel Adler Gallery, New York, in collaboration with Richard Gray Gallery, April-May 1982. – 329. Anthological exhibition by Gonzalo Armero. Barcelona, Fundació Caixa de Pensions and Madrid, Min. de Cultura, Dirección General de Bellas Artes y Archivos, 1985. – 330. Opere 1898-1951. Mostra e catalogo a cura di Enrico Baj. Studio Marconi. Milan: Electa, 1986. – 331. ARC EN CIEL FRANCIS PICABIA. Essays by André Breton, Camille Bryen, Marcel Duchamp, Edouard Jaguer, Jean-Jacques Lebel, Pierre de Massot. 1900-2000 Gallery, Paris, 1987.

D. 332. PICABIA. Special issue of *291* dedicated to Picabia. New York, no. 5-6, July-August 1915. – 333. PICABIA NUMBER. *The Little Review*, New York, vol. VIII, no. 2, Spring 1922. – 334. FIXE. Published by the review *Dau-al-set* (30th anniversary of the Picabia exhibition of 1922, Dalmau Gallery). Barcelona, August-September 1952. – 335. IN MEMORIAM FRANCIS PICABIA. Booklet published by the review *Orbes*, April 1955. – 336. PARADE POUR PICABIA-PANSAERS. Review *Temps Mêlés*, Verviers [Belgium], no. 31-33, March 1958.

E. 337. ARP (Jean). "Picabia" (Note from 1949) included in: *Jours effeuillés* [*Arp on Arp*, Bibl. 20]. – 338. DUCHAMP (Marcel). "Picabia" (Note for "La Société Anonyme, Inc.") in: *The Essential Writings of Duchamp*. Bibl. 81. – 339. BOIS (Yve-Alain). "Picabia: de Dada à Pétain". Paris: Review *Macula*, no. 1, 1976, p. 122.

OTTO AND ADYA VAN REES (1884-1957 and 1876-1959)

C. 340. REES (Otto and Adya van). *Leven en werk tot 1934*. Utrecht: Centraal Museum & The Hague: Gemeentemuseum, 1975.

GEORGES RIBEMONT-DESSAIGNES (Montpellier, June 19, 1884 – Saint-Jeannet, July 9, 1974)

A. 341. Ribemont-Dessaignes, Georges. Théâtre. *L'Empereur de Chine* and *Le Serin muet*. Paris: Au Sans Pareil, Coll. Dada, March 1921. – 342. *L'Autruche aux yeux clos*. Paris: Au Sans Pareil, 1924. – 343. *Le Bourreau du Pérou*. Paris: Au Sans Pareil, 1928. – 344. *Déjà jadis ou du Mouvement Dada à l'espace abstrait*. Paris: Julliard, Lettres Nouvelles, 1958. – 345. *Dada* (Manifestos, Poems, Articles, Projects 1915-1930). Ed. by J.-P. Begot, Paris: Champ Libre, 1974. – 346. *Dada 2* (Short Stories, Articles, Theater, Literary Chronicles 1919-1929). Ed. by Jean-Pierre Begot, Paris: Champ Libre, 1978. – 347. *Théâtre*, Paris: Gallimard, 1966.

B. 348. JOTTERAND (Franck). *Georges Ribemont-Dessaignes*. Paris: Seghers, Poètes d'aujourd'hui, 1966.

D. 349. Ribemont-Dessaignes. Review *Marginales*, Brussels, 28th year, no. 152, April 1973.

HANS RICHTER (Berlin, April 6, 1888 – Minusino-Locarno, February 1, 1976)

A. 350. Richter, Hans. *Filmgegner von heute – Filmfreunde von morgen*. Berlin: Hermann Rechendorf, 1929. – 351. *Dada Profile*. Zurich: Die Arche, 1961. – 352. *Dada : Kunst und Antikunst*. Cologne: DuMont Schauberg, 1965. – 353. Translation: *Dada: Art and Anti-Art*. New York and Toronto: Oxford Univ., 1965. – 354. RICHTER. Autobiographical text by the artist. Introduction by H. Read. Neuchâtel: Le Griffon, 1965. – 355. *Köpfe und Hinterköpfe*. Zurich, Die Arche, 1967. – 356. *Begegnungen von Dada bis heute*. Cologne: DuMont, 1973. – 357. Opera Grafica dal 1902 al 1969. Ed. by Magdalo Mussio. Milan: La Nuova Foglio, 1976.

B. 358. HANS RICHTER BY HANS RICHTER. Ed. by C. Gray, New York Chicago San Francisco: Holt Rinehart Winston, 1971.

C. 359. *Hans Richter*. Amsterdam: Stedelijk Museum, March-April 1961. – 360. HANS RICHTER BY HANS RICHTER. Text by Brian O'Doherty. New York: Byron Gallery, and Finch College Museum of Art / Contemporary Wing, 1968. – 361. Œuvres Dada de Hans Richter. Denise René Gallery, Paris, May 1975. – 362. Dessins et Portraits Dada. Les Sables d'Olonne: Musée de l'Abbaye Sainte-Croix, April-June 1978. – 363. RICHTER 1888-1976. Dadaist, Filmpionier, Maler, Theoretiker. Berlin: Akademie der Künste, 1982.

JACQUES RIGAUT (Paris, December 30, 1898 – Châtenay-Malabry, November 6, 1929)

A. 364. Rigaut, Jacques. *Papiers posthumes*. Paris: Au Sans Pareil, 1934. – 365. *Ecrits*. Ed. by Martin Kay. Paris: Gallimard, 1970.

ERIK SATIE (Honfleur, May 17, 1866 – Paris, July 1, 1925)

A. 366. Satie, Erik. *Ecrits*. Ed. by Ornella Volta. Paris: Champ Libre, 1977. New revised edition : Champ Libre, 1981. – 367. *Le Piège de Méduse*. Notes by Ornella Volta. Paris: Castor astral, 1988.

B. 368. TEMPLIER (Pierre-Daniel). *Erik Satie*. [1932] Transl. Elena S. French and David S. French. Cambridge, Massachusetts: MIT Press, 1969 and New York: Dover, 1980. – 369. MYERS (Rollo). *Erik Satie*. London: Denis Dobson, 1948; New York: Dover, 1968. – 370. REY (Anne). *Erik Satie*. Paris: Le Seuil, coll. Microcosme Solfèges, 1974. – 371. HARDLING (James). *Erik Satie*. London: Secker & Warburg, 1975. – 372. VOLTA (Ornella). *L'Ymagier d'Erik Satie*. Paris: Van de Velde-Opéra de Paris, 1979. – 373. VOLTA (Ornella) *Erik Satie*. Paris: Seghers / Humour, 1979. – 374. GILLMOR (Alan M.). *Erik Satie*. Boston: Twayne, Div. of G.K. Hall & Co, 1988. – 375. VOLTA (Ornella). *Satie Seen Through His Letters*. Ed. by Ornella Volta. Transl. Michael Bullock. Introduction by John Cage. London: Marion Boyars, 1989.

C. 376. Erik Satie e gli artisti del nostro tempo. Ed. by Ornella Volta. XXIV Festival dei due mondi. Spoleto: De Luca, June-July 1981. – 377. Erik Satie et la tradition populaire. Ed. by Ornella Volta. Paris: Fondation Erik Satie, Musée national des Arts et des Traditions populaires, May 1988.

D. 378. *La Revue Musicale*, Ed. de la NRF, no. 5, March 1924. – 379. *Erik Satie, son temps et ses amis*. Paris: Richard-Masse, *La Revue Musicale*, June 1952, no. 214. – 380. *Chronologie satiste* by Dr Roland Belicha. Paris: Richard-Masse, *La Revue Musicale*, June 1978, no. 312. – 381. *Erik Satie*. Paris: Richard-Masse, *La Revue Musicale*, Dec. 1985, no. 386-387.

CHRISTIAN SCHAD (Miesbach, Oberbayern, August 21, 1894 – Bessenbach-Keilberg, March 1982)

B. 382. *Christian Schad*. Basel: Ed. Panderma Carl Laszlo, 1972.

C. 383. SCHAD / DADA. Milan, Galleria Schwarz, February 1970. Schadographien 1918-1975. Von der Heydt-Museum Wuppertal, Feb. 1975.

KURT SCHWITTERS (Hanover, June 20, 1887 – Kendal, Ambleside, January 8, 1948)

A. 384. Schwitters, Kurt. *Anna Blume*. Dichtungen. Hanover, Steegemann, Die Silbergäule 39/40, 1919. – 385. *Die Kathedrale*. [Eight Merzlithographs.] Hanover: Steegemann, Die Silbergäule 41/42, 1920. – 386. Kurt Merz Schwitters, *Elementar. Die Blume Anna*. Berlin: Der Sturm, 1922. – 387. Kurt Merz Schwitters, *Memoiren Anna Blumes in Bleie*. Freiburg: Walter Heinrich, 1922. – 388. *Tran Nr. 30. Auguste Bolte (ein Lebertran)*. Berlin: Der Sturm, 1923. – 389. K.S. and Käte Steinitz. *Die Märchen vom Paradies*. Hanover: Aposs, 1924. – 390. Das Literarische Werk. Ed. by Friedhelm Lach. Volume I: *Lyrik*. Cologne: DuMont Schauberg, 1973. Volume 2: *Prosa 1918-1930*. *Ibid.*, 1974. Volume 3: *Prosa 1931-1948*. *Ibid.*, 1975. Volume 4: *Schauspiele und Szenen*. *Ibid.*, 1977. Volume 5: *Manifeste und kritische Prosa*. *Ibid.*, 1981. – 391. *Wir spielen, bis uns der Tod abholt*. Briefe aus fünf Jahrzehnten. Ed. by Ernst Nündel. Frankfurt/M. – Berlin: Ullstein, 1974.

B. 392. SPENGEMANN (Christof). *Die Wahrheit über Anna Blume*. *Kritik der Kunst, Kritik der Kritik, Kritik der Zeit*. Hanover: Der Zweemann, 1920. [Reprinted in Hanover: Postskriptum, 1985.] – 393. THEMERSON (Stefan). *Kurt Schwitters in England*. London: Gaberbocchus, 1958. – 394. LACH (Friedhelm). *Der Merz Künstler Kurt Schwitters*. Cologne: DuMont Schauberg, 1971. – 395. REICHARDT (Jasia). *Kurt Schwitters & Raoul Hausmann: Pin and the story of Pin*. London: Gaberbocchus, 1962. [Reissued in a new German-English edition: Ed. by Michael Erlhoff and Karl Riha. Giessen: Anabas, 1986.] – 396. SCHMALENBACH (Werner). *Kurt*

Schwitters. New York: Harry N. Abrams, n.d. – 397. STEINITZ (Kate Trauman). *Kurt Schwitters. Erinnerungen aus den Jahren 1918-1930.* Zurich: Die Arche, 1963. – 398. *Kurt Schwitters: A Portrait from Life.* Berkeley and Los Angeles: Univ. of California, 1968. – 399. ELGER (Dietmar). *Der Merzbau, Eine Werkmonographie.* Cologne: Walther König, 1984. – 400. ELDERFIELD (John). *Kurt Schwitters.* London: Thames and Hudson, 1987.

C. 401. SCHWITTERS. Contributors : Camille Bryen, Kurt Schwitters, Hans Bolliger. Paris: Berggruen and Co., April-May 1954. – 402. SCHWITTERS. Stedelijk Museum, Amsterdam, June 1956. – 403. SCHWITTERS. Gmurzynska Gallery, Cologne, Oct. 1978. – 404. KURT SCHWITTERS IN EXILE. The Late Work 1937-1948. Marlborough Fine Art, London, Oct. 1981. – 405. Kurt Schwitters. Tokyo: Seibu Museum of Art & Takanawa: Seibu Museum of Modern Art, 1983. – 406. Ausstellung zum 99 Geburtstag Sprengel Museum, Hanover: Propylaen, Feb.-April 1986. – 407. Schwitters-Archiv Stadtbibliothek Hanover. Katalog. Bearbeitet von F. Stark. Bestandsverzeichnis 1986. Nachtrag 1987.

E. 408. VORDEMBERGE-GILDEWART (Friedrich). "Kurt Schwitters". In: Dietrich Helms: Vordemberge-Gildewart, *Schriften und Vorträge.* St Gall: Erker Verlag, 1976. – 409. GABO (Naum). "Kurt Schwitters". Pinacotheca Gallery, New York, 1948. – 410. SCHWITTERS (Ernst). "Some points on Kurt Schwitters". In *Art News and Review*, vol. 10, no. 19, Oct. 1958, pp. 5-8. – 411. MON (Franz). "Zur August Bolte von Kurt Schwitters". In *Akzente*, no. 2, April 1963, pp. 238-240. – 412. HEISSENBÜTTEL (Helmut). *Versuch über die Lautsonate von Kurt Schwitters.* Akademie der Wissenschaften und der Literatur, Mainz. Abhandlungen der Klasse der Literatur, 1983, no. 6. Wiesbaden, Franz Steiner.

WALTER SERNER (Karlsbad, 1889 – August 1942)

A. 413. Serner, Walter. *Letzte Lockerung : Manifest.* Hanover: Paul Steegemann, 1920. – 414. *Gesammelte Werke* in Ten Volumes. Ed. by Thomas Milch. [Vol. 2 : *Das Hirngeschwür. Letters to Tzara.* Vol. 9 : *Letzte Lockerung. Ein Handbrevier für Hochstapler und solche die es werden wollen.*] Munich: Klaus Renner, 1982; Goldmann [Paperback], 1988.

B. 415. *Ich.* Eine Edition des Walter-Serner-Archivs. Ed. by Thomas Milch and Dr. H. Möbius in an edition of 99 numbered copies, Heidelberg, 1985. – 416. SCHROTT (Raoul). *Walter Serner und Dada.* Siegen: "Vergessene Autoren der Moderne", Universität-Gesamthochschule, 1989.

C. 417. Walter Serner. Catalogue by H. Wiesner with E. Wichner. Berlin: Literaturhaus, 1989.

PHILIPPE SOUPAULT (Chaville, August 2, 1897 – Paris, March 12, 1990)

A. 418. Soupault, Philippe. *Aquarium.* Paris: Imprimerie Birault, 1917. – 419. (and Breton, André). *Les Champs magnétiques.* Paris: Au Sans Pareil, 1920. – 420. *Rose des vents.* Paris: Au Sans Pareil, 1920. – 421. *L'Invitation au suicide.* Paris: Imprimerie Birault, 2 copies, destroyed, 1922. – 422. *Westwego.* Paris: Librairie Six, 1922. – 423. *Le Bon Apôtre.* Paris: Simon Kra, 1923. – 424. *A la Dérive.* Paris: Ferenczi, 1923. – 425. *Profils perdus.* Paris: Mercure de France, 1963. – 426. *Mémoires de l'Oubli 1897-1927 : Histoire d'un Blanc* [1927]. Paris: Lachenal & Ritter, 1986. – 427. *Mémoires de l'Oubli 1914-1923.* Paris: Lachenal & Ritter, 1981. – 428. *Mémoires de l'Oubli 1923-1926.* Paris: Lachenal & Ritter, 1986. – 429. *Ecrits sur le cinéma 1918-1931.* Paris: Ramsay, Poche-Cinéma, 1988.

B. 430. DUPUY (Henri-Jacques). *Philippe Soupault.* Paris: Seghers, Poètes d'aujourd'hui, 1957. – 431. MORLINO (Bernard). *Philippe Soupault.* Lyon: La Manufacture, 1988. – 432. FAUCHEREAU (Serge). *Philippe Soupault, voyageur magnétique.* Paris: Cercle d'art, 1989.

SOPHIE TAEUBER-ARP (Davos, January 19, 1889 – Zurich, January 13, 1943)

B. 433. STABER (Margit). *Sophie Taeuber-Arp.* Transl. Eric Schaer. Lausanne: Rencontre, 1970. – 434. LANCHNER (Carolyn). *Sophie Taeuber-Arp.* New York: The Museum of Modern Art, 1981.

C. 435. Sophie Taeuber and Jean Arp. Bern, Musée des Beaux-Arts, Sept.-Nov. 1988. – 436. Sophie Taeuber [zum 100. Geburtstag / nel centenario della nascita]. Ed. by Aargauer Kunsthaus, Aarau (Switzerland). Baden: Lars Müller, 1989.

E. 437. MIKOL (Bruno). "Figures d'art : les marionnettes de Sophie Taeuber et d'Otto Morach." Charleville-Paris, Institut international de la Marionnette / L'Age d'Homme, *PUCK La Marionnette et les autres arts*, no. 1, September 1988, pp. 44-51.

TRISTAN TZARA (Moinesti, Rumania, April 16, 1896 – Paris, December 24, 1963)

A. 438. Tzara, Tristan. *La première aventure céleste de M. Antipyrine.* Zurich: Coll. Dada, July 1916. – 439. *Vingt-cinq poèmes.* Zurich: Coll. Dada, June 1918. – 440. *Cinéma calendrier du cœur abstrait. Maisons.* Paris: Coll. Dada, Au Sans Pareil, June 1920. – 441. *La deuxième aventure céleste de M. Antipyrine* [review *Littérature* and *391*, June and November 1920]. – 442. *Le Cœur à gaz* [review *Der Sturm*, Berlin, March 1922]. – 443. *De nos oiseaux* [November 1922 and Paris: Kra, 1929]. – 444. *Faites vos jeux* [Novel published in five parts in *Les Feuilles libres*, Paris, between March-April 1923 and March-June 1924]. – 445. *Mouchoir de nuages* [Nov. 1924, review *Sélection*, Antwerp]. – 446. *Sept manifestes Dada – Lampisteries.* Paris: Budry, July 1924. – 447. American and English Editions: *Seven Dada Manifestoes and Lampisteries.* Transl. Barbara Wright. New York: Riverrun & London: John Calder, 1977. – 448. "Memoirs of Dadaism" in: Edmund Wilson, *Axel's Castle.* New York: Charles Scribner's Sons, 1931 & Collins Fontana Literature, 1961. – 449. *Œuvres complètes, I* (Complete Works, 1912-1924). Ed. by Henri Béhar. Paris: Flammarion, 1975.

B. 450. LACOTE (René). *Tristan Tzara.* Paris: Seghers, 1952. – 451. *Zurich – Dadaco – Dadaglobe: The Correspondence between Richard Huelsenbeck, Tristan Tzara and Kurt Wolff (1916-1924).* Ed. by Richard Sheppard. Scotland: Hutton Press, 1982. – 452. PETERSON (Elmer). *Tristan Tzara, Dada and Surrational Theorist.* New Brunswick, New Jersey: Rutgers Univ. Press, 1971.

C. 453. LA RENCONTRE SONIA DELAUNAY-TRISTAN TZARA. Musée d'art moderne de la Ville de Paris, April-June 1977. – 454. Catalogue de la vente de la collection Tzara. Etude Loudmer, Paris, November 20, 1988. – 455. Catalogue de la vente de la bibliothèque de Tristan Tzara. Etude Loudmer, Paris, March 4, 1989.

D. 456. Tristan Tzara. Review *Europe.* Paris, July-August 1975, no. 555-556.

HENDRIK NIKOLAAS WERKMAN (Leens, Groningen, April 29, 1882 – April 10, 1945)

B. 457. *Hommage à Werkman.* New York: George Wittenborn, 1957-1958. – 458. MARTINET (Jan). *Werkman's Call.* A Study devoted to Hendrik Werkman and *The Next Call.* Utrecht: Reflex, Galerie Gamma, 1978.

The Next Call. See Bibl. no. 472.

II. REPRINTS

459. ACTION (1920-1922, Florent Fels and Marcel Sauvage). Introduction by Walter G. Langlois and Georges Gabory. Paris: Jean-Michel Place, 1990.
460. BLAST (1914-1915, Wyndham Lewis). Introduction by Bradford Morrow. Santa Barbara: Black Sparrow Press, 1981.
461. ÇA IRA ! (1920-1923, Paul Neuhuys). Introduction by Paul Neuhuys. Brussels: Jacques Antoine, 1973.
462. DADA ZEITSCHRIFTEN (1918-1921). Hamburg: Nautilus, 1978.
463. DADA ALMANACH (Ed. by Richard Huelsenbeck, Berlin: Erich Reiss, 1920). New York: Something Else Press, 1966.
464. DADA (1916-1922, Tristan Tzara). Nice: Centre du XXe siècle, Nice Univ., 1976.
465. DADA, CABARET VOLTAIRE, DER ZELTWEG, LE CŒUR À BARBE. Reprint of the Dada magazines published in Zurich and Paris between 1916 and 1922. Introduction by Michel Giroud. Transl. Sabine Wolf and Michael Gluck. Paris: Jean-Michel Place, 1981.
466. DE STIJL (1917-1932, Theo van Doesburg, Leiden). Two volumes. Amsterdam: Athenaeum & The Hague: Bert Bakker & Amsterdam: Polak and Van Gennep, 1968.
467. G, Material zur elementaren Gestaltung (1923-1926, Hans Richter). Munich: Der Kern Verlag, 1986.
468. LITTÉRATURE (1919-1921, Aragon, Breton, Soupault; New series 1922-1924, Breton and Soupault). Foreword by Philippe Soupault. Introduction by Marguerite Bonnet. Paris: Jean-Michel Place, 1978.
469. MAINTENANT (1912-1915, Arthur Cravan). Introduction by Maria Lluïsa Borràs. Paris: Jean-Michel Place, 1977.
470. MANOMÈTRE (1922-1928, Emile Malespine). Introduction by Michel Carassou. Paris: Jean-Michel Place, 1977.
471. MECANO (1922-1923, Van Doesburg / Bonset). Vaduz: Quarto, 1979.
472. THE NEXT CALL (1923-1926, H.N. Werkman). Utrecht: Uitgeverij Reflex / Galerie Gamma, 1978.
473. NORD-SUD (1917-1918, Pierre Reverdy). Introduction by Etienne-Alain Hubert. Paris: Jean-Michel Place, 1980.
474. NUMERO UNICO FUTURISTA CAMPARI, DINAMO FUTURISTA (1931-1933, Fortunato Depero). Introduction by Giovanni Lista. Paris: Jean-Michel Place, 1979.
475. HET OVERZICHT (1921-1925, Pijnenburg, Berckelaers alias Seuphor and Peeters). Paris: Jean-Michel Place, 1976.
476. SIC (1916-1919, Pierre Albert-Birot). Introduction by Arlette Albert-Birot. Paris: Jean-Michel Place, 1980.
477. LES SOIRÉES DE PARIS (1912-1914). Geneva: Slatkine, 1971.
478. *391* (1917-1924, Francis Picabia). Introduction by Michel Sanouillet. Paris: Belfond & Eric Losfeld, 1976.
479. TROÇOS (1916-1918, J.M. Junoy and J.V. Foix). Barcelona: Leteradura, 1977.
480. LES TROIS ROSES (1918-1919, Justin-Frantz Simon). Introduction by Etienne-Alain Hubert. Vercheny: Grande Nature, 1985.

III. GENERAL WORKS

481. ADES (Dawn). *Photomontage.* London: Thames and Hudson, 1976.
482. AFFAIRE BARRES (L'). Ed. by Marguerite Bonnet. Paris: José Corti, 1987.
483. AGEE (William). *New York Dada 1910-1930.* Thomas B. Hess and John Ashbery. London, 1968.
484. ALMANACCO DADA. Antologia letteraria-artistica, Cronologia, Repertorio delle riviste. Ed. by Arturo Schwarz. Milan: Feltrinelli, 1976.
485. AMIARD-CHEVREL (Claudine). *Le Théâtre artistique de Moscou (1898-1917).* Paris: CNRS, 1979.
486. ANNÉE 1913 (L'). *Les formes esthétiques de l'œuvre d'art à la veille de la première guerre mondiale.* Ed. by Liliane Brion-Guerry, I. *Pourquoi 1913.* II. *Les revues internationales.* Paris: Klincksieck, 1971. III. *Manifestes et témoignages.* Paris: Klincksieck, 1973.
487. ARCHIVI DEL FUTURISMO. Ed. by Maria Drudi Gambillo and Teresa Fiori. Roma: De Luca & Arnoldo Mondadori, 1962. Reissued 1986.
488. AVANT-GARDE. *Vitalité et contradictions de l'avant-garde (Italie France 1909-1924). Dadaïsme, futurisme, surréalisme.* Ed. by S. Briosi and H. Hillenaar. Paris: José Corti, 1988.
489. AVANT-GARDES LITTÉRAIRES AU XXe SIÈCLE (Les). Ed. by the Centre d'étude des avant-gardes littéraires de l'Université libre de Bruxelles sous la direction de Jean Weisgerber. I. Histoire. II. Théorie. Budapest: Akademiai Kiado, 1984.
490. BABLET (Denis). *Les Révolutions scéniques du XXe siècle.* Paris: Société Internationale d'art XXe siècle, 1975.
491. BABLET (Denis) & alii. *Les Voies de la création théâtrale.* Mises en scène des années vingt et trente (Meyerhold, Taïrov, Vakhtangov, Evreinov, Radlov, Groupe L'Assaut, Pitoëff, Schiller, Honzl, Jessner, Piscator, Engel, Baty). Volume VII. Paris: CNRS, 1979.
492. BEHAR (Henri). *Etude sur le théâtre dada et surréaliste.* Paris: Gallimard, Les Essais CXXXI, 1967.
493. BOHAN (Ruth L.). *The Société Anonyme's Brooklyn Exhibition: Katherine Dreier and Modernism in America.* Iowa: UMI Research, 1982.
494. CINEMA D'AVANGUARDIA (Il). 1910-1930. Ed. by Paolo Bertetto. Venice: Marsilio, 1983.
495. COUTTS-SMITH (Kenneth). *Dada.* London: Studio Vista / Dutton Pictureback, 1970.
496. DACHY (Marc). *Des énergies transformatrices du langage.* Paris: Fondation Nationale des Arts Graphiques et Plastiques, 1980.
497. ——. *Avant-gardes et nouvelle typographie.* Paris: Min. Ed. Nat., C.N.D.P., Actualité des Arts Plastiques, 1985.
498. DADA (DAS WAR). *Dichtungen und Dokumente.* Ed. by Peter Schifferli. Munich: Deutsches Taschenbuch, 1963.
499. DADA. *Eine literarische Dokumentation.* Ed. by Richard Huelsenbeck. Rowohlt Paperback, 1964.
500. DADA. *Studies of a Movement.* Ed. by Richard Sheppard. Contents : Jane Beckett: "Dada, Van Doesburg and De Stijl." Hanne Bergius: "The Ambiguous Aesthetic of Dada: Towards a Definition of its Categories." Richard Sheppard: "Dada and Politics." Robert Short: "Paris Dada and Surrealism." Martin Sorell: A Translation of "Lettres de Guerre" with Introduction and Notes. Nicholas Zurbrugg: "Dada and the Poetry of the Contemporary Avant-Garde." Buckinghamshire: Alpha Academic, 1979.
501. DADA / Dimensions. Ed. by Stephen C. Foster. Contents: Roy F. Allen: "Zurich Dada, 1916-1919: The Proto-Phase of the Movement." Allan C. Greenberg: "The Dadaists and the Cabaret as Form and Forum." Friedhelm Lach: "Schwitters: Performance Notes." Jane Hancock: "Arp's Chance Collages." Harriett Watts: "Periods and Commas: Hans Arp's Seminal Punctuation." Charlotte Stokes: "Dadamax: Ernst in the Context of Cologne Dada." Timothy O. Benson: "The Functional and the Conventional in the Dada Philosophy of Raoul Hausmann." Estera Milman: "Dada New York: An Historiographic Analysis." Ruth L. Bohan: "Joseph Stella's *Man in Elevated (Train).*" John E. Bowlt: "H_2SO_4: Dada in Russia." Stephen C. Foster: "Johannes Baader: The Complete Dada." Peter W. Guenther: "Notes on Research in Dada and Expressionism." Ann Arbor, Michigan: UMI Research Press, 1985.
502. DADA. Monograph of a Movement, Monographie einer Bewegung, Monographie d'un mouvement. By, von, par Willy Verkauf. Teufen (Switzerland): Arthur Niggli Ltd., 1957.
503. DADA BERLIN 1916-1924. Documents d'art contemporain. Arc 2, Musée d'art moderne de la ville de Paris, 1974.
504. DADA BERLIN. Texte, Manifeste, Aktionen. Ed. with Hanne Bergius by Karl Riha. Stuttgart: Philipp Reclam, 1977.
505. DADA PAINTERS AND POETS (The). An Anthology. Ed. by Robert Motherwell. New York: Wittenborn, Schultz, 1951.
506. DADA RUSSO. L'avanguardia fuori della Rivoluzione. Ed. by Marzio Marzaduri. Bologna: Il Cavaliere azzuro, 1984.
507. DADA SPECTRUM : THE DIALECTICS OF REVOLT. Ed. by Stephen Foster and Rudolf Kuenzli. Michel Sanouillet: "Dada, A Definition." Stephen C. Foster: "Dada Criticism, Anti-Criticism and A-Criticism." Rudolf Kuenzli: "The Semiotics of Dada Poetry." Arthur Cohen: "The Typographic Revolution: Antecedents and Legacy of Dada Graphic Design." Richard Sheppard: "Dada and Mysticism: Influences and Affinities." Dickran Tashjian: "New York Dada and Primitivism." Hans J. Kleinschmidt: "Berlin Dada." Alastair Grieve: "Arp in Zurich." Mary-Ann Caws: "Dada's Temper: Our Text." Nicholas Zurbrugg: "Towards the End of the Line: Dada and Experimental Poetry Today." Ben Vautier: "The Duchamp Heritage." Richard Sheppard: Bibliography. Madison: Coda Press, Univ. of Iowa, 1979.
508. DADA AND SURREALIST FILM. Ed. by Rudolf E. Kuenzli. New York: Willis Locker & Owens, 1987.
509. DADA ZURIGO. BALL E IL CABARET VOLTAIRE. Ed. by Luisa Valeriani. Turin: Martano ed., "nadar" 1, 1970.
510. DADAS ON ART. Ed. by Lucy Lippard. New Jersey: A Spectrum Book, Prentice-Hall, 1971.
511. DIE GEBURT DES DADA. Dichtung und Chronik der Gründer. By and with Hans Arp, Richard Huelsenbeck and Tristan Tzara. Ed. by Peter Schifferli. Zurich: Schifferli / Die Arche, 1957. Reissued by Sanssouci under the title *Dada in Zurich*, 1966.
512. DEREN COKE (Van). *Avantgarde Photografie in Deutschland 1919-1939.* Munich: Schirmer / Mosel, 1982.
513. DOCUMENTS DADA. Ed. by Yves Poupard-Lieussou and Michel Sanouillet. Geneva: Weber, 1974.
514. DUPUIS (Jules-François). *Histoire désinvolte du surréalisme.* [1977]. Paris: L'Instant, 1988.
515. EINGRIFFE. Jahrbuch für gesellschaftskritische Umtriebe: Hannah Arendt, Christian Schultz-Gerstein, Hans-Magnus Enzensberger, Henryk M. Broder, Eike Geisel, Klaus Bittermann ("Die Reinkarnation der Kunst : Marcel Duchamp"), Holger Fock ("Der ultra-moderne Dichter Clément Pansaers"), Uli Becker ("Über den wiederentdeckten Dadaisten Walter Ser-

ner"), Karl-Hans Wieser ("Über den Kunstkritiker und Literaten Carl Einstein"), Harry Mulisch & alii. Berlin: Tiamat, 1988.
516. ERICKSON (John D.). *Dada: Performance, Poetry and Art.* Boston: Twayne Publishers, A Division of G. K. Hall, 1984.
517. FOUCHÉ (Pascal). *Au Sans Pareil.* Bibliothèque de Littérature française contemporaine de l'Université Paris 7, coll. L'Edition contemporaine, 1983.
518. ——. *La Sirène (1917-1937).* Bibliothèque de Littérature française contemporaine de l'Université de Paris 7, coll. L'Edition contemporaine, 1984.
519. GLAUSER (Friedrich). *Dada, Ascona und andere Erinnerungen.* Zurich: Die Arche, 1967.
520. GRAY (Camilla). *The Russian Experiment in Art 1863-1922.* Augmented edition. London: Thames and Hudson, 1986.
521. GREENBERG (Allan C.). *Artists and Revolution: Dada and the Bauhaus, 1917-1925.* Iowa: UMI Research, 1980.
522. GROSSMAN (Manuel L.). *Dada: Paradox, Mystification, and Ambiguity in European Literature.* New York: Pegasus, Bobbs-Merrill, 1971.
523. HAAS (Patrick de). *Cinéma intégral: de la peinture au cinéma dans les années vingt.* Paris: Transédition, 1986.
524. HUGNET (Georges). *L'aventure Dada (1916-1922).* Introduced by Tristan Tzara, Paris: Galerie de l'Institut, 1957. Reissued: Paris: Seghers, 1971.
525. ——. *Dictionnaire du dadaïsme.* Paris: Jean-Claude Simoën, 1976.
526. KANBARA (Tai). *Futurism, Expressionism, Dadaism.* Tokyo, 1937.
527. KNOBLAUCH (Adolf). *Dada.* Leipzig: Kurt Wolff, Der Jüngste Tag, 73/74, 1919.
528. LAST (Rex W.). *German Dadaist Literature: Kurt Schwitters, Hugo Ball, Hans Arp.* New York: Twayne, 1973.
529. LAWDER (Standish D.). *The Cubist Cinema.* Anthology of Film Archives. Series 1. New York: New York Univ., 1975.
530. LEAVENS (Ileana B.). *From "291" to Zurich: The Birth of Dada.* Ann Arbor: UMI Research, Perspectives on Dada, 1983.
531. LEMAÎTRE (Maurice). *Le lettrisme devant Dada et les nécrophages de Dada.* Paris: Centre de créativité, 1967.
532. LEMOINE (Serge). *Dada.* Paris: Hazan, 1986.
533. LINHARTOVA (Vera). *Dada et surréalisme au Japon.* Paris: Arts du Japon, Publications Orientalistes de France, 1987.
534. MATTHEWS (J.H.). *Theatre in Dada and Surrealism.* New York: Syracuse Univ., 1974.
535. MELZER (Annabelle Henkin). *Latest Rage the Big Drum: Dada and Surrealist Performance.* Iowa: UMI Research, 1980.
536. MEYER (Reinhart) & alii. *Dada in Zurich und Berlin 1916-1920.* Kronenberg-Taunus: Scriptor, 1973.
537. NAKANO (Ka.ichi). *Zen.ei shi undō shi no kenkyū.* Tokyo: Ohara shinsei-sha, 1975.
538. ——. *Modanizumu shi no jidai.* Tokyo: Hobunkan shuppan, 1986.
539. NEW STUDIES IN DADA. *Essays and documents.* Ed. by Richard Sheppard. Part I: Essays. Karin Füllner: "The Meister-Dada: The Image of Dada through the eyes of Richard Huelsenbeck." Martin Kane: "George Grosz, Constructivism Parodied." Rudolf Kuenzli: "Hans Arp's Poetics, The Sense of Dada "Nonsense". Rex Last: "Hans Arp and the Problem of Evil." Marian Malet: "Hans Arp and the Aesthetics of the Workshop." Philip Mann: "Plimplamplasko, der hohe Geist, Friedrich Maximilian Klinger, Jean-Jacques Rousseau and Hugo Ball." Richard Sheppard: "Julius Evola, Futurism and Dada: A Case of Double Misunderstanding." Part II: Inedita. [A] Four Unpublished or Partially Published Dada Manifestos (1916-1920). [B] Nineteen Letters, Telegrams and Cards from Raoul Hausmann to Tristan Tzara (1919-1921). [C] Thirty-three Letters, Telegrams and Cards from Hans Richter to Tristan Tzara and Otto Flake (1917-1926). [D] Twelve Unpublished or Partially Published Items by Johannes Baader (1918-1921). Part III: Dada. A Chronology. Driffield: Hutton Press, 1981.
540. NEW YORK DADA. Ed. by Rudolf E. Kuenzli. Contributions: Francis Naumann, Judith Zilczer, Dickran Tashjian, Craig Adcock, William Agee, Robert Reiss, Roger Conover, Willard Bohn, Kenneth Burke, Rudolf E. Kuenzli, Timothy Shipe. New York: Willis Locker & Owens, 1986.
541. OCCHIO TAGLIATO (L'). *Documenti del cinema dadaista e surrealista.* Ed. by Gianni Rondolino. "nadar" 10, Turin: Martano, 1972.
542. PIERRE (José). *Le futurisme et le dadaïsme.* Lausanne: Rencontre, 1966.
543. POEMI E SCENARI CINEMATOGRAFICI D'AVANGUARDIA. Ed. by Mario Verdone. Rome: Officina Edizioni, 1975.
544. POGGIOLI (Renato). *The Theory of the Avant-Garde.* Transl. Gerald Fitzgerald. New York: Harper and Row, Icon, 1971.
545. POUPARD-LIEUSSOU (Yves). *Dada en verve.* Choix de propos et aphorismes. Paris: Horay, 1972.
546. PROSENC (Miklavizh). *Die Dadaisten in Zürich.* Bonn: Bouvier, 1967.
547. RIHA (Karl). *Da Da war ist Dada da.* Munich-Vienna: Hanser Verlag, 1980.
548. RODARI (Florian). *Collage: Pasted, Cut and Torn Papers.* New York: Skira-Rizzoli, 1988.
549. ROTERS (Eberhard). *Berlin 1910-1933.* Fribourg: Office du Livre & Paris: Vilo, 1982.
550. RUBIN (William S.). *Dada and Surrealist Art.* New York: Abrams, 1968.
551. SAMALTANOS (Katia). *Apollinaire: Catalyst for Primitivism, Picabia, and Duchamp.* Iowa: UMI Research, 1984.
552. SANOUILLET (Michel). *Dada à Paris.* Paris: Jean-Jacques Pauvert, 1965.
553. ——. Facsimile reprint of Bibl. 552. Nice: Centre du XXe siècle, 1980.
554. ——. *Dada 1915-1923.* Translation of Bibl. 552. London and New York, 1969.
555. ——. and BAUDOUIN (Dominique). *Dada: dossier critique.* Nice: Centre du XXe siècle, Nice Univ., 1983.
556. SCHIPPERS (K.). *Holland Dada.* Amsterdam: Querido, 1974.
557. SCHNEIDER (Luis Mario). *El Estridentismo, una literatura de la estrategia.* Mexico City: Ed. de Bellas Artes, 1970.
558. SCHROTT (Raoul). *Dada Tyrol 1921-1922.* Innsbruck: Haymon, 1988.
559. SCHWARZ (Arturo). *New York Dada.* Munich: Prestel, 1974.
560. SEUPHOR (Michel). *L'art abstrait. I. 1910-1918: Origines et premiers maîtres. II. 1918-1938.* Paris: Maeght, 1971 and 1972.
561. SHATTUCK (Roger). *The Banquet Years: Henri Rousseau, Erik Satie, Alfred Jarry, Guillaume Apollinaire.* [1957] Garden City, New York: Doubleday Anchor, 1961.
562. SINN AUS UNSINN: DADA INTERNATIONAL. Ed. by Wolfgang Paulsen and Helmut G. Hermann. Bern-Munich: Franke, 1980.
563. SOCIETE ANONYME (The) AND THE DREIER BEQUEST at Yale University. A Catalogue Raisonné by Robert L. Herbert, Eleanor S. Apter, Elise K. Kenney. New Haven and London: Yale University, 1984.
564. SPENCER (Herbert). *Pioneers of Modern Typography.* London: Lund Humphries, 1969.
565. TASHJIAN (Dickran). *Skyscraper Primitives: Dada and the American Avant-garde 1910-1925.* Middletown, Connecticut: Wesleyan Univ., 1975.
566. TORRE (Guillermo de). *Literaturas europeas de vanguardia.* Madrid: Caro Raggio, 1925 and Guadarrama, 1965.
567. VERGINE (Lea). *L'altra metà dell'avanguardia.* Mostra: Milan & Stockholm: Mazzotta, 1980.
568. VILA-MATAS (Enrique). *Dada aus dem Koffer. Die verkürzte Geschichte der tragbaren Literatur.* Munich: Popa, 1988.
569. VILLEGLE (Jacques). *Urbi & orbi.* Mâcon: W, Coll. Gramma, 1986.
570. VIRMAUX (Alain and Odette). *Cravan, Vaché, Rigaut.* Suivi de "Le Vaché d'avant Breton". Choix d'écrits et de dessins. Mézières-sur-Issoire: Rougerie, 1982.
571. WALDBERG (Patrick), SANOUILLET (Michel) and LEBEL (Robert). *Dada surréalisme.* Paris and Milan: Rive Gauche Productions and Gruppo Editoriale Fabbri, 1981.
572. WATTS (Harriett Ann). *Three Painter Poets: Arp, Schwitters, Klee.* London, 1974.
573. ——. *Chance: A Perspective on Dada.* Iowa: UMI Research, 1980.

IV. CATALOGUES

(chronological order)

574. FANTASTIC ART, DADA, SURREALISM. Catalogue edited by Alfred H. Barr, Jr. Essays by Georges Hugnet. New York: The Museum of Modern Art, 1936.
575. DADA 1916-1923. Catalogue-poster designed by Marcel Duchamp, crumpled up into a ball and handed out to visitors. Contributions by Arp, Hulbeck, Levesque, Tzara. New York: Sidney Janis, 1953.
576. DADA. Dokumente einer Bewegung. Düsseldorf Kunsthalle, Sept.-Oct. 1958.
577. DADA. Amsterdam: Stedelijk Museum. Cat. 199, Dec. 1958-Feb. 1959.
578. DADA 1916-1966 / DADA IN ITALIA. By Arturo Schwarz, Lino Montagna, Daniela Palazzoli. Milan: Civici Padiglione d'Arte Contemporanea, Schwarz Gallery, June-September 1966.
579. DADA 1916-1966. Dokumente der internationalen Dada Bewegung. Ed. with notes by Hans Richter. Munich: Goethe Institut, 1966. Reissued: Cologne: Vogel + Besemer, 1970.
580. DADA. Suites no. 10. Contribution by Werner Haftmann. Geneva: Jan Krugier Gallery, February 1966.
581. DADA. Ausstellung zum 50jährigen Jubiläum / Exposition Commémorative du Cinquantenaire. Kunsthaus Zurich, Oct.-Nov. 1966 & Paris: Musée national d'art moderne, Nov. 1966-January 1967.
582. DADA, SURREALISM AND THEIR HERITAGE. By William S. Rubin. New York: The Museum of Modern Art, 1968.
583. DADA IN DRACHTEN. Franeker (Netherlands): Coopmanshûs Museum, Nov. 1971-January 1972.
584. CINÉMA DADAÏSTE ET SURRÉALISTE. Paris: Musée national d'art moderne, Centre Georges Pompidou, 1976.
585. DADA IN EUROPA, Werke und Dokumente. Städtische Galerie im Städelschen Kunstinstitut Frankfurt am Main & Berlin: Dietrich Reimer, 1977.
586. DADAISTS (ART OF THE). In conjunction with Timothy Baum. New York: Helen Serger, la boetie, inc., September-November 1977.
587. DADA Artifacts. Iowa: The University of Iowa Museum of Art, March-May 1978.
588. DADA AND SURREALISM REVIEWED. By Dawn Ades, with an introduction by David Sylvester and a supplementary essay by Elizabeth Cowling. London: Arts Council of Great Britain & Hayward Gallery, 1978.
589. THE TWENTIES IN BERLIN : Johannes Baader, George Grosz, Raoul Hausmann, Hannah Höch. Contributors: Jane Beckett, Michel Giroud, Andrei Nakov, Keith Wheldon. London: Annely Juda Fine Art, 1978.
590. PICTORIAL PHOTOGRAPHY IN BRITAIN 1900-1920. London: Arts Council of Great Britain in association with The Royal Photographic Society, 1978.
591. DADA PHOTOMONTAGEN. Photographie und Photocollage. Contributions by Richard Hiepe, Eberhard Roters, Arturo Schwarz, Werner Spies und Carl-Albrecht Haenlein. Ed. by Carl-Albrecht Haenlein. Hanover: Kestner-Gesellschaft, 1979.
592. DADA AND NEW YORK. New York: Whitney Museum of American Art, 1979.
593. DADA: BERLIN, COLOGNE, HANOVER. Contributions by Stephen Prokoposs and Hellmut Wohl. Boston: Institute of Contemporary Art, Nov. 1980-Feb.1981.
594. ESPÍRITU DADA (El). 1915-1925. Contribution by Arturo Schwarz. Caracas: Museo de Arte Contemporánea, Nov. 1980-Feb. 1981.
595. TABU DADA. Jean Crotti & Suzanne Duchamp 1915-1922. Ed. by William A. Camfield and Jean-Hubert Martin. Paris: Musée national d'art moderne, Centre Georges Pompidou, 1983.
596. ZENIT. Zenit i avangarda 20ih godina; Zenit and the Avant-garde of the Twenties, by Irina Subotić. Belgrade: Narodni muzej, Feb.-March 1983.
597. DADA in Japan. Japanische Avantgarde 1920-1970. Eine Fotodokumentation. Kunstmuseum Düsseldorf. May-June 1983.
598. DADA / CONSTRUCTIVISM. By Dawn Ades, Marc Dachy, Patrick de Haas, Andrei Nakov. London: Annely Juda Fine Art, 1984.
599. NEHMEN SIE DADA. Ed. by Bonner Kunstverein. Dada Zeitung 18.3.84.
600. MALIK VERLAG (The). 1916-1947. Berlin, Prague, New York. An Exhibition organized by James Fraser and Steven Heller. Contributions by Wieland Herzfelde and George Wyland. New York: Goethe House, in association with the Madison Campus Library Fairleigh Dickinson University, Autumn 1984.
601. DADA SURREALISM. In the Mind's Eye. Ed. by Terry Ann R. Neff. Contributors: Dawn Ades, Mary Mathews Gedo, Mary Jane Jacob, Rosalind E. Krauss, Dennis Alan Nawrocki, Lowery Stokes Sims. Chicago: Museum of Contemporary Art & New York: Abbeville, 1985.
602. DADA IN ZURICH. Ed. by Hans Bolliger, Guido Magnaguagno, Raimund Meier and the Kunsthaus. Zurich: Arche, 1985.
603. COLLAGE (The Golden Age of). Dada and Surrealism Eras, 1916-1950. In association with Timothy Baum. London: The Mayor Gallery, 1987.
604. THE DADA PERIOD IN COLOGNE. Selections from the Fick-Eggert Collection. Toronto: Art Gallery of Ontario, 1988.
605. THE WORLD ACCORDING TO DADA. Curator: Stephen C. Foster. Taipei Fine Arts Museum & Univ. of Iowa, 1988.
606. DADA Y CONSTRUCTIVISMO. By Andrei Nakov, Simón Marchán Fiz, Marc Dachy. Madrid: Centro de Arte Reina Sofía, Ministerio de Cultura, 1989.
607. DAMES IN DADA. Het aandeel van vrouwen in de DADA-Beweging. Ed. by Gioia Smid. Amsterdam: Stichting Amazone, 1989.

V. SPECIAL ISSUES

(alphabetical order)

608. ALBERT-BIROT (Pierre). *Cahiers Bleus.* Troyes: Centre culturel Thibaud de Champagne, no. 14, Winter-Spring 1979.
609. ANNI VENTI E DINTORNI. Naples: Review *es*, no. 11, September-December 1979.
610. ARP. Poète-plasticien. Paris: *Mélusine*, L'Age d'Homme, no. IX, 1988.
611. APOLLINAIRE (Guillaume) et les surréalistes. Lettres à Tristan Tzara et à André Breton. Paris: *Revue des lettres modernes*, no. 104-107, 1964.
612. DADA PANSAERS. Meeting pansaérien. Ed. by Marc Dachy. Bassac: *Plein Chant*, no. 39-40, Spring 1988.
613. DUCHAMP ET APRES. Paris: *Opus International*, no. 49, March 1974.
614. HAUSMANN ET DADA A BERLIN (Raoul). Ed. by Roberto Altmann and Jean-François Bory. Vaduz (Liechtenstein): *Apeiros*, no. 6, 1974.
615. MANIFESTE ET LE CACHÉ (Le). Paris: *Le Siècle éclaté.* Lettres Modernes / Minard, no. 1, 1974.
616. MAVO (The Age of). Special Report. Tokyo: *Art vivant*, no. 33, 1989.
617. RIBEMONT-DESSAIGNES (Georges). Brussels: *Marginales*, 28th year, no. 152, April 1973.

VI. ARTICLES

618. ARNAUD (Noël). "Les Métamorphoses historiques de Dada". Paris: Minuit, *Critique*, no. 134, July 1958.
619. BEN (Ben Vautier, called). "Dada par Ben". Paris: *Art Press*, no. 21, Nov.-Dec. 1975.
620. BERSANI (Jacques). "Dada ou la joie de vivre". Paris: Minuit, *Critique*, no. 225, February 1966.
621. BRYEN (Camille). "Arp, colloque de Meudon". Paris: *XXe siècle*, New series, no. 6, January 1956.
622. DACHY (Marc). "Pour en finir avec le futurisme". Paris: Minuit, *Critique*, no. 404, January 1981.
623. DAMIAN (Jean-Michel). "La musique et Dada. Cage, premier (et dernier?) musicien Dada ?" Paris: *Art Press*, no. 21, Nov.-Dec. 1975.
624. DÉCAUDIN (Michel). "Sur le décor des *Mamelles de Tirésias*". Paris: *Ligeia*, no. 2, July-September 1988.
625. DUFOUR (Bernard). "Portrait de l'auteur Francis Picabia". Paris: *Art Press*, no. 57, March 1982.
626. GIROUD (Michel). "Pour un art élémentaire". Paris: Transédition, *Luna-Park*, no. 8/9: Cahier 1986 : Un siècle d'avant-garde.
627. GLEIZES (Albert). "L'Affaire Dada". Paris: *Action*, no. 3, April 1920.
628. GORIÉLY (Benjamin). "Dada en Russie." Paris: *Cahiers Dada Surréalisme*, no. 1, 1966.
629. KOSTELANETZ (Richard). "Dada and the Future of Fiction". In: *The Old Fictions and the New.* Jefferson: McFarland, 1987.
630. LINHARTOVA (Vera). "Manifestes et Réflexions 1910-1941." In: *Japon des avant-gardes 1910-1970.* Paris: Centre Pompidou, 1986.
631. LE BOT (Marc). "Dada et la guerre". Paris: *Europe: Mil neuf cent quatorze*, no. 421/422, May-June 1964.
632. LOUREAU (René). "Essai d'analyse institutionnelle du manifeste dada du 22 mars 1918". In *Le Manifeste et le caché*, See Bibl. 615.

633. MEZEI (Arpad). "Réévaluer Dada". Brussels: *Gradiva*, no. 2.

634. MICHELET (Raymond). "Du surréalisme et de la contradiction". Paris: *IIIe Convoi*, no. 4, May 1947.

635. MILLET (Catherine). "Francis Picabia le diabolique". Paris: *Art Press*, no. 57, March 1982.

636. NEUHUYS (Paul). "Quelques poètes (IV)". Antwerp: *Ça Ira !*, no. 14, September 1921. See Bibl. 461.

637. OKABE (Aomi). "Action et avant-garde." In: *Japon des avantgardes 1910-1970*. Paris: Centre Pompidou, 1986.

638. PADRTA (Jiri). "Malévitch et Khlebnikov." In: *Malévitch*. Cahier des Avant-gardes. Lausanne: L'Age d'Homme, 1979.

639. PLASSARD (Didier). "Une *Orestie* dadaïste". Charleville-Paris: Institut international de la Marionnette / L'Age d'Homme, *Puck* La Marionnette et les autres arts, no. 1, September 1988.

640. ——. "Vilmos Huszár, entre *De Stijl* et Dada". Paris: *Ligeia*, no. 2, July-September 1988.

641. RIVIÈRE (Jacques). "Reconnaissance à Dada". Paris: *La Nouvelle Revue Française*, no. 83, August 1920.

642. ROCHE (Denis). "Dada soupçon mortel". Paris: *Art Press*, no. 21, Nov.-Dec. 1975.

643. SEUPHOR (Michel). "Dadakoll". Paris: *XXe siècle*, new series, no. 6, January 1956.

644. ——. "L'Internationale Dada". Paris, *L'Œil*, no. 24, Dec. 1956.

645. VAN OSTAIJEN (Paul). "Dada film : Bankruptcy Jazz (film script)". Transl. E. M. Beekman. New York: *The Drama Review*, Volume 14, number 3, no. 47.

646. VAN STRAATEN (Evert). "Ze hebben Tzara bijna doodgeslagen: Theo van Doesburg als ooggetuige van de Soirée du Cœur à barbe." The Hague: *Jong Holland*, no. 4, November 1987.

VII. WORKS CITED OR CONSULTED

647. APOLLINAIRE (Guillaume). *Apollinaire on Art*. Ed. by LeRoy C. Breunig. New York: Viking, 1950.

648. ——. *Œuvres poétiques*. Ed. by Marcel Adéma and Michel Décaudin. Paris: Gallimard, La Pléiade, 1959.

649. BANN (Stephen). *The Tradition of Constructivism*. New York: Viking, 1974.

650. BARR (Alfred H.). *Cubism and Abstract Art*. New York: The Museum of Modern Art, 1936 & 1966. Reissued: Belknap, Harvard Univ. Press, Cambridge, Massachusetts and London, England, 1986.

651. BLUMENFELD (Ervin). *Durch tausendjährige Zeit*. Erinnerungen. Berlin: Argon, 1988.

652. BORY (Jean-François). *Once Again*. Transl. Lee Hildreth. New York: New Directions, 1968.

653. BURROUGHS (William S.). *Scrapbook 3*. Printed in Xerox in 30 numbered copies. New York / Geneva: Claude Givaudan, 1979.

654. ——. *Nova Express*. New York: Grove Press, 1964.

655. ——. *The Adding Machine*. Selected Essays. New York: Seaver, 1986.

656. COMPTON (Susan P.). *The World Backwards: Russian Futurist Books 1912-1916*. London: British Library, 1978.

657. DAMASE (Jacques). *Sonia Delaunay, Rythmes et couleurs*. Paris: Hermann, 1971.

658. DEBORD (Guy-Ernest). *Rapport sur la construction des situations et sur les conditions de l'organisation et de l'action de la tendance situationniste internationale*, 1957.

659. ——. *Mémoires*. Structures portantes d'Asger Jorn. Ouvrage composé d'éléments préfabriqués. Copenhagen: Internationale Situationniste, 1959, 64 p. (printed by Permild & Rosengreen).

660. ——. *The Society of the Spectacle*. Detroit: Black and Red, 1977.

661. DIJKSTRA (Bram). *Cubism, Stieglitz, and the Early Poetry of William Carlos Williams*. New Jersey: Princeton Univ., 1969.

662. *DOCUMENTS relatifs à la fondation de l'Internationale Situationniste 1948-1957*. Ed. by Gérard Berreby. Paris: Allia, 1985.

663. EINSTEIN (Carl). *Werke*. Volume 1 : 1908-1918. Ed. by Rolf-Peter Baacke, with Jens Kwasny. Berlin: Medusa, 1980. ——. *Werke*. Volume 2 : 1919 - 1928. Ed. by Marion Schmid with Henriette Bees and Jens Kwasny. Berlin: Medusa-Wölk + Schmid, 1981. ——. *Werke*. Volume 3: 1929-1940. Ed. by Marion Schmid and Liliane Meffre. Vienna-Berlin: Medusa, 1985.

664. FAERBER (Thomas) and LUCHSINGER (Markus). *Joyce in Zurich*. Zurich: Unionsverlag, 1988.

665. FRANK (Peter). *Something Else Press: An annotated bibliography*. New York: McPherson & Company, 1983.

666. GAYRAUD (Régis) and ILIAZD (Hélène). *Iliazd 1894-1975*. Chronology written for the Iliazd exhibition. Montreal: Galerie d'art de l'Université du Québec, September 1984.

667. GLAUSER (Friedrich). *Briefe 1*. Ed. by Bernhard Echte and Manfred Papst. Zurich: Die Arche, 1989.

668. GORIÉLY (Benjamin). *Le avanguardie litterarie in Europa*. Transl. Montaldi and Maria Gregorio. Milan: Feltrinelli, 1967.

669. GROSS (Otto). *Über psychopathische Minderwertigkeiten*. Vienna-Leipzig, 1909.

670. ——. *Drei Aufsätze über den inneren Konflikt*. Bonn, 1920.

671. *Grosz-Jung-Grosz*. Ed. by Günter Bose and Erich Brinkmann with Peter Ludewig. Berlin: Brinkmann & Bose, 1980.

672. GYSIN (Brion). *Brion Gysin let the mice in*. With texts by William Burroughs & Ian Sommerville. Ed. by Jan Herman. West Glover, Vermont: Something Else Press, 1973.

673. HANSEN (Al). *A Primer of Happenings & Time / Space Art*. New York-Paris-Cologne: Something Else Press, 1965.

674. HERMANN (Frank). *Der Malik-Verlag 1916-1947*. A Bibliography. Kiel: Neuer Malik Verlag, 1988.

675. ILIAZD. *Poésie de mots inconnus*. 157 copies. Paris: Iliazd, 1949.

676. *ILIAZD and the illustrated book*. Ed. by Audrey Isselbacher. Essay by Françoise Le Gris-Bergmann. New York: The Museum of Modern Art, 1987.

677. ISOU (Isidore). *Les véritables créateurs et les falsificateurs du lettrisme, 1965-1973*. Paris: Ed. Lettrisme (no. 16-20), 1973.

678. JOOSTENS (Paul). Catalogue. Ed. by Flor Bex, Phil Mertens, Rik Sauwen. Antwerp: Internationaal Cultureel Centrum, June-September 1976.

679. JORN (Asger). *Fin de Copenhague*. Conseiller technique pour le détournement : G.-E. Debord. Copenhagen: Bauhaus Imaginiste, May 1957.

680. ——. *Ebauche d'une Méthodologie des Arts*. Paris: Internationale Situationniste, 1958, 140 p.

681. JOSEPHSON (Matthew). *Life among the Surrealists*. [Chapter 7: The Dadaists. Chapter 8: Decline and fall of Dada]. New York: Holt, Rinehart and Winston, 1962.

682. JUNG (Franz). *Revolte gegen die Lebensangst*. Berlin: Brinkmann & Bose, 1983.

683. KHLEBNIKOV (Velimir). *Tvorenia*. Ed. by M. Poliakov, V. Grigoriev and A. Parnis. Moscow: Sovietskiï Pissatiel, 1986.

684. KÎKI [Alice Prin]. *Kiki's Memoirs*. Transl. Samuel Putnam. Paris: Black Mannikin Press, 1930.

685. KLÜVER (Billy) and MARTIN (Julie). *Kiki's Paris. Artists and Lovers 1900-1930*. New York: Abrams, 1989.

686. LAFARGUE (Paul). *Le Droit à la paresse*. [1880] Introduced by Maurice Dommanget. Paris: Maspéro, 1972.

687. LIVSHITS (Benedikt). *The One and a Half Eyed Archer*. Transl. John E. Bowlt. Newtonville: Oriental Research Partners, 1977.

688. LOY (Mina). *The Last Lunar Baedecker*. Ed. and introduced by Roger L. Conover. Highlands: The Jargon Society, 1982.

689. McALMON (Robert). *Being Geniuses Together 1920-1930*. Revised with supplementary chapters and an Afterword by Kay Boyle. San Francisco: North Point Press, 1984.

690. MALIK-VERLAG (Der) 1916-1947. *Chronik eines Verlages*. Ed. by Jo Hauberg, Giuseppe de Siati, Thies Zimke. Kiel: Neuer Malik Verlag, 1986.

691. MARKOV (Vladimir). *Russian Futurism: A History*. Berkeley: Univ. of California, 1968.

692. MARTIN DU GARD (Maurice). *Les Mémorables (1918-1923)*. Paris: Flammarion, 1957.

693. MIERAU (Fritz). *Russen in Berlin 1918-1933*. Weinheim and Berlin: Quadriga, 1988.

694. MORGENTHALER (Prof. Dr. W.). *Ein Geisteskranker als Künstler*. Bern and Leipzig: Ernst Bircher, 1921.

695. ——. *Adolf Wölfli*. Transl. and introduced by Henri-Pol Bouché. Paris: Publications de la Cie de l'Art brut, Fascicule 2, 1964.

696. NOGUEZ (Dominique). *Lénine Dada*. Paris: Robert Laffont, 1989.

697. PACH (Walter). *Queer Thing, Painting*. New York and London : Harper & Brothers, 1938.

698. PAWLOWSKI (Gaston de). *Voyage au pays de la quatrième dimension*. [1912] Paris: Eugène Fasquelle, 1923.

699. PETRY (Walter). *Die dadaistische Korruption*. Hg. im Auftrag der Liga zur Bekämpfung des Dadaismus. Berlin: Leon Hirsch, 1920.

700. PISIS (Filippo de). *Futurismo Dadaismo Metafisica*. E due carteggi con Tristan Tzara e Primo Conti. Ed. by Bona de Pisis and Sandro Zanotto. Milan: Fondazione Primo Conti, Libri Scheiwiller, 1981.

701. ROTHENBERG (Jerome). *Revolution of the Word. A New Gathering of American Avant Garde Poetry 1914-1945*. New York: Seabury, 1974.

702. RUSSIAN SHOW (THE FIRST). *A Commemoration*. Catalogue by Andrei Nakov, Krystina Passuth, Peter Nisbet, Christina Lodder. London: Annely Juda Fine Art, 1983.

703. SCHLEMMER (Oskar), MOHOLY-NAGY (László), MOLNAR (Farkas). *The Theater of the Bauhaus*. Ed. and with an introduction by Walter Gropius. Transl. Arthur S. Wensinger. Middletown, Connecticut: Wesleyan Univ., 1961.

704. SEGAL (Arthur). 1875-1944. Catalogue (Kölnischer Kunstverein, Haus am Waldsee Berlin, Museum Ostdeutsche Galerie Regensburg, Museo communale d'arte Moderna Ascona, The Tel Aviv Museum). Ed. by Wulf Herzogenrath and Pavel Liska. Berlin: Argon, 1987.

705. SCHLICHTER (Rudolf). 1890-1955. Catalogue. Kunsthalle. Berlin: Frölich & Kaufmann, 1984.

706. THEVOZ (Michel). *Le langage de la rupture*. Introduction by Jean Dubuffet. Paris: Presses Universitaires de France, Perspectives critiques, 1978.

707. TSCHICHOLD (Jan). *Die Neue Typographie*. [1928] Ein Handbuch für zeitgemäss Schaffende. Reprinted in Berlin: Brinkmann & Bose, 1988.

708. ——. *Ausgewählte Schriften*. Berlin: Brinkmann & Bose, 1989.

709. TUCHOLSKY (Kurt). *Gesammelte Werke*. Ed. by Mary Gerold-Tucholsky and Fritz J. Raddatz. Volume I. Reinbeck bei Hamburg: Rowohlt, 1960.

710. THE TWENTIES IN JAPAN. Tokyo: Tokyo Metropolitan Art Museum / Asahi Shimbun, 1988.

711. VANEIGEM (Raoul). *Adresse aux vivants sur la mort qui les gouverne et l'opportunité de s'en défaire*. Paris: Seghers, 1990.

712. WILLIAMS (Emmett). *Sweethearts*. New York: Something Else Press, 1967.

713. ——. *An Anthology of Concrete Poetry*. New York-Villefranche-Frankfurt: Something Else Press, 1967.

714. WOOD (Beatrice). *I Shock Myself*. California: Ojai, 1985.

715. ZHADOVA (Larissa Alekseevna), editor. *Tatlin*. London: Thames and Hudson, 1988.

716. *Zum freien Tanz, zu reiner Kunst: Suzanne Perrottet (1889-1983), Mary Wigman (1886-1973)*. Kunsthaus Zurich, 1989.

List of Illustrations

POSTERS, LEAFLETS, AND VARIA

PHOTOGRAPHS

The Dada design on the binding and the title page is from a linocut made by Raoul Hausmann for *Club Dada*, Berlin, 1918.

The author and the publisher offer grateful thanks for their help to Mr. Timothy Baum, New York, to Mr. Ralph J. Dosch, Zurich, to the Bibliothèque littéraire Jacques Doucet, Paris, and in particular to Monsieur Paul Destribats, Paris, who has generously supplied thirty-three photographs for reproduction.

INDEX

PRINTED BY
IRL IMPRIMERIES REUNIES LAUSANNE S.A.

BOUND BY
SCHUMACHER S.A., SCHMITTEN

Printed in Switzerland